DIVORCE AND REMARRIAGE IN THE BIBLE

Divorce and Remarriage in the Bible

THE SOCIAL AND LITERARY CONTEXT

David Instone-Brewer

William B. Eerdmans Publishing Company
Grand Rapids, Michigan / Cambridge, U.K.

Wm. B. Eerdmans Publishing Co.
2140 Oak Industrial Drive N.E., Grand Rapids, Michigan 49505 /
P.O. Box 163, Cambridge CB3 9PU U.K.

Printed in the United States of America

17 16 15 12 11 10

Library of Congress Cataloging-in-Publication Data

Instone-Brewer, David.
Divorce and remarriage in the Bible: the social and literary context /
David Instone-Brewer.
p. cm.
ISBN 978-0-8028-4943-4 (pbk.: alk. paper)
1. Divorce — Biblical teaching.
2. Remarriage — Biblical teaching. I. Title.

BS680.D62 I57 2002
241′.63 — dc21

2001050813

www.eerdmans.com

Contents

Preface

Innumerable scholars and readers have interacted with me in the preparation of this work. Various aspects have been presented at conferences, and the whole of this text has been available, without the footnotes, on my website for several months. The large number of helpful comments and questions, verbally and in emails, has contributed hugely to the development of my ideas and the way they are presented here. Unfortunately I cannot name all those who have helped me, but I would like to mention a few in particular. The members and my fellow minister at Llanishen Baptist Church in Cardiff helped me to consider the practical issues at the heart of this study and encouraged me to find time for research. Later, when I took up a research post at Tyndale House in Cambridge, I was able to interact with a constant stream of doctoral and post-doctoral scholars who visited or stayed there, as well as other scholars who are resident in Cambridge. In particular, William Horbury gave much useful guidance, Gerald Bray helped me with Latin texts, and Bruce Winter introduced me to the complexities of Roman law.

Editing this work would not have been possible without the help of Olaf Olsen, who responded to my appeal on the internet for an editor who would work for nothing more than a free copy of the book. His attention to detail was truly remarkable. My wife was the second editor, who worked just as hard for even less reward.

The frequent emails from people who have read my work in progress on the web have helped me to keep focused on the practical issues. I would like to apologize to the many who have received very brief replies to their requests for pastoral help that I am not able to give. This book is not really for them, but it lays the academic foundations of a practical and sensitive pastoral response for the millions of people who are suffering from the Church's misunderstanding of this subject.

Introduction

The purpose of this book is to understand the meaning of the New Testament teaching on divorce and remarriage as it would have been understood by its original readers. This is as close as historical research can get to the elusive "authorial intent."

The conclusions, in brief, are:

- Both Jesus and Paul condemned divorce without valid grounds and discouraged divorce even for valid grounds.
- Both Jesus and Paul affirmed the Old Testament grounds for divorce.
- The Old Testament allowed divorce for adultery and for neglect or abuse.
- Both Jesus and Paul condemned remarriage after an invalid divorce, but not after a valid divorce.

These conclusions are very different from the traditional Church interpretation of the New Testament texts, which concluded that divorce with remarriage was not allowed on any grounds, and that separation was allowed only in the case of adultery, and possibly desertion by a nonbelieving spouse. The reason for this difference is that the background knowledge and assumptions of a first-century reader were already forgotten by the second century, and thus the texts were misunderstood even by the Early Church Fathers.

In order to understand the New Testament through the eyes of a first-century reader, the historical context and literary background need to be understood in great detail.

There is, of course, no such thing as a typical first-century reader. All readers come to the text with their own presuppositions. This was as true in NT times as now. However, one presupposition was shared by all first-century believers, both Jews and Christians: they all accepted that the Old Testament was God's word and was the basis for ethics.[1] The teaching of the New Testament would be tested against this groundwork. The opening chapters will therefore examine the teaching on divorce and remarriage in the Old Testament.

The first-century readers of the New Testament were not particularly interested in the original meaning of the Old Testament. They considered that God was speaking directly to them and that his words should be interpreted for their own time. The original intent of the words to the original audience of the Old Testament was of little interest to them.[2] However, the original intent of the Old Testament is important to the modern reader, if only to prevent us from reading the text through the presuppositions of our own culture. Therefore the cultural context of the Old Testament will be covered as well as the cultural context of the New Testament.

The intertestamental period is important because it helps us to understand the development of the Jewish and Greco-Roman cultures in the first century. We need insights into these cultures in order to understand how the original recipients read the New Testament. The chapters on Jesus' and Paul's teaching apply these insights to the New Testament texts.

The later chapters of the book trace the consequences of neglecting the cultural background of the text. The Early Church was soon separated from the Synagogue, and the Jewish world was itself cut off from part of its past by the destruction of Jerusalem. Background knowledge that could be taken for granted in the original readers of the New Testament disappeared from the Church. The misunderstandings that resulted, especially in the teaching on divorce and remarriage, have continued to the present. The final chapter outlines some practical pastoral responses.

In the scholarly world there are no firm conclusions, only theories that are internally coherent and that fit the facts to a greater or lesser degree. The findings that are presented here have already been debated with innumerable

1. It has been argued that Paul did not base his ethics on the Old Testament. This has been convincingly refuted by Brian Rosner in *Paul, Scripture and Ethics: A Study of 1 Corinthians 5–7*, Arbeiten zur Geschichte des antiken Judentums und des Urchristentums 22 (Leiden: Brill, 1994).

2. This does not mean that they were not interested in the context or the plain meaning of the text. In my *Techniques and Assumptions in Jewish Exegesis before 70 CE*, Texte und Studien zum antiken Judentum 30 (Tübingen: J. C. B. Mohr, 1992), I show that rabbinic Judaism in New Testament times took the context into account and always pursued the primary meaning of the text, though their idea of the primary meaning may often have been different from ours. The more extreme midrashic techniques such as lifting the text out of its context and looking for multiple layers of meaning came to rabbinic Judaism after 70 C.E. via Alexandria and Qumran, where they were already being employed in New Testament times.

scholars at conferences, in journals, over coffee at Tyndale House, and by email. There are many who remain to be convinced, but most have welcomed the clear theology of marriage that results from these conclusions, and the way that they concur with pragmatic common sense, while being based on rigorous historically contextual biblical research.

The tradition of the Church is based on a completely different interpretation. My hope is that this work will give a biblical foundation to Church leaders and individuals who are seeking to evaluate that tradition for themselves.

Further resources are available at my website, www.Instone-Brewer.com.

1. The Ancient Near East

Marriage Is a Contract

Marriage in the ancient Near East was contractual, involving payments, agreed stipulations, and penalties. If either partner broke the stipulations of the contract, the innocent partner could opt for a divorce and keep the dowry. Exact parallels to these practices are found in the Pentateuch.

The Marriage Covenant

Marriage is called a "covenant" (בּרית, *berith*) throughout the Pentateuch and the rest of the Old Testament.[1] Proverbs 2:17 speaks about the adulterous wife who "ignored the covenant made before God," and Malachi says that one of the witnesses of any "marriage covenant" is God himself (2:14). Ezekiel employs a vivid picture of God marrying the nation of Judah, in which he frequently referred to their marriage covenant (Ezek. 16:8, 59-62). He describes in intimate and overtly sexual language how God entered into marriage, including the ceremony at which he said: "I spread the edge of my cloak over you, and covered

1. Prov. 2:17; Jer. 31:32; Ezek. 16:8, 59, 60, 61, 62; Mal. 2:14. See the excellent summary in David Atkinson, *To Have and To Hold: The Marriage Covenant and the Discipline of Divorce* (London: Collins, 1979), pp. 72-100. Many commentators have tried to distance marriage from other covenants, but G. P. Hugenberger has exhaustively dealt with all these other theories (*Marriage as a Covenant: A Study of Biblical Law and Ethics Governing Marriage, Developed from the Perspective of Malachi,* Vetus Testamentum Supplement 52 [Leiden and New York: Brill, 1994]).

your nakedness: I pledged myself to you and entered into a covenant with you" (Ezek. 16:8).[2]

A marriage covenant is also referred to in many of the passages that speak about a covenant with God. The word "covenant" may mean a "marriage covenant" or a "treaty covenant," and often in these passages it means both. The marriage covenant of God with his people is, at times, almost synonymous with his treaty covenant with them. For example, the comment "I will remember my covenant with you in the days of your youth, and I will establish with you an everlasting covenant," which occurs in the description of God's marriage to Israel (Ezek. 16:60), sounds very similar to Ezekiel 37:26, which speaks about the treaty covenant of God with his people. A similar mixture of these two ideas occurs in Jeremiah 31:31-32, where the new everlasting covenant is compared with "my covenant which they broke, though I was their husband." These two concepts are sometimes mixed deliberately in order to draw out comparisons. For example, Jeremiah 11:10 appears to refer to a treaty covenant ("they have broken the covenant that I made with their ancestors") but later verses contain references to Israel as a wayward wife (Jer. 11:15, "What right has my beloved in my house, when she has done vile deeds?").

The Pentateuch also speaks of the treaty covenant of Israel in terms of a marriage. The jealousy of God is frequently referred to (Exod. 20:5; Deut. 5:9; cf. Exod. 34:14; Josh. 24:19) and in Numbers 5:14 the term "jealousy" (קנא, *qana*) is used in its technical sense of marital jealousy.[3] Also, the covenantal oath "I will be your God and you shall be my people" (Lev. 26:12; Deut. 29:13 [MT 29:12]; etc.) is very similar to the ancient Near Eastern marriage formula attested in Hosea 2:2 [MT 2:4].[4]

The concept of "covenant" is used throughout the ancient Near East for treaty covenants, covenants for hiring labor, and many other types of agree-

2. Although there are no parallels to this language outside the Bible, the similarity of Ruth 3:9 suggests that this may have been a common betrothal ceremony. Marvin H. Pope points out that "spreading one's cloak over" a woman is an Arab euphemism for sexual intimacy ("Mixed Marriage Metaphor in Ezekiel 16," in *Fortunate the Eyes That See — Essays in Honor of David Noel Freedman in Celebration of His Seventieth Birthday,* ed. Astrid Beck [Grand Rapids: Eerdmans, 1995], pp. 384-99, esp. p. 393).

3. See M. Weinfeld, "Berith," in *Theological Dictionary of the Old Testament,* ed. Johannes G. Botterweck, Helmer Ringgren, and Heinz-Josef Fabry (Grand Rapids: Eerdmans, 1974), 2:253-79, esp. p. 278.

4. See Markham J. Geller, "The Elephantine Papyri and Hosea 2.3: Evidence for the Form of the Early Jewish Divorce Writ," *Journal for the Study of Judaism* 8 (1977): 139-48; M. A. Friedman, "Israel's Response in Hosea 2.17b: 'You Are My Husband,'" *Journal of Biblical Literature* 99 (1980): 199-204. This is discussed later.

ments including marriage.[5] Although the word for "covenant" is different in different languages (Akkadian *riksu* and Hittite *ishiul,* etc.[6]), the same concept pervades the societies surrounding Israel. This concept was also later adopted by the Greco-Roman culture of the first century C.E.[7] A covenant was cemented not only by blessings and curses (benefits and penalties) but also by a concept of mutual concern and loyalty, which was often expressed as "love" even in treaty covenants.[8] The similarity of language used for treaty covenant and marriage covenant and for other agreements between two parties is also found in many ancient Near Eastern sources.[9]

The phrase "marriage covenant" was the constant and normative phrase used to describe the legal framework of marriage in the Old Testament and in its surrounding cultures.[10] Marriage covenants in the rest of the ancient Near East help us to understand the meaning of this phrase in the Old Testament.

Marriage Covenants in the Ancient Near East

The term "covenant" has a wide range of meaning in the ancient Near East, from a business agreement concerning a loan through to a national treaty with a foreign power or with a god. The primary meaning of "covenant" was an agreement between two parties that was mutually binding. Covenants could be made, kept, and broken. Covenants were implemented by document or by a ceremony. They had stipulation agreed to by both parties, and sanctions that came into force when a stipulation was broken.[11]

5. Leslie W. Pope, "Marriage: A Study of the Covenant Relationship as Found in the Old Testament," M.A. thesis, Providence Theological Seminary, 1995 (Ann Arbor, Mich.: UMI Dissertation Services, 1997), pp. 74-78.

6. Weinfeld, "Berith," pp. 254-55.

7. Weinfeld, "Berith," p. 256.

8. Leslie Pope, "Marriage," p. 78.

9. P. Kalluveettil, *Declaration and Covenant: A Comprehensive Review of Covenant Formulae from the Old Testament and the Ancient Near East* (Rome: Biblical Institute Press, 1982), pp. 79-81, has various instances where a royal marriage is also a political alliance. In these situations it is difficult to distinguish between the marriage covenant and the treaty covenant.

10. See also the analyses in David Atkinson, *To Have and To Hold,* pp. 72-100; Hugenberger, *Marriage as a Covenant;* William F. Luck, *Divorce and Remarriage: Recovering the Biblical View* (San Francisco: Harper and Row, 1987), pp. 26-66. However, Andrew Cornes (*Divorce and Remarriage: Biblical Principles and Pastoral Practice* [London: Hodder & Stoughton, 1993], pp. 164-65) disagrees. He acknowledges that the OT uses "marriage covenant," but he does not accept it as a "biblical concept" because the phrase "marriage covenant" is not used in the NT.

11. For the full range of meanings of "covenant," and a wide-ranging bibliography, see Weinfeld, "Berith," pp. 253-65.

The legal basis of marriage was called a "covenant" because, like all other types of covenant, it was an agreement between two parties that contained stipulations and sanctions. A marriage covenant, like any other covenant, included details of payment, the agreement to stipulations by two parties, a set of penalties for the party who did not keep these stipulations, and a legally binding witnessed ceremony or document that recorded all these matters.[12]

A marriage covenant in the Old Testament was like all other ancient Near Eastern covenants. The Old Testament refers to the payments involved, the stipulations of the agreement, and the penalties that ensued if these stipulations were not kept. The Old Testament also uses the same legal language for all these aspects of a marriage covenant as found in other ancient Near Eastern marriage covenants.

This system of payments and penalties, stipulations agreed upon, and the legal terminology of marriage covenants will now be examined in detail, in both the ancient Near East and the Old Testament sources. Many of these customs and terms survived into the first century C.E. and became the basis for New Testament teaching on marriage.

Payment and Penalties in Marriage Covenants

Payment varied in different cultures and at different times throughout the time period covered by the Old Testament. The Old Babylonian culture had various payments. E. M. Yamauchi[13] summarizes these as the *terḥatu* and the *sheriqtu*. The *terḥatu* or "bride-price," which sealed the betrothal, was paid by the groom to the bride's father. This averaged 10 shekels, or about 10 months wages. The *sheriqtu* or "dowry" was paid by the bride's father to the bride. The Jewish equivalent of the *terḥatu* was called the *mohar.*[14] The husband also gave the bride gifts (Gen. 24:22). The Jewish equivalent of the *sheriqtu* was known as the *nedunyah.*[15] There were many variations to this

12. Many scholars have argued that a binding oath is also a necessary part of a covenant. Hugenberger has examined this at length (*Marriage as a Covenant,* ch. 6, pp. 168-215). He concluded that this may be the case, but it is equally the case that marriage ceremonies included some kind of oath-sign, or that consummation of the marriage was itself an oath-sign.

13. Edwin M. Yamauchi, "Cultural Aspects of Marriage in the Ancient World," *Bibliotheca Sacra* 135 (1978): 241-52.

14. Gen. 24:53; Exod. 22:16-17; Hos. 3:2. Jacob was charged much more than average in Gen. 29:18.

15. See Judg. 1:14-15; 1 Kings 9:16; Tob. 7:14; 8:21; Assuan papyri (Cowley nos. 15, 18). *Nedunyah* is presumably from *neden,* or *nedah,* "gift" in Ezek. 16:33. In the Jacob story, the dowry was probably not paid, because Laban's daughters said: "Do we have any share left in the inheritance of our father? . . . Not only has he sold us, but he has used up what was paid for us." The

scheme in the city states of Old Babylon and in other ancient Near Eastern cultures.[16]

Even the gods were not immune from making such payments. When Ugaritic gods took wives, they paid a very high bride-price in keeping with their exalted status.[17] Yahweh also paid an especially high bride-price when he married Israel. However, Yahweh was pictured as paying the bride-price in a currency that was much more valuable than gold: he paid with "righteousness and justice."[18]

The purpose of these payments was to give security to the marriage, as well as being the legal seal on the marriage covenant. In some senses the covenant appears to be a sale, in which the groom buys his bride from her father.[19] However, it was understood that the father would give a dowry well in excess of the bride-price, so that the net payment was made by the bride's father to the groom. The dowry could be regarded as equivalent to the daughter's share of the family estate, held in trust for her by her husband.[20] In effect, therefore, the payment by the bride's father helped the couple to establish their home.

The dowry also gave personal security to the bride. The dowry continued to belong to the bride, so if her husband died or divorced her, she had money to

---

dowry was, in many ways, the equivalent of a daughter's portion of the estate. Perhaps Laban held back the dowry until they left home, but they realized that he had lost his wealth and would not be able to pay any dowry. Cowley nos. 15 and 18 were originally published in A. E. Cowley, *Aramaic Papyri of the Fifth Century* B.C. (Oxford: Clarendon, 1923) and are now republished as B2.6 and B6.4 in Bezalel Porten and Ada Yardeni, *Textbook of Aramaic Documents from Ancient Egypt: Newly Copied, Edited and Translated into Hebrew and English,* 4 vols. (Jerusalem: Hebrew University, 1986-96).

16. See discussions in Bezalel Porten, *Archives from Elephantine: The Life of an Ancient Jewish Military Colony* (Berkeley: University of California Press, 1968), pp. 209-10, and the useful chart in Hugenberger, *Marriage as a Covenant,* p. 242.

17. Marjo Christina Annette Korpel, *A Rift in the Clouds: Ugaritic and Hebrew Descriptions of the Divine* (Münster: Ugarit-Verlag, 1990), p. 226.

18. Hos. 2:19 [MT 2:21]; see the comparisons with Ugaritic terminology in Korpel, *A Rift in the Clouds,* p. 229. Korpel translates Hos. 2:19-20 [MT 2:21-22]: "And I will betroth you to me for ever, and I will betroth you to me, at the price of righteousness and justice, at the price of faithfulness and mercy. Yea, I will betroth you to me, at the price of reliability, and you shall know the Lord." She explains that "at the price of" is the same phrase as in 2 Sam. 3:14 where David betrothed Michal at the price of a hundred Philistine foreskins. "To know" is a euphemism for sexual intercourse (as at Gen. 4:1, 17, 25; 19:8; Num. 31:17; Judg. 21:11).

19. Leone J. Archer (*Her Price Is beyond Rubies: The Jewish Woman in Greco-Roman Palestine,* Journal for the Study of the Old Testament — Supplement Series 60 [Sheffield: Sheffield Academic Press, 1990], pp. 156-65) argues at length that the Jews did not regard marriage as a sale, at least in rabbinic times.

20. This is the conclusion in M. T. Roth, *Babylonian Marriage Agreements: 7th-3rd Centuries* B.C. (Kevalaer: Verlag Butzon & Bercker; Neukirchen-Vluyn: Neukirchener Verlag, 1989), p. 9. She studied forty-five Babylonian marriage documents, which showed a wide variety of arrangements.

live on.[21] She might also get a portion of the estate in addition to her dowry.[22] The only exception to this was when the wife caused the divorce. In some arrangements the wife would get only half the dowry in this case,[23] though usually she lost all rights to the dowry.[24]

These payments also added security to the marriage itself. The bride-price, which was paid by the groom to the bride's father, represented many months wages. This helped to ensure that marriage was not entered into lightly. The whole system of payments was weighted against divorce, because whoever caused the divorce was penalized financially. If the husband divorced his wife without cause, he usually returned the dowry, and if the wife divorced her husband without cause, she lost her right to some or all of her dowry.[25] However, if the divorce was caused by one partner breaking a stipulation in the marriage contract, the guilty partner was deemed to have caused the divorce and the innocent partner kept the dowry.[26] For example, the seventeenth century B.C.E. Babylonian high priest Enlil tried to escape the repayment of this dowry by accusing his wife of disloyalty, but his charges were found to be false.[27]

21. For example the Babylonian marriage contract no. 16 in Roth, *Babylonian Marriage Agreements,* p. 66: "Should H desire to have another wife live (in the house) in preference to W, the orchard which WF the father of W [gave her as her dowry] will belong to W" (W stands for the name of the wife, H for the name of the husband, and WF for the name of the wife's father).

22. See, for example, the Code of Hammurabi #137, in James B. Pritchard, ed., *Ancient Near Eastern Texts Relating to the Old Testament,* 3rd ed. (Princeton: Princeton University Press, 1978, 1992), p. 172: "They shall return to that woman her dowry and shall give to her part of field, garden, and goods, and she shall bring up her children — whatever is given to her children, they shall give to her a portion corresponding to that of a son." These regulations varied from city to city, but the general rule was that the bride got the whole or part of the dowry.

23. See Porten, *Archives from Elephantine,* p. 209. Although this refers to an Egyptian document, Porten assumes that this also occurred in other areas of the ancient Near East.

24. For example the Babylonian marriage contract no. 34 discussed in Roth, *Babylonian Marriage Agreements,* pp. 14, 110. This contract stipulates that the wife loses all rights to her dowry if she divorces her husband: "Should W release H her husband, she will forfeit her entire dowry in favor of H and thereby she will relinquish her means of support." For further discussion see Porten, *Archives from Elephantine,* pp. 209-10, 223.

25. The code of Hammurabi may represent the first official recognition of a woman's right to divorce when her husband is at fault, though Porten thinks that Hammurabi was establishing a middle ground in order to bring together widely disparate practices (Porten, *Archives from Elephantine,* pp. 209-10).

26. For example, some of the marriage covenants collected by Roth include the stipulation that the husband may not take a second wife (Roth, *Babylonian Marriage Agreements,* nos. 1, 2, 4, 5, 6, 8, 15, 16, 17, 19, 20, 25, 26, 30, 34). If he does, he must give his first wife a divorce, and she keeps the dowry.

27. Both the marriage certificate listing the dowry and the court records of the case have

Deuteronomy 24:1-4 is an example of these payments and penalties in action. This passage is an item of case law[28] about a man who wanted to remarry a wife whom he had divorced, and who had been married again in the meantime. The ruling states that she would now be unclean for him. The reason for this ruling has been traced by Raymond Westbrook[29] to the financial payments and penalties involved in marriage and divorce. Westbrook has pointed out that the main difference between these two marriages was the financial consequence for the woman. The first marriage ended when the man cited a valid ground for divorce, namely "a matter of indecency." The fact that he had a valid ground for the divorce meant that she lost her right to her dowry. The second marriage ended without any valid grounds for divorce, either because the man "hated/disliked" her (which was a technical term for a groundless divorce),[30] or because he died. In either case the woman would have kept her dowry. If she had not brought a dowry into this second marriage, she would nevertheless have been awarded an equivalent amount. Westbrook thus noted that this would give the first husband a financial motive for remarrying his wife, because he would then have both her new dowry and her old one. This law therefore forbids the first husband from getting financial benefit in this way.[31]

Throughout the ancient Near East, therefore, marriage covenants were

---

survived; see E. Lipinski, "The Wife's Right to Divorce in the Light of an Ancient Near Eastern Tradition," in *The Jewish Law Annual*, ed. B. S. Jackson (Leiden: Brill, 1981), 4:9-26, esp. pp. 15-16.

28. Case law is a ruling in one particular instance that then becomes the basis of other later rulings. The clearest example is the man gathering sticks on the Sabbath (Num. 15:32-36), which became the basis of laws about work on the Sabbath.

29. Raymond Westbrook, "Prohibition of Restoration of Marriage in Deuteronomy 24.1-4," in *Studies in Bible 1986*, ed. S. Japhet, Scripta Hierosolymitana 31 (Jerusalem: Magnes, 1986), pp. 387-405.

30. Westbrook argued for the technical meaning of the term **שׂנא** *(shana)* "dislike" or "hate" from many parallels in the OT and ancient Near Eastern sources. Examples he cites include an Old Babylonian marriage contract that has the parallelism "If H divorces W . . . if W hates H" (British Museum, *Cuneiform Texts from Babylonian Tablets in the British Museum* [London: British Museum, 1898-1977], 6:26a). He also found a longer version "hate and divorce," e.g., a marriage contract from Alalakh: "If W hates H and divorces him . . . ," and a Neo-Assyrian contract "if W hates H (and) divorces . . ." (Westbrook, "Prohibition of Restoration of Marriage," p. 400). This type of groundless divorce based on **שׂנא** "hate" is not permitted in the OT though it probably existed because of the influence of surrounding cultures. In Deut. 22:13-21, the man who "hates" his new bride cannot simply divorce her on this ground, so he invents a nonvirginity charge against her. Hugenberger has convincingly argued that Mal. 2:16 criticizes those who "hate (and) divorce" (*Marriage as a Covenant*, pp. 51-83).

31. For further details, see my "Deuteronomy 24.1-4 and the Origin of the Jewish Divorce Certificate," *Journal of Jewish Studies* 49 (1998): 230-43.

sealed by various payments of money. Even though some of these payments canceled each other out, when two parties paid each other different sums, they were still considered to be important and were recorded. These payments are reflected in the Old Testament and survived to the time of the New Testament in Jewish practice.

Stipulations in Marriage Covenants

The stipulations of an ancient Near Eastern marriage covenant were written down in a document, or they were stated verbally at a ceremony before witnesses. As well as these stipulations, which could vary from marriage to marriage, there were also basic rights and responsibilities that applied to every marriage. These would not normally be recorded in a marriage covenant. For example, very few marriage covenants say anything about adultery, but a death penalty for adultery is found throughout the ancient Near East.

The unwritten stipulations were more important than the written ones because they were binding on every marriage. Most marriages did not have a written covenant.[32] Written covenants were needed only if the dowry was exceptionally large or if there were unusual stipulations added. These extra stipulations varied considerably in the different marriage covenants that have survived.[33]

One additional stipulation that occurs with some regularity states that a man may not take a second wife in preference to his first.[34] Roth pointed out that this does not mean that polygamy is forbidden but only that the first wife should not be neglected in favor of the second wife.[35]

Another phrase that occurs regularly in ancient Near Eastern texts refers to the support a husband is expected to give to his wife as well as to other female de-

32. Roth, *Babylonian Marriage Agreements,* pp. 1-2. Among the tens of thousands of cuneiform documents found so far, only forty-five are marriage covenants. Roth suggests that this was because most marriages were oral ceremonies. She points out that the written documents read like literal transcripts of a spoken ceremony, e.g., "The groom said . . . then the bride's father said. . . ."

33. See examples in Roth, *Babylonian Marriage Agreements.*

34. Roth, *Babylonian Marriage Agreements,* p. 66, Document 16: "Should H desire to have another wife live (in the house) in preference to W. . . ." See also Documents 2, 15, 17, 19, 26, and 34. See also Lipit-Ishtar Lawcode #28: "If a man has turned his face away from his *first* wife . . . (but) she has not gone out of the [house], his wife which he married *as his favourite* is a second wife; he shall continue to support his *first* wife" (Lipit-Ishtar Lawcode in Pritchard, *Ancient Near Eastern Texts,* pp. 159-61).

35. Roth, *Babylonian Marriage Agreements,* p. 13.

pendents. The phrase, which is used at least five times in the extant literature, is: "he was obligated to provide **food, anointing oil and clothing** for her." There were some variations in the first item, which was sometimes grain or money.[36]

There is a clear parallel to these stipulations in Exodus 21:10-11, which records that a second wife should not be preferred over a first wife even when the first wife was a slave wife. It was generally assumed by rabbinic interpreters that this right extended to free wives as well as slave wives. This was presumably based on the logic that any right that a slave had would certainly also be shared by a free person.

This passage also lists the rights of the first wife that must not be diminished when the second wife arrives. This list of these rights in Exodus 21:10, according to most translations, is the right to food, clothing, and conjugal relations. This is very similar to the common ancient Near Eastern phrase "food, anointing oil, and clothing." There is some difficulty in the translation of the third word, **ענתה** *('onathah)*, but if it can mean "her ointment," as some argue,[37] then Exodus 21:10 would be a precise reflection of Babylonian marriage stipulations.

Sexual faithfulness is rarely listed as a stipulation in ancient Near Eastern marriage covenants. It was understood as an unwritten stipulation. All of the ancient Near Eastern law codes that have rulings about adultery prescribe capital punishment.[38] Only in cases of doubt or coercion is a lesser punishment allowed.[39] The capital punishment was applied to the man or woman or both, depending on who was considered to be guilty. It is not certain whether this punishment was compulsory. For example, the Code of Hammurabi #129 suggests that the king could pardon a wife at the husband's request:

> If the wife of a seignior has been caught while lying with another man, they shall bind them and throw them into the water. If the husband of the woman wishes to spare his wife, then the king in turn may spare his subject.[40]

36. Shalom M. Paul, "Exod. 21.10: A Threefold Maintenance Clause," *Journal of Near Eastern Studies* 28 (1969): 48-53, repeated in his *Studies in the Book of the Covenant in the Light of Cuneiform and Biblical Law,* Vetus Testamentum Supplement 17 (Leiden: Brill, 1970), pp. 52-61.

37. E.g., Paul, "Exod. 21.10: A Threefold Maintenance Clause," and Benno Jacob, *The Second Book of the Bible, Exodus,* trans. with an introduction by Walter Jacob (Hoboken, N.J.: Ktav, 1992), pp. 626-27.

38. E.g., Laws of Eshnunna #28; Code of Hammurabi #129; Middle Assyrian laws #13-14; Hittite laws #189-91, 195, in Pritchard, *Ancient Near Eastern Texts,* pp. 160-98.

39. E.g., Code of Hammurabi #130-32; Middle Assyrian laws #12, 23; in Pritchard, *Ancient Near Eastern Texts,* pp. 160-98.

40 Pritchard, *Ancient Near Eastern Texts,* p. 171. Cf. a similar law in the Hittite law #198, in Pritchard, *Ancient Near Eastern Texts,* p. 196.

This does not diminish the seriousness with which adultery was regarded. The fact that the king had to pardon her suggests that adultery was considered a crime against the state, not just against the marriage partner.

In the Old Testament, too, adultery is strongly condemned and is punishable by death.[41] It was also more than just a crime against a partner because it is one of the sexual crimes that might cause the land to "vomit" them out (Lev. 20:10, 22). In Genesis it is regarded as a crime against God (Gen. 20:6; 26:10; 39:9). Deuteronomy speaks of it as something that must be purged from the nation (Deut. 22:22, 24).[42]

A stipulation about **cleanliness in Deuteronomy 24:1** does not have any parallel in the ancient Near East. The teaching of Deuteronomy 24:1-4 has traditionally been understood to mean that one could divorce a wife for adultery. However, it is very unlikely that this passage originally referred to adultery because the punishment for adultery was death. The phrase later interpreted as referring to "adultery" is ערות דבר (*'ervat davar),* literally "nakedness of a matter." This strange phrase has been the subject of much debate by Jewish scholars up to the present day. The word ערוה (*'ervah)* occurs frequently and usually includes the connotation of sexual impropriety or sinfulness, but it is certainly not restricted to adultery. S. R. Driver[43] suggests that the phrase originally meant some improper or indecent behavior. It was used in this sense in Deuteronomy 23:14 [MT 23:15] with regard to taking care of toiletry arrangements in the camp, so that the Lord would not "turn his back" on Israel. It is also implied by the Septuagint ἄσχημον πρᾶγμα, "something unbecoming."[44] It is now impossible to decide what this referred to originally, but it is likely to be related to some matter of the cleanliness laws. It is not surprising that Israel would have an additional stipulation based on cleanliness considering the importance of cleanliness in Yahweh worship.

There are, therefore, clear parallels between the stipulations for marriage contracts in the Pentateuch and ancient Near Eastern sources, though in both

41. It is serious enough to be listed in the Decalogue (Exod. 20:14; Deut. 5:18). The punishment is death for any willing partner (Lev. 20:10; Deut. 22:22-29).

42. Deut. 22:22, 24: "put away the evil from Israel" and "put away the evil from the midst of you." See also other laws in Deuteronomy with similar injunctions (Deut. 13:5; 17:7; 19:19; 21:21; 24:7.

43. S. R. Driver, *A Critical and Exegetical Commentary on Deuteronomy,* 3rd ed. (Edinburgh: T. & T. Clark, 1902), p. 270.

44. Deut. 24:3 (LXX). Driver (*Deuteronomy,* p. 271) also pointed out that the Karaites allowed divorce only on the grounds of offenses against modesty or good taste, a change of religion, serious bodily defects, and repulsive complaints. He does not say so, but the Karaites favored literal interpretations, and perhaps they considered this to be the literal interpretation of the text.

cases the amount of extant material is limited. Written stipulations added to many marriage covenants rule out favoring a second wife, using very similar language to that found in Exodus 21:10-11. The written stipulations include obligations to provide food, clothing, and ointment, which is again paralleled in Exodus 21:10. The unwritten stipulations about faithfulness, and the death penalty for adultery, also have clear parallels in the Pentateuch.

Legal Records of Marriage Covenants

The legal mechanism and terminology used for written or spoken marriage covenants in the ancient Near East also have clear parallels in the Pentateuch.

Most marriages in the ancient Near East were enacted by **verbal ceremony**, without any written covenant.[45] One of the Middle Assyrian laws gives an insight into what might have happened at a marriage ceremony. In this example a man marries his concubine.

> #41 If a seignior wishes to veil his concubine, he shall have five (or) six of his neighbours present (and) veil[46] her in their presence (and) say, "She is my wife," (and so) she becomes his wife. A concubine who was not veiled in the presence of the men, whose husband did not say, "She is my wife," is not a wife; she is still a concubine.[47]

The main thrust of this ruling is to determine whether or not a concubine inherits from her dead husband or master. Marrying a free woman presumably involved a different ceremony, which included an agreement with her parents. A ceremony or formal covenant was necessary because simply living with a man did not make a woman his wife. For example, in the Laws of Eshnunna:[48]

> #27 If a man takes a(nother) man's daughter without asking the permission of her father and her mother and concludes no *formal contract* with her father and her mother, even though she may live in his house for a year, she is not a housewife. #28 *On the other hand,* if he concludes a formal contract with her father and her mother and cohabits with her, she is a housewife.

45. See above.

46. The veil referred to is the compulsory headdress worn in public by all decent women but forbidden to prostitutes and slaves (see rule #40).

47. The Middle Assyrian Laws, in Pritchard, *Ancient Near Eastern Texts,* pp. 180-88.

48. Pritchard, *Ancient Near Eastern Texts,* pp. 161-63. Also, The Code of Hammurabi, in Pritchard, *Ancient Near Eastern Texts,* pp. 163-80: #128 "If a seignior acquired a wife but did not draw up the contracts for her, that woman is no wife."

> When she is caught with a(nother) man, she shall die, she shall not get away alive.

The words "formal contract" (in italics) have been supplied by the translator. There is nothing in the text to suggest whether the agreement was written or oral. However, it is clear that there had to be some kind of formal agreement, probably marked by a ceremony.[49]

The words used in marriage agreements are found in the documents collected by Roth.[50] Although there is considerable variation, they generally follow the same model. In the following examples, H is the name of the husband and W is the name of the wife, while HF and WF are their fathers:

> #2 H: "Cut yourself off from any other man. Be a wife." W consented and she will cut herself off from any other man.

> #25 H: "Come to me. You will be a wife." W consented. She will live in [marriage] with H.

The contract was one of mutual consent, though this is not always clear in the written versions. Often the contracts include a request from the parents of the groom to the parents of the bride. These examples suggest that the woman was involved and had to make voluntary assent as part of the ceremony. The agreement is therefore not only between the parents and the husband but also between the man and his wife.

M. A. Friedman tried to discover the original oral formula for the marriage covenant, and he concluded that both the man and the woman took part orally in the ceremony. He found parallels to the Old Babylonian written formulae in Elephantine marriage certificates and in the OT.[51] He pointed out that

49. For further texts showing that a contract was necessary see Daniela Piattelli, "The Marriage Contract and Bill of Divorce in Ancient Hebrew Law," in *The Jewish Law Annual*, ed. B. S. Jackson (Leiden: Brill, 1981), 4:66-78, esp. p. 74.

50. Roth, *Babylonian Marriage Agreements.*

51. Friedman, "Israel's Response in Hosea 2.17b." He cited the Elephantine marriage formula "She is my wife and I am her husband from this day and forever," which is seen in obverse in the divorce formula "She is not my wife and I am not her husband" found at Elephantine and also in *Num. Rab.* 2:15, and very similarly in Hos. 2:2 [MT 2:4]: "She is not my wife and I am not her husband." Cf. also Tob. 7:12 in Codex Sinaiticus: "From henceforth you are her brother and she is your sister. She has been given to you from today and forever" (Codex Vaticanus has only "You are her brother and she is yours"). Both are here in third person because it is said by the bride's father, performing the marriage ceremony. Other ancient sources are found in Lipinski, "The Wife's Right to Divorce," pp. 14-17, and B. Meissner, *Beiträge zum altbabylonischen Privatrecht* (Leipzig: Hinrichs, 1893), nos. 89 and 90, pp. 71-72.

the formulae in written certificates are usually recorded from the point of view of the man, but the oral ceremony would be different. He found evidence that in the marriage ceremony both parties made a verbal affirmation.[52] It seems that the spoken formula was probably:

> H. "(Be) my wife, this day and forever."
> W. "(Be) my husband."[53]

The marriage covenants also recorded details of the dowry and details of divorce settlements, as well as any stipulations in addition to the normally accepted marriage stipulations. The details of **divorce settlement** are there as a warning as well as to make sure that any divorce is settled without financial wranglings. This divorce section of the marriage covenant may contain some very severe warnings and penalties, for example:

> #2 Should H marry another wife in preference to W,[54] he will give her six minas of silver and she may go [wherever she] wishes.[55] May Nabu and Marduk decree the destruction of whoever contravenes this agreement.[56]

> #5 Should W be found with another man, she will die by the dagger.[57] Should H declare "W is not my wife," H will give to W six minas of silver as her divorce settlement, and send her back to her father's house.

52. See examples in Friedman, "Israel's Response in Hosea 2.17b," p. 202. He points out that the "response" of Israel to God's invitation in Hos. 2:16-20 [MT 2:14-18] may reflect this ceremony.

53. A very early example of this formula that was not noticed by Friedman and others can be found in the Ugaritic myth of El marrying the two sisters. El tells them that if they say to him "Husband . . ." they will be his "wives for ever," but if they say "Father . . ." they will be his daughters. They respond "Husband . . ." and so they become his wives. For texts and translations see "Shachar and Shalim and the Gracious Gods" in J. C. L. Gibson, *Canaanite Myths and Legends,* 2nd ed., originally ed. G. R. Driver (Edinburgh: T. & T. Clark, 1978), pp. 28-30, 123-27, and "Dawn and Dusk (The Birth of the Gracious and Beautiful Gods)," in William W. Hallo and K. Lawson Younger, *The Context of Scripture,* vol. 1: *Canonical Compositions from the Biblical World* (Leiden: Brill, 1997), pp. 274-83. These two translations are very different. The first suggests that El seduced the two young girls, and the second that they approached him and that he made sure they were mature enough for marriage before proceeding.

54. Cf. similar wording about "a wife in preference" in #19, 17, 26, and 34.

55. Cf. also #19: "If he releases her she may go wherever she wishes." Similarly #4, 6, 15, 16, and 20.

56. These threats are found with various names, but with a fairly consistent form.

57. The reference to "die by the dagger" is common in these documents, but there is no mention made of equal punishment for the man.

#15 Should H desire to have another wife live (in the house) in preference to W, the orchard which WF [gave her as dowry] will belong to W; she may go . . . wherever she pleases.

The curse "may [a god] decree destruction" occurs usually directly after the details of the divorce settlement. However, the anger of the god is not directed against the person who divorces, but the person who causes the divorce by breaking the agreement. This would mean the person who does not provide the divorce settlement promptly. The curse is there presumably because it was difficult for a woman to get her rights through law, especially if her father was dead by the time she was divorced.

These documents show various **parallels with the Old Testament**, both in the Pentateuch and beyond. The words "she may go wherever she wishes" occur regularly.[58] These words may be reflected in the later rabbinic divorce certificate formula "you are free to marry any man."[59] The phrase "Be a wife" is similar to "She is my wife" in the wedding ceremony of the Middle Assyrian law #41, cited above. It is also similar to Hosea 2:1 [MT 2:3] and other ancient Near Eastern parallels found by Markham J. Geller.[60] The phrase "Cut yourself off from any other man" may find a parallel in Genesis 2:24: "separate from his father and mother, and cleave to his wife." Even the curses in the names of various gods may have a parallel in Malachi 2:15-16. The curse of the gods is against those who break the agreement, and the hatred of God against divorce in Malachi is directed against those who "deal treacherously" against "the wife of your covenant."[61]

58. In Roth's collection, seven marriage documents use the phrase "she may go wherever she wishes," in two slightly different versions: nos. 2 (625-23 B.C.E.); 6 (564 B.C.E.); 19 (535/4 B.C.E.); 20 (523 B.C.E.): *ašar ṣebāt;* 4 (592 B.C.E.); 15 (543 B.C.E.): *ašar maḫri;* and 16 (543 B.C.E.): corrupt. A similar formula is found in the divorce provisions of marriage documents of Egyptian Jews of the fifth century B.C.E. Two of the three marriage certificates among the Aramaic papyri of Elephantine use the phrase "She may go wherever she wishes" (ותהך לה אן זי צבית) (Cowley, *Aramaic Papyri,* p. 43): Papyrus G, also known later as Cowley 15, and Kraeling papyrus #7 (Emil G. Kraeling, *The Brooklyn Museum Aramaic Papyri: New Documents of the Fifth Century* B.C. *from the Jewish Colony at Elephantine* (New Haven: Yale University Press, 1953), pp. 206-7.

59. *m. Git.* 9:3. See my "Deuteronomy 24.1-4 and the Origin of the Jewish Divorce Certificate," and ch. 5.

60. Geller, "The Elephantine Papyri and Hosea 2.3." Hosea will be explored further in the next chapter.

61. The exact meaning of the words that follow this pronouncement in Malachi is probably impossible to decipher, but one word stands out: בגד *(bagad),* which is usually translated "treachery." This word has already been used twice in 2:14-15, where the crime that is condemned is the breaking of a covenant. The word has perhaps been picked up from Jeremiah 3 where Israel's spiritual adultery is called "treachery," and the word has already been used by Malachi in 2:11 to describe the action of someone who married the daughter of a foreign god. It

These links and similarities between the language of marriage covenants in the Bible and the ancient Near East do not suggest any kind of literary dependence. They are indications that the world of Pentateuchal literature was the same as the world of the ancient Near East. Marriage covenants in the Old Testament are very similar in almost every respect to marriage covenants in the ancient Near East. In the light of this, we will now consider what is the correct nature of a biblical "marriage covenant."

Marriage Is a "Contract"

In contemporary English, the best translation for the ancient Near Eastern concept of "covenant" (Hebrew ברית, *berith*) is the term "contract." Like a contract, an ancient Near Eastern covenant involved an agreement between two parties, sealed with a document or a ceremony, and involving an exchange of goods or rights. A biblical "marriage covenant" should therefore be understood as a "marriage contract."

There has been some reluctance among biblical scholars to recognize the contractual basis of marriage. In ancient Near Eastern studies and Jewish studies it is generally accepted that the marriage documents are called "contracts,"[62]

---

is unclear whether v. 11 refers to the nation of Judah or individuals in Judah who marry "the daughter of a foreign god." Malachi swings from speaking about the nation breaking her covenant with God, to illustrations of this in the lives of individuals who have broken their marriage covenants. Usually it is clear which he is addressing at any one point, but in this case it is more difficult. Most probably he is speaking about individuals who have married foreign women, because the nation of Judah would commit adultery "with a foreign god" and not with "the daughter of a foreign god." Whichever it is, the argument in this paper is unaffected. Malachi also used the word "treachery" in 2:10, where it clearly means the breaking of a covenant: "Why do we profane the covenant of our fathers by acting treacherously with one another?" The sin that God hates, according to Malachi, is the breaking of promises made in the marriage covenant. Therefore the NIV is as good a translation as any: "You have broken faith with her, though she is your partner, the wife of your marriage covenant." See also Hugenberger, *Marriage as a Covenant,* pp. 51-83.

62. For example, Louis M. Epstein, *The Jewish Marriage Contract: A Study in the Status of the Woman in Jewish Law* (New York: Johnson Reprint Corp., 1968); Samuel Greengus, "The Old Babylonian Marriage Contract," *Journal of the American Oriental Society* 89 (1969): 505-32; Piattelli, "The Marriage Contract"; I. Abrahams, *Studies in Pharisaism and the Gospels* (London: Macmillan, 1917), e.g., p. 74; Reuven Yaron, *Introduction to the Law of the Aramaic Papyri* (Oxford: Clarendon, 1961); Mordechai Friedman, *A Jewish Marriage in Palestine: A Cairo Geniza Study,* 2 vols., *The Ketubba Traditions of Eretz Israel* and *The Ketubba Texts* (Tel-Aviv, New York, and Jerusalem: Daf-Chen, 1980).

but some biblical scholars wish to make a distinction between a **"contract"** and a **"covenant."** This distinction will now be examined and rejected.

Paul Palmer, for example, has rejected this idea of calling a marriage a "contract."[63] He summarized the debate about the meaning of "covenant" and "contract" and concluded that contracts are legal entities enforced by penalties, whereas covenants are based on faith. He pointed out that the OT covenants between Israel and God are based on the faithfulness of God. He pointed out that marriages should also be based on trust between two people. Although it is true that there is a contractual aspect to marriage, and a legal framework for the responsibilities that marriage implies, this is less important than the covenant of marriage.

G. P. Hugenberger also argues that the Old Testament refers to a marriage covenant. He argues that the ancient Near Eastern marriage documents were not necessarily drawn up at the time of the wedding but might be drawn up when the first child was born.[64] This means that they do not represent the words spoken at a wedding, and they are simply a legal contract in addition to the marriage covenant. He suggests that there are traces of a marriage covenant formula in the Genesis formulae "bone of my bone," "one flesh," and "leave their family," all of which indicate the formation of a family covenant.[65] He also suggests that the actual words of the marriage covenant may be something like the "You are my husband" and "You are my wife." This is based on the opposite words indicating a divorce in Hosea 2:2 [MT 2:4], and several parallels in ancient Near Eastern sources.[66] This suggestion is supported by the Demotic marriage contracts that preserve other features of ancient Near Eastern marriage contracts.[67]

Although the distinction between "covenant" and "contract" is a useful one in theological language, we must take care not to read later theological development back into the Old Testament. The theological distinction between covenant and contract helps to distinguish between a relationship based on le-

63. Paul F. Palmer, "Christian Marriage: Contract or Covenant?" *Theological Studies* 33 (1972): 617-65.

64. Hugenberger, *Marriage as a Covenant,* p. 191.

65. Hugenberger, *Marriage as a Covenant,* p. 230.

66. Hugenberger, *Marriage as a Covenant,* pp. 216-37.

67. See F. L. Griffith, *Catalogue of the Demotic Papyri in the John Rylands Library, Manchester: With Facsimiles and Complete Transcriptions,* vol. 3: *Key-list, Translations, Commentaries and Indices* (Manchester: University Press, 1909), esp. pp. 115-17. Almost all the marriage contracts collected there contain the declaration by the husband: "I make you my wife." Other ancient Near Eastern features in the Demotic marriage contracts include the use of the term "hate" to mean "divorce."

galism and one based on grace and trust. The term "covenant" is useful for emphasizing the gracious aspect of God's covenant with Israel and with the Church. However, the theological development of this term should not determine the way in which Old Testament language is understood.

As originally written, there was no distinction between "covenant" and "contract." There is only one word for both (ברית), and there is no reason to believe that this one word represented more than one type of agreement. This applies not only to the OT use of the term "covenant" but also to its use in the NT and beyond into the Church Fathers. Throughout this period, the term "covenant" meant a contract that could be broken if either side reneged on their half of the agreement. In the New Testament and beyond there was also a second, entirely separate meaning of "covenant" as the "New Covenant" (i.e., New Testament). This developed alongside the traditional meaning of covenant as a contract.[68]

The theological meaning of "covenant" is an agreement that a faithful person would not break even if the partner to whom that person is in covenant breaks the stipulations of the covenant. This new meaning of "covenant" is based on the covenantal relationship between God and his people in the later prophets and the New Testament. In the later prophets, God promised that he would keep his side of the agreement whether or not his people kept theirs. God would be faithful even if his people were faithless. This irrevocable covenant was portrayed in Ezekiel 36–37 and Jeremiah 31 as a "new covenant." This is different to every other type of covenant found in the ancient Near East or in the Old Testament. It is this difference that made the "new covenant" so special.

The **covenant with Israel** at Sinai is described in the Pentateuch in terms of a treaty covenant between an empire and a vassal state. Ancient Near Eastern treaty covenants followed a common format that included historical prologue, stipulations of the covenant, divine witnesses, and curses on those who break the covenant. We find this pattern in Exodus-Leviticus, in Deuteronomy, and perhaps in Joshua 24. The only real distinction between these covenants and other extant ancient Near Eastern covenants is that the witnesses are not a collection of gods but God himself, who is also one of the parties to the covenant.[69]

68. Private communication with Petrus Grabbe before the publication of his book that surveyed the use of "Covenant" from the ancient Near East to the Early Church Fathers.

69. Another possible difference is that most ancient Near Eastern covenants lacked the blessings that accompanied the curses in OT, though these are present in Hittite covenants. For a useful summary and bibliography see James H. Walton, *Ancient Israelite Literature in Its Cultural Context: A Survey of Parallels between Biblical and Ancient Near Eastern Texts* (Grand Rapids: Zondervan, 1989), ch. 4.

The old covenant of Sinai was not as generous as the "new covenant" because it was based on the normal covenant treaty model. As normal, it ended with curses and blessings. These acted as a list of the sanctions that would be meted out if the treaty was broken, and as a reminder of the benefits of keeping the treaty. The Sinai treaty of God with Israel contained a long section of blessings and curses (Deuteronomy 27–28), and it was understood that God did indeed bring these curses on Israel when they disobeyed (Deut. 29:22-28). The "new covenant" had no curses to be meted out to the disobedient partner. God was going to be faithful forever. This "new covenant" became the basis for covenant theology.

Hugenberger acknowledged that the Old Testament word "covenant" shared the same meaning throughout the ancient Near East, but he also tried to argue that there was an extra agreement in marriage, which he called the marriage covenant. This was separate from marriage contracts that list stipulations concerning finances, divorce, and death settlements. His marriage covenant consisted of personal vows such as "You are my wife" without any contractual elements attached.

However, there is no evidence that these two aspects of marriage agreement were ever separated in Israel or anywhere else in the ancient Near East. The marriage documents that have survived either have only the financial and other stipulations, or they have both these and the personal vows. The examples of these vows cited above[70] occur in documents that list finances and stipulations like any other marriage document.

It is therefore misleading to use the term "covenant" for the legal marriage agreement in the Old Testament and ancient Near East. Marriage covenants in the ancient Near East were written and enacted exactly like any other business or diplomatic covenant. Like any other agreement, they were based on both trust and penalties. The penalties as well as the benefits of keeping the stipulations of the marriage covenant were clearly outlined. There was a recognized system of financial penalties for the partner who initiated divorce without good cause, or for the partner who broke the stipulations of the covenant. The terminology of marriage documents is also similar in all respects to other business transactions. This is all reflected in the Old Testament language and law.

Although the phrase "marriage covenant" is correct, it is misleading. Marriage "covenant" has come to mean something separate from legal restraints. The phrase "marriage contract" is therefore much better than "marriage covenant" for conveying the correct meaning in modern English. This is the normal

70. Roth, *Babylonian Marriage Agreements,* nos. 2 and 25.

phrase used by Jewish scholars when referring to legal marriage documents, and also by ancient historians when referring to ancient Near Eastern marriage law. For this reason, this book will from now on use the phrases **"marriage contract"** and "marriage covenant" synonymously when referring to the legal framework for marriage in biblical, ancient Near Eastern, and rabbinic sources.

The implication of understanding marriage as a contract is that divorce with the loss of the dowry should be regarded as the main penalty defined in this contract. Like any other contract, the ancient Near Eastern marriage contract was an agreement between two parties that also defined the penalties incurred by the party who failed to keep the agreement.

There is a general understanding throughout the ancient Near East that a wife can be divorced at will by a husband and have her dowry returned, but, if she has done wrong, she does not receive her dowry. There is also some evidence that wives were able to divorce their husbands in some situations.[71] The evidence is more sparse in these situations, but the contracts collected by Roth suggest that the woman could keep the dowry when her husband had broken a stipulation in their marriage contract. This all fits with the conclusion that marriage is a contract, and that the party who breaks the contract faces a fine, which is represented by the dowry.

Conclusions

This chapter has shown that marriage in the Pentateuch is a contract between two families and between two individuals. This contract was often recorded in a document that included the financial arrangements, the stipulations that could lead to divorce if the contract was broken, and the financial arrangements in the event of divorce. Many of these documents have been found dating from the seventh century B.C.E. The details recorded in these documents, and the language that is used to record them, find exact parallels in the Pentateuch. The Old Testament speaks of marriage as a "covenant" (ברית), which was the ancient Near Eastern term for any kind of binding agreement or contract. The correct phrase for a marriage agreement in the Old Testament is therefore a "marriage contract." Like any other contract, this contained an agreement and penalties for breaking the agreement. The penalty for breaking the marriage contract was divorce with loss of the dowry.

71. The evidence is conveniently collected in Tal Ilan, "Notes and Observations on a Newly Published Divorce Bill from the Judean Desert," *Harvard Theological Review* 89 (1996): 195-202, esp. p. 195.

2. The Pentateuch

The Divorce Certificate Allows Remarriage

The law of Moses was different from the rest of the ancient Near East with regard to the rights of women in marriage and divorce. They had greater rights within marriage, and a greater opportunity to remarry after divorce. The divorce certificate, which gave women the right to remarry, was unknown elsewhere in the ancient Near East.

Distinctiveness of the Pentateuch

Comparisons of the Pentateuch with other ancient Near Eastern sources have shown that they share the same culture with regard to marriage, divorce, and remarriage. Their customs, terminology, and laws are similar in almost all respects. This chapter will examine the distinctiveness of the Pentateuch over against the rest of the ancient Near East.

It is not possible to be definite about such distinctiveness because the documentary sources from Israel and her neighbors are fragmentary. There are still thousands of ancient Near Eastern texts waiting in museums to be translated, and perhaps countless more waiting to be unearthed. The Pentateuchal sources should also be regarded as fragmentary because we do not have a complete law code. We have various law codes, such as the Book of the Covenant (Exod. 20:22–23:33) and other less well defined codes. The two primary texts for the law on divorce[1] are pieces of case law that are not even found in the same

1. Exod. 21:10-11 and Deut. 24:1-4.

collection. There is no reason to think that the old Israelite law on divorce is preserved in the Pentateuch in its entirety or even in outline.

Because of the similarity of the Pentateuch with other ancient Near Eastern law codes, we must assume that where the Old Testament is silent, there was broad agreement with the prevailing culture. However, the Israelites were very proud that they did *not* conform to the prevailing culture of the nations surrounding them. We can therefore assume that when there was a distinctiveness between the Israelites and their neighbors, this would be likely to be recorded in the Pentateuch. One of the purposes of the Pentateuchal law was to highlight these differences.

Most of the differences that will be examined are differences in degree rather than absolute differences. In particular, women have greater rights in the Pentateuch than in the ancient Near East generally. This does not mean that women had no rights in other societies, and it does not mean that women in other societies all shared the same level of rights, but *in general* the Pentateuch offered women more rights. Unfortunately there is little evidence that these greater rights were enacted in actual practice in Israel.

Before looking at the areas where the Pentateuch is distinct from the ancient Near East, we will look at a couple of areas where, although one might expect to find a distinction, in fact there is very little difference. These are the practices of polygamy and divorce. We might expect that the Pentateuchal law would prohibit or at least limit these practices, but in the area of polygamy we find almost total silence, and in the area of divorce we find no greater restriction than that found elsewhere. The differences that *do* exist are in the rights of the wife and the divorcée.

The Monogamist Ideal

It is possible that there is an indication in Genesis 2:24 that monogamy was the ideal for marriage in the Pentateuch. Yet whatever the original intent of this passage, it is unlikely that it was interpreted in this way until almost the time of the New Testament. Many of the ancient heroes and ancestors of Israel had more than one wife, from Abraham and Jacob to David and Solomon. Although there is some criticism of the "many wives" of the kings, some of whom were foreigners, there is little or no criticism of other cases of polygamy.[2] At

2. Louis M. Epstein (*Marriage Laws in the Bible and Talmud*, Harvard Semitic Series 12 [Cambridge, Mass.: Harvard University Press, 1942], pp. 3-7) summarizes the biblical data. He points out that the Law assumed polygamy in Exod. 21:10; Deut. 21:15; Lev. 18:18. He lists among

later times monogamy was taught as an ideal (e.g., Isa. 50:1; Jer. 2:2; Ezek. 16:8; Prov. 12:4; 18:22; 19:14; 31:10-31; Ps. 128:3), but polygamy was never made illegal. The next chapter will show that even God was portrayed as married to both Israel and Judah, without any shame attached to either union.

It is unlikely that there was any teaching against polygamy in the early history of Israel. The phrase "they shall be one flesh" would probably have been interpreted to mean "they shall be one family."[3] By New Testament times there were many voices teaching that polygamy was against God's ideal. These included the Qumran sect, the translators of the LXX and Targums, and Jesus. These will be considered in chapter four. However, even in the first century C.E., polygamy was still considered to be part of traditional Jewish teaching.[4]

In practice, most men would have had only one wife due to financial reasons.[5] In the biblical text it is generally the wealthy individuals who had more than one wife. In the ancient Near Eastern sources there is also an assumption that polygamy is permissible, but that only the wealthy would actually have more than one wife.

There is therefore no discernible distinctiveness between the Pentateuch and the ancient Near Eastern sources with regard to monogamy/polygamy. The later prophets appear to prefer monogamy, and Judaism ultimately banned polygamy, but not until the eleventh century C.E.[6]

---

the polygamists of the OT, Lamech, Abraham, Nahor, Esau, Jacob, Simeon, Gideon, Elkanah, Saul, David, Solomon, Rehoboam, Jehoash, Abiah, Manasseh, and Sheharaim.

3. John Skinner (*Genesis,* International Critical Commentary [Edinburgh: T. & T. Clark, 1930], p. 70) pointed out that flesh, בשׂר *(basar),* is synonymous with "clan," "family group," in both Hebrew and Arabic usage. Cf. Lev. 25:49, "a near kinsman belonging to his flesh may redeem him."

4. S. Safrai, "Home and Family," in *The Jewish People in the First Century: Historical Geography, Political History, Social, Cultural and Religious Life and Institutions,* 2 vols., ed. S. Safrai and M. Stern with D. Flusser and W. C. van Unnick, Section 1 of Compendia Rerum Iudaicarum ad Novum Testamentum (vol. 1: Assen: Van Gorcum and Co. B. V., 1974; vol. 2: Philadelphia: Fortress Press, 1976), 2:728-92. At 2:749 Safrai cites Josephus (*Ant.* 17.14; *J.W.* 1.477), Justin Martyr (*Dialogue* 141), and some examples of polygamy in first-century rabbinic sources (*t. Yebam.* 1.10; *b. Sukk.* 27a; *b. Yebam.* 15a).

5. Epstein (*Marriage Laws,* p. 5) argued that the contrary is proved by the census in Numbers 2–3. He pointed out that if the numbers are taken literally, there was an average of one firstborn for every forty-five males, which would imply that polygamy must have been common. The census of Numbers 2–3 gives 22,273 firstborn for a population of 603,550, males over twenty — i.e., a total population of about a million. Therefore $1/45$ males are firstborn. However, as he says himself, the definition of a firstborn was the first born to a woman, not to a man (Num. 3:12: "who unlooses the womb"). Perhaps this was so during that period of Israel's history, but it is unlikely that it was generally true.

6. See chapter four for further details.

The Practice of Divorce

With the hindsight of the New Testament, Genesis 2:24 might also be interpreted as a condemnation of divorce. The rest of the Pentateuch, however, fails to speak against divorce. Abraham divorced his wife Hagar, the slave, and it is recorded as if God approved (Gen. 21:12).[7]

Although there are not multiple instances of divorce recorded in the Pentateuch, we must assume that divorce was as prevalent in Israel then as in other ancient Near Eastern societies. Several passages speak about divorce,[8] but none of them condemns or even discourages it.[9] The next chapter will show that Malachi criticized the breaking of marriage vows, though the actual process of divorce was not criticized. It is assumed in these passages that divorce happens, and no comment is made whether divorce itself is desirable or not.

Specific guidelines were given about the practice of divorce. In Exodus 21:10-11 there is the requirement in the divorce of a wife who is a slave that she must be released without any payment. Presumably this means that she did not have to buy her freedom, though it may also mean that the man did not have to pay her the equivalent of a dowry. Any other wife would be released with the repayment of her dowry, but a slave brought no dowry. Other guidelines are given about divorces in general in Deuteronomy 24:1-4: a divorced wife must be given a divorce certificate, and she must leave the marital home. Grounds for which divorce was accepted are also given in these passages. Indecency (whatever that meant) is named in Deuteronomy 24:1, and the neglect of basic provisions is implied in Exodus 21:10-11.[10] The fact that the husband in Deuteronomy 22:13-18 tried to find false grounds for divorce suggests that a groundless divorce was either not permitted or resulted in severe financial penalty.

There is much more about divorce that is not stated. There is nothing about whether these were the only grounds for divorce, or whether or when the wife should have her dowry returned. There is nothing about the rights of chil-

7. In Gen. 21:10, Sarah says, "Cast out this slave woman with her son," and in v. 12 God says, "Whatever Sarah says to you, do as she tells you." In the text, Abraham simply dismisses Hagar, but later Jewish tradition says that he also gave her a certificate of divorce (Yalkut Shimeoni Gen. Sec. 95).

8. Exod. 21:10-11; Deut. 21:14; 22:19, 29; 24:1-4.

9. Deut. 22:19, 29 forbids divorce to the man who has shamed his wife by raping her or claiming she was not a virgin. However, this is not a condemnation of divorce; it is a way of punishing the man for his crime while also providing financial security for the woman who might otherwise find it difficult to marry.

10. Later interpretations of the Pentateuch regarded "indecency" as adultery, and they translated the basic rights in Exod. 21:10-11 as food, clothing, and love.

dren to their father's estate. There is nothing about the rights of the woman after she is divorced, whether she is allowed to remarry, or where she should live after her divorce. There is no indication of the procedures for divorce, such as witnesses or other legal necessities. The lack of all these details suggests that the process of divorce followed the normal procedure found in the rest of the ancient Near East. The Pentateuch recorded only those situations where the Israelites were distinct from their neighbors.

The differences between Pentateuchal law and other ancient Near Eastern law codes lay mainly in the areas of a woman's right to remain married and remarried and of her right to divorce and remarriage. These will now be examined in detail.

Rights of Women to Divorce

This section could have been called "the rights of women within marriage," because their right to divorce acted as an enforcement of the rights that they could demand from their husband within marriage.

In the ancient Near East women were permitted to divorce their husbands, although there is little evidence that this actually happened with any frequency. Women had different degrees of rights to divorce in different city states. In Hittite law, women appear to have similar rights as men, though the text is fragmentary. What remains of code #26 reads:

> If a woman sends away a man, she shall give him . . . and . . . The man shall get his children.[11]

Other codes do not mention the right of women to divorce their husbands, though this does not mean that the right did not exist. These codes are rarely complete, and they are not at all exhaustive. A small minority of marriage certificates indicates that the wife had the right to divorce her husband.[12] According to Porten the Code of Hammurabi represents the middle ground in

11. Hittite law, in James B. Pritchard, ed., *Ancient Near Eastern Texts Relating to the Old Testament,* 3rd ed. (Princeton: Princeton University Press, 1978, 1992), p. 190.

12. E. Lipinski ("The Wife's Right to Divorce in the Light of an Ancient Near Eastern Tradition," in *The Jewish Law Annual,* ed. B. S. Jackson [Leiden: Brill, 1981], vol. 4, esp. pp. 14-17) collects a few marriage certificates that provide this right. The certificates contain sections such as: "If H ever says to W his wife, 'You are not my wife', he shall weigh out 10 shekels of silver. If W ever says to H her husband, 'You are not my husband', she shall weigh out 10 shekels of silver" (where W and H indicate the names of wife and husband, respectively).

the ancient Near East. Some city states did not allow women to divorce their husbands, and some allowed them a divorce for any reason, but the code of Hammurabi allowed women to divorce only **if their husband was at fault** in some way.[13] The method by which fault was decided was through a court made up of the city council:

> #142 If a woman so hated her husband that she has declared, "You may not have me," her record shall be investigated at her city council, and if she was careful and was not at fault, even though her husband has been going out and disparaging her greatly, that woman without incurring any blame at all, may take her dowry and go off to her father's house.
>
> #143 If she was not careful but was a gadabout, thus neglecting her house (and) humiliating her husband, they shall throw that woman into the water.

On the one hand, this sounds generous towards the woman, who is allowed to keep her dowry. On the other hand, it was a dangerous case to bring to the court because the woman faced the threat of death if the court decided against her.[14]

Women could also divorce their husbands **if they were neglected.** In the Code of Hammurabi a woman had the right to find another husband if her husband had been taken captive and had not left her sufficient means to live, though she had to return to her first husband if he returned.[15] In the Middle

13. Bezalel Porten, *Archives from Elephantine: The Life of an Ancient Jewish Military Colony* (Berkeley: University of California Press, 1968), pp. 209-10. The Hittite law is fragmentary.

14. In the Code of Hammurabi, being thrown into the river was actually regarded as a final plea to the gods, who would save the innocent. This is made clear in code #2: "If a seignior brought a charge of sorcery against a(nother) seignior, but has not proved it, the one against whom the charge of sorcery was brought, upon going to the river, shall throw himself into the river, and if the river has then overpowered him, his accuser shall take over his estate; if the river has shown that seignior to be innocent and he has accordingly come forth safe, the one who brought the charge of sorcery against him shall be put to death, while the one who threw himself into the river shall take over the estate of his accuser."

15. Code of Hammurabi #133-36, in Pritchard, *Ancient Near Eastern Texts,* p. 171:

> #133: If a seignior was taken captive, but there was sufficient to live on in his house, his wife [shall not leave her house, but she shall take care of her person by not] entering [the house of another]. #133a: If that woman did not take care of her person, but has entered the house of another, they shall prove it against that woman and throw her into the water. #134: If the seignior was taken captive and there was not sufficient to live on in his house, his wife may enter the house of another, with that woman incurring no blame at all. #135: If, when a seignior was taken captive and there was not sufficient to live on in his house, his wife has then entered the house of another before his (return) and has borne children,

Assyrian laws this is further developed into the case where a woman was deliberately neglected by a husband who had not been taken captive. She could not seek another husband until five years had lapsed:

> #36 If a woman is still living in her father's house or her husband made her live apart and her husband has gone off to the fields, without leaving her either oil or wool or clothing or food or anything at all (and) without having even an ear of grain brought to her from the field, that woman shall remain true to her husband for five years (and) not go to live with a(nother) husband. If she has sons (and) they hire themselves out and earn their living, the woman shall wait for her husband (and) not go to live with a(nother) husband. If she has no sons, she shall wait for her husband for five years; on the advent of the sixth year she may go to live with the man of her choice; her husband upon coming back may not claim her; she is free for her later husband.[16]

This law seems very harsh, particularly for a woman whose father has died and does not have sons to support her. She is required to wait for five years, supporting herself as well as she can, before she can look for another husband. Other ancient Near Eastern laws do not even grant this concession.

The Pentateuch was more generous to the woman because it did not prescribe time constraints while it allowed women to divorce their husbands on the same grounds of neglect. The grounds of neglect are defined in Exodus 21:10-11 in very similar terms to the Middle Assyrian law.[17] These rights were given to a slave, and it may be assumed that, if a slave had these rights, a free woman would also have them. However the Pentateuch is more generous than other ancient Near Eastern law codes because there is no minimum time limit set for this neglect. She did not have to starve for five years before claiming that she was being neglected.

(and) later her husband has returned and has reached his city, that woman shall return to her first husband, while the children shall go with their father.

#136: If, when a seignior deserted his city and then ran away, his wife has entered the house of another after his (departure), if that seignior has returned and wishes to take back his wife, the wife of the fugitive shall not return to her husband because he scorned his city and ran away.

16. Pritchard, *Ancient Near Eastern Texts,* p. 183.

17. Exod. 21:10 — lack of food, clothing, and oil or conjugal rights — as discussed in chapter one.

The Rights of Women to Remain Married

Another way in which women are given more equality in the Pentateuch was the right to remain married when they had been dealt with falsely.

When a virgin was raped, the general ancient Near Eastern law was for her rapist to suffer the death penalty and for her to go unpunished. For example, the Laws of Eshnunna #26:[18]

> If a man gives bride-money for a(nother) man's daughter, but another man seizes her forcibly without asking the permission of her father and her mother and deprives her of her virginity, it is a capital offence and he shall die.

The woman who is the victim is not punished, but her future is ruined. It was likely that she would remain unmarried or that she would be married with a much reduced bride-price.

In the Middle Assyrian laws there is a law that the rapist has to give up his own wife to be raped and he has to marry the raped virgin (if her father wishes it), as well as pay a bride-price for the virgin, and he may not divorce her.[19]

The Pentateuch also has a law about the woman who is raped (Deut. 22:28-29), but it is much more generous toward her than were the Middle Assyrian laws. The man who raped her must marry her, and he cannot divorce her. He must support her for life, even though she does not have to fulfill her marriage stipulations.[20] This meant that the woman was provided for and would not be a burden on her family.

The Code of Hammurabi had a concession to a **woman who was ill** with *la'bum*.[21] It is uncertain what this illness is,[22] but a woman who contracts it af-

18. E.g., the Laws of Eshnunna, in Pritchard, *Ancient Near Eastern Texts*, pp. 161-63.

19. Middle Assyrian law #55, in Pritchard, *Ancient Near Eastern Texts*, p. 185.

20. D. W. Amram (*The Jewish Law of Divorce according to Bible and Talmud* [reprint of undated original, New York: Sepher-Hermon, 1975], p. 43) points out that Josephus assumed that she could be divorced if she commits adultery. This was probably because Philo and Josephus both followed the Hittite law that a woman could be divorced for "any matter," and thus they regarded the restriction as meaning that she could be divorced only on serious grounds.

21. "#148: When a seignior married a woman and a fever *(la'bum)* has then seized her, if he has made up his mind to marry another, he may marry (her), without divorcing his wife whom the fever seized; she shall live in the house which he built and he shall continue to support her as long as she lives. #149: If that woman has refused to live in her husband's house, he shall make good her dowry to her which she brought from her father's house and then she may leave." Pritchard, *Ancient Near Eastern Texts*, p. 172.

22. T. J. Meet (in Pritchard, *Ancient Near Eastern Texts*, p. 172) translates it with the vague term "fever" while noting that this translation is uncertain.

ter she has married may not be divorced, even if her husband decides to marry someone else, unless she wishes it.

The Pentateuch does not have anything equivalent to this provision. However, it may well have been enacted in Israel along with other ancient Near Eastern laws that are not recorded in the Pentateuch. Some evidence for this lies in the rabbinic tradition that a woman who is afflicted with madness cannot be divorced.[23] Unlike other grounds for divorce, there is no scriptural basis for this.[24] It is possible that, like many other traditional regulations, this was inherited from the ancient Near Eastern heritage of the Israelites.

There is an additional right in the Pentateuch for a **woman who is accused** on her wedding night **of not being a virgin** (Deut. 22:13-19). The motive for this may be financial. If a husband could convince the city officials that his wife was not a virgin, he would lose the burden of keeping her, and he would keep her dowry. The Pentateuch makes this potentially profitable falsehood into a very risky one, because if the family can prove otherwise, her husband cannot divorce her. There is no parallel for this right in other ancient Near Eastern laws.

The question arose about women who did not *want* to marry their rapist or their mercenary husbands. In other ancient Near Eastern laws, the father could decide in the case of rape, and the wife could decide in the case of severe illness. Amram[25] points out that Philo and Josephus both assumed that in Judaism the choice lay with the woman. They do not adduce any scriptural proof for this, so it may have been a well-established traditional interpretation.

The Right of Women to a Divorce Certificate, and to Remarriage

It will be shown that the right of a woman to a divorce certificate is equivalent to the right of a woman to remarry. In fact, the purpose of the divorce certificate was to help the woman remarry.

The reference in Deuteronomy 24:1 to a divorce certificate is unique in ancient Near Eastern sources. Nowhere outside Judaism is there any reference to a divorce certificate or any other document that would be taken away by every divorced woman.[26]

23. *m. Yebam.* 14.1; *b. Yebam.* 111b-12a.

24. The debate on this mishnah in *b. Yebam.* 111b-12a reflects the concern by various rabbis that this ruling was not based on Scripture.

25. Amram, *The Jewish Law of Divorce*, pp. 42-43.

26. It is likely that some financial receipt would be handed over at the time of divorce,

The **wording on the divorce certificate** is not stated in the Pentateuch, but there are good reasons to conclude that it was similar to the wording of standard rabbinic divorce certificates: "You are allowed to marry any man you wish." This wording can be traced through Jewish divorce certificates and marriage certificates that have survived from as far back as the fifth century B.C.E., and it can then be traced through Babylonian marriage certificates and law codes back as far as the fourteenth century B.C.E.[27] This would fit all the known facts. This document would be needed by women, but not by men, because men could marry more than one woman in any case. It would have been a most valuable document for a woman to possess because it gave her the right to remarry. Without it she would be under the constant threat of her former husband, who could claim at a later date that she was still married to him and thus charge her with adultery.

The nearest possible parallel to a divorce certificate in the ancient Near Eastern literature is the **tablet proving widowhood** mentioned in the Middle Assyrian law #45:

> When a woman has been given in marriage and the enemy has captured her husband, . . . she shall complete two years and then she may go to live with the husband of her choice. They shall write a tablet for her as a widow.[28]

This was probably not given to every widow, but only to those whose widowhood was in doubt. If her husband had been captured, after two years he was presumed dead. In order to give her the rights of a widow, she needed a ruling by the city council that he should indeed be presumed dead.

In the Pentateuch this right of remarriage was already extended to all widows. In fact, widows without a son were guaranteed a new husband by the

---

but this would have been needed by the man, not the woman. The dowry, in part or whole, usually had to be repaid to the divorced woman, and presumably some kind of written or witnessed oral receipt had to be given to the man to testify that his debt had been paid. This document or witnessed testimony would be very important to the man to prevent his ex-wife from claiming that he had not repaid the dowry. This document or testimony would be kept by the husband. The only time that a woman would have needed a similar receipt would be when she initiated the divorce. In this case, in some city-states, she had to repay parts of her dowry (see Hittite law #26, in Pritchard, *Ancient Near Eastern Texts*, p. 190, cited above). Even in this situation it is unlikely that the woman would need any receipt, because what she "gave" to her ex-husband would have been part or the whole of her rights to her dowry.

27. This traditional wording is found in the Elephantine documents of the fifth century B.C.E., in Babylonian marriage documents of the sixth to seventh centuries, and in ancient Near Eastern law codes. For details see my "Deuteronomy 24.1-4 and the Origin of the Jewish Divorce Certificate," *Journal of Jewish Studies* 49 (1998): 230-43.

28. Pritchard, *Ancient Near Eastern Texts*, p. 184.

law of levirate marriage,[29] though there are details about what was done in the case of doubtful widowhood. However, the "tablet for her as a widow," which was given to a woman in this particular circumstance, was extended by the Pentateuch to every divorced woman.

The tablet of widowhood in this Middle Assyrian law is not a divorce certificate, but it is very similar in many ways. It was given to a woman to prove that her marriage had ended, and the force of it was to state that "she may go to live with the husband of her choice." This phrase is very similar to the wording of the ancient Jewish divorce certificate, which stated simply that "you are free to marry any man" (*m. Git.* 9.3). It is also similar to a phrase that occurs regularly in ancient Near Eastern marriage documents after the stipulations about divorce, stating that the divorced wife is "free to go wherever she pleases."[30] This is the same phrase that is recorded of a widow in the Middle Assyrian law #33: "she may go where she wishes."[31]

The Middle Assyrian law is preserved on clay tablets from the time of Tiglath-pileser I in the twelfth century B.C.E., but the laws on them probably go back to the fifteenth century.[32] The fact that a similar phrase can be traced through the centuries to the traditional wording of the rabbinic divorce certificate is strong evidence that we are very close to the original wording of the divorce certificate referred to in Deuteronomy 24.

The law of the divorce certificate marks a very distinctive difference between the Pentateuch and other ancient Near Eastern laws. It provided a clean and proper end to a broken marriage. In other ancient Near Eastern cultures, the man could neglect his wife and then reclaim her within five years, even if she had remarried in the meantime. The Middle Assyrian law #36 states:

> If her husband has gone off to the fields, . . . If she has gone to live with a(nother) husband before the five years and has also borne children, her husband upon coming back shall get her back and her children as well because she did not respect the marriage covenant but got married.[33]

The law of Deuteronomy 24 meant that a man could not simply reclaim his wife. He had to give her a certificate that stated that she was free to remarry.

29. Deut. 25:5-9.

30. M. T. Roth, *Babylonian Marriage Agreements: 7th-3rd Centuries B.C.* (Kevalaer: Verlag Butzon & Bercker; Neukirchen-Vluyn: Neukirchener Verlag, 1989), nos. 2, 4, 6, 15, 19, 20.

31. Pritchard, *Ancient Near Eastern Texts,* p. 182.

32. See the introduction to the Middle Assyrian laws in Pritchard, *Ancient Near Eastern Texts,* p. 180.

33. Pritchard, *Ancient Near Eastern Texts,* p. 183.

At the same time he would presumably have to settle the return of the dowry, so that the wife would have some money to live on.

Unfortunately, because of the way the law of the divorce certificate was interpreted, it actually became a way to stop women from getting divorced. The law was interpreted to mean that one could not get divorced without a divorce certificate. This meant that divorce became the prerogative of the husband because he wrote out the divorce certificate. Therefore, a provision that was meant to empower the divorced woman resulted in the enslavement of women who wished to get divorced. As will be seen in later chapters, there were ways in which a rabbinic court could force a man to write out a divorce certificate when the woman had good grounds for a divorce. However, there was, and still is, one group of women who could not get a divorce. These are those whose husbands are missing, either through misadventure during war or during travel abroad, or deliberately. These women can not remarry unless some proof is found that their husbands are dead. As long as there is a possibility that their husbands are alive, they can not be divorced without a certificate signed by their husband. The Jewish world is still struggling with this conundrum.[34]

As originally intended, the Pentateuch gave women greater freedom than any other ancient Near Eastern law. It gave divorced women the documentary evidence of their divorce, which enabled them to remarry without fear of counterclaims some time in the future from their former husbands.

The Rights of Women to Remain Remarried

According to the ancient Near Eastern law codes, a woman could be reclaimed by her first husband, even if she had remarried, since she had been left by him. The Middle Assyrian law #36 (cited above) put a limit of five years on this right. This law is not paralleled in other ancient Near Eastern codes and appears to be a humane concession, similar to the other concession in law #45 concerning the doubtful widow (cited above). This made it very difficult for a woman to remarry, and, having remarried, she was always in danger of being reclaimed by her original husband.

Her first husband could appear at any time and demand her back. This meant that another man would have had the expense of bringing up the chil-

34. The problem is well summarized in Ben-Zion (Benno) Schereschewsky, "Agunah," *Encyclopaedia Judaica,* 16 vols. (Jerusalem: Keter, 1972), 2:430-34. E. N. Dorff and A. Rosett have pointed our that the problem is shared by all modern Jewish wives who have been divorced in secular courts (*A Living Tree: The Roots and Growth of Jewish Law* [New York: Jewish Theological Seminary of America, State University of New York Press, 1988], p. 531).

dren, and then the first husband would have the financial reward of their work now that they were grown. In these circumstances it would be very difficult for a woman to remarry.

In this context, the law of Deuteronomy 24:1-4 stands in stark **contrast to other ancient Near Eastern laws**. This law forbids a man from remarrying a woman whom he has divorced. This, in effect, gives the woman the right to remain remarried to her second husband. If the Mosaic law had merely said that the first husband was not entitled to reclaim his former wife, this would not have been sufficient protection for her. Her second husband may have felt morally obliged to divorce his wife when her first husband wished to have her back. This was the normal procedure throughout the ancient Near East, and it would be difficult for the second husband to avoid the moral pressure of his neighbors who expected him to act in the time-honored way. The law therefore forbids the remarriage of a woman to her first husband, even if her second husband has divorced her.[35]

This protection of the second marriage is a further assistance under the Pentateuchal law to help a divorced woman to remarry.

The Primary Distinctiveness of the Pentateuch

Most of the differences outlined above are differences in degree rather than absolute differences. Women had *greater* rights within marriage, in divorce, and in remarriage, but these were all extensions of rights that already existed in other ancient Near Eastern law codes. The only matter of absolute distinctiveness is the divorce certificate. There is no equivalent to the divorce certificate in any ancient Near Eastern culture outside Judaism.

The purpose of the divorce certificate was to allow an abandoned woman to remarry. It was an abrogation by the man of his rights as her husband to reclaim her after abandoning her. He had to give her this certificate before he sent

35. It is unlikely that this is a complete explanation for the difficult legislation in Deut. 24:1-4 because it does not explain the words "or if he dies" in v. 3. There have been many attempts to understand this legislation. See the review by Raymond Westbrook, "Prohibition of Restoration of Marriage in Deuteronomy 24.1-4," in *Studies in Bible 1986*, ed. S. Japhet, Scripta Hierosolymitana 31 (Jerusalem: Magnes, 1986), pp. 387-405, and more recent suggestions by James H. Walton, "The Place of the *hutqattel* within the D-stem Group and Its Implications in Deuteronomy 24.4," *Hebrew Studies* 32 (1991): 7-17, and Joe M. Sprinkle, "Old Testament Perspectives on Divorce and Remarriage," *The Journal of the Evangelical Theological Society* 40 (1997): 529-50.

her from his house.[36] If she exercised this right and remarried, his right to her was then irrevocably lost.

The divorce certificate was therefore both a disincentive to divorce as well as a benefit to a divorced woman. Without the law of the certificate of divorce, a man could simply dismiss his wife from the house and then change his mind on a future occasion. The certificate made this dismissal a more significant event and gave the woman legal rights. It also slowed down the event because the man had to sit down and write out the certificate. This must have prevented many divorces that might otherwise have occurred at the climax of an argument.

Conclusions

In conclusion, when the Pentateuch is compared with the laws of surrounding cultures, its distinctiveness does not lie in the monogamist ideal or restrictions on remarriage. The Pentateuch assumes that both polygamy and divorce occur, and neither is criticized. Its distinctiveness lies in the relatively greater rights of women within marriage and remarriage, and the greater rights to divorce and remarry. The only absolute distinctiveness was the right of a woman to a divorce certificate, which affirmed that she was free to remarry. This certificate, which was a right of a few privileged women in some ancient Near Eastern legal systems, was extended by the Pentateuch to all divorced women. This certificate freed women from the fear that their ex-husbands could reclaim them after abandoning them. The wording of the ancient Near Eastern certificates was similar to the traditional rabbinic *get,* which states "you are free to marry any man you wish."

36. Deut. 24:1, 3: "He writes her a bill of divorce and puts it in her hand and sends her out of his house, and she departs out of his house." This set of phrases, in exactly the same order, occurs twice, in v. 1 and v. 3.

3. The Later Prophets

Breaking Marriage Vows Is Condemned

The later prophets speak about God as if he were married to Israel and Judah. He separates from one wife and divorces another, all the time acting in strict accord with the Pentateuchal laws. The marriage metaphor that was presented by Hosea's life and teaching was developed by Jeremiah, and then developed further by Ezekiel and Second Isaiah. A literary dependence is likely, especially from Hosea to Jeremiah and Ezekiel. These prophets present a consistent picture of God who reluctantly divorces Israel because she consistently breaks her marriage vows, and no shame is attached to God's divorce because it was Israel's and Judah's fault. Malachi's criticism of divorce is directed at those who cause the divorce by breaking their vows.

The Marriage Metaphor before Hosea

Hosea did not develop the marriage metaphor in a vacuum. Surrounding religions had many stories of gods and goddesses who married, though they normally married an individual god or demigod, and not a nation. The marriage metaphor of Yahweh has very early roots, as seen in the language of jealousy in the Decalogue and other parts of the Pentateuch.

The whole language of "jealousy," which is central to the picture of God in the Pentateuch, has the connotation of marriage.[1] The concept of jealousy is

1. God is frequently called "jealous," most significantly at Exod. 20:2-6. See the analysis in

already linked with spiritual whoredom in the Pentateuch[2] and Judges.[3] Sinai can be seen as the point at which God marries his people,[4] and Leslie W. Pope finds a reference to God collecting his bride and bringing her to him in the wilderness.[5]

The folk religion of Palestine spoke of gods who married people and nations. The Ugaritic myths include the story of two sisters who married El;[6] it dates back long before 1400 B.C.E. when it was written down. The personification of a city as the wife of a god was also very common in the ancient Near East.[7]

Hosea's Portrayal of Yahweh's Marriage Problems

Hosea developed ideas inherent in the Pentateuch and in the religion of the surrounding cultures.[8] Hosea does not say that Yahweh is like other gods, but instead he contrasts Yahweh with other gods.[9] He shows that Yahweh is interested in showing loving kindness to his people. Hosea lived out his message of

---

Raymond C. Ortlund, *Whoredom: God's Unfaithful Wife in Biblical Theology* (Leicester: Apollos, 1996), pp. 27-30.

2. Exod. 34:14-16; Lev. 17:1-7; 20:1-6; Deut. 31:16. See the analysis in Nelly Stienstra, *YHWH Is the Husband of His People: Analysis of a Biblical Metaphor with Special Reference to Translation* (Kampen: Kok Pharos, 1993), pp. 179-86, and in Ortlund, *Whoredom*, pp. 31-40.

3. Judg. 2:17; 8:27, 33 — they "play the harlot" with Gideon's Ephod and the Baals.

4. See Louis Ginzberg, *The Legends of the Jews*, trans. Henrietta Szold (Philadelphia: Jewish Publication Society of America, 1913-67), 6:36, n. 200 for covenant at Sinai as a wedding in midrashic literature.

5. Deut. 4:34-38; Exod. 15:13. See Leslie W. Pope, "Marriage: A Study of the Covenant Relationship as Found in the Old Testament," M.A. thesis, Providence Theological Seminary, 1995 (Ann Arbor, Mich.: UMI Dissertation Services, 1997), p. 93; cited in Seock-Tae Sohn, *The Divine Election of Israel* (Grand Rapids: Eerdmans, 1991), p. 44.

6. "Shachar and Shalim and the Gracious Gods," in J. C. L. Gibson, *Canaanite Myths and Legends*, 2nd ed., originally ed. G. R. Driver (Edinburgh: T. & T. Clark, 1978), pp. 28-30, 123-27, and "Dawn and Dusk (The Birth of the Gracious and Beautiful Gods)," in William W. Hallo and K. Lawson Younger, *The Context of Scripture*, vol. 1: *Canonical Compositions from the Biblical World* (Leiden: Brill, 1997), pp. 274-83.

7. See the many examples in Julie Galambush, *Jerusalem in the Book of Ezekiel: The City as Yahweh's Wife*, Society for Biblical Literature Dissertation Series 130 (Atlanta: Scholars Press, 1992), pp. 20-22.

8. C. L. Seow ("Hosea, Book of," in *Anchor Bible Dictionary* [New York: Doubleday, 1992], 3:291-97, esp. pp. 294-95) refers to the archaeological evidence for syncretism, such as the inscription that reads, "May you be blessed by YHWH of Samaria and by his Asherah."

9. Stienstra (*YHWH Is the Husband of His People*, p. 100) concludes that even though Hosea was influenced by the Ugaritic myths, or others like them, this was nevertheless a very original work.

God's love for Israel and his toleration of her constant faithlessness. By being so personally involved with his message, he was able to show the regret that God felt when he divorced Israel. He also showed that God did not end the relationship until it was already totally destroyed. God was forced into a divorce.

The events in **the life of Hosea** are difficult to reconstruct. The text of the book of Hosea has been described as the most difficult text to translate, after the book of Job.[10] This is due mainly to the use of a northern dialect of Hebrew, of which there are few other examples outside Ugaritic. The biographical elements of the first three chapters are particularly difficult to reconstruct. It is difficult to know whether the third-person account in the first chapter is describing the same events as the first-person account of chapter 3, and, if they are different events, whether they relate to the same woman. In chapter 1, Hosea is told to marry a promiscuous woman called Gomer[11] and is told to give their children names that were symbolic of God's message to Israel. This marriage ends in divorce in chapter 2 as a result of her many adulteries. In chapter 3 he is told "again" to marry an adulterous woman whom he has to purchase from the slave market. It is impossible to determine whether the word "again" refers to marrying Gomer again, or to getting married again, or to God addressing Hosea again.[12]

Most commentators assume that the redactor(s) have put these chapters together in the correct order and that chapter 3 describes a remarriage to Gomer after one of her lovers sold her into slavery. This fits well with the comparison of this marriage to Yahweh's relationship to Israel. The first marriage is preexilic, and the second is a promise of a new relationship "in the latter days" after a period of "many days without king or prince, without sacrifice" (Hos. 3:4-5). It will be argued here that the ambiguity of her identity in chapter 3 is deliberate because it fits well with the ambiguous identity of God's new bride. The new bride is in some senses Judah and in some senses Israel, because she is a reunited Judah and Israel.

In **Hosea 1**, Hosea's children act out the drama along with Hosea. The first is named "Jezreel" as a reminder of a violent incident in the past, as a portent of the eschatological "day of Jezreel" (1:11 [MT 2:2]). The second and third, which may have been illegitimate,[13] were given the ominous names "Not Loved" and

10. Seow, "Hosea," p. 292.

11. Some commentators cannot accept that God would literally ask a prophet to marry an immoral woman. They suggest that this may just have been a picture, or a dream, or that the woman was not immoral until after the marriage started (e.g., Ibn Ezra cited in Leslie W. Pope, "Marriage," p. 83, and other commentators listed on pp. 84, 90, and in Ortlund, *Whoredom*, p. 50).

12. Seow, "Hosea," p. 293.

13. Ortlund (*Whoredom*, p. 51) points out that 1:3 reads "born to him," but the lack of "to him" in vv. 6, 8 suggests they are illegitimate (cf. Gen. 21:3).

"Not My People." With the second child comes the warning that God no longer loves his people Israel, though he still loves Judah (1:6-7). With the third child comes the terrible message that not only is the marriage over, but God will also stop being their God (1:8-9). They had enjoyed a close relationship in which God not only protected them but loved them like a husband. Now he would not even be their God. Following this final blow came a glimmer of light. Hosea is able to hold out the eschatological hope of a time when Israel would be reunited to Judah, when they would again be called "Loved" and "My People" (1:10–2:1 [MT 2:1-3]).

Hosea 2 makes it clear that Israel suffers divorce.[14] The words that Yahweh speaks in verse 2 [MT v. 4], "she is not my wife and I am not her husband," are an ancient Near Eastern divorce formula.[15] Also she admits to herself that the marriage is over, because when her lovers do not support her, she decides to return to her "first husband" (v. 7 [MT v. 9]).[16] She indirectly refers to her divorce when she appeals to her lovers for the support that Yahweh has withdrawn from her. This support is described in the terms of the marriage vows of Exodus 21:10-11,

14. Some commentators cannot accept that God would carry out a divorce, even though he is blameless for the marriage breakup (e.g., those listed in Leslie W. Pope, "Marriage," pp. 91-92). Andrew Cornes (*Divorce and Remarriage: Biblical Principles and Pastoral Practice* [London: Hodder & Stoughton, 1993]) provides clear exposition of the passages about God's divorce in the prophets, but he still cannot accept that God would divorce, and so he concludes that God divorced only for a short while, and that this should not really be counted as a real divorce (see especially p. 165).

15. See M. A. Friedman, "Israel's Response in Hosea 2.17b: 'You Are My Husband,'" *Journal of Biblical Literature* 99 (1980): 199-204; Markham J. Geller, "The Elephantine Papyri and Hosea 2.3: Evidence for the Form of the Early Jewish Divorce Writ," *Journal for the Study of Judaism* 8 (1977): 139-48; Bezalel Porten, *Archives from Elephantine: The Life of an Ancient Jewish Military Colony* (Berkeley: University of California Press, 1968), p. 206; E. Neufeld, *Ancient Hebrew Marriage Laws: With Special Reference to General Semitic Laws and Customs* (London: Longmans, Green and Co., 1944), p. 180; G. P. Hugenberger, *Marriage as a Covenant: A Study of Biblical Law and Ethics Governing Marriage, Developed from the Perspective of Malachi,* Vetus Testamentum Supplement 52 (Leiden and New York: Brill, 1994), pp. 216-37; contra Leslie W. Pope, "Marriage," p. 90. None of these seem to have noticed the Old Babylonian marriage contracts in B. Meissner, *Beiträge zum altbabylonischen Privatrecht* (Leipzig, 1893), nos. 89 and 90, pp. 71-72, and in E. Lipinski, "The Wife's Right to Divorce in the Light of an Ancient Near Eastern Tradition," in *The Jewish Law Annual,* vol. 4, ed. B. S. Jackson (Leiden: Brill, 1981), where either the man or the woman can divorce using the phrase "You are not my husband/wife."

16. There are other possible references to this divorce in Hosea. The stripping naked in v. 3 is seen by some as a divorce ceremony for adulterous wives (e.g., Stienstra, *YHWH Is the Husband of His People,* p. 169, and the example in Lipinski, "The Wife's Right to Divorce," pp. 16-17). Also Reuven Yaron, "On Divorce in Old Testament Times," *Revue Internationale des Droits de l'Antiquité* 3 (1957): 117-28; Yaron (pp. 119, 121) suggests that the language in 9:15 indicates divorce.

requiring the provision of "food, clothing, and oil."[17] She describes these provisions as "my bread and my water, my wool and my flax, my oil and my drink,"[18] which had been supplied by her husband. The fact that he has stopped supplying them indicates that a divorce has taken place. This divorce is also referred to at Hosea 9:15: "I began to hate them. Because of the wickedness of their deeds I will drive them out of my house. I will love them no more." The word "hate" (**שׂנא**, *shana*) becomes a technical term for divorce when it is in a context such as this that also refers to "driving out of my house."[19]

Perhaps it should not be said that **God divorced Israel**, but instead that God *suffered* the divorce, because, although he is the one who carried it out, he was forced into it. Israel had broken every one of the marriage vows, including the most obvious, faithfulness. She was committing constant and multiple acts of adultery, which had resulted in illegitimate children. The other marriage vows, to provide food, clothing, and oil, were also broken. Normally it would be expected that the man would provide the income or the basic ingredients for the food and cloth, and the woman would make the meals and clothes. Hosea says that the best of the food, the best of the clothes (the jewelry), and the wine that Yahweh had provided for her was used by her to prepare offerings for Baal, not for Yahweh (2:8 [MT 2:10]).

The eschatological hope for Israel lay in reunification with Judah. Hosea knows nothing of the troubles ahead in Judah's relationship with Yahweh, so the implication is that Israel will share Judah's good relationship. Later prophets saw Judah become as faithless as Israel and saw her suffer separation from her husband Yahweh. The eschatological hope then became a new relationship with the united nation of Israel and Judah. It would not be merely an enlargement of Yahweh's relationship with Judah to include Israel as well. It would be a completely new relationship with a new wife.[20]

17. See chapter one. Shalom M. Paul, "Exod. 21.10: A Threefold Maintenance Clause," *Journal of Near Eastern Studies* 28 (1969): 53. Stienstra (*YHWH Is the Husband of His People,* pp. 115-16) sees this connection but fails to relate it to Exodus 21.

18. In Exod. 21:10-11, the three are usually translated as "food, clothing, and love," but the original meaning of the third term (**ענתה**) was "oil," not "love" (see ch. one).

19. Yaron, "On Divorce in Old Testament Times," pp. 117-18, 121. Raymond Westbrook, "Prohibition of Restoration of Marriage in Deuteronomy 24.1-4," in *Studies in Bible 1986,* ed. S. Japhet, Scripta Hierosolymitana 31 (Jerusalem: Magnes, 1986), pp. 399-402. Jacob J. Rabinowitz, "Marriage Contracts in Ancient Egypt in the Light of Jewish Sources," *Harvard Theological Review* 46 (1953): 91-92. It occurs in several Demotic marriage contracts (see F. L. Griffith, *Catalogue of the Demotic Papyri in the John Rylands Library, Manchester: With Facsimiles and Complete Transcriptions,* vol. 3: *Key-list, Translations, Commentaries and Indices* (Manchester: University Press, 1909), pp. 115-17.

20. Friedman ("Israel's Response in Hosea 2.17b") suggests that the wording of the new

Hosea's vision anticipates some of the newness of this relationship, even though he could not have seen the reason for it. When describing this eschatological reconciliation he uses language that fits the context of the marriage of a virgin rather than the remarriage of an adulterous divorcée. Yahweh will woo her again, "as in the days of her youth" (2:14-15 [MT 2:16-17]); he will say to her:

> 2:19 [MT 2:21] And I will betroth you to me for ever; I will betroth you to me in righteousness and in justice, in steadfast love, and in mercy. 20 [MT 22] I will betroth you to me in faithfulness; and you shall know the LORD.

These words are spoken without any hint of their difficult past relationship and with all the confidence of youth looking forward to marriage without any problems. It is as if the old relationship that broke down in such a terrible way had never happened. This could be seen as a hint that the new relationship would be with a new nation — not just with restored Israel or even with enlarged Judah, but with a completely renewed nation made up of them both. This theme is taken up in more detail by later prophets.

Jeremiah's Development of Hosea

Jeremiah developed the ideas in Hosea,[21] looking at them afresh from a completely new situation. He is speaking to Judah, not Israel, and he is speaking after Israel's exile has occurred and Judah has followed the same path of spiritual adultery. Jeremiah was active from about 627 to 586 B.C.E., but editing took

---

marriage ceremony may be preserved in 2:19 [MT 2:21], which are the words spoken to her in the wilderness in 2:14 [MT 2:16], to which she "responds" in 2:15-16 [MT 2:17-18] with the words "My husband." He shows that these are similar to the words used in an ancient Near Eastern marriage ceremony. The original vow was "My lord," בעלי, but Hosea does not like the link with the Baalim, so he says she should vow "My man," אישי. See also Hugenberger, *Marriage as a Covenant,* pp. 216-37; Porten, *Archives from Elephantine,* p. 206; Stienstra, *YHWH Is the Husband of His People,* p. 99; Leslie W. Pope, "Marriage," pp. 96-98; Ortlund, *Whoredom,* p. 70.

21. This indebtedness is summarized well in Jack R. Lundbom, "Jeremiah, Book of," in *Anchor Bible Dictionary* (New York: Doubleday, 1992), 3:717. In both prophets the covenant is like a family bond of husband to wife or father and son; sin is rooted in the lack of knowledge of Yahweh; breach of covenant is equivalent to harlotry or adultery; and Yahweh suffers hurt by having to punish his wife or child (who is called Ephraim [Jer. 31:16-20; Hos. 11:8-9]). Several instances of intertextuality between Hosea and Jeremiah 3:1–4:4 are explored (see Mary E. Shields, "Circumscribing the Prostitute: The Rhetorics of Intertextuality, Metaphor, and Gender in Jeremiah 3:1–4:4," unpublished thesis, Emory University, 1996, pp. 208, 222, 227. See also Michael Fishbane, *Biblical Interpretation in Ancient Israel* [Oxford: Clarendon, 1985], pp. 311-12; Robert P. Carroll, *Jeremiah* [London: SCM, 1986], p. 119).

place later. The state of the text of Jeremiah is somewhat uncertain, and the history of the editing is complex.[22] It is often assumed that editorial passages are interspersed with Jeremiah's work.[23]

Jeremiah addresses chiefly Judah, reminding her of the honeymoon period[24] after Sinai (2:2), and then describing at length the pitiful state she has fallen into. She is like a wild animal lusting after many mates (2:23-25; 5:8). She has forgotten her husband (2:32-37) and has been unfaithful to him by whoring after other gods (2:27-28; 5:7) and by allegiances to other nations (2:36-37). She will be shamed like a harlot (13:26), and she is threatened with divorce like her sister Israel (3:1-20). Yet in the end Israel will be restored as though she were a virgin bride once more (31:1-7), and Judah will be restored with her as one united nation (31:31-34).

Jeremiah, like Ezekiel 23, pictures God as married to two sisters,[25] which is contrary to Mosaic law (Lev. 18:18). If the allegory is applied literally, of course, God did not actually marry two sisters because the nation was united when the marriage took place. However, a normal bride does not split into two women partway through a marriage, and so for the sake of the allegory Jeremiah and Ezekiel speak as though God married two sisters.[26]

The significance of Jeremiah is his development of the differences between Israel and Judah in chapter 3. **Judah is warned** that she may suffer the same fate as Israel, who was sent away with a divorce certificate (3:6-11).

22. The LXX is often very different from the MT, and the DSS findings add to, rather than resolve, these differences. The history of the editing of the text is even more complex, with the acknowledged hand of Baruch and the inferred hand of several later editors. William L. Holladay (*A Commentary on the Book of the Prophet Jeremiah,* 2 vols. [Philadelphia: Fortress, 1986]) makes a very detailed attempt to unravel the editorial history.

23. For example, Holladay's conclusions about chapters 2-4: "By this analysis, the early recension to the north consisted of 2.4-9; 3.1-2, 4-5, 12, 14-15, 18bβ, 19, 21a, 22-23, the poetic core of vv 24-25, and 4.1-2. In the first scroll the following were added: 2.1-3, 10-25, 29-37; 3.13, 21b; and 4.3-4. In the second scroll the following were added: 2.26-28; 3.3 and 20. Later expansions were responsible for 3.6-11 and 16-18bα" (*Jeremiah,* pp. 67-68).

24. Jeremiah, like Hosea, but contrary to history and to Ezekiel, says that Israel was faithful before the marriage (see Julie Galambush, *Jerusalem in the Book of Ezekiel,* pp. 53, 81; W. McKane, *Jeremiah 1–25* [Edinburgh: T. & T. Clark, 1986], p. 28).

25. Galambush (*Jerusalem in the Book of Ezekiel,* p. 82) suggests that Jeremiah produced the idea of two sisters by playing on Hosea's plea to Israel not to entice Judah to infidelity (Hos. 4:15).

26. Walther Zimmerli suggests that the marriage to two sisters may also have been influenced by the surrounding folk religion. The two wives may relate to the mythology evident at Elephantine in which Yahweh has two consorts called Anat-Bethel and Asam-Bethel, or it may be influenced by the older Ugaritic myth of El, who seduces and impregnates two girls. See Walther Zimmerli, *Ezekiel,* 2 vols., Hermeneia (Philadelphia: Fortress, 1983), 1:482.

> Jeremiah 3 (RSV): 6 The LORD said to me in the days of King Josi'ah: "Have you seen what she did, that faithless one, Israel, how she went up on every high hill and under every green tree, and there played the harlot? 7 And I thought, 'After she has done all this she will return to me'; but she did not return, and her false sister Judah saw it. 8 She saw that for all the adulteries of that faithless one, Israel, I had sent her away with a decree of divorce; yet her false sister Judah did not fear, but she too went and played the harlot. 9 Because harlotry was so light to her, she polluted the land, committing adultery with stone and tree. 10 Yet for all this her false sister Judah did not return to me with her whole heart, but in pretense, says the LORD." 11 And the LORD said to me, "Faithless Israel has shown herself less guilty than false Judah."

This reference to a divorce certificate in verse 8 may be an allusion to the verbal divorce formula in Hosea 2:2 [MT 2:4],[27] which became a divorce certificate by the act of Hosea writing it down.

Jeremiah is keenly aware that a divorce has taken place because he sees this as an impediment to their reconciliation. In 3:1 he summarizes the law of Deuteronomy 24:1-4,[28] which states that a wife cannot remarry her first husband after she has married someone else. Although Israel has not actually married someone else in the meantime, Jeremiah says that she has done far worse because she has had many lovers.[29]

> Jeremiah 3 (RSV): 1 "If a man divorces his wife and she goes from him and becomes another man's wife, will he return to her? Would not that land be greatly polluted? You have played the harlot with many lovers; and would you return to me?" says the LORD.

This law of Deuteronomy 24 and the action of Israel appear to mean that

27. See references in n. 20 above.

28. The connection with Deut. 24:1-4 was noted as long ago as 1862. See K. H. Graf, *Der Prophet Jeremia* (Leipzig: T. O. Weigel, 1862), p. 51. There is still some debate as to the direction of the dependence. Shields ("Circumscribing the Prostitute," p. 107), after a lengthy discussion of previous scholars, concludes that they are two independent uses of a common tradition applied to two different contexts. Fishbane (*Biblical Interpretation in Ancient Israel,* pp. 307-8) concludes that the differences between them are not sufficient to remove the direct link between the two texts.

29. Holladay traces the development of this passage as a *rîb* or lawsuit between Yahweh and Israel. The lawsuit is based on Deut. 24:1-4, paraphrased in v. 1. The argument of v. 1b is "how much more" *(qal vahomer).* In v. 2 there is a call to view the evidence, and vv. 4-5a contain quotations of Israel cited by Yahweh the plaintiff. The rest of the early recension is a fourfold summons to repentance. See Holladay, *Jeremiah,* pp. 47-48 for a bibliography of this subject. Stienstra (*YHWH Is the Husband of His People,* pp. 113-14) points out that Hos. 2:7b [MT 2:9b] shows that these lovers should be regarded as husbands because Israel says to her lovers, "I will go and return to my first husband."

it will be impossible for Israel to be reconciled to God. If God were to **remarry Israel**, not only would he break his own law, but the land would be polluted. However, Hosea has predicted that God and Israel would be reconciled, and so Jeremiah now seeks to discover how this can happen. He first repeats Hosea's assertion that this reconciliation will come about when Israel and Judah are united, and then he seeks to show that the Israel who has had many lovers is not the same as the Israel who is reconciled.

> Jeremiah 3 (RSV): 18 "In those days the house of Judah shall join the house of Israel, and together they shall come from the land of the north to the land that I gave your fathers for a heritage. 19 ¶ "I thought how I would set you among my sons, and give you a pleasant land, a heritage most beauteous of all nations. And I thought you would call me, My Father, and would not turn from following me. 20 Surely, as a faithless wife leaves her husband, so have you been faithless to me, O house of Israel," says the LORD. 21 A voice on the bare heights is heard, the weeping and pleading of Israel's sons, because they have perverted their way, they have forgotten the LORD their God. 22 "Return, O faithless sons, I will heal your faithlessness." "Behold, we come to thee; for thou art the LORD our God."

Jeremiah manages to distance the reconciled Israel as far as possible from the Israel who was unfaithful to her husband. It is not Israel who is reconciled, but Israel-Judah as a united nation. Furthermore, it is not the original Israel but her "sons" who will make up part of that new nation. When Jeremiah finally reveals the new covenant, he speaks of this new bride as "the virgin Israel" (31:3-5). Jeremiah has presumably found hints for all this in Hosea. Hosea not only spoke of the new nation of united Israel and Judah, but he also introduced the idea of "sons" of Israel. Hosea said that the curse "Not my people" would be reversed to "Sons of the living God," and that these "sons of Israel" would be gathered together with Judah (Hos. 1:10-11 [MT 2:1-2]). In this way the law of Deuteronomy 24 is not broken because God does not remarry exactly the same former wife, and yet the prophecy of Hosea is also fulfilled because the future Israel will be reconciled when she becomes a new wife in unification with Judah.

The interpretation of Jeremiah 3 is made difficult by many **questions of redaction**. In particular, it is difficult to decide whether verses 1-5 are addressed to Israel or Judah. W. McKane regards verses 6-11 as a later exegesis based on verses 1-5 and verses 12-13. The exegete had assumed that these two sets of verses belonged together, and thereby came to the wrong conclusion that verses 1-5 referred to Israel.[30] William L. Holladay has also reconstructed this passage into

30. McKane, *Jeremiah*, 1:67: "It is unlikely that the interpretation of vv. 1-5 which is as-

three stages of construction.[31] He concludes that most of it was originally addressed to Israel, in two stages, and that later additions added Israel's fate as a warning to Judah. Robert P. Carroll simply points out the contradictions in the text as it stands and does not attempt a detailed reconstruction.[32]

The reconstruction by Holladay is the most persuasive, though its complexity weighs against it. By Holladay's reconstruction, the only nation that suffers a divorce is Israel. They are described as having a divorce certificate in verse 8, and their divorce and subsequent whoredom make a reconciliation impossible (vv. 1-5). If verses 1-5 refers instead to Judah, we have to assume that another divorce has already occurred that has not been referred to elsewhere, and that the warnings of the subsequent verses are too late. Holladay's reconstruction does not have these problems. Holladay concludes that the whole passage consists of revelations that may well originate with Jeremiah and that he is reusing material that was originally directed at Israel in order to warn Judah. McKane's explanation concludes that a later exegete misunderstood his material, and Carroll simply points out the contradiction of the later message of hope with the earlier message of doom, both of which suggest clumsy editing.

Whatever is concluded about the text history of Jeremiah, the text as it stands speaks of Israel as the divorcée in verses 6-11, which means that the reader understands the discussion of divorce in verses 1-5 to also refer to Israel. It has been suggested here that the whole of chapter 3 can be read as an exposition of Hosea's prophecy and as a single argument that developed sequentially. First Jeremiah outlines the problem of the law in Deuteronomy 24 as applied to Israel's divorce and reconciliation (vv. 1-5); then he uses their dire situation to warn Judah, who is being even more faithless (vv. 6-11). He also pleads with faithless Israel to return (vv. 12-20), and, when they respond, he shows how they can be reconciled because the future Israel is different from the faithless Israel (vv. 21-25). This solves the problem of the law of Deuteronomy 24, with which the chapter opened.[33]

---

sumed by vv. 6-11 is the right one, since there is no reason to suppose that vv. 1-5 relate so particularly to the former northern kingdom. If vv. 1-5 are from Jeremiah, it would be more natural to conclude that they were spoken to Judah. Nor should it be assumed that the interpretation which has been put on the poetry of vv. 12-13 by the connecting piece in v. 12 is necessarily correct."

31. First most of 3:1-5, 12-15, 18b-25 was addressed to Israel; then 3:3, 20 were added; and finally 3:6-11 and 16-18a were addressed to Judah.

32. Carroll, *Jeremiah*, p. 147, regarding 3:12-13: "Having established that in the matter of a divorce the divorcing party cannot concede to the return of the erring spouse and having created numerous images of a state of the community beyond help, the appended material on turning is quite incompatible with what precedes it."

33. Stienstra (*YHWH Is the Husband of His People*, pp. 169-70) also finds the marriage metaphor developed in Jer. 13:20-27, but this is very questionable.

Ezekiel on Judah's Breaking of the Marriage Contract

Ezekiel expanded the metaphor about Judah as an unfaithful wife into two allegories in **chapters 16 and 23.** In chapter 16 he portrays Judah as an abandoned child who is rescued by God and later married to him. She becomes grossly unfaithful and is punished, but her marriage covenant is finally restored. In chapter 23 Judah and her sister Israel were both immoral before God married them, and when they both continued their immorality, they were handed over to their lovers. Israel was killed by the Assyrians (23:10) and Judah was punished (though not killed) by the Babylonians. Both of these allegories are told in particularly stark and shocking language.[34]

The two allegories in these chapters have some significant differences. The main differences are the preoccupation with Judah in chapter 16, the lack of any reconciliation in chapter 23, and the premarital unfaithfulness in chapter 23. William H. Brownlee has suggested that the core of the differences is that chapter 23 starts the story in Egypt while chapter 16 starts in the wilderness. He suggests that Ezekiel may have prepared them for significant occasions, because chapter 23 would be most suitable at Passover, and chapter 16 would be suitable for Tabernacles (when the Sinai covenant is remembered).[35]

The premarital unfaithfulness in chapter 23 is probably influenced by Hosea, but this would not fit in with the allegory of chapter 16, so it is not mentioned there. In chapter 16 the girl is portrayed as totally abandoned and unwanted. Her parents have left her to die by infanticide, and she was rescued by God (vv. 3-6). When she was growing up, no one looked after her, and she was totally destitute, so the next time God saw her he had to clothe her nakedness (vv. 7-8). The wonder of God's concern for this abandoned orphan stands out

34. Ezekiel commonly used shocking images to get his message across. These chapters contain sexually explicit language that would have been shocking to the original readers and that cannot be translated faithfully in any Bible that will be used in worship. Some commentators have suggested that this language is not shocking when compared with that found in Ugaritic myths (see Ortlund, *Whoredom,* pp. 32, 120). However, these myths contain few sexual passages and usually employ euphemisms. R. Eliezer ben Hyrcanus forbade the public reading of Ezekiel 16, though this was as much because of the racial slur of v. 3 as the sexual tone of the language (see Marvin H. Pope, "Mixed Marriage Metaphor in Ezekiel 16," in *Fortunate the Eyes That See — Essays in Honor of David Noel Freedman in Celebration of His Seventieth Birthday,* ed. Astrid Beck [Grand Rapids: Eerdmans, 1995], pp. 389-90). Marjo Christina Annette Korpel (*A Rift in the Clouds: Ugaritic and Hebrew Descriptions of the Divine* [Münster: Ugarit-Verlag, 1990], p. 220) points out that such explicit language was already used to a lesser extent by Hosea, especially in 11:8, which she translates as "my organs of heat are aroused."

35. William H. Brownlee, *Ezekiel 1–19,* Word Biblical Commentary 28 (Waco: Word Books, 1986), p. 220.

when he clothes her. He does not merely cover her nakedness, but he does so with his own coat, as in a betrothal,[36] and then he swears a marriage covenant with her.

In both chapters, unfaithfulness soon follows. The description of the breakdown of the marriages is inspired both by Hosea and by the **divorce law of Exodus 21:10-11.** Hosea describes how Israel offered to Baal the food, jewelry, and oil that had been given to her by God as part of their mutual marriage obligations in Exodus 21:10. This argument is developed much further by Ezekiel, who describes how Israel and Judah were presented with these things and who details the way in which they gave them to their lovers.

In chapter 16 the newly married bride has the best food, clothes, and oil lavished on her:

> Ezekiel 16 (RSV): 9 "Then I bathed you with water and washed off your blood from you, and anointed you with oil. 10 I clothed you also with embroidered cloth and shod you with leather, I swathed you in fine linen and covered you with silk. 11 And I decked you with ornaments, and put bracelets on your arms, and a chain on your neck. 12 And I put a ring on your nose, and earrings in your ears, and a beautiful crown upon your head. 13 Thus you were decked with gold and silver; and your raiment was of fine linen, and silk, and embroidered cloth; you ate fine flour and honey and oil. You grew exceedingly beautiful, and came to regal estate."

The lengthy list of rich food, wealthy apparel, and lovingly applied oil[37] serves to emphasize that God went far beyond what was required by law. He is required to give her clothes but lavishes beautiful cloth and jewelry on her.[38] His bride was not only cared for but had everything in abundance.

Yet when she takes lovers, she gives all these gifts to them, instead of using them to make clothes and meals for her husband and herself. In describing this, Ezekiel again follows the categories of food, clothing, and oil as in Exodus 21:10:

36. It is generally agreed that this was part of a betrothal ceremony, as in Ruth (e.g., Hugenberger, *Marriage as a Covenant,* p. 240; M. Greenberg, *Ezekiel 1–20,* Anchor Bible 22 [Garden City: Doubleday, 1983], p. 277). Some regard it as euphemistic for a sexual encounter (e.g., Marvin H. Pope, "Mixed Marriage Metaphor in Ezekiel 16," pp. 393-94; Brownlee, *Ezekiel 1–19,* p. 220).

37. The anointing with oil in v. 9 may indicate both love and oil. The earliest meaning of **ענתה** in Exod. 21:10 was oil, but it later came to be understood as love (as discussed in chapter one). Ezekiel may mark a transition in the understanding, and so he indicates both meanings to emphasize that whatever interpretation is understood, God fulfilled it completely.

38. Galambush (*Jerusalem in the Book of Ezekiel,* p. 83) points out that the vocabulary of the clothing is influenced by the descriptions of the tabernacle in Exodus.

> Ezekiel 16 (RSV): 16 "You took some of your garments, and made for yourself gaily decked shrines, and on them played the harlot; the like has never been, nor ever shall be. 17 You also took your fair jewels of my gold and of my silver, which I had given you, and made for yourself images of men, and with them played the harlot; 18 and you took your embroidered garments to cover them, and set my oil and my incense before them. 19 Also my bread which I gave you — I fed you with fine flour and oil and honey — you set before them for a pleasing odor," says the Lord GOD.

All of this adds up to three **grounds for divorce**. By listing God's gifts to her and her gifts to the idols with such clear allusions to the list in Exodus 21:10, Ezekiel is emphasizing that she has broken her marriage covenant. God has more than fulfilled these three obligations, but she has broken all three by failing to give reciprocal support to her husband.

Adultery, another ground for divorce, is also emphasized. In chapter 23 it is almost the sole subject under discussion, and in chapter 16 it is also very prominent. It is the first thing named in her downfall, just before the passage about the food, clothing, and oil:

> Ezekiel 16 (RSV): 15 "But you trusted in your beauty, and played the harlot because of your renown, and lavished your harlotries on any passer-by."

Ezekiel comes back to the subject of her unfaithfulness after listing her failures with regard to food, clothing, and oil. From verse 23 onwards he describes at length how she acted like a prostitute. But before this there is a further charge that may possibly be another ground for divorce.

In verses 20-21 Ezekiel says that Judah has sacrificed her children to idols. This may refer to a literal practice of child sacrifice (as in 23:37-39), or it may describe the way in which her liaisons with other nations caused the whole nation to follow idols. Either way, it is difficult to see how it fits into the context of what Ezekiel is saying in this chapter. One possible solution is that he regards this as deliberate childlessness, which is a ground for divorce. Procreation was regarded as an obligation in marriage in the earliest rabbinic traditions.[39] It was based on the words "Be fruitful and multiply" (Gen. 1:22, 28), which is a direct command and therefore has the force of God's law. It is not known when this traditional interpretation started, but it is possible that Ezekiel is alluding to it

39. It was an established tradition in the time of the School disputes of Hillel and Shammai, because although they argued about how many children were necessary, they did not dispute the fact that a married couple were obliged to have children (*m. Yebam.* 6.6).

here. Deliberate childlessness would be regarded as a breach of the law of Moses and therefore as a breach of the marriage contract.

Despite all this, Ezekiel says that God chose not to end the marriage contract that he has with Judah. At the end of the chapter, after Ezekiel has shown that Judah has broken every stipulation of the marriage covenant, God says that he will remember and renew his covenant with her after she has been punished:

> Ezekiel 16 (RSV): 58 "You bear the penalty of your lewdness and your abominations," says the LORD. 59 "Yea," thus says the Lord GOD: "I will deal with you as you have done, who have despised the oath in breaking the covenant, 60 yet I will remember my covenant with you in the days of your youth, and I will establish with you an everlasting covenant. 61 Then you will remember your ways, and be ashamed when I take your sisters, both your elder and your younger, and give them to you as daughters, but not on account of the covenant with you. 62 I will establish my covenant with you, and you shall know that I am the LORD."

This covenant refers both to the Sinai covenant and more specifically to a marriage covenant. The marriage covenant is most clearly referred to in verse 8:[40]

> Ezekiel 16 (RSV): 8 ". . . I spread my skirt over you, and covered your nakedness: yea, I plighted my troth to you and entered into a covenant with you," says the Lord GOD, "and you became mine."

Julie Galambush[41] points out that Ezekiel appears at first to have no future hope for Jerusalem. After the fall of Jerusalem at the end of Ezekiel 24, the city is never again mentioned by name in Ezekiel. However, Yahweh promises renewal to "the mountains of Israel" (36:8-15), "my people" (37:13), "Judah and the house of Israel" (37:16), and the people as a whole (37:26-27). Ezekiel in chapters 40–44 sees a hope for the people but distances the new bride from the old by abandoning the city and projecting a completely new Jerusalem.

Ezekiel has shown that God had every right to end this marriage if he wished, but he did not. He does not suggest that God is being righteous in this matter, nor that God would be unrighteous to end the covenant. There is no similar mercy extended to Israel, who is linked with Sodom in her punishment (16:46-50) even though she did not sin as much as Judah (16:51), and whose marriage ends when God gives her into the hands of her lovers (23:9). The whole

40. Greenberg (*Ezekiel*, p. 220) argues that this is not a marriage covenant, but Hugenberger (*Marriage as a Covenant*, pp. 308-9) convincingly refutes him.

41. Galambush, *Jerusalem in the Book of Ezekiel*, pp. 86, 145.

chapter describes an undeserved love towards someone who was utterly abandoned, and who was rescued again after letting herself fall as far as anyone can fall. Ezekiel showed that she had broken every stipulation of her marriage contract so that he could emphasize the undeserved mercy God showed her.

Isaiah on Yahweh's Divorce Certificate

Isaiah uses the metaphor of Israel as an adulteress and later as an abandoned wife. He says that she has not been divorced, but she had suffered a period of separation that will come to an end.

Most of the references to this metaphor are in Second Isaiah. There is only one possible reference to the metaphor in the opening chapters, when Jerusalem is called the "faithful city" who "has become a harlot" (1:21). In later chapters there are clear references to Israel or Jerusalem as a wife who has not been divorced (50:1) though she has been "forsaken" (54:4-7) and will be married again (62:4-5).

It is often difficult to decide to whom Isaiah is referring when he uses terms such as "Israel." Before chapter 40 "Israel" can refer to the ten tribes, but later the names **"Israel," "Jacob," and "Judah"** are used interchangeably, even with "Jerusalem" or "Zion." For example:

> Isaiah 48 (RSV): 1 "Hear this, O house of Jacob, who are called by the name of Israel, and who came forth from the loins of Judah; who swear by the name of the Lord, and confess the God of Israel, but not in truth or right."

> Isaiah 59 (RSV): 20 "And he will come to Zion as Redeemer, to those in Jacob who turn from transgression," says the Lord.

Occasionally there appears to be reference to the former tribes joining with Judah, as in the description of the people gathered from the four points of the earth (43:5-6), but even this must be limited to those who have survived the exile ("the preserved ones of Israel," 49:6). Generally speaking, the only exile that is described is the one to Babylon. They return across the desert (40:3-4), with the help of Cyrus (41:25-27; 44:28; 45:1), traveling from Babylon (43:14; 48:20). Although Isaiah may have a wider concept of the identity of Israel, most of the time he is addressing only the exiles in Babylon.

We must therefore assume that everything referring to "Israel" or "Jacob" in Second Isaiah[42] is addressed to Judah, unless it is clearly indicated otherwise.

42. I use the term Second Isaiah as shorthand for the chapters after ch. 1–39. This does

Consequently, Isaiah, unlike Hosea, Ezekiel, and Jeremiah, does not distinguish between the two wives Israel and Judah. Also unlike Jeremiah and Ezekiel, he interacts very little with Hosea, though he does not seem to be ignorant of Hosea's prophecies.

His reference to a **divorce certificate** in 50:1 may even be regarded as opposition to a popular interpretation of Hosea. The people in exile had lost hope, and much of Second Isaiah's message to them is that God still loves them and will rescue them. In their hopelessness they looked at the message of Hosea and concluded that God had divorced them as he had divorced Israel. Isaiah challenges them to produce the divorce certificate.

> Isaiah 50 (RSV): 1 Thus says the LORD: "Where is your mother's bill of divorce, with which I put her away? Or which of my creditors is it to whom I have sold you? Behold, for your iniquities you were sold, and for your transgressions your mother was put away."

> Isaiah 50 (GNB): 1 "Do you think I sent my people away like a man who divorces his wife? Where, then, are the papers of divorce? Do you think I sold you into captivity like a man who sells his children as slaves? No, you went away captive because of your sins; you were sent away because of your crimes."

The Good News Bible, like many commentators, treats the phrase about the divorce certificate as a rhetorical question.[43] This fits well in the context, which is a series of rhetorical questions continuing into verse 2 and the rest of the chapter. Not all the questions in this section are rhetorical (the opening of v. 2 is probably not), so the matter of the divorce certificate could be a straightforward question. In this case Isaiah would be taking the matter seriously and asking for the certificate as proof that Judah was divorced.[44] However, this question is in parallel with the following question, which is undoubtedly rhetorical, because otherwise it describes God as one who sold the nation like a pack of slaves in order to pay off his

---

not imply or deny anything about the authorship, other than the obvious fact that there are differences in style and situation.

43. The thinking behind this translation is outlined in Herbert G. Grether, "Translating the Questions in Isaiah 50," *Bible Translator* 24 (1973): 240-43.

44. Grether could find only one commentator who did not regard this question as rhetorical (see Claus Westermann, *Isaiah 40–66*, Old Testament Library [London: SCM, 1969]). Since that time Norman H. Snaith has also followed this line ("Isaiah 40–66: A Study of the Teaching of the Second Isaiah and Its Consequences," in *Studies on the Second Part of the Book of Isaiah*, Supplements to Vetus Testamentum 14 [Leiden: Brill, 1977]). See also Stienstra, *YHWH Is the Husband of His People*, pp. 170-71.

creditors. Therefore it appears that Isaiah is pointing out the absurdity of believing that God had divorced Judah or had sold her into slavery.

Whether or not this question is rhetorical, Isaiah does not believe that Judah has been divorced. The tribes in the first exile (whom the other prophets call Israel) *are* spoken of as divorced in Hosea, Jeremiah, and perhaps in Ezekiel,[45] but Isaiah is not speaking about these tribes. He makes no reference to the fate of these tribes in distinction to the fate of the other tribes, and he appears to be uninterested in them until all the tribes are gathered together.

Isaiah argues that God has not divorced Judah but has put her away because of her sins (50:1). This is a small distinction because the word (שׁלח, *shalach*) "put away" is normally a technical term for divorce. Isaiah appears to be saying that although God has sent her away, this is not a legal divorce because he has not given her a divorce certificate. It could be said that Israel's divorce certificate is found in the words of Hosea 2:2 [MT 2:4], which is a written version of the oral divorce formula commonly used in the ancient Near East.[46] Yet there is no equivalent certificate to be found for Judah.

It might be suggested that Isaiah has rescued Judah from divorce by a legal technicality. In order to allay this suspicion, Isaiah points out in chapter 54 that it was God's plan to **abandon her** only for a short period, and that he was planning to be reconciled with her again in the future.

> Isaiah 54 (RSV): 4 "Fear not, for you will not be ashamed; be not confounded, for you will not be put to shame; for you will forget the shame of your youth, and the reproach of your widowhood you will remember no more. 5 For your Maker is your husband, the LORD of hosts is his name; and the Holy One of Israel is your Redeemer, the God of the whole earth he is called. 6 For the LORD has called you like a wife forsaken and grieved in spirit, like a wife of youth when she is cast off," says your God. 7 "For a brief moment I forsook you, but with great compassion I will gather you."

Judah is like a wife who has been completely abandoned, and so she is called a "widow" in the ancient Near Eastern sense of "a woman without support from any man."[47] She is utterly without support, but this will be reversed when God gathers her people back to the land again. It is the *land* that will then be "married" to him.

45. Israel is not mentioned much by Ezekiel, but in ch. 23 Israel is killed (23:10) while Judah is only punished.

46. See n. 20 above.

47. See Guillaume Cardascia, *Les Lois Assyriennes* (Paris: Cerf, 1969), p. 180 on Middle Assyrian laws #33, 45.

> Isaiah 62 (RSV): 4 You shall no more be termed Forsaken, and your land shall no more be termed Desolate; but you shall be called My delight is in her, and your land Married; for the LORD delights in you, and your land shall be married. 5 For as a young man marries a virgin, so shall your sons marry you,[48] and as the bridegroom rejoices over the bride, so shall your God rejoice over you.

Isaiah speaks of the reconciled bride as a "virgin" (**בתולה**, *bethulah*), which is what Hosea and Jeremiah have already hinted at (Hos. 2:15 [MT 2:17]; Jer. 31:1-7). This is not part of the imagery that Isaiah has been developing. There is no natural progression from the image of a wife who returns to her husband after many years when she has been abandoned by her lovers to the image of a young virgin bride.[49] The fact that this startling vocabulary has been introduced without warning or explanation suggests that it has been inspired by Hosea. The authority for this idea comes from the hints already found in Hosea that the reconciliation of Israel would be at a new wedding. This is the most forceful way in which Isaiah can show that God has forgiven her unfaithfulness completely. The period of abandonment is not only over, but it is as if it had never happened.

A Consistent Picture of God's Divorce

Hosea, Jeremiah, Ezekiel, and Isaiah present a consistent and coherent extended metaphor about Yahweh's marriage to Israel and Judah. There are many differences in emphases and in the extent of the development of this metaphor, but they do not disagree with each other in substance. The greatest disagreement is actually between Ezekiel chapters 16 and 23, with the former saying that the brides were faithful initially and the latter saying that they were faithless even before the marriage started. These and other minor differences may be accounted for as differences in emphasis rather than differences in substance.

The basis of this agreement can be found in their use of a **common source in Hosea.** Jeremiah and Ezekiel make more or less obvious allusions to the idea if not the words of Hosea. Isaiah is sometimes in debate with ideas from Hosea and sometimes develops ideas that originated with Hosea.

48. "Sons" could be translated as "builders," which would remove a moral problem from this picture (see Stienstra, *YHWH Is the Husband of His People,* pp. 176-77).

49. Stienstra (*YHWH Is the Husband of His People,* pp. 176-77) suggests that this may mean little more than "your wedding will be as joyful as that of a virgin," but the language seems too forceful for that.

Galambush has pointed out that the concept of a city as the wife of a god was so commonplace in ancient Near Eastern literature that it no longer had the force of a metaphor.[50] However, the concept of such a wife having an adulterous relationship was unknown. She suggests that this extension of the metaphor would have been impossible in a polytheistic culture, but in Israel it was a natural extension of the marriage metaphor.

The other idea introduced by Hosea was the distinction between Israel and Judah and their subsequent reunification, and all the ramifications of that reunification. Hosea portrayed Israel as the faithless partner who is divorced, but who regains her husband when she is reunited with Judah, who is still married to him. As far as Israel is concerned, this is like a remarriage, though it is spoken of in such glowing terms that it seems as though it were her first marriage (Hos. 2.14-15 [MT 2:16-17]).

By the time of Jeremiah and Ezekiel, it was clear that Judah was just as unfaithful as Israel. They both regard Judah as *more* wicked because she had been warned by Israel's fate. They also conclude that her fate would not be as permanent as Israel's. Neither of them makes any attempt to explain why God should be merciful to Judah and not to Israel, and both of them emphasize that the punishment of Judah was less than she deserved. Both of them see the salvation of Israel and Judah in the reunification of the two nations, which would be followed by a remarriage and reconciliation of Israel-Judah with their husband.

It is left to Isaiah to try to justify this difference between Israel and Judah. He points out that Israel had a written divorce certificate in Hosea 2:2 [MT 2:4], but Judah was never given a certificate. He appears to argue that if Judah did not have a certificate, she was not divorced. In arguing this way, Isaiah is treating the metaphor in a very literal sense, as though this marriage was a proper, legally binding contract.

The **literal interpretation of this marriage** by Isaiah is mirrored also in Jeremiah and Ezekiel. Jeremiah is just as concerned about legality in 3:1, where he struggles to understand the law of Deuteronomy 24:1-4 in the context of Israel's remarriage. Ezekiel also treats the law of Exodus 21:10-11 in a very literal way to demonstrate that Judah has broken the terms of her marriage contract. Hosea is also literal but in a very different way. The very literal actions that Hosea is asked to perform are carried out in order to demonstrate something he believed about God. It is not clear whether he believed that God had actually entered into a marriage contract, in the literal way that later prophets saw it, but he does seem to believe that God's feelings towards Israel were literally like his own. When God says to him, "Go again, love a woman who is beloved of a par-

50. Galambush, *Jerusalem in the Book of Ezekiel,* pp. 22-26.

amour and is an adulteress; even as the Lord loves the people of Israel, though they turn to other gods," one gets the impression that Hosea is being asked to do this terribly difficult thing because it is the only way that God can express the hurt that he himself feels.

It appears that these prophets (with the possible exception of Hosea) believed that God really had literally entered a marriage contract with Israel and Judah. This was easy to accept in the ancient Near East, where the concept of a god married to a city, and thus to the nation, was commonplace. It was also easy for the prophets to argue that the nations had been unfaithful. This language had been used already in the Pentateuch. What was much more difficult was the consequential idea that God suffered as a result of this and that he was forced into a divorce of one wife and the abandonment of the other. However, rather than treating the marriage merely as a metaphor, with the limitations of a metaphor, the prophets explored the consequences of regarding this relationship as a literal marriage contract.

The difficulties they had to face up to were that God was more merciful to Judah, who was more unfaithful than Israel, and that Israel would be remarried to God after she had been divorced and had had many lovers. Both of these difficulties found a solution in the unification of the two nations, after which there would be a reconciliation and remarriage. This event was described as though it were the first marriage of a virgin bride, as though the new united nation was a completely new individual without the murky past of either of her component nations. Jeremiah distanced the new united nation from her past by speaking of Israel's "sons" (3:19), though this tends to obscure the feminine character of the bride. Isaiah was more successful when he spoke of the new bride as the "land" (62:4), and Ezekiel envisioned a complete transformation of the city, the land, and the religion. This effectively included both former faithless sisters without identifying the new bride with their faithless ways. It is Ezekiel's vision in particular that is taken up in the New Testament as a picture of the new bride of Christ.

These prophets have therefore developed a picture of God that is more than a metaphor. Beginning from the revelation of the covenant at Sinai and the experiences of Hosea, they concluded that Yahweh had a real marriage contract with Israel and Judah, and that Yahweh was a divorcé.

The prophets all laid the blame for the divorce on the woman Israel. She was portrayed as having broken her marriage vows in every possible way. All the prophets spoke of the sexual unfaithfulness of Israel (except Second Isaiah who appeared to ignore the ten tribes), and most of them also listed her failed obligations with regard to food, clothing, and oil. In contrast, God was shown to have showered her with love and provided her with the most expensive food, clothing, and oil. Instead of using these commodities to prepare meals and garments for him, in accordance with her marriage vows, Israel gave them to her lovers, the other gods. Judah followed suit and did even worse than Israel (according to Jeremiah and Ezekiel).

The main message of this metaphor was not that God is a divorcé but that Israel and Judah had broken their marriage vows. God's anger and hurt at these broken vows was applied by Malachi to all marriages, and not just to God's own marriage.

Malachi on God's Hatred of Divorce

There is no evidence that Malachi was writing in response to Hosea and the other prophets who developed Hosea's theme. Malachi does not use the metaphor of God married to his people,[51] even when he is accusing the people of breaking their covenant with God (e.g., 2:4-9). Malachi speaks about divorce more generally, as part of his criticism of those who break covenant promises.

It is possible that Malachi is referring to Judah's marriage to God in a sideways glance. The main message of Malachi is that Judah has failed to keep their covenant with God. Despite God's love for them (1:2-5) they have shown him nothing but disrespect (1:6-14). God warns them that this disrespect is a breaking of the covenant (2:1-10, especially v. 5). He lists a number of specific areas in which they have broken the covenant: three of them are described in detail (2:10-16; 3:8-10), and others are simply listed (3:5). In the rest of the book he asks Judah to choose between judgment and mercy; the outcome will depend on how well they keep the Sinai covenant (4:4).

The three matters of **covenant breaking** that are dealt with in detail are marriages to idolatrous foreign wives (2:11-12), breaking marriage vows (2:14-16), and nonpayment of tithes (3:8-10). The other offenses listed in 3:5 are magic, adultery, perjury, and the oppression of employees, widows, orphans, and foreigners. Although we are concerned here only with the second offense,

51. It is possible that Mal. 2:11 is speaking about the nation marrying "the daughter of a strange god," but the context suggests that it refers to individuals who marry foreign wives (cf. v. 12: "May Yahweh cut off the man who does it"). See the discussion in Hugenberger (*Marriage as a Covenant*, p. 35), who calls this the "traditional" interpretation. Abel Isaksson (*Marriage and Ministry in the New Temple: A Study with Special Reference to Mt. 19.13*[sic]*-12 and 1 Cor. 11.3-16*, trans. Neil Tomkinson and Jean Gray, Acta Seminarii Neotestamentici Upsaliensis 24 [Lund: Gleerup; Copenhagen: Munksgaard, 1965], p. 31) argues that the whole of vv. 11-16 refers to God's marriage and that the "bride of your youth" is Israel. However, even with the difficulties of translating this passage, it is clear that the man is accused of being unfaithful to the woman in this passage.

of breaking marriage vows, it is important to note the others. The defense of foreigners shows that the foreign wives were despised not because they were non-Israelite but because they led people into idolatry,[52] and the separate mention of adultery may suggest that this was the main way in which marriage vows were being broken.

Some scholars have suggested[53] that there may be a strong link between the marriage to idolatrous wives and the breaking of marriage vows made to the "wife of your youth." Perhaps some men were divorcing the wife whom they married when they were young in order to marry a rich foreign women. In this case their unfaithfulness would consist of abandoning their wives by divorcing them without proper grounds. They would, in effect, be breaking their vows to sustain their wives with food, clothing, and oil (love). However, all this is conjecture, and there is no indication in the passage about the precise way in which the marriage covenant was being broken. The only thing that is mentioned is that these people were being "faithless" to the wives of their youths or the wives of their covenant.

The passage about breaking marriage vows in **Malachi 2:14-16** is very difficult to translate. G. P. Hugenberger has analyzed many of the issues involved in painstaking detail,[54] and thus his translation is given here, along with a more traditional version:

> Malachi 2 (RSV): 14 . . . The LORD was witness to the covenant between you and the wife of your youth, to whom you have been faithless, though she is your companion and your wife by covenant. 15 Has not the one God made and sustained for us the spirit of life? And what does he desire? Godly offspring. So take heed to yourselves, and let none be faithless to the wife of his youth. 16 "For I hate divorce," says the LORD the God of Israel, "and covering one's garment with violence," says the LORD of hosts. So take heed to yourselves and do not be faithless.

52. As implied by the phrase "the daughter of a strange God" in 2:11. See also the previous note.

53. Called the "traditional" view in Hugenberger, *Marriage as a Covenant,* pp. 101-5, where it is also criticized as relying too much on conjecture.

54. Hugenberger, *Marriage as a Covenant.* He admits that he has not discussed all the possible translations for v. 15, but in his defense he cites A. S. van der Woude, who said "Mal. 2.15 is one of the most difficult passages of the whole Old Testament. It would be a hopeless task to record all the attempts that have been made to explain this verse" ("Malachi's Struggle for a Pure Community: Reflections on Malachi 2.10-16," in *Tradition and Re-interpretation in Jewish and Early Christian Literature: Essays in Honour of Jürgen C. H. Lebram,* ed. J. W. van Henten, H. J. de Jonge, P. T. van Rooden, and J. W. Wesselius, Studia Post-Biblica 36 [Leiden: Brill, 1986], p. 69).

> Malachi 2 (Hugenberger):[55] 14 . . . The Lord was witness between you and the wife of your youth, against whom you have been faithless though she is your companion and your wife by covenant. 15 Did He not make [you/them] one, with a remnant of the spirit belonging to it? And what was the One seeking? A godly seed! Therefore watch out for your lives and do not act faithlessly against the wife of your youth. 16 "If one hates and divorces [merely on the grounds of aversion]," says Yahweh, God of Israel, "he covers his garment [i.e. visibly defiles himself] with violence," says Yahweh of hosts. Therefore take heed to yourself and do not be faithless [against your wife].

The main differences between Hugenberger and the more traditional translations are in the first half of verse 15 and the first few words of verse 16. In verse 15 he finds an allusion to Genesis 2:23-24 and the covenant of one flesh, though he resists the revocalization of "remnant" to "flesh," which would produce the phrase "Did he not make one flesh?" He argues that this interpretation fits in well with the whole concept of marriage covenants in these verses. However, the translation of this portion of the passage is so difficult that it is best left as inconclusive. The second half of the verse is more straightforward and continues to emphasize faithfulness to marriage vows.

The translation of verse 16a is more important, not only because it changes the sense of the verse substantially but also because it replaces the well-known and much-quoted phrase "'I hate divorce,' says the Lord." Hugenberger's translation is based on reading the Hebrew text without emendation. The Hebrew reads "he hates divorce" (שׂנא שלח), which most translations emend to "I hate divorce."[56] Hugenberger relies on Raymond Westbrook,[57] who pointed out the parallel with ancient Near Eastern texts that use the phrase "He hates [and] divorces." He showed that this phrase meant "he divorces without adequate grounds." This was a legal distinction between a divorce that was based on grounds such as adultery or neglect (which resulted in a financial penalty for the guilty partner) and a divorce where no grounds

55. Hugenberger, *Marriage as a Covenant,* v. 14 at p. 27; v. 15 at p. 126; v. 16 at p. 76.

56. The Qumran Cave 4 Scroll of the Minor Prophets emended שׂנא שלח "if/for he hates divorce" to שׂנתה שלח "if you hate, divorce," which is followed by *Targum Pseudo-Jonathan* "But if you hate her, release her" (ארי אם סנית לה פטרה) and also by the Vulgate and LXX[WL]. This emendation is typical of Qumran literature where כי is often changed to כי אם (see P. R. Davies, *The Damascus Document: An Interpretation of the "Damascus Document,"* Journal for the Study of the Old Testament, Supplement 25 (Sheffield: Sheffield Academic Press, 1983), pp. 234-38). This may also be reflected in Sir. 7:26: "Hast thou a wife, abhor her not (אל תתעבה), but trust not thyself to one that hateth thee," which in the Greek reads "do not divorce her," μὴ ἐκβάλῃς αὐτήν instead of אל תתעבה.

57. Westbrook, "Prohibition of Restoration of Marriage."

could be cited (which resulted in a financial penalty for the person bringing the divorce).

Either way, verse 16 shows that God is against the person who **breaks** one's **marriage vows**. The more traditional interpretations may seem to suggest that God is against divorce of any kind, but the context clearly shows that this is not so. The constantly reiterated theme of these verses is faithfulness to the terms of the marriage covenant. Criticism is not directed at the person who carries out the divorce but at the person who causes the divorce by not being faithful to the marriage covenant.

This is the emphasis of verse 14, where God is seen as the witness at the marriage, and, in particular, a witness to the covenant vows. It is not clear what verse 15 is emphasizing, but the conclusion of this verse is also that one should be faithful to one's first bride ("the bride of your youth"). In verse 16 the difficulty of "I/he hates divorce" is made more difficult by the following phrase about "covering one's garment with violence." This is probably best seen as a metaphor for the inner state of the man.[58] Therefore verse 16 is condemning the violence done to persons when they are divorced without adequate grounds. This, too, is condemned as unfaithfulness at the end of the verse.

The term "unfaithfulness" (**בגד**, *bagad*) is used at the conclusion of each of these verses and is the central theme of this condemnation. The whole passage of 2:10-16 is structured around this word. It introduces the idea in verse 10 that Judah's covenant unfaithfulness to God is reflected in their behavior to each other: "Why do we act unfaithfully to each other to profane the covenant of our fathers?" Then verse 11 applies it to those who marry foreign idolatrous wives: "Judah has been unfaithful. . . ." The word is often translated "treacherous," which helps to imply the breaking of a treaty. It occurs only forty-three times in the OT and is used overwhelmingly for violations of covenants, as S. Erlandsson summarizes: "It is used when the OT writer wants to say that a man does not honor an agreement, or commits adultery, or breaks a covenant or some other ordinance given by God."[59] It is used for those who break the Sinai covenant,[60] for those who break a betrothal covenant,[61] and for those who break a marriage covenant.[62]

58. Cf. Jer. 2:34: "On your skirts is found the lifeblood of guiltless poor"; Ps. 73:6: "violence covers them as a garment."

59. S. Erlandsson, "Bāghadh," *Theological Dictionary of the Old Testament,* ed. Johannes G. Botterweck, Helmer Ringgren, and Heinz-Josef Fabry, 8 vols. (Grand Rapids: Eerdmans, 1974), 1:470-73, esp. p. 470.

60. 1 Sam. 14:33; Ps. 119:158.

61. Exod. 21:8 — a man who buys a female bondservant from her father, saying that he will marry her, but then changes his mind.

62. Jer. 3:20; 9:2 — Judah as the adulterous wife.

Malachi's condemnation of divorce is therefore directed at the person who breaks the marriage covenant. This is the emphasis found in each of the three verses in the repeated use of the term "unfaithfulness" (בגד). This fits well with the context of the section of which these verses are part (vv. 10-16), where faithlessness in human covenants is used to illustrate faithlessness towards God's covenant. It also fits in well with the thrust of the whole book, which is a call back to covenant faithfulness.

Conclusions

The prophets Hosea, Jeremiah, Ezekiel, and Isaiah present a consistent and coherent picture of God who was married to the nation of Israel, and then to the sisters Israel and Judah (when the nation split up). Israel was unfaithful and was divorced. Judah was even more unfaithful, but God was merciful and separated for a period, then sought reconciliation. The eschatological hope includes a reconciliation and remarriage of God to Judah and Israel when they will be united again. The pain that God felt in this experience of divorce is expressed in Malachi, where he condemns all those who break their marriage vows.

4. Intertestamental Period

Increasing Rights for Women

In the Intertestamental period there were various changes that increased both the rights of women and the security of marriages within Judaism. Women who were divorced without good cause had a guarantee that their dowry would be returned to them, so that they had some degree of financial independence. Polygamy and divorce were starting to be criticized. Outside Judaism, in the Greco-Roman world, divorce became easier to initiate by both men and women, and this began to affect Diaspora Jews. These changes are seen especially in the documents unearthed at Qumran and at Elephantine in Egypt, as well as in the Mishnah, which records early developments of the marriage contract.

Polygamy in Israel

Polygamy was allowed in Mosaic law,[1] but there were also caveats such as the warning that kings should not marry too many wives. Polygamy is nowhere spoken of with approval, and many passages indicate that monogamy is the ideal.[2] There is no evidence that polygamy was widespread in Israel, except perhaps

1. Exod. 21:10-11; Deut. 21:15-17. Polygamy may also be implied in the laws that a man who seduces an unbetrothed virgin (Exod. 22:16) or rapes her (Deut. 22:28-29) must marry her, because they do not state that the man must be unmarried.

2. Cf. Isa. 50:1; Jer. 2:2; Ezek. 16:8; Prov. 12:4; 18:22; 19:14; 31:10-31; Ps. 128:3 (listed in Louis M. Epstein, *Marriage Laws in the Bible and Talmud,* Harvard Semitic Series 12 [Cambridge, Mass.: Harvard University Press, 1942], p. 4).

after times of war when the male population was diminished.[3] In the OT, polygamy is almost always related to childlessness[4] and is often associated with problems.[5] Leaders and kings like Gideon, Samson, David, and Solomon had many wives, probably to imitate leaders in other countries.[6] In New Testament times there is very little evidence of polygamy, but this may be due simply to the rarity of family records from that time.[7] It had generally been assumed that only the very rich practiced polygamy, but one set of family documents that has survived from the second century C.E. shows a middle-class example of polygamy.[8] The rabbinic writings assume that polygamy occurs and contain much legislation concerning it,[9] but many people were unhappy with the

3. See Isa. 3:25; 4:1. Nelly Stienstra (*YHWH Is the Husband of His People: Analysis of a Biblical Metaphor with Special Reference to Translation* [Kampen: Kok Pharos, 1993], p. 79) points out that even when war made an imbalance of the women:men ratio, polygamy was seen as a shameful response to it.

4. E.g., Sarah and Hagar (Gen 16:1-4). Elkanah also had a second wife because his favorite (perhaps his first) couldn't conceive (1 Samuel 1). Jacob was a special case because of Laban's trick (Gen. 29:15-30). This mirrors the situation in other ancient Near Eastern countries (see G. P. Hugenberger, *Marriage as a Covenant: A Study of Biblical Law and Ethics Governing Marriage, Developed from the Perspective of Malachi,* Vetus Testamentum Supplement 52 [Leiden and New York: Brill, 1994], pp. 108-12).

5. Stienstra (*YHWH Is the Husband of His People,* p. 82) lists Hagar and Sarah (Gen. 16:4-6); Rachel and Leah (Gen. 30:14-16); Peninnah and Hannah (1 Sam. 1:6-8). She also lists laws that imply problems with polygamy: Lev. 18:18 says not to marry two sisters because this may cause rivalry (cf. the story of Rachel and Leah); Deut. 21:15-17 says the son of a favorite wife should not rob the firstborn of his rights (cf. the story of Joseph); Exod. 21:10-11 assumes there will be problems of neglect for the first wife. She also cites the *Targum of Ruth* 4:6, which has Ruth's kinsman redeemer say: "On this ground I cannot redeem it, because I have a wife already, and I have no desire to take another, lest there should be contention in my house."

6. Cf. 1 Sam. 8:5; 8:19-20 — criticized in Deut. 17:17.

7. Polygamy was recognized as permitted (Josephus, *Ant.* 17.14: "For it is our ancestral custom that a man may have several wives at the same time"; also *J.W.* 1.477) and Justin Martyr says that Jews practiced it (*Dialogue* 141). There are a few first-century examples of bigamy, mainly among the rich. Epstein (*Marriage Laws,* p. 17) lists Herod Archelaus, Herod Antipas (Josephus, *Ant.* 17.350); from priest's families, Alubai, Caiaphas, and Josephus (*t. Yebam.* 1.10; *b. Yebam.* 15b; *y. Yebam.* 1.5, 3a; Josephus, *Life* 75); from the Rabbis, Abba b. Rabban Simeon b. Gamaliel I (*b. Yebam.* 15a), R. Tarphon (*t. Ketub.* 5.1), Rab and R. Nahman (*b. Yoma* 18b; *b. Yebam.* 37b).

8. The documents of the Babatha family dating from 93-132 C.E. have been found in a cave at Nahal Hever. Babatha was widowed when young, and her second husband already had a wife. See Naphtali Lewis, Yigael Yadin, and Jonas C. Greenfield, eds., *The Documents from the Bar Kokhba Period in the Cave of Letters: Greek Papyri* (Jerusalem: Israel Exploration Society, Hebrew University of Jerusalem, Shrine of the Book, 1989), p. 22.

9. Epstein lists (*Marriage Laws,* p. 18) teaching on the co-wife (Zareh), which is discussed frequently (e.g. *m. Yebam.* 1 passim); on the interval between marriages (*b. Ketub.* 93b — less than one day!); on the fact that wives should know each other, lest their children marry each

practice.[10] Polygamy was eventually prohibited in Judaism in the eleventh century,[11] though it had probably ceased to be practiced long before this.

A move towards monogamy started very early, as evidenced by a gloss in the Septuagint and other early versions at Genesis 2:24, which read "and they two shall become one flesh." The word "two" is not present in the Masoretic text, but it is found very widely in ancient versions.[12] This gloss was included in the text when Jesus and Paul cited it.[13] Although this gloss was widespread, it did not cause the Hebrew text to be changed. Even at Qumran, when they were amassing arguments against polygamy (see below), the text was not quoted in this form,[14] and there is no example of the Hebrew text being quoted with the word "two" in it.[15]

It appears that this gloss was a very common addition to the text, and that it was recognized as a comment on the text rather than a variant of it. This means that the purpose of the addition must have been obvious to the reader. The gloss affirmed that a marriage is made between only two individuals, and thus polygamy is an aberration.

Qumran Exegetes Prohibited Polygamy

The Dead Sea Scrolls show that some sections of Judaism actually forbade polygamy. The sectarians at Qumran differed from the rest of Judaism over several

---

other (*b. Yoma* 18b); and on compelling a second wife if the first is barren (*b. Yebam.* 21b; *b. Soṭa* 24a).

10. The rabbinic writings have many negative comments about it. Epstein (*Marriage Laws*, p. 19) lists *b. 'Abot* 2.5: "He who multiplies wives multiplies witchcraft"; *b. Yebam.* 44a — polygamy creates strife in a house; *b. Yebam.* 44a — no more than four wives are permitted so that each gets her conjugal rights at least each month.

11. The Herem of R. Gershom of Mayence (960-1040) finally prohibited it (Responsa, "Asheri" 42.1), probably in 1030 at Worms (the document has not survived). Previously the marriage contract had prohibited polygamy without the wife's consent, but this Herem prohibits it even with the wife's consent.

12. Septuagint, Syriac Peshitta, Samaritan Pentateuch, Vulgate, *Targum Pseudo-Jonathan*, and *Targum Neofiti*. It is missing from *Targum Onqelos* (which is often corrected back to the Masoretic text).

13. Matt. 19:5; Mark 10:8; 1 Cor. 6:16.

14. This variant is not used in the Damascus document when it argues for monogamy at CD 4.20–5.6. This may have been in order to argue the point more effectively with Palestinian exegetes who did not accept the use of variants as part of a proof (see my "Nomological Exegesis in Qumran 'Divorce' Texts," *Revue de Qumran* 18 [1998]: 561-79).

15. The text is not found at Qumran, so we have only the witnesses of rabbinic literature, much of which is late, though it is cited by Aqiba (*b. Sanh.* 58a, early second century) and Hananiah (*Gen. Rab.* 18:5, mid-second century).

matters concerning worship, cleanliness, and other laws. They separated from the worship of other Jews because of differences of interpretation concerning the religious calendar. Many of them separated physically from other Jews, living apart in the desert, because of their concern over cleanliness. Many also lived celibate lives,[16] but they were still interested in matters of marriage, and especially polygamy. These matters were discussed in their writings particularly when they were criticizing the practices of others.

In the Damascus Document (CD 4.19–5.5),[17] the sectarians **criticize the** "builders of the wall," which may be a reference to the **Pharisees** or non-Qumran Jews in general.[18] They accuse them of sexual sin and of polluting the temple.[19] They presumably thought that they polluted the temple by going there when they were themselves polluted. They were polluted by two sexual taboos: menstrual blood and marrying close relatives.

One of the two main criticisms that the Damascus Document brought against the Pharisees concerned the practice of polygamy, which they regarded as a sexual sin. The Qumran exegetes regarded Leviticus 18:18 as a proof text outlawing polygamy.

CD 4.20–5.6[20]

. . . They are caught by two (snares). By sexual sin (**זנות**), (namely) taking (21) two wives in their lives (**בחייהם**), while the foundation of creation is "male and female he created them" [Gen. 1:27]. (5.1) And those who entered (Noah's) ark went in two by two into the ark [Gen. 7:9]. And of the prince it is written, (2) "Let him not multiply wives for himself" [Deut. 17:17]. And

16. The Manual of Discipline found at Qumran suggests that the community was celibate, though an appendix to it (1QSa 1.8-11) and the Damascus Document (CD 7.7-8) suggest that at least some members were married.

17. The Damascus Document is named after its references to Damascus. It was first discovered in the Cairo Geniza, so it was called CD for Cairo: Damascus.

18. The "wall" may be a reference to the "fence" that the Pharisees put around the law (*m. 'Abot* 1.1). The fence was the system of rabbinic laws that amplified and specified what the biblical law said and what it implied. By keeping all these rabbinic laws, one would be certain to fulfill all the biblical laws, and so they were a "fence" to protect one from trespassing a biblical law. James H. Charlesworth suggests that the similar phrase at CD 8.12 may also refer to the Pharisees (*The Dead Sea Scrolls: Hebrew, Aramaic, and Greek Texts with English Translations,* 2 vols. [Tübingen: Mohr, 1995], p. 29). In the same passage they are also called "whitewash-daubers," which has interesting NT parallels (Matt. 23:27; Acts 23:3).

19. These are two of the three sins listed in CD 4.17, the other being of arrogance or materialism, which was perhaps reserved for the Sadducees.

20. Based on Charlesworth, *The Dead Sea Scrolls.* This portion only exists in the Geniza MS A. The Damascus Document has been found in Qumran fragments 6Q15 and 4Q226-273 but only a couple of words from this passage are found in these fragments.

David did not read the sealed book of the Torah which (3) was in the Ark (of the Covenant), for it was not opened in Israel since the day of the death of Eleazar (4) and Joshua and the elders. For (their successors) worshipped the Ashtoreth, and that which had been revealed was hidden (5) until Zadok arose, so David's works were accepted, with the exception of Uriah's blood, (6) and God forgave him for them.

The phrase "taking two wives in their lives" has a masculine suffix for "their," and thus it appears to criticize any man who takes two wives within his own lifetime. This would include those who practice polygamy, remarriage after divorce, or remarriage after widowhood. This led some early commentators like Solomon Schechter to argue that this virtually prohibited divorce because it did not allow divorcés to remarry.[21] Other early commentators like Chaim Rabin suggested that "in their *(masc.)* lives" was an allusion to Leviticus 18:18, and thus it should be read as "in their *(fem.)* lives."[22] This would mean that divorce and remarriage was possible but only after the former wife had died.

The publication of the **Temple Scroll** appeared to support this emendation.[23] The Temple Scroll is an expanded rewriting of Torah law. The expansions are not arbitrary additions to the text but are based on the exegesis of other biblical texts, which are sometimes alluded to and are sometimes just assumed to be part of the reader's general knowledge. The Temple Scroll may not have been written by the same group that wrote the Damascus Document, but they help to illuminate each other. Column 57 of the Temple Scroll is equivalent to Deuteronomy 17:14-20 concerning kings, and, like the Damascus Document, it uses Leviticus 18:18 as a proof text for monogamy.

21. Solomon Schechter, *Documents of Jewish Sectaries* (Cambridge: Cambridge University Press, 1910; reprinted New York: Ktav Publishing House, 1970), p. xvii. For a full bibliography and an analysis of the exegesis of this passage see my "Nomological Exegesis in Qumran 'Divorce' Texts."

22. I.e., בחייהן instead of בחייהם, e.g., Chaim Rabin, *The Zadokite Documents* (Oxford: Clarendon, 1954), pp. 16-17. It should be noted that Schechter probably realized this too, though he does not say so in his commentary, because in his introduction he concluded that CD prohibited "marrying a second wife, as long as the first wife is alive though she had been divorced" (*Documents of Jewish Sectaries,* p. xvii). Yigael Yadin (*The Temple Scroll,* 3 vols. [Jerusalem: Israel Exploration Society, 1983], 1:356) says "most of the early scholars" read it this way.

23. According to Yadin (*The Temple Scroll,* 1:356), only Jerome Murphy-O'Conner still defends the masculine reading since the publication of the Temple Scroll. He has carried on a long debate with Yadin.

Column 57.15-19[24]

15 . . . And he [the king] shall not take a wife from all (16) the daughters of the nations, but from his father's house he shall take unto himself a wife, (17) from the family of his father. And he shall not take upon her another wife, for (18) she alone shall be with him all the days of her life (כול ימי חייה). But should she die, he may take (19) unto himself another (wife) from the house of his father, from his family.

This section of the Temple Scroll concerns the king's wife and is an expansion of Deuteronomy 17:17: "And he shall not multiply wives for himself, lest his heart turn away." The Temple Scroll interprets this as an injunction against polygamy, whereas the standard rabbinic interpretation is that one may not take more than eighteen wives.[25] The Temple Scroll's author seems to interpret the phrase "lest his heart turn away" in the light of Deuteronomy 7:3-4[26] and 1 Kings 11:1-2, which say that Israel's hearts will be turned away by foreign women, as Solomon's was. Therefore, the Temple Scroll says, the king may marry only an Israelite and may take only one wife. In order to justify the interpretation "one wife" rather than "few wives," the Temple Scroll alludes to Leviticus 18:18 with the phrase "all the days of her life."[27] Leviticus 18:18 says that one may not marry the sister of one's wife (or former wife) while she is still alive. In order to apply this law to the king, the Temple Scroll emphasizes that the whole of Israel is one family: "he shall not take a wife from all the daughters of the nations, but from his father's house."[28]

It is impossible to know whether the Temple Scroll regarded monogamy as mandatory for all Jews, but they would at least have regarded the king as an example to look up to and probably to emulate. It is unfortunate that the section regarding Deuteronomy 21:15-17 (which allows polygamy for the ordinary

24. Based on Yadin, *The Temple Scroll,* 2:258.

25. See R. Judah at *m. Sanh.* 2.4 and the Palestinian Targum. This is probably based on the tradition that David had eighteen wives (*b. Sanh.* 21a; *y. Sanh.* 2.6 [20c]).

26. Cf. Lawrence H. Schiffman, "Laws Pertaining to Women in the Temple Scroll," in *The Dead Sea Scrolls: Forty Years of Research,* ed. D. Dimant and U. Rappaport (Leiden: Brill, 1992), pp. 210-28, esp. p. 213.

27. Yadin (*The Temple Scroll,* 1:355, 2:300) suggests that Lev. 18:18 was cited at the top of column 57, which is missing.

28. This detail is greatly emphasized in this short passage: "from his father's house . . . from the family of his father. . . . But should she die, he may take unto himself another (wife) from the house of his father, from his family." It was natural to regard God as the father of Israel (as at Isa. 63:16; Jer. 31:9) when the context concerned turning away to other gods. Schiffman ("Laws Pertaining to Women in the Temple Scroll," pp. 214-15) says that the main emphasis was to make the king like a high priest, who may not marry a non-Israelite.

Israelite) is not preserved — it would have been at the start of column 54, which is missing.

In the Damascus Document, the allusion to Leviticus 18:18 is not accompanied by any explanation. There is not even the briefest of explanations, as found in the Temple Scroll. It is assumed that the reader understands the text and its importance. It is followed by texts that strengthen the argument against polygamy. The examples of Adam and Noah's Ark are used to show that God ordained one wife to one husband.[29] There then follows a long explanation of King David's polygamy, arguing that he was ignorant of the law because it was hidden during his time.

The authors of both the Damascus Document and the Temple Scroll were therefore highly critical of polygamy. They regarded it as sexual immorality, as contrary to the ideals shown in the examples of the Creator, of Adam, and of Noah's Ark, as well as contrary to a command in Torah at Leviticus 18:18. Their use of this text must have been well known because they do not attempt to exegete it clearly. Their very brief use of this text will now be explored with regard to the implications for their teaching on divorce and remarriage.

Qumran Exegetes Did Not Criticize Divorce or Remarriage

The phrase **"taking two wives in their lives"** is very difficult to interpret. Originally, as already stated, this was interpreted to mean that divorce was effectively prohibited because a man could not remarry during his lifetime. After the publication of the Temple Scroll, there was a general consensus that the emendation proposed by Rabin and others was correct. They emended בחייהם "in their [*masculine*] lives" to read בחייהן "in their [*feminine*] lives." This portion of the Damascus Document is preserved in only one manuscript: MS A of the Geniza Zadokite fragments. This is a very well preserved manuscript in a clear square script, and there is no doubt that the text itself reads בחייהם.[30] Thus, one must assume a scribal error in order to make this emendation. This emendation is also difficult to accept because the new reading produces new problems in interpretation.

If the emended reading is accepted, it would imply that a divorced man cannot remarry unless his former wife has died. This has huge implications,

29. Evald Lövestam ("Divorce and Remarriage in the New Testament," in *The Jewish Law Annual*, ed. B. S. Jackson [Leiden: Brill, 1981], 4:50) pointed out that these two passages are linked by the words "male and female" (זכר ונקבה), which occur immediately after the text cited from Gen. 7:9.

30. See the photographs in Magen Broshi, *The Damascus Document Reconsidered* (Jerusalem: Israel Exploration Society, 1992).

which are not explored in the Qumran documents. These two passages are the only places where Leviticus 18:18 is used in this way, and neither passage says anything about divorce. There is no further teaching about divorce anywhere else in the Qumran documents other than a couple of references that appear to be neutral about divorce.[31] Even given the fragmentary nature of the texts, one would expect to find further teaching on this point. It is likely that there were far more cases of divorce than of polygamy, and thus this matter would have been of far greater practical importance than the teaching on polygamy. Also, as Louis Ginzberg[32] has pointed out, if the Qumran community believed that remarriage was prohibited, this would have formed a far more effective criticism of their opponents. If they believed that remarriage before the death of a former wife was invalid, they could have charged their opponents with committing and condoning adultery, which was a far greater offense than polygamy.

The three references to **divorce in** the **Qumran** documents appear to allow divorce, and certainly do not condemn it. They do not say anything about restrictions to remarriage after divorce. In the Temple Scroll there is a brief reference to the nature of a vow made by a divorcée:

Temple Scroll 54.4-5[33]
But any vow of a widow or of a divorced woman, anything by which she has bound herself (5) shall stand against her, according to all that proceeded out of her mouth.

Another reference in the Temple Scroll forbids a rapist who has married his victim from ever divorcing her (as in Deut. 22:29), which suggests that divorce was normally allowed:

Temple Scroll 66.8-11
If a man violates a young virgin who is not betrothed, and she suits him according to the Law and he lies with her and they are discovered, the man who lay with her will give the girl's father fifty silver shekels and she will be his wife, since he raped her, and he cannot dismiss her all his life.

In the Damascus Document there is a longer reference that is very fragmentary. It concerns the role of the examiner, who governed many aspects of personal life for the members of the community:

31. Temple Scroll 54.4 and CD 13.17, which are explored below.

32. Louis Ginzberg, *An Unknown Jewish Sect* (New York: Jewish Theological Seminary of America, 1978), p. 131.

33. Based on Yadin, *The Temple Scroll*, 2:399.

CD 13.15-17[34]

Let no man do anything involving buying and selling without informing (16) the Examiner in the camp. He shall do (it) [ ] and not [ ] (17) and so for one divorcing and he [ ] (18) humility and with loving mercy.

This has been reconstructed by Lawrence H. Schiffman to read as follows:

> And let no one do anything in regard to buying or selling unless he has made (it) known to the examiner who is (in charge of) the camp, and does so with (his) counsel, lest they e[rr. And thus] for a[ny]one who ma[rr]ies a wo[man], i[t] (must be)[with] (his) counsel. And thus (also) for one who divorces (his wife). And he (the examiner) shall [instruct their sons and their daughters with a spirit of] humility and with lovingkindness.

Schiffman concludes that the Qumran community allowed divorce. Rabin, who is more cautious with his reconstruction, points out that there is no evidence from this passage that divorce is accompanied by a warning, or by any special regulations concerning remarriage.[35]

Schiffman and Jerome Murphy-O'Conner are the only scholars who still defend the unemended reading "in their [*masculine*] lives." Murphy-O'Conner had a running debate with Yigael Yadin in *Revue biblique* in which he reasserted the idea that Qumran condemned all remarriage, but he admits that this interpretation does not fit well with the Temple Scroll text. Schiffman proposed a new reason for the plural masculine, that it indicated that the law applied to both male and female — that is, that both a man and a woman are prohibited from remarrying their spouse after a divorce.[36] This is a very plausible explanation because it takes into account both the text in Leviticus, which certainly does imply a feminine suffix, and the principle in the Damascus Document of equal application of laws to both male and female, which is spelled out in the section following the prohibition of polygamy:

34. Based on Charlesworth, *The Dead Sea Scrolls.*

35. Rabin, *The Zadokite Documents,* regarding CD 4.20. He reconstructs CD 13.15-17 as: "And let no man make a partnership for trade unless he informs | the overseer in the camp and makes a *written* agreement, and let him not (. . . | . . .) the council. And likewise with regard to him that divorces *his wife* and he (. . . | . . .) they shall answer him, and 'with merciful love.'" Rabin suggested that למגרש could be "common land," but this is ruled out by the newly published 4Q266 (of col. 8, lines 6-7) that suggests the words apply to the children of the man whom he first admonishes, and who then reply to him. See Tom Holmén, "Divorce in CD.4.20–5.2 and in 11Q 57.17-18: Some Remarks on the Pertinence of the Question," *Revue de Qumran* 18 (1998): 403.

36. Schiffman, "Laws Pertaining to Women in the Temple Scroll," p. 217.

CD 5.6-11[37]

. . . And they also continuously polluted the sanctuary by not (7) separating according to the Torah, and they habitually lay with a woman who sees blood of flowing; and they marry (8) each one his brother's daughter or sister's daughter. But Moses said, "To (9) your mother's sister you may not draw near, for she is your mother's near relation" [Lev. 18:13]. Now the precept of incest is written (10) from the point of view of males, but the same (law) applies to women, so if a brother's daughter uncovers the nakedness of a brother or (11) her father, she is a (forbidden) close relationship.

The Law said that an aunt and nephew should not marry (Lev. 18:13), but it did not say that an uncle and a niece should not marry. The Damascus Document said that this law should have equal application to male and female, and thus this law would rule out marriages to a niece as well as a nephew. The same conclusion, though without stating the reasoning, is found at 11QTemple 66.16-17. This principle of equal application is expressed by the words "(it) is written from the point of view of males, but the same (law) applies to women." This statement is not justified in any way, and thus it is assumed that the reader would understand it and agree with it as an accepted principle for interpreting Scripture.

Ginzberg's Explanation of "During Their Lives"

Ginzberg, who was one of the first commentators on the Damascus Document, proposed an explanation that is even more convincing and that seems to have been relatively ignored.[38] This may be partly because the explanation was presented in a complex way, and partly because the explanation was slightly incomplete. He pointed out that if this principle of equal application to male and female were applied to Leviticus 18:18, that would explain why the Qumran exegetes interpreted it in the way that they did. He also implied that this would mean that they did not forbid remarriage of those who were divorced. Unfortunately he did not expound this explanation very completely, and he failed to point out that this exegesis is implied by the exact words used in CD 4.20.

The law of Leviticus 18:18 states:

37. Based on Charlesworth, *The Dead Sea Scrolls.*

38. Ginzberg, *An Unknown Jewish Sect,* pp. 19-20.

> You shall not take a wife with her sister to be a rival, to uncover her nakedness beside her, during her life.

> ואשה אל־אחתה לא תקח לצרר לגלות ערותה עליה בחייה

By the principle of equal application, this law would also teach that a woman may not marry her husband's brother during the lifetime of her first husband. The word "during [his] life" would imply that she would be able to marry him after her husband died. However, this would break the law stated earlier in Leviticus 18:16 that a man cannot marry the wife of his brother after he has died.[39] Ginzberg proposed that the Qumran exegetes, in order to get around this difficulty, read the word "sister" (**אחתה**) as "other," which is linguistically possible,[40] so that this law forbade a man from marrying another woman besides his wife.[41]

In CD 4.20, this exegesis is implied by the word "during their [*masculine plural*] lives." The plural is used so that it includes both male and female, and it points to the principle of equal application. This particular word is chosen from the text of Leviticus 18:18 because it is this word that demonstrates the untenability of the traditional interpretation. If the word "during their life" were missing, the law would not imply that a woman may marry her dead sister's husband, and there would be no need to read **אחתה** as "other" rather than the more normal "sister."

Ginzberg also criticized those who said that the Damascus Document prohibited remarriage before the death of a former partner. He answered them with the words: "Naturally, however, he is permitted to marry a second woman after he is divorced from his first wife, since he thus has only one wife. The addition of **בחייהם** (= **בחייהן**) in our text is borrowed from Scripture and means only that this prohibition of marriage differs from all the others in so far as it is in force only so long as a man lives with his first wife

39. The law actually says simply that he cannot marry the wife of his brother, but it is self-evident that this is true during his brother's lifetime, and so this law is always interpreted to apply after his death.

40. He cites examples at Exod. 26:5, 6, 17. However, the Qumran exegetes were probably not influenced by biblical Hebrew as much as by the Aramaic **אחר** "another."

41. The Karaites also used this same principle of equality, and they dealt with Lev. 18:18 in a similar way, but they had difficulty with Deut. 21:15-17, which allowed polygamy. Aaron ben Elijah of Nicomedia said that Lev. 18:18 prohibited a second marriage only if it was the husband's intention to neglect his first wife, based on "to be a rival" (**לצרר**) (*Našim* 9.164d). Toviah ben Eliezer said that Deut. 21:15-17 applied only where the second wife was a captive woman (*Midrash Leqah Tov* to Deut. 21:15). See Schiffman, "Laws Pertaining to Women in the Temple Scroll," p. 217; Ginzberg, *An Unknown Jewish Sect*, p. 19.

in marital union."[42] This rather compact answer can perhaps be unpacked as follows.

The law of Leviticus 18:18 (according to the Qumran exegetes) concerns a man who has a wife and wants to take another, which is prohibited unless the first wife has died. If a man is divorced from his first wife, he no longer has a wife, and so this law does not apply to him. We can see that this interpretation was in the minds of the Qumran exegetes in the way they summarize the teaching of Leviticus 18:18 with the words "taking two wives during their lives." This phrase reminds the reader that Leviticus 18:18 is emphatically speaking about being married to two wives at once: "You shall not take a wife **with** her sister **to be a rival**, to uncover her nakedness **beside** her, during her life."

The authors of the Temple Scroll passage also accepted the principle of equal application to male and female, and they also used Leviticus 18:18 as a proof text against polygamy, but they may have used different reasoning to get there.

The Temple Scroll has a justification for the principle of equal application to male and female rights at the end of the last column. It lists various forbidden degrees of sexual relations, some of which are specifically mentioned in Leviticus 18 and some which are not. In the following, those that are not mentioned in Leviticus are in italics:

> **Temple Scroll 66.12-17**
> A man shall not take his father's wife, nor shall he uncover his father's skirt. A man shall not take (13) his brother's wife, nor shall he uncover *his brother's skirt, be it his father's son or his mother's son,* for this is impurity. (14) A man shall not take his sister, his father's daughter or his mother's daughter, for this is an abomination. A (15) man shall not take his father's sister or his mother's sister, for it is wickedness. A man (16) shall not take (17) his *brother's daughter or his sister's daughter,* for it is an abomination. A [man] shall not [ ]

Leviticus named the nakedness of one's mother, father, sister, and half-sister, but not brother or half-brother, which the Temple Scroll specifically adds. This addition was presumably based on the principle of equal application. The Temple Scroll then listed aunts from both families, as in Leviticus, and added nieces of a brother or sister. Like the Damascus Document, the Temple Scroll infers from the prohibition of marrying an aunt that a niece cannot marry her uncle. In the Damascus Document the principle of equal application is specifically referred to at this point. It is clear that the Temple Scroll is arguing in exactly the same way.

42. Ginzberg, *An Unknown Jewish Sect,* p. 20.

The Temple Scroll also used Leviticus 18:18 for a similar purpose as the Damascus Document, but via a slightly different route. They both saw that there was something strange about Leviticus 18:18 because the principle of equal application made it seem like a contradiction of verse 16. The Temple Scroll also read אחתה as "other," like the Damascus Document, and paraphrased Leviticus 18:18 as follows (the shared vocabulary is in italics):

> And he shall not *take with her another wife*, for she alone shall be with him all the days of *her life*.
>
> ולוא יקח עליה אשה אחרת כי היאה לבדה תהיה עמו כול ימי חייה

Unlike the Damascus Document, the Temple Scroll exegetes also gave a new emphasis to the idea of אחתה as "sister." They understood "sister" as "fellow Israelite" so that the text not only prohibited polygamy but also assumed that one would marry only an Israelite. This is given great emphasis in the Temple Scroll passage: ". . . from his father's house . . . from the family of his father . . . another (wife) from the house of his father, from his family." If the primary meaning of אחתה is regarded as "other," then exegetes are entitled to point out that this is an unusual word and to look for a reason for it.[43] The reason they found is that a wife should be taken only from among one's "sisters," and so one should not marry a non-Israelite.

This extra meaning, that the "other" wife would be a sister, did not constitute a new law that could be applied to all Israelites. It applied to the king because he would be expected to demonstrate the highest morals and conform not only to the laws of Scripture but also to the norms demonstrated by Scripture.

Similarly the Temple Scroll assumed that the king would not divorce his wife. After their paraphrase of "in her lifetime" they added "But should she die, he may take to himself another. . . ." They cannot argue that "in her lifetime" is a prohibition of divorce any more than it is a command to remarry after a first wife has died. The only command in Leviticus 18:18 is the negative one either against polygamy or against marrying two sisters (depending how one reads אחתה). Yet they could argue that "in her lifetime" demonstrates the scriptural assumption that marriage lasts for a lifetime. The king would be expected to live up to this ideal, and the other people might be expected to emulate him, but this exegesis could not negate the Law with regard to divorce.

43. This is an exegetical technique that is found in early rabbinic exegesis (see my *Techniques and Assumptions in Jewish Exegesis before 70* CE, Texte und Studien zum antiken Judentum 30 [Tübingen: J. C. B. Mohr, 1993], pp. 20-21).

The conclusion of this lengthy excursus is that the Qumran documents do not say anything significant about divorce or remarriage. Ginzberg's explanation for the text of CD 4.20 is comprehensive and coherent. It allows the text to be understood in an unemended form and without any of the difficulties associated with other texts. Other explanations require the assumption that the Qumran exegetes had a doctrine about forbidding remarriage, which is not stated in this passage or any other passage, and which is based on the implications of a single word. They also assume that the Qumran exegetes used Leviticus 18:18 as a proof text, torn out of its context and twisted to conform to their own purposes. Ginzberg's explanation shows that they had a coherent approach to exegesis that took the text seriously. The text that they used had (as they understood it) a direct bearing on the matter of polygamy. When this exegesis is placed behind the Temple Scroll text, it strengthens the argument by providing a reasoned exegesis for prohibiting marriage to non-Israelites.

Therefore the text in the Damascus Document has no implications with regard to remarriage after divorce because the text, as the Qumran exegetes specifically state, applies to someone who takes two wives. The Temple Scroll text assumes that the king will not divorce his wife, and this might be seen as a moral example to others, but it does not prohibit divorce or remarriage for the general population.

Divorce by Jewish Women Becomes Easier outside Israel

Divorce became easier for women in most ancient societies during the last two centuries B.C.E. and the first century C.E. In the **Greco-Roman world**, women were almost equal to men in their right to divorce. In Jewish law women had equal standing with men in most areas, except with regard to reproductive functions.[44] This meant that married women were subject to their husbands in most matters, including divorce. However, they did have a limited right to force their husbands to divorce them. This will be explored in the next chapter. In the Diaspora, Jewish women were starting to share an equal right to divorce their husbands, as seen at Elephantine in Egypt (see below).

In classical Greek culture and in early Roman society divorce was almost unknown.[45] The most ancient form of Roman marriage held women in total

44. See Judith R. Wegner, *Chattel or Person? The Status of Women in the Mishnah* (Oxford: Oxford University Press, 1988).

45. Plutarch, *Lives* I:395: "Just as our Greek historians recorded the names of those who first slew kinsfolk, or made war on their brothers, or were parricides, or matricides, so the

subjection to their husbands.[46] This was abandoned by the third century B.C.E. in favor of "free marriage." Augustus tried to reassert traditional values by making laws in 18 B.C.E. that rewarded those who married and produced children, and by making adultery a crime. These laws had little effect[47] because they relied on private prosecution, and gradually divorce became more common. By New Testament times a social revolution had taken place that enabled women and men to divorce at will, without citing any grounds.[48] A woman would lose her dowry if she was divorced for adultery, and a man would have to return the dowry plus a half if he committed adultery, but divorce for other grounds was without any penalty.[49]

Marriage was assumed to be a matter of mutual consent, and when that consent broke down, the marriage would end.[50] This meant that either partner could end the marriage at any point by walking out or by declaring that the marriage had ended,[51] and even a declaration was technically not necessary.[52]

Romans make record of the fact that Spurius Carvilius [Ruga] was the first to divorce his wife, two hundred and thirty years after the founding of Rome [231 B.C.E.], there being no precedent for it."

46. Twelve Tablets, 451-450 B.C.E. See Deborah F. Sawyer, *Women and Religion in the First Christian Centuries* (London: Routledge, 1996), p. 19.

47. Augustus imposed the laws *de adulteriis* and *de maritandis ordinibus,* which encouraged marriage and birth and opposed adultery, and the law *lulia de adulteriis,* which laid down that a divorce must be witnessed in the presence of seven Roman citizens over the age of puberty. See Alfredo M. Rabello, "Divorce of Jews in the Roman Empire," in *The Jewish Law Annual,* ed. B. S. Jackson (Leiden: Brill, 1981), 4:79-102, esp. p. 83; Suzanne Dixon, *The Roman Family* (Baltimore and London: Johns Hopkins University Press, 1992), p. 79.

48. *Institutes of Gaius,* I sect. 137. See D. W. Amram, *The Jewish Law of Divorce according to Bible and Talmud* (reprint of undated original, New York: Sepher-Hermon, 1975), p. 61. A written *repudium* was not needed until the late third century C.E. (see B. Cohen, *Jewish and Roman Law: A Comparative Study,* 2 vols. [New York: Jewish Theological Seminary of America, 1966], pp. 384-85).

49. Dixon, *The Roman Family,* p. 66.

50. Gaius, a jurist of the second century, defined divorce in the 11th book *ad edictum provinciale* as "The term *divortium* is derived either from the *difference* of minds (of the parties), or from the fact that the parties who are tearing the marriage asunder are going their *different* ways" (*Dig.* 24.2.2.pr). He said it was wrong to bind yourself not to divorce or to pay a penalty on divorce: "It is dishonourable to bind together a marriage whether existing or anticipated, by means of a penal bond" (*Dig.* 45.1.134). Cited in Rabello, "Divorce of Jews in the Roman Empire," pp. 79-80.

51. See the many references in Craig S. Keener, . . . *And Marries Another: Divorce and Remarriage in the Teaching of the New Testament* (Peabody, Mass.: Hendrickson, 1991), p. 51.

52. Cicero deals with an example that shows that divorce needed no ceremony and did not even require the partner to be informed. He recounts the case of a Roman citizen who left his pregnant wife in Spain and set up house with another woman in Rome without having told

Adultery was common, though it was still shameful, and it was considered by some to make divorce compulsory.[53] A divorce did not require court proceedings, though sometimes a refusal to return dowry resulted in a court case.[54]

As a result, divorce was very common in the Greco-Roman world, especially among the wealthier classes.[55] In practice the number of divorces probably did not exceed 30 percent of marriages, even in the first century C.E. when it was at its height.[56] It is difficult to know whether it was also common among the poorer classes, about whom we know much less. It is possible that financial constraints or more traditional moral standards may have held marriages together, but it is likely that the practices of the wealthy reflected the practices of all strata of society.

---

his intentions to his first wife. His sudden death and the birth of a son to both women posed the question as to which son was illegitimate. Cicero considered that, although it was not legally necessary to give notice of a divorce, the man should have done so (*De Oratore I,* 40.183; cited in Rabello, "Divorce of Jews in the Roman Empire," p. 80). Another example is Messalina, the wife of emperor Claudius, who celebrated a wedding with her lover Silius. She had not sent Claudius a formal notice of divorce, so someone who heard about the wedding came to tell the emperor the news that he was divorced. This divorce-by-separation continued at least till Diocletian, who ruled in 294 C.E. that "even though a bill of repudiation was not delivered or known to the husband, the marriage is dissolved." All this changed when Constantine, in his first constitution in 331 C.E., ruled that divorce was legal only if one's spouse was guilty of serious crime (see Rabello, "Divorce of Jews in the Roman Empire," p. 84).

53. The legislation of Augustus penalized husbands who did not divorce their adulterous wife, though this legislation was generally ineffective. See also the references in Keener, . . . *And Marries Another,* pp. 31, 52.

54. Dixon, *The Roman Family,* p. 61; Susan Treggiari, "Divorce Roman Style: How Easy and How Frequent Was It?" in *Marriage, Divorce and Children in Ancient Rome,* ed. Beryl Rawson (Oxford: Clarendon, 1991), pp. 38-39.

55. Seneca complained that there are women who do not number the years by consuls but by husbands; they divorce to marry and they marry to divorce (*De beneficiis* 3.16.2). Martial remarks, concerning a woman who in thirty days had married and divorced ten husbands: "Women who marry so often do not contract marriages; in law it is adultery" (*Epigrammata* 6.7; cited in Rabello, "Divorce of Jews in the Roman Empire," p. 82). See also references in Keener, . . . *And Marries Another,* p. 51; K. R. Bradley, "Remarriage and the Structure of the Upper Class Roman Family," in *Marriage, Divorce and Children in Ancient Rome,* ed. Beryl Rawson (Oxford: Clarendon, 1991), pp. 79-93, esp. pp. 81-84.

56. A study of women of the senatorial aristocracy from the Augustan period to around 200 C.E. found 51 out of 562 showed evidence of divorce. There are far fewer divorces in the second than the first century (see Judith Evans Grubbs, "'Pagan' and 'Christian' Marriage: The State of the Question," *Journal of Early Christian Studies* 2 [1994]: 361-412, esp. p. 367).

Divorces by Jewish Men and Women at Elephantine

A large body of papyri has been unearthed at Elephantine in Egypt, including marriage contracts and documents relating to divorce. They consist of the documents of a few Jewish families living in this Greek society in the fifth century B.C.E. They give a detailed insight into how Jewish customs were affected by a Gentile environment.[57] The collection includes a betrothal contract,[58] seven marriage contracts (though four of these are very fragmentary),[59] two documents concerning payment of the divorce settlement,[60] and many other commercial and family documents.

There are no divorce certificates, and it appears from the wording of the marriage contract that divorce was carried out orally. The documents concerning divorce deal only with matters of money still owed after a divorce. One of these documents appears to concern the return of the dowry or part of it,[61] but in the other document it is unclear what the payment is for, though it is related to the divorce settlement.[62] Neither of these documents mentions the freedom of the wife to remarry whomever she wishes, or other phrases that are normally

57. The marriage and divorce texts are published with useful commentary by A. E. Cowley (*Aramaic Papyri of the Fifth Century* B.C. [Oxford: Clarendon, 1923]) and Emil G. Kraeling (*The Brooklyn Museum Aramaic Papyri: New Documents of the Fifth Century* B.C. *from the Jewish Colony at Elephantine* [New Haven: Yale University Press, 1953]). These and the other texts from Elephantine have been reedited and translated in Bezalel Porten and Ada Yardeni, *Textbook of Aramaic Documents from Ancient Egypt: Newly Copied, Edited and Translated into Hebrew and English*, 4 vols. (Jerusalem: Hebrew University, 1986-96). The traditional numbering is based on the collections of Cowley (C1 etc.) and Kraeling (K1 etc.), but the later numbering used by Porten and Yardeni (B1.1 etc.) is more useful because it groups together texts that belong to the same family archive or the same type of document. The two main family archives belonged to Mibtahiah (B2.1-11 [471-410 B.C.E.]) and Anani (B3.1-13 [456-402 B.C.E.]). Marriage contracts that are not part of these archives are collected as B6.1-4.

58. C48 = B2.5 — a very small fragment that includes the words "your daughter to take her for wifehood" (Porten and Yardeni, *Textbook of Aramaic Documents*, p. 29).

59. Three marriage contracts are mostly complete (C15 = B2.6 concerning a divorcée; K2 = B3.3 concerning a slave girl; K7 = B3.8 concerning a freed woman) and four are fragmentary (K14 = B6.1; C36 = B6.2; C46 = B6.3; C18 = B6.4).

60. C14 = B2.8; C35 = B4.6.

61. C35 = B4.6: "You have a claim on me for silver, 2 shekels, that is silver, 1 stater, from part of the silver and the goods which (are written) on your document of wifehood" (based on Porten and Yardeni, *Textbook of Aramaic Documents*, pp. 114-15). The divorce payment is normally 7.5 shekels (see C15 = B2.6; K2 = B3.3; K7 = B3.8).

62. C14 = B2.8: "<Name of husband> said to <name of wife>: about the suit which we made in Syene, a litigation about silver and grain and raiment and bronze and iron — all the goods and property — and the wifehood document" (based on Porten and Yardeni, *Textbook of Aramaic Documents*, pp. 38-39).

found in divorce certificates. The otherwise relative completeness of the family archives makes it fairly safe to say that divorce certificates were not normally used by this community.

The three **marriage contracts** that are substantially complete use wording that is very similar, and so it is safe to assume that they record the standard wording of marriage contracts in that community.[63] The standard wording is:[64]

> On <date>, <name of husband> said to <name of father/guardian> saying: I came to <place of meeting> (and asked you) to give me <name of wife> for wifehood. She is my wife and I am her husband from this day and forever.[65]
>
> I gave you (as) *mohar* for <name of wife>: <list of goods and/or money>. It came into you and your heart was satisfied herein.[66]
>
> <Name of wife> brought to me in her hand: <list of goods and money>. It came to me and my heart was satisfied herein.[67]
>
> Tomorrow or (the) next day, should <the husband> stand up in an assembly and say: "I hated my wife <name of wife>, she shall not be my wife," silver of hatred is on his head. He shall give <his wife> silver, 7 shekels 2 quarters, and all that she brought in her hand she shall take out, from straw to string.[68]
>
> Tomorrow or (the) next day, should <the wife> stand up in an assembly and say: "I hated you; I will not be your wife," silver of hatred is on her head. She shall give to <her husband> silver, 7 shekels 2 quarters, and all that she brought in her hand she shall take out, from straw to string.[69]
>
> Tomorrow or the next day, should <the husband> die not having a child,

63. This is a fairly close-knit community. Of the five contracts for which we know the scribe who wrote them, two were written by Nathan, and three by his son Mauziah.

64. Based on the text of Porten and Yardeni, *Textbook of Aramaic Documents*. This text is put together from the various contracts, with major variations noted in the footnotes. Personal names and places have been replaced by generic terms in angled brackets, e.g., <name of wife>. It is unlikely that the scribes used a template like this one because there are too many minor variations in wording and in order of the paragraphs.

65. C15 = B2.6; K2 = B3.3; K7 = B3.8; K14 = B6.1.

66. C15 = B2.6; K7 = B3.8; K14 = B6.1. This is missing from K2 = B3.3 because she was a servant.

67. C15 = B2.6; K2 = B3.3; K7 = B3.8. The money comes from the father or guardian. In C15 = B2.6 the bride contributes some of the dowry herself because she is a divorcée and has money of her own.

68. C15 = B2.6; K2 = B3.3; K7 = B3.8 with slight variations.

69. C15 = B2.6; K2 = B3.3; K7 = B3.8 with slight variations.

male or female by <his wife>, it is <the wife> who has right to all the goods which he has. Tomorrow or (the next) day, should <the wife> die not having a child, male or female, by <her husband>, it is <the husband> who shall inherit from her goods.[70]

And whoever shall stand up against <the wife> to evict her from the house of <the husband> and his goods and his property, shall give her silver, 20 karsh,[71] and do to her the law of this document.[72]

And <the wife> shall not be able to take another man beside <her husband>. And if she do thus, it is hatred. They shall do to her the law of hatred.[73] And <the husband> shall not be able to take another woman beside <his wife>. And if he do thus, it is hatred. He shall do to her the law of hatred.[74]

And moreover <the husband> shall not be able not to do (i.e., to refuse) to <name of wife> his wife the law of one or two of his colleagues' wives.[75] And if he not do thus (i.e., if he refuse), it is hatred. He shall do to her the law of hatred. And moreover, <the wife> shall not be able not to do (i.e., to refuse) to <name of husband> her husband the law of one or two (of her colleagues'

70. C15 = B2.6; K2 = B3.3; K7 = B3.8; C46 = B6.3 with slight variations.

71. One karsh = 10 shekels.

72. C15 = B2.6; K2 = B3.3; K7 = B3.8; C46 = B6.3. In K2 = B3.3 the fine and wording are significantly different — probably because she was a servant — but it still speaks of evicting or divorcing (גרש).

73. This passive "they shall do to her the law of hatred" is probably what made I. Abrahams (*Studies in Pharisaism and the Gospels* [London: Macmillan, 1917], p. 67) conclude that women at Elephantine could not truly declare a divorce, but they could claim one. However, this passive occurs only in K7 = B3.8. The same passive is not used with regard to women divorcing husbands for neglecting their conjugal rights ("she shall do to him the law of hatred" — see the next paragraph), though it must be admitted that there is only one contract for those words too.

74. K7 = B3.8; C18 = B6.4; C15 = B2.6. C15 = B2.6 forbids polygamy only by the husband and speaks in the first person, using completely different language: "And I shall not be able to say: I have another wife beside <name of wife> and other children besides the children whom <the wife> shall bear to me. If I say: I have other children and wife beside <name> and her children, I shall give to <the wife> silver, 20 karsh by the stone-weights of the king. And I shall not be able to release my goods and my property from <name of wife>. And should I remove them from her, I shall give to <the wife> silver, 20 karsh by the stone-weights of the king." C18 = B6.4 also forbids polygamy by the husband only, but it uses the same wording as K7 = B3.8, and the fragmentary nature of this document means that it may also have included a prohibition for the wife.

75. This is a euphemism for conjugal rights. This is similar to the wording in later *ketuboth:* "come to you as the way of all the world" (cf. Mordechai Friedman, *A Jewish Marriage in Palestine: A Cairo Geniza Study,* 2 vols., *The Ketubba Traditions of Eretz Israel* and *The Ketubba Texts* [Tel-Aviv, New York, and Jerusalem: Daf-Chen, 1980], 1:178).

husbands). And if she not do for him, it is hatred. She shall do to him the law of hatred.[76]

<Name of scribe> wrote. And the witnesses herein: <list of names>[77]

This contract has many similarities with Old Babylonian and other ancient Near Eastern marriage contracts, and a few similarities to later Jewish *ketuboth* (marriage contracts). If these are typical of fifth-century B.C.E. contracts, we must conclude that either the Jewish *ketubah* changed a great deal during the next few centuries or the Jews at Elephantine had lost most of their Jewish roots. The latter is confirmed to some extent by Hillel who, in the first century B.C.E., recognized that the marriage contracts of Egyptian Jews were different to those of Palestinian Jews.[78]

They have some very significant similarities with other ancient Near Eastern marriage contracts. The oral vow "She is my wife and I am her husband from this day and forever" is very similar to that found throughout the ancient Near East in many sources.[79] The term "forever" does not imply that a divorce could not take place. It is used in all kinds of legal contracts concerning sales and debts, as well as marriages.[80] It did not imply that a marriage was immutable or eternal any more than a contract for supply of goods precluded reselling them. The prohibition of a second wife was also found in a significant proportion of ancient Near Eastern marriage contracts.[81] The use of the term "hate" (**שׂנא**, *shana*) was a common word for "divorce" in the ancient Near East[82] and did not indicate revulsion or anger.

76. K7 = B3.8; C18 = B6.4. K7 = B3.8 misses the final phrase "she shall do to him the law of hatred."

77. C15 = B2.6; K2 = B3.3; K7 = B3.8; C46 = B6.3; C18 = B6.4.

78. The unique phrase that Hillel identified in Alexandrian *ketuboth* was "When you will enter my house you will be my wife," which came immediately before the common *ketubah* phrase "in accord with the law of Moses and Israel" (*t. Ketub.* 4.9). This phrase does not occur in any of the Elephantine documents, though it is similar to a phrase in the *ketubah* implied in Tob. 7:13: "Behold, take her to yourself after the law of Moses and lead her away to your father." See the discussion below.

79. Such as Middle Assyrian law #41 and others cited in chapter one.

80. B2.3, 11; 3.4, 7, 11-12; cf. B2.4; 3.5.

81. Of M. T. Roth's forty-five marriage certificates, fifteen have a clause anticipating what will happen if the husband divorces his wife because he wants to marry another woman (nos. 1, 2, 4, 5, 6, 8, 15, 16, 17, 19, 20, 25, 26, 30, 34; in M. T. Roth, *Babylonian Marriage Agreements: 7th-3rd Centuries B.C.* [Kevalaer: Verlag Butzon & Bercker; Neukirchen-Vluyn: Neukirchener Verlag, 1989]).

82. Reuven Yaron, "On Divorce in Old Testament Times," *Revue Internationale des Droits de l'Antiquité* 3 (1957): 117-19. Raymond Westbrook, "Prohibition of Restoration of Marriage in

These contracts also show features that are very unusual in ancient Near Eastern marriage contracts, especially the **almost total equality of men and women.**[83] These equalities included equal rights to divorce, equal inheritance rights, equal conjugal rights, and equal rights to demand monogamy from their spouse. The last of these suggests links with the Greco-Roman world rather than the ancient Near East. The Greco-Roman world, unlike the ancient Near East, held to a strict monogamy, but the other aspects of equality did not develop this far in the Greco-Roman world until about the third century B.C.E.[84]

The only difference between the sexes in the Elephantine marriage contracts is with regard to money. The ancient practices of providing a purchase price (the *mohar*) and presenting a dowry continued to occupy the majority of the contract, as they did in ancient Near Eastern contracts and in *ketuboth.* When divorce came, the dowry went with the woman. This was not an inequality because the dowry was considered as the woman's property.

The most remarkable feature of these contracts was the **oral divorce** that could be enacted by the woman as well as the man. Both husbands and wives could declare in the Assembly that they "hated" their spouse and that they were willing to pay the price of a divorce. Emil G. Kraeling suggested that this price may have been a court fee because it is not the same as the amount of the *mohar* and it is a fixed rate of 7.5 shekels.[85]

This form of divorce by oral declaration was not the same as the Roman free marriage, which could be ended by either partner. A Roman marriage could be ended by simply walking out of the marital home or expelling the spouse who did not own the house (as noted above). At Elephantine this possi-

---

Deuteronomy 24.1-4," in *Studies in Bible 1986*, ed. S. Japhet, Scripta Hierosolymitana 31 (Jerusalem: Magnes, 1986), pp. 387-405. Jacob J. Rabinowitz, "Marriage Contracts in Ancient Egypt in the Light of Jewish Sources," *Harvard Theological Review* 46 (1953): 91-92. The term occurs in several Demotic marriage contracts (see F. L. Griffith, *Catalogue of the Demotic Papyri in the John Rylands Library, Manchester: With Facsimiles and Complete Transcriptions*, vol. 3: *Key-list, Translations, Commentaries and Indices* [Manchester: University Press, 1909], pp. 115-17).

83. E. Lipinski ("The Wife's Right to Divorce in the Light of an Ancient Near Eastern Tradition," in *The Jewish Law Annual*, vol. 4, ed. B. S. Jackson [Leiden: Brill, 1981], pp. 9-26) collected a handful of early Semitic ancient Near Eastern marriage contracts that do show equality of divorce rights for men and women. He pointed out that the terminology of these contracts shows such substantial similarities to the Elephantine contracts that they may be considered as their precursors. He said that they were not influenced by Egyptian divorce certificates because Egyptian divorce documentation has survived from the 19th Dynasty (1320-1200 B.C.E.), but there is no divorce on the wife's initiative.

84. See Sawyer, *Women and Religion*, pp. 15-19.

85. Kraeling, *The Brooklyn Museum Aramaic Papyri*, p. 202.

bility is specifically ruled out by a fine that is imposed if a woman is expelled from the house, presumably without a public ceremony of divorce.

The Elephantine marriage contracts are therefore a strange mixture of ancient Near Eastern forms and trends in the Greco-Roman world but are influenced by a high regard for the rights of women. It is impossible to know how widespread these developments were. The contracts that have survived come from a relatively small community that may have had isolated customs or may have been representative of the vast majority of surrounding cultures. The rarity of documents surviving from that period makes it impossible to conclude how common these developments were.

Development of the Jewish Marriage Contract

Equality between men and women was also gradually established in Judaism, as far as was possible within the law of Moses. The Law allowed only the man to write out a divorce certificate, but the rabbinic court gradually took on more power to force a man to do so when the wife wanted a divorce. These changes culminated in the eleventh century when Rabbi Gershom of Mayence decreed an end to the theoretical right of a husband to divorce his wife when he pleased. If either partner could show good cause, the guilty partner could be forced to divorce. This is a development of a principle that underlies mishnaic Judaism, that the innocent partner should decide whether or not to proceed with a divorce. These changes could be introduced because they were already present in embryonic form in the principles of biblical divorce law and in the traditional marriage contract, as detailed in the next chapter.

The earliest recognizable Jewish marriage contract is the one referred to **Tobit.** Some have argued that the Jewish marriage contract is much older than this, and certainly it is likely that the Jews used contracts similar to those found in other ancient Near Eastern sources. However, Tobit preserves the first occurrence of phrases that became a fixed part of the traditional *ketubah,* though it is not strictly correct to call it a *ketubah* until after the reform of Simeon ben Shetah (see below).

The earliest Jewish marriage contract, according to the Babylonian Talmud, was in the time of Moses, though Rashi says it was even older.[86] The marriage contracts at Elephantine are similar to the Jewish marriage contract, but they bear more resemblance to the ancient Near Eastern contracts.[87] However,

86. See *b. Yebam.* 89a; *b. Ketub.* 10a. Rashi said that the difference between Ketura's sons and Sarah's son was that Sarah had a *ketubah* (Rashi on Gen. 25:6).

87. See the discussion above and Yaron, "On Divorce in Old Testament Times," pp. 117-18;

the marriage contract mentioned in Tobit 7:13 contains two phrases that are later enshrined in Jewish *ketuboth:* "according to the law of Moses" and "lead her away to [the house of] your father." The former phrase is found in almost every Jewish marriage contract that has been preserved, other than Greek ones.[88] The latter phrase is one that was typical in Alexandrian *ketuboth,* according to a story about Hillel.[89] This takes the traditional wording back to about 200 B.C.E.[90] though the practice of giving a marriage contract is undoubtedly much older.

Discouragement of Divorce by Simeon ben Shetah

The first recorded ruling about marriage contracts in rabbinic literature is attributed to Simeon ben Shetah in the first century B.C.E. The record of his ruling contains information about two rulings that preceded his, both of which had time to become established practice before they were changed. This suggests that Jewish law concerning marriage contracts goes back at least a couple of centuries B.C.E.[91]

Markham J. Geller, "New Sources for the Origins of the Rabbinic Ketubah," *Hebrew Union College Annual* 49 (1978): 227-45, esp. pp. 228, 240; Bezalel Porten, *Archives from Elephantine: The Life of an Ancient Jewish Military Colony* (Berkeley: University of California Press, 1968), p. 209.

88. Hannah Cotton, "A Cancelled Marriage Contract from the Judaean Desert *(XHev/Se Gr. 2),*" *Journal of Roman Studies* 84 (1994): 82.

89. Hillel examined an Alexandrian *ketubah* for the phrase "when you will enter my house" (*t. Ketub.* 4.9: "Hillel the Elder made an exegesis of ordinary language. When the Alexandrians would betroth a woman, afterward someone else would come along and grab her right out of the market. Such an incident came before the sages, and they considered declaring the children to be *mamzers* (illegitimate children). Hillel the Elder said to them: Show me the marriage contract of your mothers. They showed them to him and written in them was the following language: When you will enter my house you will be my wife in accord with the law of Moses and Israel").

90. Joseph Klausner (*Jesus of Nazareth: His Life, Times, & Teaching,* trans. Herbert Danby [New York: Menorah, 1979; London: Allen & Unwin, 1925], p. 195) argues that the traditional wording goes back further than the Maccabean times because of the archaic Hebrew phrases in it.

91. Michael Satlow ("Reconsidering the Rabbinic *ketubah* Payment," in *The Jewish Family in Antiquity,* ed. Shaye J. D. Cohen [Atlanta: Scholars Press, 1993], pp. 133-51) argues that the idea of *ketubah* payments was invented at Yavneh at the end of the first century C.E. This is based mainly on silence and is contrary to the custom already seen at Elephantine. He recognizes this and argues, rather weakly, that it fell into disuse and was revived at Yavneh. He considers the tradition of Simeon ben Shetah to be a justification of the policy by attributing it to an earlier authority. However, it is more likely that these reforms followed similar reforms in Egypt, where marriage contracts evolved with the same three stages recorded in rabbinic traditions — i.e., (1)

Simeon ben Shetah allowed a groom to forgo paying the money that was formerly paid to a bride's father, but the groom became personally liable for paying this money if he divorced his wife. The role of the ***ketubah*** or marriage contract became so tied up with recording the goods and money that comprised this payment that the payment itself came to be called the *ketubah*. The purpose of this change was to discourage divorces, which were becoming too common.

> *t. Ketub.* 12.1: In earlier times, when [the property set aside for payment of] her marriage contract was in her father's hands, it was a light thing in his [the husband's] eyes to divorce her. Simeon ben Shetah therefore ordained that [property to cover] her marriage contract should be with her husband. And he therefore writes for her "All property which I have is liable and obligated for the payment of your marriage contract."

Simeon ben Shetah is attributed with reforming this law, but this change occurred in various stages, and only the latter stages should properly be attributed to him. Two previous stages are recorded in the Babylonian and Jerusalem Talmuds,[92] though these accounts are complicated and appear to be chronologically confused.[93]

Originally the groom paid a *mohar* of 200 *zuzin* (sacred shekels) for a virgin and 100 for a widow or divorcée. This was given to the bride's father as payment for his daughter. The first change to the marriage law was to give this money to the bride but to have it held in trust at her father's house against the time she was divorced or widowed. This still meant that it was costly to get married but relatively cost-free to get divorced, and thus people were reluctant to marry, and many were too hasty to divorce. A later change allowed the bride to

---

the sum was handed to the father of the bride by the bridegroom; (2) (about 230 B.C.E.) the sum was handed to the bride; and (3) the sum is paid fictitiously and only on the dissolution of the marriage (see Pieter Willem Pestman, *Marriage and Matrimonial Property in Ancient Egypt: A Contribution to Establishing the Legal Position of the Woman*, Papyrologica Lugduno-Batava 9 [Leiden: Brill, 1961], pp. 15-20, 108-114). By the time of the first surviving marriage contracts in the early second century C.E., these reforms are all fully in place. The lack of marriage contracts for earlier periods should not make us conclude that rabbis at Yavneh reinvented exactly the same reforms as those started in Egypt.

92. *b. Ketub.* 82b; *y. Ketub.* 8.11, 32b.

93. The account here is based on the analysis by Leone J. Archer (*Her Price Is beyond Rubies: The Jewish Woman in Greco-Roman Palestine*, Journal for the Study of the Old Testament — Supplement Series 60 [Sheffield: Sheffield Academic Press, 1990], pp. 159-166) and Menachem Elon (*Jewish Law: History, Sources, Principles*, 4 vols. [Philadelphia: Jewish Publication Society, 1994], pp. 559-60).

turn the money into goods (such as metal pots or ornaments) that were kept and used by the married couple.[94] This meant that marriage was still costly and that the price of divorce included the loss of the goods that were part of the home; thus, divorce was personally costly for the husband.

The next change in the law allowed the money to be invested in the family business. This meant that there was no longer any tangible set of utensils or ornaments that would be given to the woman on divorce or widowhood; instead she would receive a sum of money. The husband was made personally liable for this sum of money, which had to be paid whether his business did well or not. He had to pay out of his personal property if necessary. The final change allowed the *mohar* to be paid by promise alone. No money needed to be exchanged because the money would, in any case, become part of the groom's financial property. Yet he, or his estate, was still liable for the repayment of this money on his wife's divorce or widowhood.

The two final changes can properly be attributed to Simeon ben Shetah. They resulted in making marriage much less costly, but they also made **divorce** correspondingly **more costly**. Somewhere during this process of changes the term *mohar* was replaced by *ketubah,* and the *ketubah* came to include the dowry settlement as well as the *mohar.* The dowry is the gift from the bride's father to the bride; it remained the property of the bride but was used by the couple while they were married. When the status of the *mohar* changed, the *mohar* and the *dowry* were both very similar as far as the marriage contract was concerned, because they both had to be paid to the wife or her children when the marriage ended by divorce or death. Therefore, they both came to be included in the term *ketubah.*

All this finally had the effect of making marriage much less costly, and it made divorce more costly. In some cases it made divorce prohibitively expensive if the father had given a large enough dowry.[95] The amount of dowry could vary enormously, and so the *ketubah* varied accordingly. The rabbis set a minimum payment of 50 *zuzin,*[96] but the payment could be a large fortune if the bride's father was wealthy.[97] These changes also encouraged fathers to give a

94. Geller ("New Sources for the Origins of the Rabbinic Ketubah," p. 229) points out that three Seleucid contracts have been discovered that illustrate this stage. He also says that Demotic contracts before 536 B.C.E. record gifts to the bride's father, but after this the gifts are given to the bride: "I give you. . . ." He speculates that this influenced the similar change brought about by Simeon ben Shetah (p. 240).

95. *b. Git.* 57a refers to a man who hesitated before divorcing his wife "because she had a big marriage settlement."

96. *m. Ketub.* 6.5 — this was paid by the community if the bride's father could not afford it.

97. Large dowries attracted many suitors (see *b. Ketub.* 54a-b; 66a-b; *b. B. Meṣ.* 104b;

more generous dowry and thereby helped to provide financial security for the wife if she was divorced.

Conclusions

The many changes in divorce law during the Intertestamental period added up to greater rights for women but also greater instability of marriage. Divorce became more common, and both men and women started to be able to demand a divorce. The reforms of Simeon ben Shetah tried to discourage divorce among Jews, but they also resulted in greater financial security for divorced women, and so divorce was no longer perceived as calamitous or cruel. All these changes form the background for the debate in Judaism concerning the grounds for divorce, which is discussed in the next chapter.

b. Yebam. 67a). Young men were warned not to be influenced by the size of a dowry (see Sir. 25:21-22; cf. 7:19; Josephus, *Ag. Ap.* 2.200; *b. Qidd.* 70a).

5. Rabbinic Teaching

Increasing Grounds for Divorce

By the first century C.E. there was general agreement in rabbinic Judaism[1] concerning most aspects of divorce and remarriage. The rabbis agreed that the grounds for divorce were childlessness, material neglect, emotional neglect, and unfaithfulness. Divorce was generally regarded as undesirable but sometimes necessary. Divorce was enacted by the man, though a court could persuade a man to enact a divorce when his wife demonstrated that she had sufficient grounds for a divorce. Remarriage was generally accepted, but if it followed an invalid divorce, it was treated as adultery. The rabbis also agreed on the financial penalties for divorce when marriage vows were broken. The main dispute concerned a new interpretation of Deuteronomy 24:1 by which the Hillelites allowed divorce for "any matter." This new groundless divorce was much easier to enact and very quickly became the form of divorce used by almost all Jews.

Divorces by Women

Only a man could enact a divorce, but this did not mean that women could not initiate a divorce. If a woman could show a court of rabbis that she had suffi-

1. The terms "rabbi" and "rabbinic" (with a lowercase "r") are used to refer to those who passed on the traditions that were later encapsulated in rabbinic literature such as the Talmud and Midrash. Jews did not ordain people with the title "Rabbi" until after 70 C.E. (except for a few highly respected Pharisees among the priests), and so this title (with an uppercase "R") is best restricted to post-NT times.

cient grounds for a divorce, the court could persuade her husband to divorce her.

The principle that divorce could be enacted only by a man was based on the law that said that a man should write out the *get* or "divorce certificate" (Deut. 24:1). This resulted in the principle that a man had to enter into divorce voluntarily, but a woman could be divorced against her will, as stated in the maxim:

> The man who divorces his wife is not equivalent to a woman who receives a divorce, for a woman goes forth willingly or unwillingly, but a man puts his wife away only willingly.[2]

However, it came to be recognized that **a woman could force a man to divorce her** if he broke his marriage vows or other obligations in the marriage contract. The marriage contract enshrined both the grounds and the authority for a woman to get a divorce.[3] If the terms of the contract were broken, the injured party, man or woman, was within his or her rights to terminate the contract with a divorce.[4] The promises spoken and implied in the marriage contract thereby became the grounds for divorce. The rabbinic court would make sure that the woman could be released from the marriage contract if the husband broke any of its terms.

The court had a difficult task because theoretically the husband had to voluntarily divorce his wife. The court therefore "persuaded" him by means of fines (by increasing the *ketubah*) until he was technically bankrupt, or even by using force. The nature of this force is not specified, but talmudic commentators suggested that if persuasion failed, then whips were used.[5] Another diffi-

2. *m. Yebam.* 14.1.

3. *t. Ketub.* 12.3: "Should there be no marriage contract at all? But if that were the case, then a woman would go forth both when she wants and when she does not want to do so, but a man would put her forth only when he wants to do so." This implied that a marriage contract made them equal by enabling a woman to initiate a divorce when the man did not want it.

4. This is the practical effect of the various rabbinic rulings explored below, but this general principle was not accepted until the sixteenth-century authoritative *Shulhan ʿAruk,* which states: "Where either of the parties, however, shows good cause for divorce, the marriage will be dissolved against the will of the guilty party" (*Shulhan ʿAruk, Eben ha-ʾEzer,* 119.6, gloss). The Talmud has inequalities that go against this principle, such as the inability of a wife to get a divorce from her unfaithful husband (see below).

5. The Mishnah says, "They compel him until he says: I will it" (*m. ʿArak.* 5.6). A divorce imposed by a Gentile court was invalid unless the husband was beaten into agreeing that he wanted a divorce (*m. Git.* 9.8: "A *get* imposed by a court — in the case of an Israelite court it is valid, and in the case of a gentile court it is invalid. In the case of gentiles they beat him and say to him: Do what the Israelites tell you to do. And it is valid"). In the Talmud of *m. Ketub.* 7.10

culty was that the man had to be present. If he abandoned his wife and went abroad where he could not be found, he could not be forced to give her a divorce certificate, even though the court agreed that she should have one.[6]

Evidence that women brought petitions for divorce in the first century is found in the Mishnah and in a recently discovered divorce document. The Mishnah records the results of detailed discussions that appear to originate from demands for divorce brought by women to the courts. These are discussions about how to define the practical application of the marriage vows that were based on the threefold obligations to feed, clothe, and love in Exodus 21:10-11. The practical application of these obligations was investigated in great detail during the first century, as will be shown below.

A recently published **divorce certificate** or *get* dating from the early second century appears to have been **written by or for a woman** to her husband. This was discovered in the Judean Desert in 1951 but it was not published till 1995.[7] It is known variously as the Ṣe'elim *get,* or Papyrus Ṣe'elim 13. Its existence was disclosed by J. T. Milik in 1957,[8] and it has been the subject of much conjecture and debate. Several authors had suggested, even before publication,

---

R. Abba suggests that persuasion was by words in cases where the wife was permitted to allow the marriage to continue if she wished, and by whips where the wife was not given this option. The cases where she had the option were those that were based on rabbinic rulings (such as cases of boils, smell, etc.), and those where she had no option were those based on scriptural rulings (presumably incestuous marriages, etc.) (*b. Ketub.* 77ab). However, it is possible that these Amoraim did not really know what the pre–70 C.E. situation was. In modern Israel the rabbinic courts can imprison a husband till he gives a *get,* but this does not always work, and the husband can extort money from his wife in return for writing a *get* (see Mark Washofsky, "The Recalcitrant Husband: The Problem of Definition," in *The Jewish Law Annual,* ed. B. S. Jackson [Leiden: Brill, 1981], 4:144-66, esp. pp. 145-46).

6. Outside Israel there is the additional problem that the rabbinic courts have little coercive force, though secular judges in some countries such as the United States tend to uphold these decisions. However, rabbinic courts will not allow women to remarry if they are abandoned or have a civil divorce without a Jewish divorce certificate. They are known as *agunot* and are a growing problem for modern Judaism.

7. J. T. Milik did not publish it with the rest of the finds from Murabba'at in Pierre Benoit, Jozef T. Milik, and Roland de Vaux, *Les grottes de Murabba'at,* Discoveries in the Judaean Desert 2 (Oxford: Clarendon, 1961). He passed it to Jonas Greenfield, who died in 1995 after passing it to Ada Yardeni, who published it in a thin booklet of all the readable Ṣe'elim papyri, *Naḥal Ṣe'elim Documents* (Jerusalem: Israel Exploration Society and Ben Gurion University in the Negev Press, 1995). The Ṣe'elim *get* is called Papyrus Ṣe'elim 13. It was first published with a translation by Tal Ilan in "Notes and Observations on a Newly Published Divorce Bill," *Harvard Theological Review* 89 (1996): 195-202.

8. J. T. Milik, "Le travail d'édition des manuscrits Désert de Juda," in *Volume du Congres, Strasbourg, 1956,* Vetus Testamentum Supplements 4 (Leiden: Brill, 1957), pp. 17-26. It is mentioned in one short paragraph on p. 21.

that this document implied the ability of women to gain a divorce, and these authors pointed to the other evidence in Mishnah and in the Elephantine documents.[9] Some orthodox scholars maintained that it could not be what Milik claimed and that it must be either addressed to the woman, or it must be a receipt from her for her *ketubah.*[10] This dispute delayed publication of the document for some time, and it has continued since its publication. However, the document is clearly addressed *to* the husband, and it uses the language of a standard divorce certificate:

> On the 20th of Sivan, year 3 of Israel's freedom. In the name of Simon bar Kosibar, the Nasi of Israel . . . I do not have . . . **I, Shelamzion, daughter of Joseph Qebshan** of Ein Gedi, with you, **Eleazar son of Hananiah who had been the husband before this time,** that **this is from me to you a bill of divorce and release.** . . . I do not have with you . . . Eleazar anything (I wish for?), as is my duty and remains upon me. I Shelamzion (accept) all that is written (in this document). Shelamzion present, lent her hand writing(?). Mattat son of Simon by her order . . . son of Simon, witness. Masbala, son of Simon, witness. (Translation by Tal Ilan with my emphases)

This text employs precisely the formulae found in other divorce certificates, and the layout of the whole document, with date, names, and witnesses,

9. Several articles in *The Jewish Law Annual,* vol. 4, ed. B. S. Jackson (Leiden: Brill, 1981), argued for the right of women to force a divorce from their husbands. E. Lipinski ("The Wife's Right to Divorce," pp. 9-26) argued mainly from the ancient Near Eastern background, in which it was possible for women to sometimes gain a divorce, but he also cites the Ṣe'elim *get.* Alfredo M. Rabello ("Divorce of Jews in the Roman Empire," pp. 79-102) argues on pp. 93-99 from a woman's rights under Roman law, but he points out that later rabbis enforced these rights (*m. Git.* 9.8). M. A. Friedman ("Divorce upon the Wife's Demand As Reflected in MSS from Cairo Geniza," pp. 103-26) showed that the medieval commentators also understood the Mishnah in this way. Shmuel Shilo ("Impotence as a Ground for Divorce: To the End of the Period of the Rishonim," pp. 129-43) argued from the laws regarding a husband's impotence in talmudic times. Finally, Mark Washofsky ("The Recalcitrant Husband," pp. 144-66) showed that this law allows a woman to divorce her husband even in modern Israel.

10. In particular Ada Yardeni, who was much influenced by Greenfield, who lectured many times on the Ṣe'elim *get,* calling it a receipt of a *get.* Yardeni has a long footnote in her publication of the *get* that says: "The nature of the document was decided by reading **די** at the beginning of line 6, and undermines Milik's opinion that it is a divorce bill . . ." (*Naḥal Ṣe'elim Documents,* p. 55, translated from Hebrew in Tal Ilan, "Notes and Observations on a Newly Published Divorce Bill," p. 197). More recently Adriel Schremer ("Divorce in Papyrus Ṣe'elim 13 Once Again: A Reply to Tal Ilan," *Harvard Theological Review* 91 [1998]: 193-202) argued that it was written by a husband; I replied to this in "Jewish Women Divorcing Their Husbands in Early Judaism: The Background to Papyrus Ṣe'elim 13," *Harvard Theological Review* 92 (1999): 349-57.

mirrors exactly what is found in other documents. There is no hint in rabbinic literature that a woman could actually write a divorce certificate and send it to her husband,[11] and it is unlikely that this was standard practice. Normally women would not write a divorce certificate such as this one, but they would ask a court to persuade their husbands to write one.

Perhaps this nonrabbinic practice was influenced by the Greco-Roman world where women could initiate a divorce, as wealthy Jewish women in the first century are known to have done.[12] It may also have come into Palestine from Jewish communities in Egypt. Philo seems to suggest that women can divorce their husbands,[13] and the Elephantine documents show that women had been able to do so since the fifth century B.C.E.

The Elephantine marriage certificates give men and women the equal right to a divorce by publicly stating that they "hate" their partner and by paying them compensation.[14] Ze'ev W. Falk suggested that they were able to demand this right in their marriage certificates because there were too few women in the military outpost of Elephantine, and he also found parallels for this practice by women in later Palestinian rulings.[15]

Even before the announcement of the Ṣe'elim *get,* there was a consensus

11. The reference in *m. Git.* 2.5 to a woman writing a *get* does not mean that a woman can write it on her own behalf. It means that anyone, even the wife, can write the certificate at the husband's request.

12. Josephus recorded that Salome divorced her husband by issuing a *repudium* — a Roman divorce certificate: "Some time afterwards Salome had occasion to quarrel with Costobarus and soon sent him a document dissolving their marriage, which was not in accordance with Jewish law. For it is (only) the man who is permitted by us to do this, and not even a divorced woman may marry again on her own initiative unless her former husband consents. Salome, however, did not choose to follow her country's law but acted on her own authority and repudiated her marriage, telling her brother Herod that she had separated from her husband out of loyalty to Herod himself" (Josephus, *Ant.* 15.259-60, Loeb). Other women in the Herodian family were likewise known to divorce their husbands (Herodias — Josephus, *Ant.* 18.109-11; Berenice, Drusilla, and Mariamme — Josephus, *Ant.* 20.141-47). Even Josephus's own wife walked out before he could divorce her, but without giving him a divorce certificate of any kind (*Life* 415).

13. Philo, *Spec. Leg.* 3.30: "Another commandment is that if a woman after parting from her husband for any cause whatever, marries another . . . she has broken with the rules that bound her in the past and cast them into oblivion" (Loeb, 1984).

14. See details in the previous chapter.

15. Ze'ev W. Falk, *Introduction to Jewish Law of the Second Commonwealth,* 2 vols. (Leiden: Brill, 1972, 1978), 2:310-11. He refers to *y. Ketub.* 5.9, 30b (5.10 in the Leiden and Vatican MSS): "Said R. Yose, 'In the case of those who write in the marriage settlement, "If he should hate", "If she should hate", this is a stipulation concerning a monetary matter, and such a stipulation remains in effect [despite the circumstances of the break-up of the marriage].'"

that women could, under many circumstances, gain a divorce from their husbands within first-century Palestinian Judaism.[16] Since its publication there are few who would argue against this consensus.[17] The internal evidence of the Mishnah suggests that there were several cases where women brought appeals for divorce to rabbinic courts in or before the first century, based on the obligations in Exodus 21:10-11. It appears that some women also took the law into their own hands, so to speak, and issued their own divorce certificates, as evidenced by the one example that has survived. It is unknown whether this would have had legal weight in any rabbinic courts outside Egypt, but the language is clearly based on the traditional Jewish *get,* and so one must assume that some Jewish courts in Palestine recognized this practice.

16. The right of women to divorce was concluded by several authors before the announcement of the Ṣe'elim *get.* The article "Divorce," in *Jewish Encyclopaedia* (New York and London: Funk & Wagnalls Co., 1905), 4:624-28, gave the standard opinion that a woman could demand a divorce for refusal of conjugal rights or impotence. I. Abrahams (*Studies in Pharisaism and the Gospels* [London: Macmillan, 1917], p. 77) confirmed that this right extended to women whose husbands neglected to support them. Louis M. Epstein (*The Jewish Marriage Contract: A Study in the Status of the Woman in Jewish Law* [New York: Johnson Reprint Corp., 1968 (1942)], pp. 201-5) has a long discussion that concludes that the rights seen in Elephantine and Roman law were enshrined to a lesser degree in early rabbinic practice and in biblical law. Others, writing after Milik's announcement but before the publication of the Ṣe'elim *get,* argued in the same way without appearing to know anything about the new document. Ernst Bammel ("Markus 10.11f. und das jüdische Eherecht," *Zeitschrift für die neutestamentliche Wissenschaft* 61 [1970]: 95-101) argued mainly from the Elephantine documents and did not cite Milik. Hugh Montefiore (in an appendix "Jesus on Divorce & Remarriage," in the Anglican Synod's *Marriage, Divorce & the Church — the Report of a Commission Appointed by the Archbishop of Canterbury to Prepare a Statement on the Christian Doctrine of Marriage* [London: SPCK, 1971], pp. 79-80) argued from the obligations of Exodus 21. Similarly Ben-Zion (Benno) Schereschewsky ("Divorce," *Encyclopaedia Judaica,* 16 vols. [Jerusalem: Keter Publishing House, 1972], 6:122-24) argued from the Exod. 21:10-11 obligations, citing the rabbinic discussions based on this. D. W. Amram (*The Jewish Law of Divorce according to the Bible and Talmud* [New York: Sepher-Hermon, 1975 (reprint of undated original)], pp. 57-58) discussed the ways in which a husband was forced to grant a divorce. David Atkinson (*To Have and To Hold: The Marriage Covenant and the Discipline of Divorce* [London: Collins, 1979], p. 109) concluded that a wife could write her own divorce certificate after gaining permission from a rabbinic court, but the rabbinic texts he cites do not support this. Perhaps he knew about the Ṣe'elim *get,* but just as the previous authors, he does not refer to it.

17. Bernadette J. Brooten laid out the arguments in "Könnten Frauen im alten Judentum die Scheidung betreiben? Überlegung zu Mk 10,11-12 und 1 Kor 7,10-11," *Evangelische Theologie* 42 (1982): 65-80. There was a brief reply in H. Weder, "Perspective der Frauen," *Evangelische Theologie* 43 (1983): 175-78, but Brooten responded in detail in "Zur Debatte über das Scheidungsrecht der jüdischen Frau," *Evangelische Theologie* 43 (1983): 466-78. Tal Ilan wrote *Jewish Women in Greco-Roman Palestine: An Inquiry into Image and Status* (Peabody, Mass.: Hendrickson, 1996) before the publication of the Ṣe'elim *get* but was able to argue convincingly from Josephus and rabbinic sources that such a document might be possible (see esp. p. 146).

Infertility as a Ground for Divorce

Infertility was a ground for divorce because the primary purpose of marriage was regarded as procreation. One of the 613 laws identified in the Torah by rabbinic Judaism was "be fruitful and multiply and fill the earth" (Gen. 1:28). On the basis of this law, all Jews were expected to marry and have children. Marriage might be avoided to study Torah,[18] or because of financial difficulties,[19] but this happened rarely.[20]

This interpretation of Genesis 1:28 must be dated very early, because the schools of Hillel and Shammai had two debates on this matter. Both debates were based on the assumption that children are a necessary part of marriage and that marriage is a good thing precisely because it produces children and helps to fill the earth. Neither debate actually cited Genesis 1:28, though this reference was later added to an introduction of one of the debates. Both the schools agreed that marriage exists to fulfill this command.[21] Josephus said that procreation was the sole purpose for Jewish marriage,[22] and he said that even some Essenes recognized that marriage was necessary for procreation.[23]

18. Simeon b. Azzai (first century) chose not to marry "because my soul lusts for the Torah," though this was frowned on by many. When he praised married life and fulfillment of "be fruitful and multiply," they said he "is very good at expounding but not at fulfilling" (*t. Yebam.* 8.4; *Gen. Rab.* 34.14; *b. Yebam.* 63b; cf. *y. Soṭa* 1.2, 16c).

19. *m. Ketub.* 13.5.

20. Some scholars assume that all good Jews got married, and so Paul and even Jesus must have been married. See William E. Phipps, *Was Jesus Married? The Distortion of Sexuality in the Christian Tradition* (New York: Harper & Row, 1970); William E. Phipps, "Is Paul's Attitude toward Sexual Relations Contained in 1 Cor. 7.1?" *New Testament Studies* 28 (1982): 125-31; Josephine M. Ford, "Levirate Marriage in St. Paul (1 Cor. VII)," *New Testament Studies* 10 (1963-64): 361-65.

21. In *m. Git.* 4.5 (parallels in *m. ʿEd.* 1.13 and several in the Talmuds). Isa. 45:18 was cited by the school of Shammai to prove that a half-slave should be redeemed to allow him to marry, and the school of Hillel agreed when faced with this argument. In *t. Yebam.* 8.4 (parallels in *m. Yebam.* 6.6 and Talmuds). Gen. 1:28 was cited in the introduction to a school debate about how many children were necessary. The school of Shammai cited the example of Moses who had two sons (1 Chron. 23:15), and the school of Hillel cited the example of God himself, who had one son and one daughter (Gen. 5:2). Both assumed that children were necessary. Later rabbis also said that marriage stopped you from thinking about sex all day, which could distract you from Torah study (*b. Qidd.* 29b). They also allowed marriage to a woman known to be infertile, but this was only if the man already had a fertile wife, and it was not allowed for priests (*m. Yebam.* 6.5-6; *t. Yebam.* 8.5-6; *b. Yebam.* 64b-65a; *Sifra Emor* 1.7, 94b).

22. Josephus, *Ag. Ap.* 2.199. This did not mean that procreation was the sole reason for sexual activity. Early rabbis allowed contraception for women too young to bear children safely, and for pregnant or nursing mothers; R. Meir (second century) added that *coitus interruptus* could be used (*t. Nid.* 2.6).

23. Josephus, *J.W.* 2.160-61. Abel Isaksson (*Marriage and Ministry in the New Temple: A*

As a consequence, any couple who did not have children within ten years of marriage was expected to divorce. Each party was to remarry someone with whom they might be fertile.[24] Divorce in such situations was regarded as regrettable, and some rabbis argued against it.[25] Simeon ben Yohai, a very devout second-century rabbi, went to great lengths to help a couple avoid such a divorce.[26] Philo was also very sympathetic to such couples and said that if they continued in an infertile marriage, they "deserve our pardon."[27] It is likely that this ruling was rarely enforced.[28]

Divorce for impotence was later restricted because it was felt that women could misuse it to gain a divorce from their husbands. An undatable debate in *Mishnah Nedarim* says that they used to allow a woman to demand a divorce if she claimed her husband was impotent, or if she took a vow of celibacy, but that

---

Study with Special Reference to Mt.19.13[sic]-12 and 1.Cor.11.3-16, trans. Neil Tomkinson and Jean Gray, Acta Seminarii Neotestamentici Upsaliensis 24 [Lund: Gleerup; Copenhagen: Munksgaard, 1965], esp. pp. 46-62) argues that even the Qumran sect taught this, though they allowed men to separate from their wives at age twenty-five.

24. Rabbinic literature does not record the scriptural reason for this, but it is likely to be based on the ten years that Abraham waited after the promise of a son (at the vision when he entered Canaan) until taking Hagar (Gen. 16:3). This is the basis cited by the Karaites (Benjamin al-Nahawandi, *The Book of Rules,* section VI: On Marriage, in Leon Nemoy, *Karaite Anthology: Excerpts from the Early Literature* [New Haven and London: Yale University Press, 1952], p. 27).

25. *b. Ketub.* 77ab has a debate between R. Judah and R. Tahlifa b. Abimi about the words of Samuel. According to Judah he said: "If a man married a woman and lived with her ten years and she bore no child he cannot be compelled [to divorce her]," but according to Tahlifa he said ". . . he may be compelled." This ruling regarding the ten years fell into disuse (*Eben ha-'Ezer* 1.3 gloss 154.10).

26. *Song of Sol. Rab.* 1:31. Simeon met with the couple and persuaded them to have a feast with much wine, saying that the marriage started with a feast and should end with a feast. The feast resulted in a rediscovery of their love for each other, and eventually a child was born, which was attributed to Simeon's prayers. A touching detail is that the man told his wife during the feast that she could take anything she wished out of the marital home, and so she waited until he was asleep and bundled him onto a donkey and took him, because she considered that her husband was far more precious than any material wealth.

27. Philo, *Spec. Leg.* 3.35: "Those who marry maidens in ignorance at the time of their capacity or incapacity for successful motherhood, and later refuse to dismiss them, when prolonged childlessness shows them to be barren, deserve our pardon. Familiarity, that most constraining influence, is too strong for them, and they are unable to rid themselves of the charm of old affection imprinted on their souls by long companionship. But those who sue for marriage with women whose sterility has already been proved with other husbands, do but copulate like pigs or goats — their name should be inscribed in the lists of the impious as adversaries of God" (Loeb, 1984).

28. Elizabeth and Zechariah are a New Testament example of a couple who stayed together even though they were childless (Luke 1:5-7).

later they allowed this only after they had done all they could to dissuade the woman.[29] Men could also use it as an excuse. R. Judah ruled that a man who divorces his wife for sterility may not remarry her.[30] This suggests that some men were using sterility as an excuse, and that it became obvious when they wanted to remarry the same woman.

Related to this is the ruling that a woman may be granted a divorce if her husband took part in a smelly occupation, or if he had personal defects that made him repulsive to her.[31] This applied only if the smell or deformity repulsed her. The reason for this ruling is likely to be related to the presumed inability of the couple to have children if the wife found her husband to be repulsive. It is uncertain that this ruling was used in the first century. The Mishnah lists examples of men who were forced to divorce their wives because of blemishes such as boils or polyps, or because they were coppersmiths and tanners whose smell was offensive, but the datable portions of these passages are relatively late.[32]

Therefore, in New Testament times lack of children was a permissible ground of divorce but not perhaps a compulsory one. The Shammaites as well as the Hillelites recognized that childbearing was the prime motive for marriage, and they would therefore be disposed to grant divorce in this situation. However, there was likely some reluctance to do so.

29. *m. Ned.* 11.12: "Aforetimes they did rule: Three sorts of women go forth and collect their marriage contract: She who says: 'I am unclean to you' [i.e. a priest's wife who was violated]; 'Heaven knows what is between you and me' [i.e. impotence]; 'I am removed from all the Jews' [a vow to abstain from intercourse]. They reverted to the rule: so that a woman should not covet someone else and spoil [her relationship with] her husband, but she who says 'I am unclean to you' must bring proof for the claim; 'Heaven [knows] what is between you and me' let them find a way to appease her; 'I am removed from all the Jews' let him annul his share [in the vow] so that she may have sexual relations with him, but let her be removed from all other Jews."

30. *m. Git.* 4.8: "He who divorces his wife because of sterility. R. Judah says He may not remarry her. And the Sages say He may remarry her."

31. *m. Ketub.* 7.10: "And these are the ones whom they force to put her away: he who is afflicted with boils, or who has a polypus or who collects [dog excrement] or a coppersmith or a tanner, whether these [blemishes] were present before they were married or whether after they were married they made their appearance. And concerning all of them did R. Meir say: Even though he made a condition with her [that the marriage is valid despite these blemishes], she still can claim: I thought that I could take it, but now I find I cannot take it." The comment of Meir shows that the thinking behind the ruling concerned whether or not the woman had feelings of revulsion, presumably because this would prevent childbearing.

32. *m. Ketub.* 7.9 mentions Rabban Simeon b. Gamaliel (presumably II) and R. Meir, both of whom are active about 140-165 C.E.

Unfaithfulness as a Ground for Divorce

Adultery, when it happened, was treated extremely seriously. Theoretically this was still a capital offense in the first century C.E., though there is no record of this ever being applied.[33] The normal punishment was divorce without repayment of the *ketubah*. Even a man who had married a woman whom he had raped and who could not normally divorce her was permitted to put her away if she became unfaithful.[34]

Actual adultery was probably rare, and it was almost impossible to prove because two trustworthy eyewitnesses to the act were needed.[35] Philo seemed to assume that adultery was impossible for men to prove, and that this was why God had provided the rite of the suspected adulteress.[36] **Suspected adultery** was much more common. Even a faint rumor had to be treated as suspected adultery, and a woman who was alone in a room with a man was presumed to have committed adultery until proved innocent by the rite of Bitter Water.[37]

33. Although the death penalty for adultery was probably never inflicted in the New Testament era, Josephus's casual assertion that the penalty for adultery was death (*Ag. Ap.* 2.25), and the Mishnah's references to it (*m. Sanh.* 7.2; 6.4; 7.3) suggest that this penalty was generally known. Louis M. Epstein (*Sex Laws and Customs in Judaism* [American Academy of Jewish Research, 1948; reprinted New York: Ktav, 1967], p. 195) suggested that this penalty may even have been practiced in Philo's day (*de Joseph* 44: "the husband may kill the adulterer"). The only possible record of an example is the incident in John 8. It is well known that the right of Jews to carry out capital offenses ended around 30 C.E. (*b. Sanh.* 41a; *y. Sanh.* 18a, 24b), and it is often assumed that it ended much earlier. However, R. H. Charles (*The Teaching of the New Testament on Divorce* [London: Williams & Norgate, 1921], p. 5) argued that it carried on at least until the first century C.E., when it was used by Eliezer b. Zadok (*m. Sanh.* 7.2), though after 30 C.E. the husband was compelled to divorce his adulterous wife (*m. Soṭa* 6.1) The story of Susanna shows full approval of the death penalty for an adulterous wife (44-45), though Slavonic Enoch says that Noah's brother Nir divorced his adulterous wife (71:6-7).

34. *m. Ketub.* 3.5: "[one who has raped and has to marry his victim]. . . . If a matter of unchastity [דבר ערוה] turned out to pertain to her, or if she is not appropriate to enter into the Israelite congregation, he is not permitted to confirm her as his wife [but, if he has married her, he must divorce her], since it is said, *And she will be a wife to him* (Deut. 22.29) — a wife appropriate for him."

35. As in the story of Susanna. Falk (*Introduction to Jewish Law,* p. 293) concludes that adultery was almost impossible to prove, and so the death penalty was only theoretical.

36. Philo, *Spec. Leg.* 3.52: "Adulteries detected on the spot or established by clear evidence are condemned by the law. But when they are a matter of suspicion, the law did not think good to have them tried by men, but brought them before the tribunal of nature. For men can arbitrate on open matters, but God on the hidden also, since He alone can see clearly into the soul. So the law says to the husband who suspects his wife . . ." (Loeb, 1984).

37. *m. Soṭa* 6.1: "He who expressed jealous [suspicion about someone] to his wife but she went aside [with him] in secret, even if he heard [that she had done so] from a bird flying by, he

The rite of Bitter Water supposedly became too common shortly before 70 C.E. so that the practice was abandoned by Yohanan b. Zakkai.[38] However, it is more likely that the practice was abandoned after 70 C.E. when it could no longer be performed without the temple, and thus this tradition cannot be used as firm evidence that suspected adultery became common.

Some references in the Mishnah imply that adultery necessitated divorce, but this teaching probably started after the rite of Bitter Water ended. The texts cited in proof of this are frequently later than the first century or relate to other matters,[39] though opinion may have been moving in this direction during the first century. The following is the only text that can be said to represent this opinion in first-century sources.

> Just as the water puts her to the proof, so the water puts him [the lover] to the proof, since it is said *And it shall come . . . And it shall come . . .* (Num. 5:22; 5:24). Just as she is prohibited to the husband, so she is prohibited to the lover, since it is said *defiled . . . And defiled . . .* (Num. 5:27, 29) — the words of R. Aqiba. Said R. Joshua, Thus did Zekhariah b. Hakatzsab expound. Rabbi says: The two times at which, *defiled . . . And defiled . . .* are stated in this section refer, one to the husband and one to the lover. (*m. Soṭa* 5.1)

---

puts her away but pays off her marriage contract — the words of R. Eliezer [b. Hyrcanus, 80-120]." Sexual urge was recognized to be strong in both men and women, but it was assumed that women could not control it. "A woman prefers one *qab* [of material wealth] and sexual fulfilment (תפלות) to nine *qabs* and abstinence" (*m. Soṭa* 3.4). "What is the reason [that a man cannot be alone with two women]? As it is taught by the School of Eliyahu, because women are light-headed" (*b. Qidd.* 80b based on *m. Qidd.* 4.12, and in a different context in *b. Šabb.* 33b). "Men also have strong urges which they must guard against — a priest who brings the meal offering for the suspected adulteress must guard against touching her, in case he is aroused" (*y. Soṭa* 3.1, 18c).

38. *m. Soṭa* 9.9: "When adulterers became many, the ordeal of the bitter water was cancelled. And Rn. Yohanan b. Zakkai cancelled it since it is said *I will not punish your daughters when they commit whoredom, nor your daughters-in-law when they commit adultery, for they themselves go apart with whores* (Hos. 4.14)." Ilan (*Jewish Women in Greco-Roman Palestine,* pp. 136-38) suggests that this represents a controversy between some like Yohanan who wanted to abandon this rite even before 70 C.E. and others who stoutly defended it.

39. Abrahams (*Studies in Pharisaism and the Gospels,* pp. 72-75) cites *m. Ned.* 11.12 (which deals with impotence) and *m. Soṭa* 5.1. More Jewish and Roman sources are cited by Marcus Bockmuehl ("Matthew 5.32; 19.9 in the Light of Pre-Rabbinic Halakhah," *New Testament Studies* 35 [1989]: 292) and Epstein (*The Jewish Marriage Contract,* pp. 210-11), but they are all later than the first century C.E. The Jerusalem Talmud (1.2, 16b) seems to say that the Shammaites regarded the test as compulsory for all suspect women with the implication that any women guilty of adultery must be divorced, but this reads a later presupposition into an earlier time.

The first saying is a simple reminder that both the woman and her lover are found guilty or innocent by the rite of Bitter Water, and the duplication of words in the Scripture text is adduced as evidence of this. This is followed by an exposition based on another repeated word, which is used to show that both the lover and her husband are forbidden to her if she is guilty. This is expounded by three different authorities, the earliest of whom, Zekhariah b. Hakatzsab, dates this exposition to before 70 C.E. The fact that two other very influential authorities, Aqiba and Rabbi,[40] are named in support suggests that this exposition was not entirely accepted.

Although it might have been expected that a husband would **divorce** a suspected adulteress, this **was not compulsory before 70** C.E. R. Ze'ira records the opinion of the "men of Jerusalem" before the destruction:

> Come and hear: R. Josiah said: Three things did Ze'ira tell me as emanating from the men of Jerusalem: If a husband retracted his warning [to a suspected adulteress] the warning is retracted. . . .[41]

Before 70 C.E., when the rite was still performed, it was assumed that a guilty woman would die, and so there was no need to divorce her. The suspected adulteress or *sotah* had to bring a meal offering to the temple. There the priest reproved her, loosened her hair and clothes, and gave her the bitter water to drink. This was made bitter with the ink from the curse with which she swore her innocence (Num. 5:23). Torah taught that the guilty woman would suffer those curses, which the rabbis regarded as equivalent to a death penalty.

It is unclear how well this worked. One teaching about the suspected adulteress was that her former good deeds could postpone her death. Ilan suggested that this teaching arose from cases where definite proof of guilt was found later, but the woman had suffered no harm.[42]

The only suspected adulteress who was excused from the Bitter Water ritual was the one who admitted her crime, the one who was pregnant, or the one who had had relations with her husband in the meantime.[43] In these cases the

40. I.e., Judah the Prince.

41. *b. Soṭa* 25a (also at *b. Sanh.* 88a; *Sipre* 218). R. Ze'ira was from the first generation after 70 C.E., and so the "men of Jerusalem" would have predated the destruction of that city.

42. Ilan, *Jewish Women in Greco-Roman Palestine,* pp. 138-40. See especially *m. Soṭa* 3.4: "Ben Azzai says: A man should teach Torah to his daughter, for if she drinks the water she should know that [if nothing happens] it is her merit which has suspended [her punishment]."

43. *m. Soṭa* 4.3: "'A woman who was pregnant by another husband [who died or divorced her] and a woman who was giving suck to a child by another husband do not undergo the ordeal of drinking the bitter water and do not receive the marriage contract' — the words of

husband could chose to divorce her or separate from her for a while (in case a child was born of unknown parentage) and then take her back. Later rabbis, who could not use this rite to confirm guilt, took a harder line and expected a husband to divorce a suspected adulteress.[44]

Although divorce may not have been compulsory, it was generally assumed that a husband would *want* to divorce an unfaithful wife. If she was proved guilty, he would keep her *ketubah.* This became a motive for framing at least one wife.[45] Yet even if the adultery was only suspected without evidence, the man was still encouraged to divorce his wife or his betrothed even though he would lose the *ketubah.*[46]

Joseph, in the New Testament, is an example of someone who was generous enough to take back his apparently unfaithful partner (Matt. 1:19). Although the angelic message may have convinced Joseph of Mary's innocence, in the eyes of the community she had been unfaithful to him. The rite of suspected adultery would not have been applicable, even if Joseph had wanted to carry it out, because it was not given to pregnant women. Instead, Joseph simply abstained from relations with his wife, in accordance with rabbinic teaching, and returned to her after the child was born.

R. Meir. And Sages say 'He has the power to set her apart and then to take her back after a while.'" Any husband who had relations before the trial would invalidate the trial; *m. Soṭa* 4.2: "[If] her husband had sexual relations with her on the way [to Jerusalem], she receives her marriage contract and does not undergo the ordeal of drinking the bitter water."

44. See *m. Soṭa* 4.3 (n. 43) and 6.1 (n. 37) above. In the former, Meir represents the late second century C.E., while the Sages are anonymous traditions from much earlier times. In the case of priests, the wife was certainly prohibited to her husband if there was even a possibility that she had been violated: "A city which was overcome by siege, all the priest girls found therein are invalid [to return to their husbands]" (*m. Ketub.* 2.9). Yet there is no evidence that nonpriests were obliged to put away an unfaithful wife before talmudic times.

45. A man tried to avoid paying her *ketubah* by framing his wife with adultery. "There was a man who wanted to divorce his wife but hesitated because her *ketubah* was worth a great deal. He accordingly invited his friends and gave them a good feast and made them drunk and put them all in one bed. He then brought the white of an egg and scattered it among them and brought in witnesses. There was a certain elder there of the disciples of Shammai the Elder, named Baba b. Buta who said: This is what I have been taught by Shammai the Elder, that the white of an egg contracts when brought near the fire, but semen becomes faint from the fire. They tested it and found that it was so, and they brought the man to the rabbinical court and flogged him and made him pay her *ketubah*" (*b. Git.* 57a).

46. See *m. Soṭa* 6.1 cited in n. 37 above. The *ketubah* was lost even for a betrothed, though later rabbis allowed a man to give only the minimum 200 *zuz* (or 100 for a widow), and not any additional amount that was assumed to be conditional on her marrying him (*m. Ketub.* 5.1). In later times the man could divorce a suspected adulteress and keep the *ketubah* (see *m. Soṭa* 4.3 cited in n. 43 above).

Although a man could divorce his wife for adultery, **a woman could not divorce her husband for adultery** because the law allowing polygamy made it technically impossible for a man to be sexually unfaithful to his wife.[47] The fact that a husband could have more than one wife meant that he did not have to promise to be faithful to his wife when he married. This did not mean that a man could not be guilty of adultery, but if he committed adultery it was an offense against the other woman's husband, and not against his own wife. If he committed fornication with an unmarried woman, the offense was against the woman's father with whom he had failed to make a contract. This did not mean that women were chattels to be bought and sold, because a woman could not be married against her will,[48] but a technical inequality very definitely existed in this area.

A woman could also be divorced for **encouraging adultery**, even though no adultery took place. Encouragement could involve as little as going out of the house with her hair loose or her arms bare.

> *m. Ketub.* 7.6: These are they that are put away without their *ketubah:* a wife that transgresses the law of Moses and Jewish custom. . . . And what is Jewish custom? If she goes out with her hair unbound, or spins in public, or speaks with any man.
>
> *t. Ketub.* 7.6 adds: and she who goes out with both her sides (shoulders) bare . . . and bathes in a public bath with any man.

The wording of this passage relates the offense to breaking part of the marriage contract, which included the words "in accord with the law of Moses and Israel."[49] Both men and women were assumed to have a strong sexual urge, and men were enticed through their eyes, so that looking at a woman could be equivalent to adultery.

> He who looks at a woman's heel, it is as if he looked at the place of her pudenda, and if he looks there, it is as if he had intercourse with her. (*y. Ḥal.* 2.4, 58c; cf. Matt. 5:27-28)

A woman who encouraged adultery by revealing too much of her beauty could therefore be divorced without keeping her *ketubah.* These offenses were regarded as equivalent to adultery. Later Amoraim said that even the Sham-

47. See Epstein, *The Jewish Marriage Contract.*

48. A girl under twelve and a half could be forced to marry, but a woman could not.

49. These words are attested in the earliest marriage contracts, including that of Tobit (7:13-15) and the Alexandrian contract examined by Hillel (*t. Ketub.* 4.9).

maites, whose traditions said that divorce based on Deuteronomy 24:1-4 had to involve actual adultery, and not just "unseemly matters," regarded "going forth with her hair disheveled" and "her arms uncovered" as equivalent to adultery.[50]

Therefore, a man could divorce his wife without repaying her *ketubah* if he could show that she had committed adultery or did anything that might result in adultery. He was also expected to divorce a suspected adulteress and give her the *ketubah,* though this was probably not compulsory before 70 C.E. when the Bitter Water ritual could still test her guilt or innocence. In contrast, a wife could not gain a divorce by claiming her husband had been unfaithful. Most divorces pursued by women were therefore based on the obligations of marriage found in Exodus 21:10-11, which will now be discussed.

Grounds for Divorce in Exodus 21:10-11

Exodus 21.10-11 does not, at first glance, have much to do with divorce. It is a law about how someone should treat his slave wife when he marries a second, free wife.

> Exodus 21:10-11: If he takes another wife to himself, he shall not diminish [the first wife's] food, her clothing, or her marital rights. And if he does not do these three things for her, she shall go out for nothing, without payment of money.

This law states that the rights of the slave wife must not be diminished, and that, if they are, the slave wife must be given her freedom. The meaning of the three words "food, clothing, and love" in Exodus 21:10 is not clear. The first word שארה, *she'arah,* is literally "her flesh." This is usually understood to mean "her food," and perhaps to refer particularly to rich food because meat was not eaten on a regular basis.[51] It has also been suggested that this could refer to her

50. *y. Soṭa* 1.2, 16b: "For lo, it has been taught on the authority of the School of Shammai, 'I know [as grounds for divorce] only the case of the woman who goes forth [from marriage] by reason of having committed adultery. How do I know [the law pertaining to] her who goes forth [in public] with her hair dishevelled, her clothing in shambles [so that her skin shows], and her arms uncovered?' Scripture says, '. . . because he has found some indecency in her' (Deut. 24.1). [The term 'some' is understood to encompass the offences listed.]" (Jacob Neusner's translation and glosses).

51. Though Umberto Cassuto (*A Commentary on the Book of Exodus* [Jerusalem: Magnes Press, 1967], pp. 268-69) suggests that this is a hangover from a nomadic society where meat was the staple diet.

"portion,"[52] her physical well-being[53] or even sexual satisfaction.[54] However, the consistent understanding of the ancient translators is that it means something like "food" or "provisions."[55] The second word כסותה, *kesuthah,* is less difficult and is almost certainly "her clothing," though "accommodation" in the sense of "covering" has been suggested.[56] The third word ענתה, *ʿonathah,* is much more difficult. A wide variety of translations has been offered, including "her abode,"[57] "her right of parenthood,"[58] her "nuptial gift,"[59] her food,[60] and "ointment."[61] However, the ancient translations are in agreement that this term means something like "marital duty."[62]

The interpretation of these words by first-century Jews is the most important consideration for this present study. They provide the best indication of how an original reader of the New Testament would have understood this text. The early and later rabbis were in almost unanimous agreement with the ancient translations of the LXX and Targums that these words should be interpreted as "food, clothing, and conjugal rights." There was virtual unanimity even for the difficult third term "conjugal rights," among early and later Jewish interpreters.[63] The earlier talmudic commentators appear to show some disagreement about the interpretation of the individual words, but they agree that the contents of the list are food, clothing, and conjugal rights.[64]

The exegetical steps by which this law about a slave wife **became the basis of general divorce law** is not preserved, but they can be inferred fairly easily. The most common exegetical rule before 70 C.E. was *qol vahomer.*[65] This is the

52. Based on its meaning "remainder" (personal communication with Dr. Paul Wegner).

53. John I. Durham, *Exodus,* Word Biblical Commentary (Waco: Word Books, 1987), p. 313.

54. Perhaps reflected in the Vulgate translation *nuptias.* This is the interpretation of R. Eleazar and R. Judah, who read the third word as being "her time," i.e., food (*b. Ketub.* 47b; *Mekilta* at Exod. 21:10-11).

55. See *Targum Onqelos,* Jerusalem Targum, Peshitta, and LXX at Exod. 21:10-11.

56. Durham, *Exodus,* p. 313 (from כסות as "covering").

57. Cassuto, *Book of Exodus,* p. 268. Cf. "living quarters" in Peshitta.

58. Durham, *Exodus,* p. 313.

59. From the Vulgate that has *pretium pudicitiae,* the gift given on the morning after the wedding night.

60. The interpretation of R. Eleazar and R. Judah, as noted above in n. 54.

61. As discussed in chapter one.

62. See LXX, *Targum Onqelos,* and Jerusalem Targum at Exod. 21:10-11.

63. See below for the schools of Hillel and Shammai. Later rabbis include R. Ishmael, Saadiah, Rashi, Ibn Ezra, and Ramban.

64. See the debate in *b. Ketub.* 47b-48a.

65. See my *Techniques and Assumptions in Jewish Exegesis before 70 CE,* Texte und Studien zum antiken Judentum 30 (Tübingen: J. C. B. Mohr, 1993).

argument from major to minor that is common to all cultures. In English it is usually expressed: "If that is true, then surely this is also true." In terms of this law the argument would go as follows:

> If a slave wife has these rights, then surely a free wife would also have equivalent rights.
>
> And:
>
> If a wife has these rights, then surely a husband would also have equivalent rights.

As a result of this argument, the rights of the slave wife were found to be the rights of both partners in a marriage contract. The rights named in this law are threefold: the right to food, to clothing, and to marital love. The penalty if these rights were not provided is freedom. For a slave wife this would mean her freedom from the marriage and also her emancipation from slavery without any payment. For a free wife or a husband it would mean freedom from the marriage without payment or forfeiture of the *ketubah*. The discussions in rabbinic literature (as seen below) are careful to point out that men and women have equal obligations and rights in these areas.

This passage affected Jewish divorce laws in many ways. It not only provided three of the valid grounds for divorce, but it also caused the rabbis to compare the divorce certificate to an emancipation certificate for release from slavery. They pointed out that the wording of the two certificates was very similar,[66] and they produced a long list of other similarities and differences.[67] The reason for making this comparison was not stated anywhere, but a Jewish wife

66. *m. Git.* 9.3: "The essence of a *get:* Lo, you are permitted to any man. Rabbi Judah said: And this shall be to you from me a writ of divorce and bill of release and *get* of dismissal that you may be married to any man you wish." The "bill of release" is a deliberate reference to the similarity to freedom from slavery. The Mishnah immediately following this compares the wording of a *get* with the wording of a document for freeing a slave: "The text of a writ of emancipation: Lo, you are a free girl, lo, you are your own [possession]." See also later in this chapter.

67. *m. Git.* 1.4: "All the same are writs of divorce for women and writs of emancipation for slaves. . . ." Various examples of similarities between divorce certificates and emancipation certificates follow, e.g., 1.5: "All documents which are drawn up in gentile registries, even if their signatures are gentiles', are valid, except for writs of divorce for women and writs of emancipation for slaves." Then, at *m. Git.* 1.6: "For writs of divorce for women but not for writs of emancipation of slaves. . . ." This is followed by various examples of dissimilarity, such as 1.6: "If he wanted not to support his slave, he has the right to make such a decision, but not to support his wife he has no right."

was not similar to a slave in early Judaism,[68] and so the most likely reason is the use of Exodus 21:10-11 as a basis of divorce law.

Much of the **mishnaic discussions** about divorce was based on an exposition of Exodus 21:10-11, especially with regard to the grounds for divorce. Divorces brought by women to the court would almost always be based on this text. Men could also bring a case based on this text if they did not want to forfeit the *ketubah* and they could not prove adultery, but most men would bring a case based on the ground of "any matter," which is discussed below. Rabbinic literature preserves detailed discussions concerning the exact limits for gaining a divorce on the grounds in Exodus 21:10-11.

The existence of these discussions suggests that such cases occurred regularly. While it is true that rabbis often debated issues that had no practical importance, these mainly concerned more reputable and edifying subjects such as the sacrificial system or the dimensions of the temple. Matters of housekeeping and sexual activity were not discussed by choice but when necessity dictated. Even talking to a woman was to be avoided,[69] and so it is unlikely that the sages would willingly meditate on the number of times a wife should have new clothes or how often she could demand her conjugal rights without actual cases to necessitate these discussions.

There are no records of disputes among the rabbis about any of these grounds for divorce based on Exodus 21:10-11 except in matters of detail. The schools of Hillel and Shammai disputed about the length of time by which emotional neglect could be defined, and later rabbis disputed other details, but the principles appear to have been universally accepted from a very early date. From at least the beginning of the first century it was recognized that the obligations of Exodus 21:10-11 could form the basis of a claim for divorce.

The obligations in Exodus 21:10-11 are threefold, but they were classified in rabbinic sources under two headings: **material neglect and emotional neglect**. Material neglect consisted of neglect of either food or clothing, or both. This classification reflects a natural division of cases as well as the division of discussions in rabbinic literature. Early rabbinic legislation (as seen below) merged the rulings about food and clothing and treated the matter of conjugal obligations separately.[70] These two classes were dealt with differently. As seen

68. See the analysis in Judith R. Wegner, *Chattel or Person? The Status of Women in the Mishnah* (Oxford: Oxford University Press, 1988), pp. 75-77.

69. "Talk not much with womankind" is the famous saying of Yose b. Yohanan of Jerusalem (*m. 'Abot* 1.5), which the Tannaim took to include his wife. The Talmud explained it is to avoid adultery (*b. Ned.* 20a).

70. See especially *m. Ketub.* 5.5, which lists the woman's material obligations as "grinding flour, baking bread, laundry, preparing meals, feeding the baby, making the bed, working in

below, cases of material neglect normally led to divorce, but cases of emotional neglect were normally dealt with by attempted conciliation and fines, in the hope that divorce could be avoided.

Material Neglect as a Ground for Divorce

Exodus 21:10-11 defined the material obligations simply as an undiminished supply of food and clothing. Rabbinic courts had to define these obligations more specifically when they were faced with actual applications for divorce based on the ground of material neglect.

Although both partners had equal obligations, they were interpreted in different ways for men and women. Men had to provide the food and material, or the money for purchasing them, while women had to prepare the meals and items of clothing.

Mishnah Ketuboth defines the type of work expected of a wife:

> These are the kinds of labour which a woman performs for her husband: she grinds flour, bakes bread, does laundry, prepares meals, feeds her child, makes the bed, works in wool. (*m. Ketub.* 5.5)

Three of these items could be summarized as preparing food for her husband, and three could be summarized as preparing clothing. The remaining one, feeding her child, may be related to preparing food or is perhaps related to the command "fill the earth." It is mentioned specifically because of the discussion that follows about work that her bond servant can do on her behalf.

> If she brought with her a single slave girl, she does not grind, bake bread or do laundry. If two, she does not prepare meals and does not feed her child. If three, she does not make the bed for him and does not work in wool. If she brought four, she sits on a throne. (*m. Ketub.* 5.5)

This ruling can be dated before 70 C.E. because it is followed by a comment by Eliezer ben Hyrcanus (80-120 C.E.).[71]

---

wool." Although some of these relate to food and some to clothing, there is no attempt to say which is which. They are all treated as part of a single ruling. The Mishnah then goes on to the man's conjugal obligations (5.6), then the woman's conjugal obligations (5.7), and then the man's material obligations (5.8). Paul used this same classification. He merged the food and clothing obligations into a single "concern about the material things of the world" (1 Cor. 7:32-34) while treating the conjugal obligations separately (1 Cor. 7:3-5).

71. The text continues: "R. Eliezer says, Even if she brought him a hundred slave girls, he

The amount of food and clothing that the husband must provide is also defined carefully. It is listed as the amount of food he must pay for if his wife is being cared for by someone else for a period. This is presumably because the case that prompted this ruling was brought by a woman whose husband had gone on a trip and left her in the care of someone but had not left adequate funds.

> He who maintains his wife by a third party may not provide for her less than two *qabs* of wheat or four *qabs* of barley [per week]. Said R. Yose, Only Ishmael ruled that barley may be given her for he was near Edom. And one pays over to her a half-*qab* of pulse, a half-*log* of oil, and a *qab* of dried figs or a *maneh* of fig cake. And if he does not have it, he provides instead fruit of some other type. And he gives her a bed, a cover and a mat. And he gives her a cap for her head, and a girdle for her loins, and shoes from one festival season to the next, and clothing worth fifty zuz from one year to the next. And they do not give her either new ones in the sunny season or old ones in the rainy season. But they provide for her clothing for fifty zuz in the rainy season and she clothes herself with the remnants in the sunny season. And the rags remain hers. (*m. Ketub.* 5.8)

The discussions of this tradition by Ishmael b. Elisha (120-140 C.E.) and Yose b. Halafta (140-165 C.E.) help to date it at least to the early second century, and the reference to the practice of giving shoes at the festivals probably means that it dates back to the time of festival pilgrimages to Jerusalem before 70 C.E.

Some further specifications follow in *Mishnah Ketuboth* 5.9 that are more difficult to date and that were probably added on later. These include the money that a man must provide for his wife's other "needs" and the weight of wool that a wife is expected to spin. It also states that while a wife is nursing a baby, the obligation of spinning is removed and the obligated portion of food is increased. It also states that a wealthy man is required to give more support.

Material support was not limited just to food and clothes, as named in Scripture. These two matters formed the basis of legal definitions, but it was recognized that other matters of material support were also important.

A related principle was that a wife should expect a standard of living similar to or better than the one she was brought up with. This was summarized in the maxim that "She rises with him but does not go down with him."[72] She

---

forces her to work in wool, for idleness leads to unchastity [זמה — carnal thoughts]. Rn. Simeon b. Gamaliel says, Also, He who prohibits his wife by a vow from performing any labour, puts her away and pays off her marriage contract. For idleness leads to boredom."

72. This is quoted in *b. Ketub.* 48a as an old tradition. It also occurs in various other places.

could not be forced to live in a lesser dwelling than the one in which she was brought up.[73] This principle was established at a fairly early stage, though details continued to be worked out by later rabbis.

Another matter related to material neglect was that a wife should not be expected to live in the Diaspora if she had been married in Israel, though someone married in the Diaspora could be brought to live in Israel without asking her permission, and she could be moved to Jerusalem, but not from Jerusalem.[74] Within Israel there were also limits about how far she could be moved away from her family.[75]

Some of these details exhibit sensitivity and care for the well-being of the wife, but others appear to be very insensitive and were clearly not designed for marriage guidance or as a handbook for household management. Any marriage based on legalistic rules, such as the amount to be spent on footwear annually, would not last long. These are the kinds of details that would be recorded as legal definitions that arose from actual applications for divorce based on Exodus 21:10-11, and not as notes for helping failing marriages. The fact that these details were recorded in the Mishnah suggests that such cases were brought, and it is clear from the types of rulings that are given that cases were brought by both men and women, and that they were treated equally.

73. *m. Ketub.* 13.10: "With respect to marriages, the following three provinces are considered as distinct countries: Judaea, and beyond the Jordan and Galilee. They can not take out from one town to another town [in another country] nor from one city to another city, but in the same country they may take out from one town to another town or from one city to another city, but not from a town to a city or from a city to a town. They can take from a bad dwelling to a good dwelling, but not from a good dwelling to a bad dwelling. Rn. Simeon b. Gamaliel [140-165] says Not even from a bad dwelling to a good dwelling, since the good dwelling may be trying [because of too much change]." This tradition is dependent on the next one (cited in the next note), which can be dated before 70 C.E.

74. *m. Ketub.* 13.11: "All can be compelled to move to the Land of Israel but no one may be compelled to move out. All may be compelled to go up to Jerusalem but none can be made to leave, whether they be men or women." The reference to the desirability of living in Jerusalem makes it likely that this is a pre-70 tradition.

75. Falk (*Introduction to Jewish Law,* p. 292) pointed out that originally one could not move a wife to another town: "None may take forth [his wife] from one town to another" (*m. Ketub.* 13.10). This was probably a pre-Hasmonean rule, when everyone lived in one's own town and among one's own family. In the wake of conquests and enlargement of the kingdom, new opportunities were opened for choosing a place of residence, so the ruling was changed to allow a wife to be moved, but only within the same country.

Emotional Neglect as a Ground for Divorce

The regulations about conjugal obligations were defined in as much detail as the material obligations, and the obligations for both men and women are discussed.

> He who takes a vow not to have sexual relations with his wife: The School of Shammai says, For two weeks, and the School of Hillel says, For one week. Disciples go forth for Torah study without consent for 30 days. Workers go for one week. The sexual duty of which the Torah speaks [Exod. 21:10]: those without work, every day; workers, twice a week; ass drivers, once a week; camel drivers, once in thirty days; sailors, once in six months — the words of R. Eliezer. (*m. Ketub.* 5.6)

> She who rebels against her husband [regarding sexual duty] they deduct from her marriage contract seven denars a week. R. Judah says Seven tropaics. How long does one continue to deduct? — until her entire marriage contract [is voided]. R. Yose says, He continues to deduct for an inheritance may come from some other source from which he will collect what is due him. And similarly the rule for the man who rebels against his wife [regarding sexual duty] — they add three denars a week to her marriage contract. R. Judah says, Three tropaics. (*m. Ketub.* 5.7)

The ruling of *m. Ketub.* 5.6 can be dated before 70 C.E. both because it is a school debate[76] and because it is commented on by Eliezer ben Hyrcanus (80-120 C.E.). It shows that there were clear guidelines about how long a man could abstain from sexual relations with his wife. The lengths of time were based presumably on pragmatic reasons. A camel driver was likely to be away for a month, a sailor for 6 months, and an ass driver for a week. To some extent this may be an anti-Sadducean ruling because those who were richer among them would be regarded as being without work, and they were given what would have been considered a punitive amount of conjugal duty. In contrast, the rabbis allowed themselves up to thirty days of abstinence because they were devoted to Torah study.

There is no equivalent rule about how long a woman could abstain. It is likely that women did abstain in order to devote themselves to times of prayer

76. School debates can usually be assumed to be pre-70 C.E. because the Shammaites were all but wiped out by 70 C.E. Although an occasional Shammaite is referred to after this date, they do not pose any kind of threat to the dominance of the Hillelites, who effectively form normative Judaism from that time onward.

(as suggested by 1 Cor. 7:3-5), and there are clear penalties for a wife who refused too long (see below), but this limit is never defined. This may indicate that there were far fewer such cases brought by men than women.

The penalty for a "rebellious" man or woman who refused conjugal rights was not divorce but a fine. It appears that the rabbis were reluctant to actually allow a divorce on this ground to either a man or a woman. A woman could be fined by having her *ketubah* reduced, and a man could be fined by having it increased. This had no practical consequences until either divorce or death occurred, when the *ketubah* was returned to the wife or her children (or to the husband if the wife was adulterous or neglectful). It had the effect of bringing the husband and wife back to the court at regular intervals so that their fine could be increased, and so that they could be persuaded to relent. One might expect that the man or woman would be punished by divorce without her *ketubah,* as for material neglect, but instead the rabbis appear to allow a gradual process in the hope that the "rebellious" partner will change his or her mind.

It is difficult to date this ruling about the "rebellious" husband or wife before 70 C.E. because both R. Judah b. Ilai and Yose b. Halafta taught about 140-165 C.E. However, the principle of fines appears to be well established, and the debate concerns merely the amount of money, which had to be adjusted periodically when currency values changed. Therefore, it is likely that this practice dates back to at least the first century C.E. It is interesting that the equality of men and women is established fairly closely in this debate. The woman was fined a little more than the man, perhaps as an indication of the "proper" bias towards the man, but one might have expected a more extreme bias.

It is significant that there is no mention of *forcing* conjugal rights. It was assumed that the right course of action was not force but fines. Both husband and wife had an obligation to take part in marriage acts, but neither could be forced to do so. The man could not force his wife, or vice versa, and the illegality of marital rape became well established in Judaism at a relatively early stage.[77]

Emotional neglect probably included much more than just lack of conjugal rights. **Cruelty and humiliation** were also recognized as grounds for divorce and are related to emotional neglect in the Mishnah. Traditions relating to this cannot be dated, so it is not possible to say with certainty that they relate to first-century practice, but there is no reason to believe that they do not. Several

77. *b. 'Erub.* 100b has third-century C.E. traditions condemning men who force themselves on their wives.

examples of cruelty are given in *m. Ketub.* 7.2-5,[78] presumably based on actual cases.

A husband could abrogate a vow made by his wife, and could enforce a vow on his wife.[79] To refuse to abrogate a vow, or to impose demeaning or demanding conditions on her before he did so, was considered unnecessarily cruel. One example was a husband who made his wife vow not to attend any house of feasting or of mourning, which was regarded by the court as making her virtually a prisoner. Another was a man who forced his wife to publicly repeat a private conversation which was demeaning to her. In these cases the husbands were warned to release their wives from the vow or divorce them with a full payment of their *ketubah*. Petty matters were also recorded, such as the husband who demanded that his wife humiliate herself by the public and messy act of drawing water and pouring it on a dunghill.[80] Even minor matters were taken seriously, such as the wife who was not allowed to wear a certain type of adornment.

All the cases listed above are found in a collection of cases concerning vows. The Mishnah tends to collect rulings in groups defined by a common word or a common theme, probably because of its oral-law origins. There were presumably many other cases of cruelty and neglect that were not considered significant enough to be preserved as case law.

It is difficult to know if wife beating would have been classed together with these acts of cruelty. It was treated like any other criminal act of assault, except for a minor beating, which the court decided was necessary for disciplin-

78. Some examples from *m. Ketub.* 7.2-5 are:

> *m. Ketub.* 7.2: "If one accepted the vow of his wife that she would not taste some kind of fruit, he must divorce her and give her her *ketubah*. . . ."
>
> *m. Ketub.* 7.3: "If one accepted the vow of his wife that she would not put on some kind of adornment. . . ."
>
> *m. Ketub.* 7.5a: "If one set a vow upon his wife that she was not to go to a house of mourning or to a house of feasting he must divorce her and grant her her *ketubah*, because he closes all [doors] against her. But if he would urge, Because of some other matter, it is permitted."
>
> *m. Ketub.* 7.5b: "If he said to her, On condition that you shall say to so-and-so what you said to me, or What I said to you, or That you draw water and empty it on a dunghill — he must divorce her and give her her *ketubah*."

79. This applied only to certain types of vows, listed in *m. Ned.* 11.1 and *t. Ned.* 7.1. Wegner (*Chattel or Person?* p. 57) suggests that these relate to matters that might remove her from marital and household activities. This included abstention from bathing and self-adornment.

80. Wegner (*Chattel or Person?* p. 82) suggested that this was a euphemism for a contraceptive technique, or perhaps it represents a sexual perversion.

ing the wife.[81] In post-talmudic Judaism it is clearly named as a ground for divorce[82] but there is no record that this was cited for divorce in early Judaism, though it is likely that the courts would look favorably on such cases.

The wife could also be cruel, though in different ways. Immediately following this list of ways in which a husband could be cruel follows a list of reasons why a husband could divorce his wife without returning her *ketubah,* which could also be regarded as matters of cruelty or deliberate malice.[83] These included deliberately making him unclean by giving him food that had not been tithed or not warning him that her period had started. These were presumably seen as acts of cruelty, because there was little chance that he would ever know if the food he was eating had been tithed or not, unless she flaunted the fact after he had finished his meal.[84] Cruelty also included humiliations such as her behaving improperly in public or cursing his parents.

These acts of cruelty, which individually seem so petty, can mount up to an intolerable marriage. The grounds for divorce are not specified, except to say that some of them involve breaking the laws of Israel and Jewish custom.[85] It seems likely that these acts of cruelty were considered as part of emotional neglect, and that they justified divorce in these cases by extrapolating from the obligations of Exodus 21:10-11.

It is not certain that these matters of cruelty were regarded in the same category as emotional neglect. One difference is that, unlike other forms of emotional neglect, cruelty resulted in divorce rather than a protracted series of fines. However, the introduction to this list of cases of cruelty does suggest that the final editor of the Mishnah wished to regard them as emotional neglect.

81. An undatable tradition in *t. B. Qam.* 9.14.

82. *Eben ha-'Ezer* 154.3 gloss.

83. *m. Ketub.* 7.6: "And these are they that are divorced without their *ketubah:* she who transgresses the Law of Moses and Jewish custom. And what is meant by the Law of Moses? — If she gave him food that had not been tithed, or if she had sexual intercourse with him when she was a menstruant, or if she did not separate the priest's share of the dough, or if she made a vow and did not fulfil it. And what is meant here by Jewish custom? — if she set forth with her hair loose, or if she was spinning in the street, or if she conversed with all men. Abba Saul [140-165] says: Also, if she cursed his parents to his face. R. Tarphon [120-140] says: Also if she was a loud-voiced woman. What is meant here by a loud-voiced woman? — such a one who speaks in her house so that her neighbours hear her voice."

84. It was recognized that usually lapses of tithing or menstrual contamination would go unnoticed by anyone except the wife. For this reason women were threatened with the saying in *m. Šabb.* 2.6: "For three transgressions women die in childbirth: for carelessness with respect to [the laws of] the menstruant (Lev. 15.19ff.), and with respect to [the law of separating] *hallah* [dough offering taken from a batch of dough before baking it (Num. 15.20)], and with respect to the lighting of the [Sabbath] lamp [an obligation in *m. Šabb.* 2.1, not found in Scripture]."

85. *m. Ketub.* 7.6 (cited in n. 83 above).

They are introduced by the ruling that if someone used a vow to deny his wife any benefit from him, he nevertheless had to provide her material needs through a guardian. This situation could continue for a month, but then he had to divorce her, giving her the *ketubah*.[86] The divorce was presumably necessary because he was neglecting her emotional rights. Her material rights would continue to be supplied through a guardian, but she would still suffer emotional neglect, and the court ruled that he had to offer her a divorce after one month of this willful emotional neglect. After this ruling follows the list of various forms of cruelty outlined above, most of which also relate to vows. The facts that the editor chose to put these matters in the tractate dealing with the marriage contract and that he placed the vow that clearly concerns emotional neglect at the front of the list suggest that they were regarded as aspects of emotional neglect.

In summary, the law of Exodus 21:10-11 was used to apply for divorces in New Testament times by both men and women. The law was applied in two categories — material neglect and emotional neglect. The material matters of food and clothing were grouped together, and emotional neglect appears to be have been widened to include cruelty by both the wife and the husband. If a man or woman succeeded in showing that a partner had neglected his or her material or emotional needs, a divorce could be granted and the *ketubah* could be kept. The early rabbis were in agreement about the validity of all these grounds for divorce.

The No-fault "Any Matter" Divorce

The main area of disagreement about divorce among the rabbinic groups of the first century concerned the new type of divorce invented by the Hillelites, called the "any matter" divorce. The other dispute concerned procedures for writing and presenting a divorce certificate, which were of interest mainly to scribes and lawyers. In contrast, the dispute about the new "any matter" divorces was of interest to the general population because it had widespread repercussions. It has also become well known in New Testament studies because Jesus' opinion was sought on this matter (as will be discussed in the next chapter). The debate was recorded (in a highly abbreviated way) in the Mishnah:

86. *m. Ketub.* 7.1: "If one placed his wife under a vow not to derive any benefit from him, he must appoint a guardian up to thirty days; if for a longer period, he must divorce her and give her her *ketubah*. R. Judah says, In the case of an Israelite, if for one month, he may continue to keep her as wife, but if for two months, he must divorce her and grant her her *ketubah;* and in the case of a priest, if for two months, he may continue to keep her as a wife, but if for three months, he must divorce her and give her her *ketubah*."

> The School of Shammai say: A man should not divorce his wife unless he found in her a matter of indecency (דבר ערוה), as it is said: *For he finds in her an indecent matter* (ערות דבר). And the School of Hillel say, Even if she spoiled his dish, since it says *For he finds in her an indecent matter* (ערות דבר).[87]

The debate was based on differing interpretations of an unusual phrase in Deuteronomy 24:1 — ערות דבר, *'ervat davar.* This could perhaps be translated as "matter of indecency," though it is strange that the word "indecency" is in the construct form rather than the word "matter." Reading the phrase literally produces "indecency of a matter," or perhaps "nakedness of a matter." There was also another difficulty, as far as the rabbis were concerned, because the word דבר ("matter") is apparently superfluous.

The Hillelites and Shammaites followed two completely different routes to understand this unusual phrase. The Hillelites concluded that the strangeness of the phrase suggested that there was an extra meaning hidden in it. This was a common technique in early rabbinic exegesis.[88] They therefore concluded that the two words referred to two different grounds for divorce — "indecency" and "a matter." This meant one could base a divorce on an act of "indecency" or on "a matter," which meant "any matter." Because "any matter" encompassed all other grounds for divorce, this single ground could be used by anyone seeking a divorce.

The Shammaites took the two words to mean "a matter of indecency," by which they understood the phrase to mean "adultery." In their ruling they quoted the text of Deuteronomy 24:1, but they reversed the order of the two contentious words to emphasize their interpretation, though they also quoted the text in its normal form. In this way they indicated that although they recognized that the text said ערות דבר "indecency of a matter," one should read it as דבר ערוה "a matter of indecency."[89]

When this tradition is read by itself, it would appear to suggest that the Shammaites allowed divorce only on the grounds of adultery. However, we have seen above that the Shammaites also accepted the three obligations of Exodus 21:10-11 as valid grounds for divorce.[90] Therefore, although their words "a man may not divorce his wife unless he finds indecency in her" appear at first glance

87. *m. Git.* 9.10; cf. *Sifré Deut.* 269; *y. Soṭa* 1.2, 16b.

88. Instone-Brewer, *Techniques and Assumptions,* pp. 20, 74, 131.

89. For a detailed examination of the exegesis, see my *Techniques and Assumptions,* pp. 136-38.

90. The Shammaites debated with Hillel about how long a man could neglect his wife's conjugal rights (see above), but there was no debate about whether or not she had such rights.

to mean that divorce could be *only* on the grounds of adultery, they cannot be read this narrowly. The phrase should be understood in the context of the debate in which it is spoken, which was a debate about the meaning of Deuteronomy 24. The Hillelites argued from Deuteronomy 24:1 that divorce could be on the grounds of "any matter" or "indecency"; the Shammaites replied, "No, this text allows divorce only for 'a matter of indecency.'"[91]

This debate carried on into the second century when Aqiba added:

> R. Aqiba says, Even if he found someone else prettier than she, since it says *And it shall be if she find no favour in his eyes.* (*m. Git.* 9.10)

Aqiba, in the early second century, gave added weight to Hillel's argument by pointing out that the contentious phrase in Deuteronomy is preceded by "She does not find favor in his eyes because he found in her. . . ." He pointed out that "does not find favor in his eyes" could mean something as petty as her declining beauty.[92] This could not, in any way, be described as "indecency," and so it lends weight to the idea that "matter" means "any matter," as the Hillelites argued. Actually, there was little need for Aqiba to give this support because by the second century the Shammaites had almost all disappeared, and the Hillelites had won the day.

The second matter on which Hillelites and Shammaites disagreed was the complexity of **the stages involved in getting a divorce**. The Shammaites said that once a divorce certificate was written, it could be given to the wife at any time; the Hillelites said that it had to be written just before handing it to her, and there were many rules about how it should be given and about the fulfillment of conditions that might be attached to the divorce.[93]

91. See *m. Git.* 9.10, cited above. Jesus used very similar words in the same context. This will be explored in the next chapter. Even when this Shammaite ruling is quoted outside the context of this debate, as in *y. Soṭa* 1.2, 16b, it must be viewed in the overall context of divorce debates in rabbinic literature.

92. Michael L. Satlow ("'One Who Loves His Wife Like Himself': Love in Rabbinic Marriage," *Journal of Jewish Studies* 49 [1998]: 73) suggests that Aqiba focuses on חן, which "although employed idiomatically in this biblical phrase, can mean 'beauty'" (see *b. Yebam.* 63a, citing Ben Sira; *y. Git.* 5.2, 46d; Marcus Jastrow, *A Dictionary of the Targumim, the Talmud Babli, and Yerushalmi, and the Midrashic Literature* [New York: Pardes Publishing House, 1950], p. 481).

93. *m. Git.* 8.4: "The School of Shammai says: A man dismisses his wife with an old writ of divorce. And the School of Hillel prohibits it. And what is an old writ of divorce? It is any writ of divorce, after the writing of which, the man continued alone with her." This is made more explicit in *m. Git.* 8.9: "He who divorced his wife and spent a night with her in an inn — the School of Shammai says: She does not require a second writ of divorce from him. And the School of Hillel says: She requires a second writ of divorce from him." The many regulations about how the writ of divorce is presented are dealt with in *m. Git.* 8.1-8. These are summarized

The Hillelites interpreted the three phrases that accompany the mention of the divorce certificate in Deuteronomy 24:1-4 ("writes her a certificate of divorce," "puts it in her hand," and "sends her out of his house") as separate acts, all of which were necessary for a valid divorce. The three stages were the writing of the *get,* putting it into her hand or her agent's hand, and sending her away. Each of these stages had a large number of associated regulations.[94] The Hillelites also said that the divorce was not valid until any other conditions specified in the *get* or the *ketubah* had been fulfilled. The Shammaites, in contrast, said that the whole process of divorce was encompassed in the writing of the *get,* and that once this was done the woman was a divorcée.[95]

The most likely reason for the complexity of the Hillelite procedure was the ease with which someone could get an "any matter" divorce in a Hillelite court. Unlike a Shammaite court, the Hillelites did not require any evidence of grounds for divorce, so without these regulations, the husband might simply hand his wife a pre-prepared *get* in a fit of anger and dismiss her. To prevent this, the Hillelites introduced the need to prepare a *get* at the time of divorce and made sure that the *get* was given in person to the wife, or given to an agent who would give it to her in person. All this helped to slow down the process and helped to engineer a meeting at which reconciliation might occur.

The Hillelite divorce was already common in the first century B.C.E. The reforms of Simeon ben Shetah in the previous century (described in the previous chapter) were probably introduced mainly as a result of the Hillelite "any matter" divorce, which effectively allowed divorce at the whim of the husband. These reforms, like the extra rules about writing and delivering the *get,* helped to discourage hasty divorces. They made it financially disadvantageous for a husband to divorce his wife without grounds and provided some financial security for a woman divorced in this way.

The various hurdles of writing a certificate and the intricate rules about how to deliver it to a wife quickly became institutionalized. More importantly, the Hillelite interpretation was favored by the common people who wished to

---

well by Amram, *The Jewish Law of Divorce,* pp. 171-86. There is a long discussion concerning the conditional writ of divorce in *m. Git.* 7.3-8.

94. For example, if the certificate was given to her by throwing it, and it landed at her feet but she was standing inside his house, it was deemed that he had not yet given it to her. But if she was standing outside his house, and it landed nearer to her than to him, then he had succeeded in giving it to her (*m. Git.* 8.1-2).

95. Even if the man changed his mind, or if he never put the divorce certificate in her hand, and she never left, she would nevertheless be regarded as having been divorced and reconciled. As a result she could not marry a priest if she was later widowed before the rest of the divorce procedure was carried out (*m. Git.* 8.8).

avoid the arguments and uncertainties of trying to bring to court evidence of grounds for divorce. The Shammaite position quickly became one of only theoretical importance.

The Normal Rabbinic Divorce

It is unlikely that many of the ordinary people chose to follow the Shammaite teaching on divorce. It is difficult to know how much influence the Shammaites ever had among the common people, because we know their teachings only through the writings of their rivals, the Hillelites. For some reason, the only teaching that survived the destruction of 70 C.E. was Hillelite. Perhaps this reflects the fact that the only leader of note to survive was Yohanan b. Zakkai, a Hillelite, or perhaps the Shammaites were already in general decline anyway. From their rulings it appears that they normally adopted the more strict position, while the Hillelites tended to bend to accommodate the difficulties faced by ordinary people.

In the matter of divorce the Shammaites must have been almost totally cut out of the legal process even before 70 C.E. because their position was so much stricter than the Hillelite one. Almost no one who was wanting a divorce would choose a Shammaite judge when he knew that a Hillelite judge would approve an "any matter" divorce without requiring any evidence. Shammaite judges would require evidence of neglect, unfaithfulness, or infertility. With a court made up of Hillelite judges one could ask for an "any matter" divorce and there would be no need to bring proof of any kind, and so there was no need to share one's shame with one's neighbors.

The only occasion when someone might want to go to a Shammaite court would be when one wanted to prove adultery or some serious ground of neglect against one's wife and thereby keep the *ketubah.* In a Hillelite court this practice might be looked down on as greedy. It was not in the interests of the community for a woman to be divorced without her *ketubah.* Even if she had a family, they would be unlikely to take her back, and so her support would fall on the community purse.[96] Someone who wanted to keep the *ketubah* by proving adultery would therefore go to a Shammaite court where divorce was not allowed for "any matter." Here it was expected that fault be proven, in which case the *ketubah* would be forfeited. There is evidence of only one case in rabbinic literature of a man attempting to prove adultery, and this was heard in a

96. For details of community support for the poor see Keith F. Nickle, *The Collection: A Study in Paul's Strategy* (London: SCM, 1966), pp. 93-94.

Shammaite court, as one would expect.[97] This case was not successful, and, given the high standard of evidence that was demanded, it is unlikely that any such case would ever be successful.

Philo and Josephus assumed that the Hillelite "any matter" divorce was the only type of divorce in use.

> Philo *Special Laws* 3.30: Another commandment is that if a woman after parting from her husband for any cause whatever . . .
>
> Josephus *Life* 426-27: At this period I divorced my wife, being displeased at her behavior.
>
> Josephus *Antiquities* 4.253: He who desires to be divorced from the wife who is living with him, for whatsoever cause (and with mortals many such may arise), must certify in writing. . . .[98]

The "any matter" divorce was not only the most common form of divorce, but it was also considered to be the most righteous form. An appearance in court was considered to be a shameful thing for a woman.[99] When R. Yose the Galilean wanted to divorce his wife, he decided that he couldn't afford to because she had a large *ketubah* settlement. He did not think of going to court to claim material or emotional neglect, and although his colleagues saw her mistreat him, they didn't suggest this either. Instead, they made a collection to help him pay the settlement.[100]

Joseph, the father of Jesus, was also planning to use a Hillelite "any matter" divorce. Matthew records that Joseph wished to avoid bringing shame on Mary and to divorce her quietly (Matt. 1:19). An "any matter" divorce required no public trial, no evidence brought by witnesses, and very little fuss. Matthew says that Joseph was planning this because he was a righteous man.

A normal rabbinic divorce would involve a court, but this could still be a quiet and relatively private procedure, so long as it was a Hillelite court. The court that enacted a divorce was the local **"court of three."** This was a collection of three local rabbis or scribes or, in the case of some trials, priests.[101]

97. See *b. Git.* 57a cited in n. 45 above. The court is not described as Shammaite, but the fact that the ruling was based on a Shammaite tradition makes this almost certain.

98. Translations from the Loeb Classical Library series.

99. According to an Amoraic source in *b. Ketub.* 97b, but presumably this would also have been true in earlier times.

100. *y. Ketub.* 11.3, 34b; *Gen. Rab.* 17.3.

101. *m. Sanh.* 1.1: "Property cases [are decided] by three [judges]." Discussions follow about what "property cases" include. *m. Sanh.* 1.3: ". . . [Property pledged as security for] vows of

They were able to judge all cases of property except anything that involved capital punishment.[102] The litigant(s) could choose the judges and even the town in which he wanted to appoint a court.[103] In most divorces the judges would all be chosen by the husband. The only exception would be where a wife called the court to argue that she had grounds for a divorce. These courts were recognized by all branches of Judaism, though the Shammaites demanded the use of these courts in some cases for which the Hillelites were happy to avoid their use.[104]

A divorce did not require a court unless there was a dispute about the *ketubah* inheritance or the grounds for the divorce. However, it was usually safer to conduct a divorce through a court because of the large amount of money involved. Any misunderstanding could result in later legal action that could bankrupt the former husband. Also, a mistake in the divorce procedure

---

valuation, in the case of movables, is evaluated by three. R. Judah says One of them must be a priest."

102. *m. Sanh.* 1.4: "Cases involving the death penalty are judged before twenty-three [judges]. . . ."

103. See the case in *m. Git.* 4.1: "He who sent a writ of divorce to his wife and overtook the messenger . . . it is null. . . . If [he reached her] after the writ of divorce reached her possession, he no longer has the power to annul it." 4.2: "At first [such a husband] would set up [עוֹשֶׂה] a court in some other place and annul it. Rn. Gamaliel [II] ordained that people should not do so, for the good order of the world." When there was more than one litigant, they both chose a judge and the third was either mutually agreed upon or chosen by the other two judges (*m. Sanh.* 3.1: "Property cases are [decided] by three [judges]. This litigant chooses one, and that litigant chooses one, and then the two of them choose one more — the words of R. Meir. And the sages say The two judges choose one more").

104. E.g., *m. Yebam.* 13.1: "The School of Shammai says, Only those who are betrothed can exercise the prerogative of refusal, but the School of Hillel says, Both betrothed and married. The School of Shammai says, Against a husband and not against a brother-in-law [if her husband died before she refused him], but the School of Hillel says, Both against a husband and against a brother-in-law. The School of Shammai says [She must perform a proper rite of *ḥalitzah* — taking off the shoe] in his presence, but the School of Hillel says, Whether in his presence or not in his presence. The house of Shammai say Before the Court, but the School of Hillel says, Before the Court or not before the Court. The School of Hillel said to the School of Shammai, So long as she is a minor she may exercise the prerogative of refusal even four or five times. The School of Shammai says to them, The daughters of Israel are not public property — but she can exercise the prerogative of refusal and wait until she grows up [when she can perform *ḥalitzah*] or she can exercise the prerogative of refusal and be married." This indicates that the courts and proper procedures were more important for the Shammaites than the Hillelites. They wanted the proper *ḥalitzah* performed, and in the presence of the court. This is very likely to be early because the Shammaites appear to win. They have the last word, even though the structure of the debate suggests the Hillelites should be last, and they win by showing the absurdity of the Hillelite position.

could mean that the divorce was invalid and thus any subsequent marriage by the woman would be adulterous.[105]

A divorce involved two documents and several actions, any one of which could invalidate the divorce if not carried out properly. The most important document was the *get* or "divorce certificate." This had to be written out by the man or by someone on his behalf. The other document was the receipt or *quittance,* which the divorced woman gave to her husband to affirm that she had received full payment of her *ketubah.* If this was lost or faulty, the woman's family could sue the husband for this money.[106] In cases where the *ketubah* was forfeited by the wife because of her misconduct, it was even more important that a court should be involved because they had to rule that the man need not pay. Without this ruling the woman's family could sue for the *ketubah* at a later date.

Therefore, the vast majority of first-century Jewish divorces were "any matter" divorces in a Hillelite court. It is unlikely that there were many, if any, successful cases proven against an adulteress, and so for practical purposes it could be said that all divorces brought by men against their wives were "any matter" divorces. The relatively rare cases where women sought to gain a divorce from their husbands could not be based on this ground. They would therefore bring cases based on Exodus 21:10, which could be heard in Hillelite, Shammaite, or a mixed court because all branches of Judaism recognized divorce on these grounds of neglect.

Remarriage of Widows and Divorcées

Remarriage was normal and even expected after divorce or widowhood, though many women found it advantageous to remain single. If their finances were sufficient, a life being single gave them more freedom than married life.

Women were normally betrothed before the age of puberty, which came at twelve and a half years,[107] or whenever the signs of puberty appeared.[108] Fathers were encouraged to avoid immorality by marrying both boys and girls while they were still minors,[109] though pregnancy was to be avoided until after

105. This is explored more fully below.

106. An example of this is suggested in *m. Ketub.* 9.9: "If a woman produced a *get* but did not have the *ketubah* with her, she must receive her *ketubah;* but if she did not have with her a *get* and she says My *get* is lost, and he says My receipt is lost. . . ." This is not an early text, but it shows what could happen.

107. *m. Nid.* 5.6-8.

108. As defined in *m. Nid.* 5.8.

109. R. Aqiba interpreted "Do not profane your daughter by making her a prostitute"

age twelve.[110] Eighteen was also a good age to marry,[111] but God was said to be disturbed if someone was not married by age twenty.[112] Inscriptional data confirm that these guidelines were followed.[113]

A girl's father had absolute control over her until she was an adult. He could annul any of her vows, and he had the right to anything she earned or found.[114] He could also betroth her to someone against her will, and she could not refuse marriage.[115] However, if her father was dead and her mother or brothers had arranged the marriage, she could refuse her husband as soon as she became an adult.[116] An adult woman could not be married against her will, but most were betrothed before they had any choice.

A divorcée or widow was therefore in a very different situation from that of a young woman before her first marriage. She was now free to marry (or not marry) whomever she wished. This right was enshrined in wording that had to appear in every divorce certificate: **"You are free to marry any man you wish."**

(Lev. 19:29) as referring to "him who delays in marrying off a daughter who has already passed through puberty" (*b. Sanh.* 76a). Boys were also to be married at twelve (*Lam. Rab.* 1.2; cf. *y. Qidd.* 1.7, 61a).

110. R. Simeon b. Yohai: "Everyone who lets his daughter be married as a minor diminishes the increase of mankind, loses his wealth and ends up guilty of bloodshed" (*'Abot R. Nat.* B 48). Minors were allowed to use a contraceptive: "Three kinds of women may use an absorbent: a minor, a pregnant woman and a nursing mother. A minor because otherwise she might become pregnant and die as a result. . . . And what is the age of such a minor? For the age of eleven years and one day until the age of twelve years and one day."

111. *m. 'Abot* 5.21.

112. *b. Qidd.* 29b: "Until the age of twenty, the Holy One, blessed be He, sits and waits. When will he take a wife? As soon as one attains twenty and has not married, He exclaims, Blasted be his bones!"

113. See A. M. Okorie, "Divorce and Remarriage among the Jews in the Time of Jesus," *DELTION BIBLIKWN MELETWN* 25 (1996): 64.

114. *m. Nid.* 5.7. Judith Wegner infers from *m. Ketub.* 4.4 that he did not even have a legal obligation to feed or clothe her (*Chattel or Person?* p. 33), or presumably to bury her or ransom her when kidnapped.

115. Though R. Eleazar disagreed with this. He said: "A father is forbidden to betroth his daughter to another while she is a minor. He must wait until she grows up and says I want to marry so-and-so" (*b. Qidd.* 41a).

116. Ilan (*Jewish Women in Greco-Roman Palestine,* p. 84) lists five examples of this in early rabbinic literature: the wife of Pishon the camel-driver in a case disputed by Beth Hillel and Beth Shammai (*y. Yebam.* 13.1, 13c; *b. Yebam.* 107b); an orphan who brought her case before R. Judah b. Baba (*t. Yebam.* 13.5); R. Ishmael's daughter-in-law who repudiated "while her son was sitting on her shoulders" (*y. Yebam.* 1.2, 2d; 3.1, 13c; or his daughter according to *b. Nid.* 52a), showing that one could still repudiate after having children; two women who brought cases to R. Judah the Patriarch — the daughter-in-law of Abdan, a close associate of Judah (*b. Yebam.* 108a), and a woman whose husband went to "a country beyond the sea" (*b. Yebam.* 107b).

This wording is found in early traditions in the Mishnah and also in all extant divorce certificates. It can be traced back through the fifth-century Egyptian Jewish documents, the sixth to seventh centuries, and in ancient Near Eastern law codes of the fourteenth century B.C.E.[117] In the Mishnah these words are called the "essence" of the *get* because they were seen as central to its purpose:

m. Git. 9.3:

The essence of a *get:*		גופו של גט
Lo, you are permitted to any man.	[in Hebrew]	הרי את מותרת לכל אדם
Rabbi Judah said:		רבי יהודה אומר
And this shall be to you from me	[in Aramaic]	ודין דיהוי ליכי מינאי
a writ of divorce		ספר תירוכין
and bill of release		ואגרת שבוקין
and *get* of dismissal		וגט פטורין
that you may be married		למהך להתנסבא
to any man you wish.		לכל גבר דתצביין

The comment by R. Judah b. Illai (140-165 C.E.) helps to date this fairly early. A brief Hebrew form is followed by R. Judah citing an expanded Aramaic version of the words. This Aramaic version is similar to the form that became enshrined in the standard Ashkenazi *get.*[118] It is unclear from this Mishnah whether the Aramaic version (which contains the reference to a "bill of release") is an amplification of the shorter Hebrew formula or whether the Hebrew is a

117. See chapter two and details in my "Deuteronomy 24.1-4 and the Origin of the Jewish Divorce Certificate," *Journal of Jewish Studies* 49 (1998): 230-43.

118. The modern Askenazi *get* retains these ideas: "On the . . . day of the week, the . . . day of the month of . . . in the year . . . from the creation of the world according to the calendar reckoning we are accustomed to count here, in the city . . . (which is also known as . . .), which is located on the river . . . (and on the river . . .), and situated near wells of water . . . (also known as . . .), I, . . . (also known as. . .), the son of . . . (also known as . . .), who today am present in the city . . . (which is also known as . . .), which is located on the river . . . (and on the river . . .), and situated near wells of water, do willingly consent, being under no restraint, to release, to set free, and put aside thee, my wife, . . . (also known as . . .), daughter of . . . (also known as . . .), who art today in the city of . . . (which is also known as . . .), which is located on the river (and on the river . . .), and situated near wells of water, who has been my wife from before. Thus do I set free, release thee, and put thee aside, in order that thou may have permission and the authority over thyself to go and marry any man thou may desire. No person may hinder thee from this day onward, and thou art permitted to every man. This shall be for thee from me a bill of dismissal, a letter of release, and a document of freedom, in accordance with the laws of Moses and Israel" (Schereschewsky, "Divorce"). This *get* is an expansion of the mishnaic phrase "you are permitted to any man," with several additions to help identify the individuals, and an addition that the man is making this decision of his own free will.

contracted form for scholars to memorize. The second possibility is more likely correct, as shown by a first-century *get* found at Masada that is dated at 72 C.E. This *get* records the Aramaic words almost exactly as prescribed by R. Judah:[119]

that you are free on your part	די את רשׂיא בנפשכי
to go and become the wife	למהך ולמהי אנת
of any Jewish man that you wish.	לכול גבר יהודי די תצבין
And this is to be for you from me	ובו[די]ן להוי לכי מני
a writ of divorce and a *get* of release.	ספר תרכין וגט שׂבקין

Therefore the longer and shorter forms are both early, and it is difficult to decide which came first. The shorter form can be traced back to an earlier date, but the precise wording of the shorter form preserved in the Mishnah indicates that it may have been constructed as a summary of the longer form. It contains all the details that are made explicit in the longer version: the fact that this was a *written certificate,*[120] that she was *permitted*[121] to *become a wife,* and that she may marry any man *whom she wishes.*[122] The word "permitted" would imply "permitted to marry" (as at *m. Yebam.* 1.2[123]), and the word "any" in the phrase

119. Originally published in Benoit, Milik, and de Vaux, *Les grottes de Murabba'at,* pp. 104-9. The *get* is known as *Papyrus Murabba'at* 20 or *PMur.* 20, or the "*get* from the Judean Desert." For more details see Ilan, "Notes and Observations on a Newly Published Divorce Bill," and Leone J. Archer, *Her Price Is beyond Rubies: The Jewish Woman in Greco-Roman Palestine,* Journal for the Study of the Old Testament, Supplement Series 60 (Sheffield: Sheffield Academic Press, 1990), pp. 291-92.

120. The three phrases "writ of divorce" (ספר תירוכין), "bill of release" (אגרת שבוקין), and "*get* of dismissal" (גט פטורין) are all translations of the phrase "certificate of divorce" (ספר כריתת) in Deut. 24:1, 3, as found in the Targums of *Pseudo-Jonathan, Neofiti,* and *Onqelos,* respectively.

121. "To be permitted" in *m. Git.* 9.3 is מותרת from נתר, "to loose, untie," which is also used in Targum Deut. 24:4. This is the equivalent of רשׂיא from רשׂי "to have authority, permission" in the Masada *get.*

122. The Masada *get* adds a detail that is not in R. Judah's longer version, when it says "any *Jewish* man." This addition is found in an anonymous discussion in *m. Git.* 9.2, which should probably also be dated early, on the basis of the Masada *get.* This mishnah rules that the only exception to "any man" that can be made in a *get* is that which is already ruled out, such as marriage to her ex-husband's father or brother, to her own brother, to a bondman, or to a non-Jew. This word "Jewish" was therefore an allowable addition to the essential formula. Any other addition, such as "except so-and-so," made the *get* invalid.

123. "To be permitted" (מותרת) is used as an abbreviation for "permitted to marry" in *m. Yebam.* 1.2: "If one's daughter or any other woman from all these prohibited degrees were married to his brother who had yet another wife, and his daughter died or was divorced, and afterwards his brother died, then her fellow-wife is permitted (מותרת)."

"any man" would imply "any man you wish." The term *get* (גט, "certificate") would by itself imply a written document. In addition, the word "lo" links it to the certificate of emancipation, which also started in this way,[124] and thereby to all the rules that these two types of certificate shared, such as how they should be written and delivered.[125] This summary would therefore encompass the whole of the traditional Aramaic wording and could become the essence of the law to be memorized.

It was not strictly true that a divorcée could marry anyone she wished. She could not marry her lover, or the person with whom she was suspected of committing adultery.[126] She could not marry a former husband if she had been married in the meantime,[127] and she could not marry a priest.[128] Also, it was often added to her divorce certificate that she could marry only a Jew because of the rule against mixed marriages. This restriction is found in the Masada *get* and in mishnaic guidelines.[129]

This right to remarry was regarded as the personal permission given by the husband to his former wife. Even though the words were standard and occurred in every divorce certificate, they were still regarded as an important message from the former husband and as necessary for his wife to be able to remarry. Josephus makes this clear when he tells about how Salome ignored Jewish law by divorcing her husband without receiving from him a proper divorce certificate:

124. *m. Git.* 9.3.

125. *m. Git.* 1.4.

126. "He who is suspected [of intercourse] with a married woman, and they [the court] dissolved the marriage with her [new] husband, even though he married [the woman], he must put her out" (*m. Yebam.* 2.8). This tradition is undated, but the same principle is behind the pre–70 C.E. text at *m. Soṭa* 5.1, which is discussed above. Wegner (*Chattel or Person?* p. 33) suggests that this was not strictly enforced because it is not biblical. Similar restrictions ensured that no one who helped cause the divorce could benefit from it, and so she could not marry the man who acted as agent for her husband delivering her bill of divorce or a sage who pronounced her forbidden to her husband because of a vow she had taken (*m. Yebam.* 2.9-10).

127. On the basis of Deut. 24:1-4. Yet even if she hadn't remarried in the meantime, it was severely criticized: "Four are they whom the mind cannot endure. These are . . . and some say: The man who divorces his wife the first time and the second and brings her back" (*b. Pesaḥ.* 113b). Nevertheless some examples survived: the Judean Desert *ketubah* of Salome whom Elai b. Shimeon took back and remarried after divorcing her (Benoit, Milik, and de Vaux, *Les grottes de Murabba'at,* pp. 243-54); a man from Saidan divorced his wife as a result of an oath, but the Sages permitted him to take her back (*m. Git.* 4.7); and a girl married as a minor who was divorced and later remarried (*t. Yebam.* 13.5).

128. Lev. 21:7.

129. *m. Git.* 9.2.

> Salome had occasion to quarrel with Costobarus and soon sent him a document dissolving their marriage, which was not in accordance with Jewish law. For it is (only) the man who is permitted by us to do this, and not even a divorced woman may marry again on her own initiative unless her former husband consents.[130]

Widows, unlike divorcées, had an automatic right to remarry. Paul refers to this right of widows to remarry when he cites the words of the divorce certificate. He applies this to widows, even including a Christian version of the common clause in a divorce certificate that one may remarry "only a Jew":

> 1 Cor. 7:39:
> She is free to marry whichever man she wishes, (but) only in the Lord.
> ἐλευθέρα ἐστὶν ᾧ θέλει γαμηθῆναι, μόνον ἐν κυρίῳ

It is significant that Paul quotes the wording of a divorce certificate in order to establish the rights of a widow. Remarriage was a fundamental right of a divorcée because she had a certificate proving her right, whereas a widow often had to provide her own proof that her husband was dead. That is why a conscientious husband often gave a wife a conditional divorce certificate before going on a long journey, so if he did not return she could use the divorce certificate rather than try to find proof that he was dead.[131]

This right of remarriage did not just mean that she could accept an offer of marriage from whomever she wished. It appears that it was acceptable for a woman to request that a man marry her, even without the intermediary services of a relative.[132] It was normally assumed that a widow or divorced woman would wish to remarry, especially if she were young. It was thought to be shameful to the woman if she were not married.[133]

A widow who had not given her husband a male son was obligated by Scripture to marry his brother in a levirate marriage, although he could refuse

130. Josephus, *Ant.* 15.259-60 (Loeb).

131. In *m. Git.* 7.7-9 there are various regulations about writing a conditional divorce certificate that becomes effective only if the husband does not return during a specified period.

132. Ilan (*Jewish Women in Greco-Roman Palestine*, pp. 80-81) found three examples of women who asked their husbands to marry them. Two of them had greater freedom because they were wealthy (*b. Ketub.* 22a: "great woman who was great in beauty"; and Rachel, daughter of Kalba Sabua, who chose to marry poor R. Aqiba [*b. Ned.* 50a; *b. Ketub.* 62b]). The third was a simple widow who wanted a husband to care for her son (*t. B. Qam.* 8.16; *b. B. Qam.* 80a).

133. A second-century C.E. tradition, which probably reflects earlier thought, says: "More than a man wants to marry, a woman wants to get married. And further, because the shame of a woman [at not being married] is greater than the shame of a man" (*t. Ketub.* 12.3).

by the publicly humiliating ceremony of *ḥalitzah.*[134] It is possible that the law of levirate marriage had been generally abandoned by the first century and that men were expected to perform the *ḥalitzah.*[135] A childless woman was under more moral pressure to remarry than one who had children, though it was recognized that the law "be fruitful and multiply" was addressed to Adam, and so men had to have children, but women did not.[136] Judith is an example of a woman who was widowed but did not remarry, despite many offers (Jdt. 16:22), even though she had no children (Jdt. 16:24). A childless man, however, was still expected to try to raise a family, even if he was elderly.[137]

There was no stigma involved in marrying a divorcée or widow[138] unless the woman was divorced for adultery.[139] However, a second marriage was often treated as a relatively unimportant event, and the breakup of a first marriage was more momentous than consequent breakups.[140] The wedding ceremony was a less costly affair, the price of the *ketubah* was half that of a virgin. The man was assumed to be less enthusiastic about the wedding, and so it was normally held on a Thursday, in order to encourage him to spend at least a long weekend with his wife rather than return immediately to work.[141] A remarried

134. Deut. 25:5-10. She has to publicly pull a sandal off his foot, spit in his face, and declare that he is unwilling to take her.

135. See the discussion in Falk, *Introduction to Jewish Law,* pp. 317-18. This was especially true in the Diaspora. It is possible that Paul was telling widows that they need not submit to levirate marriages (see Ford, "Levirate Marriage in St. Paul").

136. *m. Yebam.* 6.6: "[Only] the man is commanded to be fruitful and multiply, but not the woman."

137. A man should not remarry in less than a year, unless he has no children (*baraita* in *b. Mo'ed Qaṭ.* 23a). Even an older man is expected to remarry: "R. Yannai said in the name of R. Shmuel bar Nahman, 'If you had no children in your youth, take a wife in your old age and raise children'" (*Gen. Rab.* 61.3).

138. There is a suggestion that one might not want to marry a divorced woman in case one's children are thought more likely to divorce: "They are the daughters of a divorced woman, why was their mother divorced?" (*m. Ned.* 9.9). This was not, however, considered an important barrier.

139. R. Meir (ca. 150 C.E.) said, "He who marries her that is divorced from her husband because of her evil conduct, is worthy of death; for he has taken a wicked woman into his house" (*b. Git.* 90b).

140. *b. Sanh.* 22a-b has a long discussion that starts with second-century C.E. sources but probably reflects earlier opinion. It starts with: "Rabbi Eliezer said, 'Anyone who divorces his first wife, even the altar sheds tears for him, as it is written, "And this you do as well; You cover the altar of the Lord with tears, weeping and moaning, so that He refuses to regard the oblation any more and to accept what you offer" [Mal. 3:13], and it is written, "But you ask, Because of what?" Because the Lord is a witness between you and the wife of your youth with whom you have broken faith, though she is your partner and covenanted spouse [Mal. 2:14].'"

141. If he married on a Wednesday, as normal, he would be tempted to work on Thursday and Friday, but if he married on a Thursday, it was hoped he would take the single day off.

woman would often be someone's second wife, as in the case of Babatha, whose documents were preserved in the Judean desert.[142]

The rabbinic system encouraged the remarriage of a divorcée or widow. The *ketubah* was set at half that of a virgin. The system also allowed a lower level of evidence in cases that prevented a woman from remarrying. From the time of Rabban Gamaliel the Elder in the first century, only a single witness was needed to establish that a husband was dead.[143] A divorcée who came to a town where she was not known did not even have to bring proof of her divorce. If she said that she was married and divorced, it was assumed that she was telling the truth.[144] If a rumor started that a so-called virgin was actually married, another rumor that she was also divorced was sufficient proof that she was available for remarriage.[145]

A woman with a substantial *ketubah* may not have wished to remarry, though a woman with the basic *ketubah* may have been forced to find financial support in a new marriage. The minimum *ketubah* of 200 *zuz* was about eight months wages for a day laborer,[146] and this alone would not support her. The common phrase for a divorcée or widow was that she would "return to her father's house" because she did not have sufficient income to be a householder in her own right. However, if her father or husband had added to the *ketubah*, or if she had inherited other wealth, she might prefer her independence.[147]

While a woman was married, any money she earned was controlled by her husband,[148] and she was expected always to be available to tend to house-

142. Babatha got remarried to Judah Khthusion who was already married to Mariamme and had a daughter from her.

143. *m. Yebam.* 16.7. Similarly R. Tarphon (*t. Yebam.* 14.10; *y. Yebam.* 16.5, 15d; cf. *m. Yebam.* 16.6), and Abba Yudan of Saidan relates that Gentile witnesses were permitted (*t. Yebam.* 14.7-8; *b. Yebam.* 126a). The Sages allowed evidence of the *bat qol* (*m. Yebam.* 16.6; cf. *t. Yebam.* 14.7). Rabbi permitted evidence of women (*b. Yebam.* 115a; cf. *m. Yebam.* 16.7). Even a criminal about to be hung was believed when he said he had killed a woman's husband (*t. Yebam.* 4.5; *y. Yebam.* 2.11, 4b; *b. Yebam.* 25b). The Sages confirmed that the ruling of Beth Hillel allowing the testimony of a woman who claimed her husband had died was based on an actual case (*m. Yebam.* 15.2; *b. Yebam.* 116b).

144. *m. Ketub.* 2.5 — it was assumed that if she wanted to hide the truth, she would not have mentioned that she was married.

145. *m. Git.* 9.9.

146. Matt. 20:2, 9. See Joachim Jeremias, *Jerusalem in the Time of Jesus* (London: SCM, 1969), p. 111.

147. The documents from the Judean Desert illustrate the variety of contracts. Salome daughter of Yohanan Galgoula had a *ketubah* of the standard 200 denarii, but Shelamzion, Babatha's step-daughter, had 500, and another was set at 2,000.

148. *m. Ketub.* 6.1.

hold duties.[149] An unmarried woman, however, could do business in her own name and had greater freedom of movement. Women were equal to men in almost every way in rabbinic Judaism, except in the realm of their fertility.[150] They could even be witnesses in court, so long as it concerned a matter within their area of expertise.[151] They could own land and goods in their own name and trade from their doorways in the communal courtyard.[152] A widow or divorcée may therefore have been happy to remain unmarried, but while they were fertile they were encouraged to remarry, both in the New Testament and in rabbinic Judaism.[153]

Remarriage Was Adulterous after an Invalid Divorce

There were a few circumstances where a woman could remarry without being properly divorced or widowed, or without having been properly married. Although these cases must have been rare, they were treated with utmost seriousness because she was technically guilty of adultery or fornication. Even though she was only "technically" guilty, she suffered the same consequences as if she had been deliberately immoral.

This was not the same as crimes that were considered morally equivalent to adultery, such as lust or touching a woman.[154] In those cases, although the

149. She was excused all positive laws that required fulfillment at a particular time, presumably to make sure that she could carry out her domestic duties (*m. Qidd.* 1.7-8).

150. This is the general conclusion of Wegner (*Chattel or Person?* esp. pp. 87-88, 115-27). They could also be seen as unequal in worship, but this was because they were not *required* to fulfill time-critical duties, and thus they could not do so on behalf of others. This meant that they could not read the Torah or lead prayers on behalf of the congregation (*m. Roš. Haš.* 3.8; *t. Meg.* 3.11; see Wegner, *Chattel or Person?* pp. 150-58).

151. Women could not be compelled to testify (*m. Šeb.* 4.1), and it was assumed that they would not be asked (*m. Sanh.* 3.4 does not include women in a list of possible witnesses). Yet their testimony was accepted, especially with regard to matters in which they might be considered to be knowledgeable, such as virginity. If they were the only witnesses who could declare that a woman had not been raped or that a husband had died, their testimony was accepted by the court (*m. Ketub.* 2.6; *m. Yebam.* 15.2). They could also swear that they had not embezzled goods in their care, just like a man (*m. Šeb.* 8.1; *m. B. Meṣ.* 7.8). See the useful discussion in Wegner, *Chattel or Person?* pp. 120-27.

152. Women could be stall-keepers (*m. Ketub.* 9.4), selling from a common courtyard (*m. B. Bat.* 2.3) or in their houses (*m. Šeb.* 7.8).

153. 1 Tim. 5:14. There is no similar injunction in rabbinic literature, but several factors, as detailed above, made it easier to marry a widow or divorcée than a virgin.

154. Jesus ruled that lust was equivalent to adultery (Matt. 5:28). This is paralleled in later rabbinic literature such as *Pesiq. R.* 24 (124b): "He who commits adultery with the eyes is called

person was considered to be morally guilty of adultery, there was no mention of punishment.[155] In the cases of **technical adultery**, which are described below, the woman suffers exactly the same punishments as a woman guilty of deliberate adultery. This does not include the death penalty, which fell into disuse in the beginning of the first century,[156] except in instances of mob rule such as described in John 8.

If a husband allocated an inadequate *ketubah* to her in the marriage certificate, the certificate was invalid.[157] The minimum was 200 *zuz* for a virgin and 100 *zuz* for a divorcée or widow, though it was customary to add to this according to one's means. After the reforms of Simeon ben Shetah[158] there was no

---

an adulterer"; and "He who touches the little finger of a woman is as one who touches a certain spot" (*b. Ber.* 24a).

155. Similarly, there were many crimes that made one morally guilty of murder. In the Talmud they are said to be "as if (כאילו) they had murdered." Examples include forgetting a halakah (*m. 'Abot* 2.10) or shaming someone in public (*b. B. Meṣ.* 58b; *b. Sanh.* 107a) or withholding wages (*b. B. Meṣ.* 112a) or robbing a poor man (*b. B. Qam.* 119a) or failing to procreate (Eliezer: *b. Yebam.* 63b; *b. Nid.* 13a) or not visiting the sick (*b. Ned.* 40a) or not escorting a stranger through danger (*b. Soṭa* 46b) or postponing alms on a feast day (*b. Sanh.* 35a). There is no mention of punishment of any kind, except in the world to come (*b. Sanh.* 107a). This is in contrast with Jesus' ruling that calling someone "fool" should result in a court appearance (Matt. 5:22). The use of כאילו more commonly indicates real equivalence that includes real consequences, such as when three women share a bed and one issues blood, it is "as if" they are all menstruants, whether they are expecting to menstruate or not (*m. Nid.* 9.5).

156. According to the Talmud, the death penalty was abolished soon after 30 C.E. ("forty years before the destruction of the Temple," *b. Šabb.* 15a; *b. Sanh.* 41a; *b. 'Abod. Zar.* 8a). Capital punishment was still administered outside the legal system, by the mob (e.g., John 8) or by zealous individuals (e.g., *m. Sanh.* 9.6). Sometimes the death penalty may have been carried out with semi-official authority, such as the beating to death of a priest who brought uncleanness into the temple (*m. Sanh.* 9.6). Most of this is undatable, and the reference to "40 years before the destruction of the Temple" may be figurative because several other events are dated to this time (*b. Yoma* 39a; cf. *b. Roš. Haš.* 31b). However, it is significant that there is no record of official death penalties, and rabbinic literature argues strongly against the use of the death penalty (*b. Nid.* 44b-45a; *m. Yebam.* 1.13), presumably to cover up the inability to carry it out. Some rabbinic rulings would make no sense if the death penalty were carried out for adultery: e.g., the rule that an unfaithful wife cannot marry her lover (*m. Soṭa* 5.1) and that if such a marriage took place, they had to divorce (*m. Yebam.* 2.8). There is one recorded death penalty for adultery (*m. Sanh.* 7.2, an old saying passed on by Eliezer b. Zadok, ca. 80-120 C.E.), but the woman was burned (instead of strangled as the law demanded), and thus this was probably a mob killing. Josephus's casual assertion that the penalty for adultery was death is probably an antiquarian note rather than a record of experience (*Ag. Ap.* 2.25). See the discussions in Epstein, *Sex Laws and Customs in Judaism*, pp. 201-2, 210-11; Abrahams, *Studies in Pharisaism and the Gospels*, p. 73.

157. This type of problem, unlike the others discussed here, could affect a first marriage as well as a remarriage.

158. See details in the previous chapter.

excuse for this amount to be less than the specified minimum because it had to be paid only if the husband divorced her without grounds, or if he died. If he assigned less than the minimum, and it was not noticed at the wedding, the marriage contract could retroactively be declared invalid.

R. Meir said the consequence of this was that the husband had been committing fornication because he had not been married.[159] It is possible that R. Meir's comment is hyperbole, because the woman could, nevertheless, get her full minimum *ketubah* by applying to a court.[160] However, the following examples suggest that he was simply stating the literal status of the crime.

Other examples of circumstances that could create an adulterous remarriage included a woman's remarriage after an invalid divorce. Two long passages in the Mishnah list the large number of consequences, which are the same as those that would be suffered by the woman if she had deliberately committed adultery. Even though the adultery happened by accident, and the fault (if any) belonged to the husband or the scribe or a witness who made an error, she still suffered almost the full consequences of the crime of adultery. One passage deals with cases where the woman is not properly divorced because of a technical problem with her divorce certificate.[161] The husband (or his scribe) may have made a mistake in writing the date or the name of the town, and this made the divorce certificate invalid. The other passage deals with the more difficult subject of proof that her husband is dead, if he died a long way from home. If news comes that he is dead and she remarries, and then if he returns, she has technically committed adultery with her new "husband."[162]

The consequences that are listed are the same in both passages. The following version of *Mishnah Gittin* 8.5 is based on Judith Wegner's translation, which includes extensive explanatory glosses:[163]

> If [the husband or his scribe] write [the writ of divorce] specifying the date of an inappropriate dynasty [i.e. he dated the writ by a dynasty not in power at the time and place of the divorce], [such as] the dynasty of the Medes or of the Greeks, or [if he wrote] specifying "so-and-so many years

159. *m. Ketub.* 5.1: "Anyone who assigns less than 200 to a virgin or one *maneh* to a widow it is as if he committed fornications" (בעילת זנות). This could also be translated "prostitution," which might be applicable because he was offering to pay a woman who was not his wife.

160. *m. Ketub.* 4.7: "If one had not written out a marriage settlement for her, if she be a virgin she may claim 200 or if she be a widow, one *maneh*, for that is a condition established by the Court."

161. *m. Git.* 8.5.

162. *m. Yebam.* 10.1.

163. Wegner, *Chattel or Person?* pp. 65-66.

after the building of the Temple" or "after the destruction of the Temple" [i.e. without specifying the ruling dynasty], [or] if [the scribe] was in the East [i.e. Babylonia] and [erroneously] wrote "in the West" or in the West [i.e. in the Land of Israel] and he wrote "in the East" [the following results ensue]: [The wife who remarried on the strength of the invalid *get*] must leave both men. [i.e. her first husband must divorce her for her technical adultery, and her second 'husband,' now recognised as her lover, must likewise send her away]. And she requires a writ of divorce from both men. [i.e. she needs a writ not only from the genuine husband but also from the spurious 'husband' for the sake of appearances.] And she is not entitled to [collect] *ketubah* money [from either man]. [i.e. she cannot collect from the first because her technical adultery forfeits her right to her marriage portion, and she cannot collect from the second because she was never validly married to him at all]. Nor [is she entitled to] usufruct [i.e. the accumulated interest on her property administered by the husband during the marriage]. Nor [may she receive] maintenance [any longer from either man]. [i.e. because she is no longer married to the one and was never married to the other]. Nor [may she receive indemnity for] depreciation [on her property]. [i.e. property administered by the husband during the marriage on condition that on divorce or widowhood she receive indemnity for any loss in value while the property remained in his hands]. [She cannot claim the aforesaid entitlements] from either husband. [i.e. she loses these rights against the first husband because the sages regard her as an adulteress. As for the second man, because she was never his legal wife, he never owed her these things in the first place.] If she has taken [any of the aforesaid entitlements] from either man, she must restore [them for she had no right to them]. And any child [of hers] by either man is illegitimate *(mamzer)*. [i.e. any child of the second 'husband' as well as any child she may bear to her first husband if she illegally returns to him on discovering her mistake will have the caste status of a *mamzer*]. And neither man may incur cultic pollution on her account. [i.e. if either man happens to be a member of the priestly caste and the woman dies, the husband may not contract cultic impurity by burying her corpse even though priests normally have a dispensation from this rule on the death of close relatives (Lev. 21.2)]. And neither man has a right to what she finds or to [the proceeds of] her labour, nor [has he the power] to annul her vows. [i.e. just as the woman loses her rights against both husbands, they lose their normal rights over her as wife. These, of course, are normally far fewer in number and value than the rights lost by the wife.] If she is an Israelite's daughter, she is disqualified from [subsequent] marriage into the priestly caste. [i.e. a member of the priestly caste may not marry a divorcee or an adulteress (Lev. 21.7)]. [If she is] a Levite's daughter, [she is disqualified] from eating tithe food [if she returns to her father's house]. [i.e. this penalty is imposed by the sages by analogy with mGit. 8.5 but without any basis in Scripture.] [If she is] a *kohen's* daughter [she is disqualified] from eating *terumah* food (heave-offerings) [should she return to live in her father's house]. [i.e. normally the daughter of a *kohen* who becomes widowed or divorced may return to her father's household and partake of priestly rations donated by Israelites to the priestly caste (Lev. 22.13). But this woman's "adultery" has "profaned" her father's holiness, so she loses the privilege (Lev. 21.9)]. And her heirs [begotten] of either man cannot inherit her *ketubah.* [i.e. if she dies before the two men divorce her, her children by both men lose their right to inherit her marriage portion on the father's subsequent death in the normal way (mKet. 4.10)]. And if either man dies [without male issue before divorcing her] his brother must release her [by *ḥalitzah*] and may not consummate levirate union [with her]. [i.e. if either man dies before giving the woman a writ of divorce, she is in the status of divorced-and-not-divorced and subject to the same rules as the doubtful widow discussed earlier]. If [her husband] had altered his name or her name or the name of his city or her city [in the writ of divorce] she must likewise leave both [the first husband and the one she married in error] and all of these [foregoing] conditions [apply] to her.

Therefore, a woman who had remarried and whose divorce was discovered to have been invalid could not continue to be married to either husband, and any children she had by them since the time of the "adultery" were considered as illegitimate. She had to be divorced by her new husband and by her first husband. She was divorced by her new husband for the sake of appearances, so there was no doubt that this marriage was over, and she lost her *ketubah* because she was considered an adulteress. She was also divorced by her first husband because her subsequent marriage to another man made her ineligible to him, according to the law of Deuteronomy 24:1-4. In this divorce she also lost her *ketubah* because she was treated as the guilty party.

There were also other circumstances that could lead to an adulterous remarriage. If a woman carried out a levirate marriage and later discovered that the marriage was invalid because they were blood relatives, the remarriage would be declared adulterous.[164] In the first century it was also possible to be given a divorce certificate that had already been declared null. The husband could send a divorce certificate via a messenger and then set up a court to annul

164. *m. Git.* 8.5-6.

it before it was delivered.[165] If the wife lived in a different town, she might not know that the divorce had been annulled and might remarry. The first-century Rabban Gamaliel said that this could not be allowed any longer. Later rabbis said that he did this to prevent the birth of illegitimate children.[166]

Some rabbis in the second century said that the punishment was unduly harsh, though they removed only the more extreme elements.[167] The rabbis appeared to recognize that the woman was innocent, but they found themselves unable to remove all the unfortunate consequences of her "adultery." They recognized that the man went entirely unpunished even though he was sometimes the cause of the problem.

One circumstance that might have caused this same problem was a divorce that had been approved by Hillelites but not by Shammaites. This might be expected to result in a remarriage that was considered adulterous by the Shammaites. However, this did not happen, because the **Hillelites and Shammaites** had a policy of **mutual recognition** of each other's rulings. This

165. *m. Git.* 4.1-2: "He who sent a writ of divorce to his wife and overtook the messenger . . . it is null. . . . If [he reached her] after the writ of divorce reached her possession, he no longer has the power to annul it. At first [such a husband] would set up a court in some other place and annul it. Rn. Gamaliel ordained that people should not do so, for the good order of the world."

166. *b. Git.* 33a: "To prevent abuses. What is referred to? R. Yohanan said: To prevent illegitimacy [ממזרים]."

167. These comments, which follow identically the consequence listed above, are found in *m. Yebam.* 10.1. The rendition is based on Wegner (*Chattel or Person?* pp. 66-67): "R. Yose rules that her *ketubah* [is a lien] on her first husband's property [i.e., because the first marriage remains valid until dissolved and the wife's honest mistake does not forfeit her right or that of her heirs to receive this money]. And R. Eleazar rules that the first [husband] has a right to what she finds and to [the proceeds of] her handiwork, and to annul her vows [i.e., because the first marriage remains valid until divorce and the true husband should not lose his rights in it]. R. Simeon rules that [with respect to the true husband, the rules of levirate marriage remain in force, so that] her intercourse [to consummate levirate union] or her *ḥalitza* release by the first husband's brother [if her returned husband now dies without male issue before divorcing her] exempts her co-wife [from levirate marriage and from *ḥalitza*] [i.e., this is so because, in R. Simeon's view, the first marriage remained valid, so she is a true levirate widow, and the levir's action in either marrying or releasing her exempts her co-wives by virtue of *m. Yebam.* 4.11]. And [R. Simeon further rules that] any issue from [the returned husband, before he divorces her] is not illegitimate *(mamzer)* [despite the intervening union that she has contracted with the levir] [i.e., R. Simeon considers the first marriage valid unless and until the first husband divorces her]. And [furthermore, in Simeon's view] if she remarried without [asking] permission [of the court] [i.e., in reliance on the testimony of two witnesses that her husband was dead, so that the court's permission was not needed] she is permitted to return to him [the first husband]. [i.e., Simeon restricted the penalty of adultery to a wife who only had one witness, and got special permission from a court to remarry. Even though the court gave her permission, Simeon still regards her as more culpable than a woman who waited for two witnesses.]"

meant that despite differences in matters of cleanliness and laws of divorce and marriage, they could still eat together and intermarry.

> Although the School of Shammai differed from the School of Hillel in regard to associate wives, sisters, a woman whose marriage is in doubt, an old bill of divorce, one who marries a woman with something worth a *peruṭa*, and a man who divorces his wife but she spends the night with him at the same inn, nevertheless the Shammaites did not refrain from marrying women from Hillelite families, nor the Hillelites women from Shammaite families.[168]

Marriages and divorces that were approved in a Shammaite court were also recognized as valid in a Hillelite court, and vice versa.[169] If one school had not recognized a marriage, the descendants of that marriage would have been counted as illegitimate for the next ten generations, and if they did not recognize a divorce, a subsequent remarriage would have been regarded as adultery and the children of that marriage would also be illegitimate. Therefore, if they did not recognize each other's rulings, the two communities would very soon find it impossible to intermarry because of fears of illegitimacy. It appears that they adopted a pragmatic approach to differences of opinion and decided to recognize each other's court rulings. This enabled them to live with each other in close proximity.

In the second century, this type of agreement presumably lapsed, because the schools of Hillel and Shammai ceased to exist. It is likely that the Rabbinate at Yavneh attempted to enforce a universally recognized set of circumstances that could be regarded as technical adultery. This is indicated by the order in which the final editor(s) of the Mishnah arranged the traditions at the end of tractate *Gittin*. *Gittin* 8.4-9 is an amalgamation of two sources that have been merged in an unexpected way. One source, which is a pair of Hillelite-Shammaite debates about uncertain divorces, has been split up so that the introduction to the debates occurs at 8.4 and the debates themselves at 8.8-9. The other source, which is a series of rulings about circumstances that lead to tech-

168. *t. Yebam.* 1.10; cf. *y. Yebam.* 1.6, 3b; *y. Qidd.* 1.1, 58d; *b. Yebam.* 14b; *m. 'Ed.* 4.8; *m. Yebam.* 4.1. A later tradition criticized disciples of the two schools who did not recognize each other's rulings: *b. Soṭa* 47b = *b. Sanh.* 88b: "When the disciples of Shammai and Hillel multiplied, who had not sufficiently served [discipleship], dissension increased in Israel and the Torah was made like two Torahs."

169. This may be due to the principle that "one Court cannot render void the word of another unless it is greater in wisdom and in number" (*m. 'Ed.* 1.5). However, this may be later than the schools, and each school might well have considered itself superior in wisdom to the others.

nical adultery, has also been split up by the insertion of the pair of Hillelite-Shammaite debates. The most likely explanation is that the editor(s) wished to show that the types of uncertain divorce in these Hillelite-Shammaite debates were subject to the rulings about technical adultery. The editor(s) may have realized that these two schools would have ignored the consequences of technical adultery in these circumstances, because of their mutual acceptance of their differences. However, the editor(s) wished to emphasize that technical adultery would no longer be ignored in these circumstances, and thus they inserted these rulings into a group of other rulings that were all subject to the consequences of technical adultery.

Therefore, a woman in the first century who remarried after an invalid divorce was treated as an adulteress even if the circumstances were completely outside her control, though this did not apply to matters where the schools disagreed. Children of the marriage were regarded as illegitimate, and she lost her rights to her *ketubah*. The next chapter will explore the way that Jesus declared all "any matter" divorces as invalid. He did not recognize the authority of other rulings, and so he declared that virtually every remarriage was a case of adultery.

Conclusions

Divorce in the rabbinic world of the first century could be based on the grounds of infertility, sexual unfaithfulness, or material and emotional neglect. Women were able to ask a court to persuade their husbands to divorce them if they suffered neglect. The Hillelites also allowed groundless divorces by interpreting the word דבר in Deuteronomy 24:1 as "[any] matter," but the Shammaites (and Jesus) said that "any matter" divorces were invalid. There was little stigma attached to divorce, and remarriage after a divorce was expected, though remarriage after an invalid divorce was considered to be adultery in a literal sense.

6. Jesus' Teaching

Divorce on Biblical Grounds Only

The Gospel accounts of Jesus' teaching on divorce are portrayed in Matthew 19 and Mark 10 as a debate with the Pharisees. The concluding statement on the matter is found in Matthew 5:32 and Luke 16:18. The highly abbreviated form of these accounts requires considerable unpacking, which is only possible by knowing what could be omitted because it was "obvious" to a first-century Jew. Fortunately the same subjects are debated in rabbinic literature and the Dead Sea Scrolls, which use very similar methods of abbreviation.

The Question

Mark 10:2: And Pharisees came up and in order to test him asked, "Is it lawful for a man to divorce his wife?"

2 Καὶ προσελθόντες Φαρισαῖοι[1] ἐπηρώτων αὐτὸν εἰ ἔξεστιν ἀνδρὶ γυναῖκα ἀπολῦσαι, πειράζοντες αὐτόν.

1. MS D omits Καὶ προσελθόντες Φαρισαῖοι and some editors of the United Bible Societies' text think that the phrase was assimilated from Matthew (Bruce Metzger, *A Textual Commentary on the Greek New Testament: A Companion Volume to the United Bible Societies' Greek New Testament,* 2nd ed. [Stuttgart: Deutsche Bibelgesellschaft, 1994], at Mark 10:2).

Matt. 19:3: And Pharisees came up to him and tested him by asking, "Is it lawful for a person to divorce his wife **for any matter**?"

3 Καὶ προσῆλθον αὐτῷ Φαρισαῖοι πειράζοντες αὐτὸν καὶ λέγοντες: εἰ ἔξεστιν ἀνθρώπῳ[2] **ἀπολῦσαι τὴν γυναῖκα αὐτοῦ κατὰ πᾶσαν αἰτίαν;**

The main differences between the accounts in Mark and Matthew, as marked in bold throughout this chapter, are the inclusion of the phrases **"for any matter"** and **"except for** (**a matter of**) **indecency"** in Matthew, the first of which occurs in this opening question. Most commentators have concluded that these phrases have been added by Matthew because the latter phrase is present in both Matthew 5:32 and 19:9, while they are absent from the parallels in Luke 16:18 and Mark 10:12. Although I will agree that Matthew has probably added these phrases to the tradition that he received, I will also argue that he has correctly reinserted something that was present in the original debate. These phrases (or their equivalent) were removed when the debate was summarized for oral or written transmission. They were so obvious and well known to the original audience that they were considered superfluous. They would have been mentally inserted whether they were included or not.

The phrases "any matter" and "except indecency" were the phrases that encapsulated the positions of the Hillelites and Shammaites, respectively, in their debate about the meaning of **ערות דבר**, *'ervat dabar,* in Deuteronomy 24:1 (as discussed in the previous chapter).

> The School of Shammai says: A man should not divorce his wife <u>except</u> if he found <u>indecency</u> in her, since it says: *For he found in her an indecent matter* [Deut. 24:1].
>
> And the School of Hillel said: Even if she spoiled his dish, since it says: <u>*[Any] matter.*</u>
>
> (*Sifré Deut.* 269.
> See also *m. Git.* 9.10; *y. Soṭa* 1.2, 16b)

These phrases would be well known by a large proportion of the Jewish population because they were the basis of divorce law. The phrase "any matter" is found in a very similar form in Philo and Josephus.[3] These legal phrases would

2. Some important MSS omit ἀνθρώπῳ (א B L 579 700), and one minuscule imports ἀνδρὶ from Mark. Metzger (*Textual Commentary,* at Matt. 19:3) points out these are mainly Alexandrian MSS, which might have preferred a more concise literary style, though he admits that scribes would be more likely to add the word than omit it.

3. Philo, *Spec. Leg.* 3.30 (2.304) καθ' ἣν ἂν τύχῃ πρόφασιν; Josephus, *Ant.* 4.253 καθ' ἁσδηποτοῦν αἰτίας.

have been as well known as similar legal phrases today, such as "irreconcilable differences," "decree absolute," "joint custody," and "maintenance." The phrases "any matter" and "a matter of indecency" were very important for lay persons to understand *before* they went to see a legal expert because their understanding of these would determine which legal expert they went to visit. If they wanted to punish an unfaithful partner through divorce, they would choose to go to a Shammaite court that would apply the interpretation "for a matter of indecency." If they wanted a divorce for a lesser matter or they did not want to go through the difficult and humiliating procedure of proving adultery or other faults, they would go to a Hillelite court that would apply the interpretation "for any matter." This is dealt with in greater detail in the previous chapter. Therefore this debate between the Hillelites and Shammaites, and these phrases that summarize the debate, would be well known by anyone who had a divorce in one's family or circle of friends.

First-century Jewish readers would have mentally inserted the phrase "for any matter" into the question that the Pharisees asked Jesus, whether or not it occurred in the text. They would have done this not only because they were familiar with the debate, but also because the question made no sense without it. The question "Is it lawful to divorce a wife?" could be answered only by "Yes, it says so in the Law." This question would make sense only if there was a portion of the Jewish world that did not allow divorce under any circumstances, so that the question would mean "Are you one of those who does not allow divorce?" However, as far as we know there was no such group. Some early commentators on the Qumran material concluded that those sectarians did not allow remarriage, and a few scholars suggested that perhaps they also forbade divorce, but, as was shown in chapter four, it is now clear that the Qumran community allowed divorce.[4]

If someone asked in a modern church context, "Do you believe in the Second Coming?" there would be no necessity to add the phrase "of Jesus Christ." Strictly speaking, the question is nonsense without this additional phrase, but the question is perfectly acceptable because everyone would mentally add the phrase "of Jesus Christ." Similarly, if someone asked "Should women have equality?" it would be unnecessary to add the phrase "in employment and education." However, if the question had been asked a century ago, the implied additional phrase would have been "in voting rights." Thus, a good historian who was reporting such a debate would add the phrase "in voting rights" even though it is likely that the original questioner omitted it. This is equivalent to Matthew's ad-

4. W. D. Davies struggles with this problem in his commentary. He regards this as a major reason for concluding that this whole debate is a post-Easter invention, though he thinks that it may still be possible to argue otherwise. See W. D. Davies and Dale C. Allison, *A Critical and Exegetical Commentary on the Gospel according to Saint Matthew*, 3 vols., International Critical Commentary (Edinburgh: T. & T. Clark, 1988-97).

dition of the phrase "for any matter" for the sake of his readers who were no longer entirely familiar with the terms of this debate within rabbinic Judaism.

The progression of the debate in the Gospels confirms that the phrase "for any matter" was implied in the opening question. The Pharisees harken back to the interpretation of Deuteronomy 24:1 when they bring up Moses' divorce certificate, because Deuteronomy 24:1-4 is the only text that deals with it. The phrase "any matter" will be discussed in more detail below, together with the exception clause.

Before Jesus gave an answer to their question, he diverted the debate into other matters concerning marriage and divorce, matters that he felt were more important.

Digression on Monogamy and Lifelong Marriage

Mark 10:6-9: But from the beginning of creation, *"He made them male and female"* [Gen. 1:27]. (7) *"For this reason a man shall leave his father and mother and be joined to his wife,* (8) *and the two shall become one flesh"* [Gen. 2:24]. So they are no longer two but one flesh. (9) What therefore God has joined together, let not man separate.

6 ἀπὸ δὲ ἀρχῆς κτίσεως ἄρσεν καὶ θῆλυ ἐποίησεν αὐτούς:[5] 7 ἕνεκεν τούτου καταλείψει ἄνθρωπος τὸν πατέρα **αὐτοῦ** καὶ τὴν μητέρα [καὶ **προσκολληθήσεται πρὸς** τὴν γυναῖκα αὐτοῦ],[6] 8 καὶ ἔσονται οἱ δύο εἰς σάρκα μίαν: ὥστε οὐκέτι εἰσὶν δύο ἀλλὰ μία σάρξ. 9 ὃ οὖν ὁ θεὸς συνέζευξεν ἄνθρωπος μὴ χωριζέτω.

Matt. 19:4-6: **He answered, Have you not read that** he who created them from the beginning *made them male and female* [Gen. 1:27], (5) **and said,** *"For this reason a man shall leave his father and mother and be joined to his wife, and the two shall become one flesh"* [Gen. 2:24]? (6) So they are no longer *two* but *one flesh.* What therefore God has joined together, let not man separate.

4 **ὁ δὲ ἀποκριθεὶς εἶπεν: οὐκ ἀνέγνωτε ὅτι** ὁ κτίσας[7] ἀπ' ἀρχῆς ἄρσεν

5. Several MSS read ὁ θεός instead of αὐτούς. Metzger (*Textual Commentary,* at Mark 10:6) suggests that a scribe wanted to make clear that "he" is not a reference to Moses, who was the last named subject.

6. Most MSS retain this phrase (missing only in ℵ B Ψ). Perhaps a scribe missed it due to the two occurrences of καὶ or perhaps it was assimilated from Matt. 19:5 or from Gen. 2:24.

7. Almost all MSS read ποιήσας instead of κτίσας (which is only in B Θ 1 124 700). Metzger (*Textual Commentary,* at Matt. 19:4) thinks it more likely that a scribe would change the

καὶ θῆλυ ἐποίησεν αὐτούς; **5 καὶ εἶπεν**: ἕνεκα τούτου καταλείψει ἄνθρωπος τὸν πατέρα καὶ τὴν μητέρα καὶ κολληθήσεται[8] τῇ γυναικὶ αὐτοῦ, καὶ ἔσονται οἱ δύο εἰς σάρκα μίαν. 6 ὥστε οὐκέτι εἰσὶν δύο ἀλλὰ σὰρξ μία. ὃ οὖν ὁ θεὸς συνέζευξεν ἄνθρωπος μὴ χωριζέτω.

Jesus did not appear at first to be interested in answering the question about the interpretation of Deuteronomy 24:1. He was more concerned with reminding the Pharisees that marriage was meant to be monogamous and lifelong. He used Genesis, partly because he wanted to point to the "beginning," and probably also because this was the standard proof text for monogamy. Polygamy was allowed in rabbinic Judaism, but it was beginning to fall out of favor, and there were groups within Judaism who disapproved of polygamy or even disallowed it.

The use of **Genesis 2:24** to prove monogamy was by this time very widespread, as indicated by the presence of the word "two" in almost all the ancient versions except the Hebrew.[9] It is possible that there was a Hebrew text that contained this variant, but the widespread use of this variant in ancient versions in contrast to the most influential Hebrew text suggests that there was either a theological reason for including it or a contrary theological reason for the rabbis to exclude it. The actual situation was probably a mixture of these two. The significant point, as far as the Gospel text is concerned, is that this variant text is used very self-consciously, with the additional comment "So they are no longer two but one" emphasizing the presence of the word "two."

The two texts, Genesis 1:27 and 2:24, are linked so that a single conclusion can be drawn from them. The activity of God in the first text is inferred in the second text, and thus it is God who joins them together. This type of exegesis was common in early rabbinic Judaism and was later called *gezerah shavah.*[10] The link between the two texts is presumably the next few words in Genesis 2:24-25: "the two were naked, the man and his wife." This exegesis would have been obvious to any intelligent listener and was not normally accompanied by any kind of explanation when it occurred in rabbinic literature or in the Targums.

The first text, Genesis 1:27, was part of a **standard proof for monogamy**, as seen in the Damascus Document:

---

text to ποιήσας, which conforms with the LXX, than change the text to κτίσας, which fits better with the Hebrew "create."

8. Many MSS read προσκολληθήσεται (א C G K L M Y Δ Π f1 118 124 1071 33 565 579 700 1424 τ), which agrees with Mark.

9. See chapter four for a discussion of polygamy and the use of this text.

10. See my *Techniques and Assumptions in Jewish Exegesis before 70 C.E.*, Texte und Studien zum antiken Judentum 30 (Tübingen: J. C. B. Mohr, 1992), pp. 17-18.

> CD 4.20–5.6:[11] . . . They are caught by two (snares). By sexual sin (זנות), (namely) taking (21) two wives in their lives, while the foundation of creation (ויסוד הבריאה) is "male and female he created them" [Gen. 1:27]. (5.1) And those who entered (Noah's) ark went in two by two into the ark [Gen. 7:9].

The two texts, Genesis 1:27 and 7:9, were cited together in order to prove that the writers' opponents, who allow polygamy, are guilty of breaking the Law. The texts are cited without any explanation, so this exegesis was probably well known. The two texts are linked by the words "male and female" (זכר ונקבה), which occur immediately after the text cited from Genesis 7:9.[12] This is exactly the same kind of linkage seen between Genesis 1:27 and 2:24 in the Gospel debate.

By linking the two texts the exegete can infer that "male and female" in 1:27 is further defined by the phrase "two by two" in 7:9. This means that the use of this phrase in 1:27 implied that marriage involved only two people. Marriage is not actually mentioned in 1:27, but in the following verse God tells the male and female to multiply. This verse was the basis of the rabbinic law that all men should marry and have children, and so marriage is implied in 1:27.

It is likely that these texts formed a well-known proof for monogamy. This is suggested by the fact that the wording in Mark and the Damascus Document is very similar. Both Mark and the Damascus Document cite exactly the same portion of Genesis 1:27, and they both precede the quotation with a very similar phrase. Mark refers to "the beginning of creation" (ἀρχῆς κτίσεως), while the Damascus Document used the phrase "the foundation of creation" (יסוד הבריאה); they are semantically identical.[13] In Matthew this similarity is

11. Based on James H. Charlesworth, *The Dead Sea Scrolls: Hebrew, Aramaic, and Greek Texts with English Translations,* 2 vols. (Tübingen: J. C. B. Mohr, 1995). This portion exists only in the Geniza MS A. CD has been found in Qumran fragments 6Q15 and 4Q226-73, but only a couple of words from this passage are found in these fragments.

12. This was pointed out in Evald Lövestam, "Divorce and Remarriage in the New Testament," in *The Jewish Law Annual,* ed. B. S. Jackson (Leiden: Brill, 1981), 4:50.

13. See F. F. Bruce, *Biblical Exegesis in the Qumran Texts* (London: Tyndale, 1959), p. 33. The phrases are not identical, and neither one uses the vocabulary of Genesis in Greek or Hebrew, but they are semantically equivalent. If this phrase in Mark was based on Genesis, one might expect the use of ποιέω (as in Gen. 1:1 LXX) instead of κτίσις for creation. However, κτίσις is common in Wisdom Literature (it occurs with ἀρχή in Prov. 8:22; Sir. 24:9; 36:14; 39:25; Pss. of Sol. 18:12), and phrases identical to ἀρχῆς κτίσεως are found in Mark 13:19; 2 Pet. 3:4, and one very similar to it is in Rev. 3:14. If this phrase in the Damascus Document was based on Genesis, one might expect the use of ברא, "create," instead of יסד, "found." The use of יסד may have been influenced by its use in Ezek. 13:14, which is alluded to in CD 8.12. In CD 8.12 the "builders

somewhat obscured because the phrase is changed to "he created them from the beginning." It is possible that this similarity occurred because Mark or Jesus was aware of the Damascus Document, but it is more likely that this was a widely known exegetical tradition.

This exegesis had great force because it showed that God himself put males and females together in pairs. From the opening phrase "beginning of creation" it might be supposed that the force of the argument lay in the fact that this is how it was done "in the beginning," but the emphasis was more likely to be on an act of God in creation. In other words, if God did something one way, we should follow his example. The same type of argument, based on an example given by God, is found in a Hillel-Shammai debate about how many children one has to have before one has fulfilled the command to "increase and multiply" (Gen. 1:28). The Shammaites argued that "two children" were sufficient based on the example of Moses (Exod. 18:2-3). The Hillelites said "a male and female" were sufficient, based on the example of God. The Hillelites won the debate because they cited a higher example than Moses.[14]

It is therefore likely that the use of Genesis 1:27 in this Gospel passage was due to this popular exegesis, which was normally linked with Genesis 7:9. The text was used for teaching that God joined males and females in pairs. The emphasis was on the fact that this was how it was in the beginning, when God the creator made everything perfect. The second half of this pair of proof texts, Genesis 7:9, has been lost in the abbreviated argument in the Gospels.

One might try to guess why the text from Genesis 7:9 was omitted. Perhaps this omission was deliberate, on the assumption that the audience would be able to supply the missing text mentally. However, this assumption supposes a very sophisticated audience. More likely the text was omitted in the mistaken belief that it was not necessary for the argument. A more generous conclusion would be that it was omitted knowing that any learned person would be able to fill the gap mentally, and that an unlearned person would not miss what was omitted. Whatever the reason, the text of Genesis 7:9 is not, strictly speaking, necessary for understanding the force of Jesus' argument.

---

of the wall" are also called the "whitewash-daubers" (טחי התפל; cf. Ezek. 13:14: טחתם תפל; cf. also NT parallels at Matt. 23:27; Acts 23:3), and these same "builders of the wall" are being addressed in CD 4.19. Therefore both Mark and the Damascus Document had influences that moved them away from the obvious vocabulary of Gen. 1:1.

14. *t. Yebam.* 8.4; *m. Yebam.* 6.6; *y. Yebam.* 6.6, 7c; *b. Yebam.* 61b-62a. Different versions have different rulings for the Shammaites. The Mishnah and Jerusalem Talmud have "two sons." The Babylonian Talmud has "2 males and 2 females." The Tosephta has two opinions: Nathan said it was "two children," and Jonathan said it was "male and female" (while Hillelite was "male or female").

What follows is an attempt to reconstruct the unabbreviated version. It would contain a reference to Genesis 7:9, and it might also have an extended quotation from Genesis 2:24, as suggested above. Therefore, a fuller version of Jesus' argument for monogamy might be:

> From the beginning of creation *"He made them male and female"* [Gen. 1:27], and those who entered (Noah's) ark *"went in two by two . . . into the ark, male and female"*[Gen. 7:9]. When taken together, these texts show that God created human males and females in pairs. Scripture also says: *"For this reason a man shall leave his father and mother and be joined to his wife, and they shall become one flesh, and the* two *were naked, the man and woman"* [Gen. 2:24-25]. This shows that they have been joined by God. So they are no longer two but one flesh. What therefore God has joined together, let not man separate.

The argument has three stages that flow naturally from one to the next. First, Jesus put together Genesis 1:27 and 7:9 in a well-established way to show that human "male and female" groups should be made up of two people, not three or more in a polygamous marriage. Then he moved to another standard proof text for monogamy based on "two" in Genesis 2:24-25, which was linked to the previous verses by a phrase similar to "male and female."

Jesus then combined these two standard proofs for monogamy in order to argue something new: that marriage should be lifelong. In the first proof based on Genesis 1:27 and 7:9, the male and female are joined together by God — God put the animals together and brought them to the ark in pairs, and God created the man and woman and blessed them and told them to multiply. In the second proof for monogamy, based on Genesis 2:24-25, we are not told who joins them together as one flesh. By taking the two proofs together, one can conclude that they have been joined by God.

This leads into Jesus' final and startling statement: Whom God has joined, **let no man separate**. The word "separate" (χωρίζω) is a standard term meaning "to divorce," with almost exactly the same semantic field as the word ἀπολύω, "to divorce" (literally, "to release"), which was used in the Pharisees' question to Jesus. The word χωρίζω was probably used because it formed a better antonym to "join." If ἀπολύω had been used, the meaning would have been something like "Whom God has bound, let no one release." The picture of God's activity in Genesis 1:27 is much more that of someone who "joins" than someone who "binds." In verse 27 God has the role of a parent who finds a spouse for his child, and in verse 28 God is like the priest or rabbi who "blesses" them when he joins them at their wedding.

The couple bind themselves to each other by means of the vows in a marriage contract, and so it is not God who binds them but they who bind themselves. Malachi portrays God as the witness to these vows (Mal. 2:14), as one who urges them to be faithful to their vows (v. 15), and even as one who is angry when the vows are broken (v. 16). God is not portrayed as one who "binds" them together. God "joins" them together, but they "bind" themselves.

This distinction between "joining" and "binding" is emphasized in the use of the imperative "let no one separate." Many commentators understand this as though it read "no one **can** separate," but both Matthew and Mark use the imperative χωριζέτω, which implies that it is possible for couples to separate, but they are being asked or commanded not to. Jesus asked or commanded them to keep their marriage vows and not to break up the marriage in which God has joined them together. They have bound themselves by marriage vows, and they have been joined together by God. Jesus implied that it is a sin to break the marriage bond by breaking these vows.[15]

As far as Jesus was concerned, this is a suitable answer to the Pharisees' question, but they are not satisfied. Jesus wanted to emphasize that marriage is lifelong, and he felt that this was far more important than arguing about the allowable grounds for divorce. However, he had not provided his thoughts on the meaning of Deuteronomy 24:1, and so the Pharisees asked another question to bring him back to the topic that interested them.

Moses' Teaching

> Mark 10:3-5: **He answered them,** What did Moses command you? (4) They said, Moses allowed a man to write a certificate of divorce, and to put her away. (5) But Jesus said to them, For your hardness of heart he wrote you this commandment.
>
> 3 **ὁ δὲ ἀποκριθεὶς εἶπεν αὐτοῖς:** τί ὑμῖν ἐνετείλατο Μωϋσῆς; 4 οἱ δὲ εἶπαν: ἐπέτρεψεν Μωϋσῆς βιβλίον ἀποστασίου γράψαι καὶ ἀπολῦσαι.

15. David Daube (*The New Testament and Rabbinic Judaism* [London: Athlone, 1956], p. 73) proposed a very different explanation of the word "joined." He suggested that this is a reference to the rabbinic haggada about the androgynous Adam, who had both male and female organs before Eve was created. This was deduced from the mixing of singular and plural in Gen. 1:27: "God created him; male and female he created them." This tradition was known to Philo, and rabbis tell us that the LXX said "a male with his female parts created he them" or "male and female created he him" (*Gen. Rab.* 1:26-27; *Mek. Exod.* 12:40). No surviving LXX manuscripts contain this wording. This may possibly be an underlying theme, but it does not fit in with the overall theme of Jesus' exposition.

5 ὁ δὲ Ἰησοῦς εἶπεν αὐτοῖς· πρὸς τὴν σκληροκαρδίαν ὑμῶν ἔγραψεν ὑμῖν τὴν ἐντολὴν ταύτην.

Matt. 19:7-8: **They said to him,** Why then did Moses command one to give a certificate of divorce, and to put her away? (8) He said to them, For your hardness of heart Moses allowed you **to divorce your wives, but from the beginning it was not so.**

7 **λέγουσιν αὐτῷ**· τί οὖν Μωϋσῆς ἐνετείλατο δοῦναι βιβλίον ἀποστασίου καὶ ἀπολῦσαι [**αὐτήν**];[16] 8 λέγει αὐτοῖς ὅτι Μωϋσῆς πρὸς τὴν σκληροκαρδίαν ὑμῶν ἐπέτρεψεν ὑμῖν **ἀπολῦσαι τὰς γυναῖκας ὑμῶν, ἀπ' ἀρχῆς δὲ οὐ γέγονεν οὕτως.**

Matthew and Mark use the material at the beginning of this section differently. In Matthew the Pharisees asked Jesus a further question to bring him back to the subject of their original question after he had digressed. In Mark this is a question asked by Jesus immediately following the original question from the Pharisees.[17] This difference will be discussed later in the chapter with regard to deciding which account is closer to the original interaction between Jesus and the Pharisees. It will be suggested below that Matthew is likely to be closer to the original because

a. Mark's account is smoother and more suitable for presentation in a sermon, while Matthew's account is more like a debate, and
b. Mark's version loses the subtle force of the difference between "command" and "allow."[18]

In Mark the word **"command"** is put on the lips of Jesus, and the Pharisees answered using the word **"allow,"** which is the reverse of Matthew's ac-

16. The MS evidence for this is equivocal.

17. Robert H. Gundry (*Matthew: A Commentary on His Handbook for a Mixed Church under Persecution* [Grand Rapids: Eerdmans, 1994], p. 379) discusses another difference: Mark speaks about *writing* a divorce certificate while Matthew speaks about *giving* it. The Shammaites probably regarded the writing of the divorce certificate as the only necessary act in divorce, while the Hillelites said that three acts were necessary: writing, giving, and sending away. This Shammaite doctrine is difficult to establish, but it seems to be implied in their debate about when a man may change his mind (*m. Git.* 8.8). However, both Gospel writers also mention "and release her," which implies in this context "send her away," and thus it cannot be said that Jesus sides with the Shammaites in Mark with regard to this matter.

18. Gundry (*Matthew,* p. 379) argues that Mark's version is original because Matthew's shows signs of his typical editing style. However, he also concedes that Matthew's version makes more sense and may reflect the original debate.

count. Mark's account has to have the words this way because Jesus was responding to the question "Is it lawful for a man to divorce his wife?" It would be inappropriate for Jesus to respond with "What did Moses allow?" because anything the Law said was regarded as a command. In Matthew the Pharisees use "command," but they could equally well have said "allow." It is therefore significant in Matthew that the Pharisees speak about Moses' command, and that Jesus answers that Moses "allowed" them to divorce.[19]

There was only one situation in which the early rabbis thought that Moses "commanded" divorce. This was the case of adultery, as dealt with in Deuteronomy 24:1-4. In early Judaism it was generally considered necessary to divorce a wife even if she was only suspected of adultery. In the previous chapter we saw that divorce was not actually compulsory for suspected adultery until after 70 C.E., but it was generally considered to be the correct thing to do, and presumably it was already starting to be regarded as compulsory by many rabbis. The text to prove this would have been Deuteronomy 24:1 because this speaks about giving a divorce certificate to a woman who was guilty of a "matter of indecency." Although there was a dispute about the exact meaning of this phrase, there was general agreement that it included adultery.[20]

The Pharisees introduced this teaching about compulsory divorce on the grounds of adultery at this point in order to counter Jesus' argument that God wants marriage to be lifelong. They were saying, in effect, that the Law "commands" divorce in some situations, and so marriage cannot be regarded as lifelong. This reply also brought Jesus back to the text in Deuteronomy 24:1 about which the Pharisees wanted to ask Jesus. This was a very strong argument used to force Jesus to answer their question. By arguing that Moses "commanded" divorce for adultery, they left no room for Jesus to say that a pious person could avoid divorce.

Jesus answered that Moses did not "command" divorce, but he "allowed" it. The implication is that even in a case of adultery, divorce is not mandatory.

19. This distinction between "command" and "permit" was first noted by Abel Isaksson, *Marriage and Ministry in the New Temple: A Study with Special Reference to Mt.19.13[sic]-12 and 1.Cor.11.3-16,* trans. Neil Tomkinson and Jean Gray, Acta Seminarii Neotestamentici Upsaliensis 24 (Lund: Gleerup; Copenhagen: Munksgaard, 1965), pp. 102, 121.

20. In modern translations, there is no command to give a divorce certificate because Deut. 24:1-4 is treated as a series of conditions: "IF a man marries, and IF she doesn't find favor, and IF he writes a divorce certificate, etc., and IF she remarries, and IF he divorces her or dies, THEN her first husband cannot remarry her." This is the translation assumed in the LXX, but Matt. 5:31, 1 Cor. 7:15, and Josephus, *Ant.* 4.253 all assume that it means: "Whoever divorces his wife, let him give her a certificate of divorce." See Andrew Warren, "Did Moses Permit Divorce? Modal *weqatal* as Key to New Testament Readings of Deuteronomy 24:1-4," *Tyndale Bulletin* 49 (1998): 46.

The text in Deuteronomy 24:1 is completely ambiguous. It could be translated as either "he should" or "he may."[21] The Pharisees who were debating with Jesus interpreted it as "should," or perhaps "must," while Jesus interpreted it as "may."

This teaching prompts a further question: What about adultery that is persistent and unrepentant? Jesus' comment on **"hardness of heart"** answered that question. The "hardness of heart" comment is also treated differently by Mark and Matthew, though the difference is minor. Mark has positioned it before the digression on monogamy, where he used it as an introduction to a discussion of the sinless ideal. Matthew put it after this digression, and thus it became a summary; he completed the summary by adding "but from the beginning it was not so."

Jesus says that Moses allowed divorce because of human stubbornness. "Hardness of heart" has been interpreted by some as if it means "sinfulness,"[22] but the Old Testament use of the word suggests that "stubbornness" would be a closer meaning for a first-century Jew. The word used for "hardness of heart" (σκληροκαρδίαν) is a combination of σκληρός, "hard" or "stubborn," and καρδία, "heart." This combined word occurs elsewhere only in Mark 16:14 (the stubborn disbelief of the disciples), and in a few OT texts where it means "stubbornness."[23] The two words occur as a phrase in contexts that indicate stubbornness.[24] There is no occurrence of the word or phrase in any context that might suggest that it meant "sinfulness."[25]

By itself, the concept of "stubbornness" is unexpected and ambiguous in this context. Does it mean that stubbornness was a ground for divorce, or that the person who initiated the divorce was acting stubbornly? Or does it suggest that the Israelites were stubbornly demanding that Moses allow them to divorce, or that they were stubbornly refusing to give divorce certificates to their former wives? The only one of these for which there is any evidence is the last. As was seen in chapter two, wives were not able to remarry in the ancient Near

21. See Warren, "Did Moses Permit Divorce?" He concludes that the grammar is ambiguous but a linguistic analysis supports Jesus' interpretation.

22. Davies and Allison (*Saint Matthew*, pp. 14-15) are clearer than most.

23. Deut. 10:16 and Jer. 4:4, both concerning the need to circumcise one's heart; Prov. 17:20, concerning the man who does not prosper; Ezek. 3:7, concerning Israel who refuse to listen; Sir. 16:10, concerning the stubborn multitude. The Hebrew equivalent is קשׁה or חזק, "harden" with לב "heart." This occurs frequently, and always with the meaning of "stubborn," though occasionally this has the good sense of "strong-willed" or "courageous" (e.g., 2 Sam. 13:28; Ps. 27:14).

24. Deut. 2:30; 2 Chron. 36:13; Ps. 95:8; Isa. 63:17; Acts 7:51; Rom. 2:5; Heb. 3:8, 15; 4:7.

25. Rom. 2:5 might be an exception, but the sense of "stubborn" fits just as well.

East without a specific release by their former husbands, and Moses' law of the divorce certificate forced Israelite husbands to do this. However, it is very unlikely that Jesus would refer to this ancient context of which none of his contemporaries would have been aware.

It is likely that the phrase "hardness of heart" is an allusion to an Old Testament text because the word is an invention of the Septuagint. It is possible that it refers to Psalm 95:8, which speaks of the stubbornness of the Israelites in the wilderness, but there is nothing there to explain the link between stubbornness and divorce. It is much more likely that it is a reference to the stubbornness in **Jeremiah 4:4 LXX**, which has a very clear link with the subject of divorce in general and Deuteronomy 24:1 specifically:

> Circumcise yourselves to your God and circumcise your hardness of heart.
>
> περιτμήθητε τῷ θεῷ ὑμῶν καὶ περιτέμεσθε τὴν σκληροκαρδίαν.

This occurs after the appeal to Judah in chapter 3 to heed the warning of what happened to Israel, who was divorced by God. The chapter opens with the only clear allusion to Deuteronomy 24:1-4 in the Old Testament:

> Jer. 3:1: If a man divorces his wife and she goes from him and becomes another man's wife, will he return to her? Would not that land be greatly polluted? You have played the harlot with many lovers; and would you return to me? says the LORD.

Jeremiah went on to describe how Israel was divorced because of her adulteries and because she stubbornly refused to repent:

> v. 3: . . . you have a harlot's brow,[26] you refuse to be ashamed.
>
> v. 13: Only acknowledge your guilt, that you rebelled against the LORD your God and scattered your favors among strangers under every green tree, and that you have not obeyed my voice, says the LORD.
>
> v. 17: . . . they shall no more stubbornly follow their own evil heart.
>
> v. 20: Surely, as an unfaithful wife leaves her husband, so have you been unfaithful to me, O house of Israel, says the LORD.

26. Cf. Ezek. 3:7: "all the house of Israel are of a **hard forehead** and of a stubborn heart." LXX reads πᾶς ὁ οἶκος Ἰσραὴλ φιλόνεικοί εἰσι καὶ σκληροκάρδιοι, "all the house of Israel are stubborn and hard-hearted."

If this is the context to which Jesus was alluding, the stubbornness is that of the unfaithful partner who refused to repent. This fits very well into the context of Jesus' teaching that divorce is not compulsory.

The Pharisees were suggesting that Moses "commanded" divorce in the case of adultery, but Jesus said that divorce was "allowed," not "commanded," by Moses. The innocent partner could forgive the unfaithful one and decide not to divorce him or her. Jesus appeared to imply that the divorce law should only be used if the guilty partner was stubbornly refusing to repent and give up the adulterous behavior, as in the case of Israel in Jeremiah.

This agrees with **Jesus' teaching on forgiveness** in Luke:[27]

> Luke 17:3-4: Take heed to yourselves; if your brother sins, rebuke him, and if he repents, forgive him; (4) and if he sins against you seven times in the day, and turns to you seven times, and says, "I repent," you must forgive him.

A modern reader might regard this as a very difficult ethical standard, but a contemporary first-century Jew would probably regard this as thoroughly scandalous. Some of this scandal is seen in Hosea, when he is told to marry an adulterous woman and take her back when she is unfaithful to him. Despite the fact that this was supposed to portray God's attitude of forgiveness to Israel, it was still very difficult for Hosea to face the public scandal of such an action. It was considered very suspect when a man refused to divorce his unfaithful wife, which is why Joseph is described as righteous for wanting to divorce Mary, who appeared to be unfaithful (Matt. 1:19). As seen in the previous chapter, even a case of technical adultery was treated with severe penalties. Perhaps the reason for this was the possibility that adultery could produce illegitimate children.

Jesus was less concerned with illegitimacy and the religious propriety of the time than with the principle that marriage was meant to be lifelong. Both partners should do all they can to make sure that their marriage survives. This means that both partners should take care to fulfill their marriage vows, but also that they should be ready to forgive a partner who breaks the marriage vows and subsequently repents. However, divorce is "allowed" if one partner stubbornly continues to break the vows, as Israel did when God divorced her.

Jesus had still not answered the original question. Finally, after he had spoken about many matters about which he was not asked, he answered the specific question that he *was* asked.

27. The version in Matt. 18:21-22 does not mention anything about repenting, but it should probably be inferred.

Answering the Question

Mark 10:10-12: **And in the house the disciples asked him again about this matter.** (11) **And he said to them,** Whoever divorces his wife and marries another, commits adultery **against her;** (12) **and if she divorces her husband and marries another, she commits adultery.**

10 **Καὶ εἰς τὴν οἰκίαν πάλιν οἱ μαθηταὶ περὶ τούτου ἐπηρώτων αὐτόν.**
11 **καὶ λέγει αὐτοῖς:** ὃς ἄν ἀπολύσῃ τὴν γυναῖκα αὐτοῦ καὶ γαμήσῃ
ἄλλην[28] μοιχᾶται **ἐπ' αὐτήν:**[29] 12 **καὶ ἐὰν αὐτὴ ἀπολύσασα τὸν ἄνδρα
αὐτῆς γαμήσῃ ἄλλον μοιχᾶται.**[30]

Matt. 19:9: **And I say to you:** whoever divorces his wife, ***unless for indecency,*** and marries another, commits adultery.

9 **λέγω δὲ ὑμῖν** ὅτι ὃς ἄν ἀπολύσῃ τὴν γυναῖκα αὐτοῦ **μὴ ἐπὶ πορνείᾳ**[31]
καὶ γαμήσῃ ἄλλην μοιχᾶται.[32]

Luke 16:18: **Every one** who divorces his wife and marries **a different one** commits adultery, **and he who marries a *woman divorced* from her husband commits adultery.**

18 **Πᾶς** ὁ ἀπολύων τὴν γυναῖκα αὐτοῦ καὶ γαμῶν **ἑτέραν** μοιχεύει, **καὶ ὁ ἀπολελυμένην ἀπὸ ἀνδρὸς γαμῶν μοιχεύει.**

Matt. 5:31-32: It was also said, "Whoever divorces his wife, let him give her a certificate of divorce." (32) But I say to you that every one who divorces his wife, ***except for*** **a matter of *indecency,* makes her an adulteress; and whoever marries *a divorced woman* commits adultery.**

31 Ἐρρέθη δέ: ὃς ἂν ἀπολύσῃ τὴν γυναῖκα αὐτοῦ, δότω αὐτῇ

28. The omission of "and marries another" in W is probably just an error, as is shown by its presence in the related family 1, 209 (see D. Parker, *The Living Text of the Gospels* [Cambridge: Cambridge University Press, 1997], p. 79).

29. The difficult term "against her" is omitted by a couple of MSS of W (1, 2542) and the Sinaitic Syriac.

30. A few MSS swap the clauses, starting with "If a woman divorces her husband . . ." then "and if a man divorces his wife . . ." (W [1, 2542]).

31. Some MSS harmonize with Matt. 5:32 to various degrees, especially adding λόγου, "a matter of" (B D f1 f13 33 69 788 1346). Some have "makes her an adulteress" instead of "commits adultery" (C* N f1 B).

32. Most MSS add καὶ ὁ ἀπολελυμένην γαμήσας, μοιχᾶται, "and he who marries a divorced woman commits adultery" (this, and variants, is found in all MSS except ℵ C D L S 2 69). Metzger (*Textual Commentary,* at Matt. 19:9) suggests that this was assimilated from Matt. 5:32.

ἀποστάσιον. 32 ἐγὼ δὲ λέγω ὑμῖν ὅτι **πᾶς ὁ** ἀπολύων τὴν γυναῖκα αὐτοῦ **παρεκτὸς λόγου πορνείας ποιεῖ αὐτὴν μοιχευθῆναι, καὶ ὃς ἐὰν ἀπολελυμένην γαμήσῃ, μοιχᾶται.**[33]

The answer was presented in various versions, which have been subjected to diverse degrees of abbreviation. The process of abbreviation will be discussed below. There is also a difference between Matthew and Mark concerning the recipients of this answer: Mark gives this answer to the disciples in private; Matthew implies that it was given in public, to the Pharisees, and that the next section on optional marriage (Matt. 19:10-12) was given to the disciples in private. This difference will be discussed below, with regard to which version came first.

The meaning of the answer that Jesus gave has been the subject of much debate, mainly because it is inherently difficult. At first glance it appears to be illogical and to contradict Pauline teaching. It appears to be illogical because it charges a person who remarries with the very specific crime of "adultery," which a remarried person is not guilty of in any known legal system. It appears to contradict Pauline teaching because Paul seems to allow divorce, and possibly remarriage, in only one circumstance: when someone has been deserted by an unbelieving partner (1 Cor. 7:15). It appears that Jesus does not allow for divorce, or he allows it in only one circumstance, which is different from Paul's.

Putting aside, for the moment, the differences in the various versions of the answer, the core of Jesus' answer was:

> "Whoever divorces his wife and marries another commits adultery."

The difficulty in this answer lies in the word **"commit adultery"** (**μοιχεύω**). The word and its cognates occur twenty-seven times in the New Testament and very frequently in the Septuagint and other literature, always with the specific meaning of illegal sexual activity with a person who is married to someone else.[34] It is used for translating the commandment "Do not commit

33. καὶ ὃς ἐὰν ἀπολελυμένην γαμήσῃ, μοιχᾶται is omitted by D and a few other MSS. Metzger (*Textual Commentary,* at Matt. 5:32) suggests that a pedantic scribe felt it was superfluous.

34. The survey of contemporary literature by F. Hauck ("μοιχάω," in *Theological Dictionary of the New Testament,* ed. Gerhard Kittel, 10 vols. [Grand Rapids: Eerdmans, 1964-95], 4:729-35) has no examples of other meanings. The only possible exceptions are found in the rule of Jesus and various rabbis that someone who lusts after a woman has committed adultery with her. Yet here, too, adultery is taken in the strict sense of illegal sexual relations with someone else's spouse, though the sexual activity is not physical. Jesus' ruling in Matt. 5:28 is paralleled in *Pesiq. R.* 24 (124b): "He who commits adultery with the eyes is called an adulterer"; *b. Ber.* 24a: "He who touches the little finger of a woman is as one who touches a certain spot."

adultery" (Matt. 5:27; 19:18; Mark 10:19; Luke 18:20; James 2:11) and for accusing the woman "caught in adultery" (John 8:3-4), and in one text the term is helpfully defined for us:

> Rom. 7:3: Accordingly, she will be shown to be an adulteress (μοιχαλίδα) if she lives with another man while her husband is alive.

Bruce Malina complained that this is as illogical as saying "Everyone who sells his TV set and buys another commits theft."[35] It may be more accurate to say that it is equivalent to: **"whoever repossesses someone's car and sells him another, commits theft."** The act of adultery can be compared to stealing another person's property, especially in a society where marriage contracts are written out like a deed of purchase. Repossessing a car is perfectly legal, but it carries a social stigma, much as divorce did. An onlooker is never sure whether there was deliberate failure to keep up the payments, or whether the purchaser's finances suddenly changed and he was unable to pay. Similarly, selling another car to him might make people gossip, like remarrying after a divorce. Although it is perfectly legal to sell him another car, one wonders if the seller is taking advantage of him. As a result, one may call the seller "avaricious" or "mercenary," but one cannot call him a thief. Similarly, a person who has legally divorced and legally remarried, might be called inconstant or immoral, but he cannot be called an adulterer.

A few commentators have suggested that divorce was valid but remarriage was not, so that the person who takes another wife is committing adultery.[36] However, this would again fall outside the normal meaning of "adultery," which always involved illegal sex with a married person. If the divorce was valid, this was not adultery but fornication (i.e., sex with an unmarried person).

The solution that almost all commentators have found is to assume that the divorce was invalid. This solution works very well, because if **the divorce was invalid,** the person was still legally married to the first partner, so the second marriage was adulterous. This solution will now be examined for all **four scenarios** that are described in the various versions of Jesus' answer:

35. Bruce J. Malina, *The New Testament World: Insights from Cultural Anthropology,* rev. ed. (Louisville: Westminster/John Knox, 1993), p. 120.

36. This is usually based on the earlier understanding of the so-called "divorce" texts found in Qumran documents, as discussed in chapter four. These were thought by some earlier commentators to show that the Qumran community allowed divorce but not remarriage. It is now becoming clear that divorce was accepted at Qumran, and the subject of the "divorce" texts was polygamy.

1. A man who marries an invalidly divorced woman commits adultery (Luke 16:18; Matt. 5:32).
2. A man who invalidly divorces his wife causes her to commit adultery (Matt. 5:32; variants of Matt. 19:9).
3. A man who invalidly divorces his wife and marries another commits adultery (Mark 10:11; Matt. 19:9; Luke 16:18).
4. A woman who invalidly divorces her husband and marries another commits adultery (Mark 10:12).

The first scenario would be recognized by anyone in Jewish society. As outlined in the previous chapter, a woman who accidentally married two men in this way was treated as an adulteress in a very literal way, even if the fault was not hers. Even if she did not know that her divorce was invalid when the marriage took place, she would suffer all the penalties of someone who deliberately committed adultery.[37]

The second scenario assumes that the woman would remarry.[38] Many commentators have assumed that it was virtually certain that a divorced woman would remarry for financial reasons. It could be said, therefore, that her ex-husband was forcing her to remarry, and thus he could be said to be responsible. However, as seen in the previous chapter, it was quite likely that a divorced woman would wish to remain unmarried. Many women had sufficient financial security in their *ketubah,* especially if this had been added to by their father. Divorced women also had considerable freedom that they might not wish to give up by remarrying.

These factors are not really a problem here. Matthew 5:32 is not trying to state a case in water-tight legal terms. It is an abbreviation down to the barest minimum, which was the normal way to record legal rulings (see below). It is clearly implied in the same verse that the invalidly divorced woman commits adultery only if she remarries. The force of this phrase is not that the woman will inevitably commit adultery. It is teaching that *if* she remarries, and thereby commits adultery, then a portion of the blame lies with the man. This emphasizes a point that was insufficiently stated in rabbinic literature: the woman who is guilty of technical adultery is not often to blame. As outlined in the pre-

37. As stated in the previous chapter, this did not include the death penalty, which fell into disuse before the first century C.E., except in cases of mob rule, as described in John 8.

38. A few commentators, such as Parker *(The Living Text of the Gospels),* say that the woman is "made to appear like an adulteress" by being divorced. However, it was well known that divorce could be for "any matter," and if the husband suspected adultery, the correct course of action was to subject her to the rite of *sorah,* for the suspected adulteress. Therefore, the fact of a divorce did not imply the woman had been unfaithful.

vious chapter, invalid divorces were usually caused by a mistake by the husband or the scribe, not by the wife.

The third scenario would be difficult for most Jews at the time to accept because it was technically impossible for a man to commit adultery by marrying an unmarried woman. He was allowed more than one wife, and so it was no crime for him to remarry, even if his divorce to his first wife was invalid. However, Jesus had already stated his belief in monogamy, which meant that a man had to be validly divorced before he could remarry. Strictly speaking one might say that he was guilty of polygamy rather than adultery when he married his second wife. Yet Jesus was making the point very strongly. He was saying not only that polygamy was immoral but that it was illegal. He gave scriptural proofs that polygamy was against God's will. This meant that the man's second marriage was invalid, and thus he was cohabiting with an unmarried woman.

Cohabiting with an unmarried woman was not, strictly speaking, adultery, because adultery was a crime against the husband of a woman. It was regarded as immoral, but it did not fall within the definition of the legal term "adultery." When a man married, he could not vow exclusive faithfulness because he was allowed more than one wife. This meant that one could not commit adultery against a wife, only against a husband. Mark added a phrase that indicates why this situation was nevertheless called "adultery." He pointed out that the man was committing adultery "against her" (Mark 10:11), that is, against his wife.[39] In a polygamous society, adultery is always against the husband. Mark was pointing out that one of the consequences of Jesus' teaching about monogamy was that adultery was no longer a crime just against a husband, but also against a wife. The husband could no longer hide behind the fact that technically he had not vowed exclusive faithfulness when he married. Marriage was meant to be monogamous, which meant that both husband and wife owed exclusive faithfulness to each other, and either could be the victim of adultery.

In the fourth scenario most commentators argue that Mark was addressing a non-Jewish context since Jewish women were not able to divorce their husbands. However, as seen in the previous chapter, it was perfectly proper for a woman to bring a divorce case to a Jewish court, and there are indications that this was practiced in the first century. Strictly speaking, the divorce was still carried out by the man because, if the court decided in the woman's favor, they would force the man to write her a divorce certificate. However, apart from ac-

39. This translation, which is found in the RSV and other versions, is defended well by John Nolland ("The Gospel Prohibition of Divorce: Tradition History and Meaning," *Journal for the Study of the New Testament* 58 [1995]: 19-35).

tually providing the certificate, the whole process of divorce could be carried out by the wife. She could decide whether or not to proceed with a divorce or whether to forgive her husband when he broke the marriage vow, and she could call the court and present the facts in court. There is even some evidence that she could hire a scribe to write out a divorce certificate on her husband's behalf. An early 2nd century divorce certificate has been discovered in a Judean desert cave which was written by a scribe on behalf of a woman who wanted to divorce her husband.[40] The wording is very similar to the type of certificate used by men who divorced their wives for "any matter." It is becoming increasingly evident that Jewish life in Palestine did not always conform to the rabbinic rules.

Many commentators have found significance in the fact that only Mark mentions divorce initiated by a woman, and they argue that Mark was writing to non-Jewish readers. They say that Jewish women could not divorce their husbands, which is mistaken, as shown above. However, it was not really necessary to spell out to a Jew that women as well as men were liable to this command. Jewish women were liable to all the negative commandments to which men were liable (*m. Qidd.* 1.7). If a man was prohibited from remarrying after an invalid divorce, it would be assumed by any Jew that a woman was similarly prohibited.

Therefore, the assumption that Jesus refers to invalid divorce fits all the four scenarios named in the various versions of Jesus' answer. This solution makes Jesus' answer consistent and understandable by any contemporary listener. What is *not* clear in this answer is the *reason* why the divorces should be considered invalid. The clue to this lies in the exception clause.

The Exception

Matt. 19:9: except for indecency

μὴ ἐπὶ πορνείᾳ

Matt. 5:32: except for a matter of indecency

παρεκτὸς λόγου πορνείας

It was argued above, with regard to the question, that the extra clause "for any matter" that is present in Matthew was necessary for the question to make

40. See the discussion of papyrus Ṣe'elim 13 in the previous chapter. Nolland ("The Gospel Prohibition of Divorce," p. 31) has suggested that the curious use of the passive ἀπολύσασα may indicate that the woman has gone to the rabbinic court and forced herself to "be divorced."

sense. If the clause had been omitted, most intelligent Jews of the day would have mentally added it. It will be argued here that the same is true of the exception clause, which is also found only in Matthew. The question of whether Matthew has added it or Mark has removed it will be discussed below, but I suggest that its inclusion is so obvious in this context that any intelligent Jew would have mentally supplied it if it were missing.

I would similarly add an exception to Jesus' words at Matthew 5:28: "But I say to you that anyone who looks at a woman lustfully has already committed adultery with her in his heart." We mentally add the words "except for his wife." We regard this exception as unnecessary, because one cannot commit "adultery" with one's wife, and because we see nothing wrong with sexual lust within marriage. Some of the early Church Fathers gave "adultery" a broader meaning, and they felt that lust *was* harmful even within marriage. Theophilus therefore felt constrained to add an exception clause to this verse and quoted it as: "Whosoever looks on a woman who is not his own wife, to lust after her, has committed adultery with her already in his heart."[41] Similarly, there is overwhelming need to add an exception to Matthew 5:22: "Whoever is angry with his brother is liable to judgment," because otherwise Jesus himself is guilty.[42] Many manuscripts have added "without cause" (εἰκῇ) in order to supply this exception,[43] though only the most legalistic readers would regard it as necessary.

It is not unusual for Matthew to add material that doesn't appear in Mark, and it is not contradictory for Matthew to add an exception to what appears in Mark as an absolute statement. In Mark 8:11-12 the Pharisees asked Jesus for a sign, to which he replied: "Amen, I say to you, no sign shall be given to this generation." This absolute statement has an exception in Matthew 12:39: "No sign shall be given to (this generation) except [εἰ μὴ] the sign of the prophet Jonah."

In the analogy used above, of a man who repossesses someone's car and then sells him another, the question might be: **"Is it lawful to repossess someone's car?"** This question makes no sense because the answer is obvious: a vendor has every right to repossess a car if the loan repayments are not kept up. Yet suppose this question was asked in a state that had just passed a new law that extended the rights of repossession. The new law stated that any car salesman could, for any reason, repossess a car that had not yet been fully paid for, and he only need return the deposit. This type of new law would create a lot of debate. In that context, if someone asked "Is it lawful to repossess someone's car?" any-

41. Theophilus, "To Autolycus," *Early Church Fathers* 3.13.

42. Jesus was "angry" in Mark 3:5, and he called the Pharisees "fools" in Matt. 23:17, 19.

43. $\aleph^2$ D L W Θ and others.

one hearing this question would mentally add the words "for any reason," or "unless repayments were suspended."

This analogy is not perfect, but the new Hillelite divorce law in the first century C.E. was actually fairly similar to this supposed situation. A Hillelite court allowed a husband to divorce his wife, for any reason, and he needed only to return the dowry. Any money that his wife had earned during their marriage, or any goods that she had made, all belonged to him. The work and wages of his wife during their marriage, to which she lost all rights when she was divorced, are like the payments that someone makes on a car loan, which are lost when the car is repossessed.

The new Hillelite ruling[44] did not require any valid grounds for the divorce and allowed divorce for any reason. Therefore when contemporary Jews heard the question "Is it lawful to divorce your wife?" they would have mentally added the words "for any reason." Similarly, when they heard the reply "Whoever divorces his wife . . . ," they would have mentally added the phrase "except for valid grounds."

Another analogous situation would be someone from Arizona who visits New York and asks **"Is it lawful to carry a handgun?"** In Arizona an adult can carry a handgun without needing a license, while in New York only law enforcement officers and certain security agents with a special license can carry one. The New Yorker will therefore answer: "No one can carry a handgun, and if they do so, and injure someone, they will be guilty of attempted murder." The New Yorker could have added "except for law enforcement officers," but he correctly assumed that this was unnecessary, though if he had been speaking to an Englishman he might have done so. He might also have added that "If a law enforcement officer accidentally kills someone, when he is carrying a gun legally, he is guilty only of manslaughter." Again, this is unnecessary because the point has been made that someone who carries a gun illegally cannot argue that he injured someone accidentally.

One final analogy will bring the comparison back to the subject of divorce and remarriage. Suppose a Muslim from a traditional Islamic country brings his family to live in a Western country, and he wishes to divorce his wife. He knows that in traditional Islamic law he only needs to say to his wife in Arabic: "I divorce you. I divorce you. I divorce you," and the divorce is complete. Yet he has heard that divorce is somewhat more complicated in Western law, and so he goes to ask the Imam in his local mosque about divorce. He asks:

44. The procedure of divorce for any cause was already widespread, as was seen by Philo (*Spec. Leg.* 3.30), Josephus (*Ant.* 4.253), and Sirach (25:26), but the Hillelite exegesis gave it a new validity that it lacked before.

"Is it lawful for me to divorce my wife in this country?" The long answer to this question would be: "No, you can't divorce her unless you have valid grounds, and if you carry out the traditional Islamic divorce and then remarry, you are committing adultery." Yet the questioner knows that divorce is possible (it is often referred to in Friday sermons about the decadence of the West), and so the Imam will probably give a shorter answer, such as, "No, you can't divorce her, and if you do, and remarry, you will be committing adultery."

In all of these analogies the two speakers share some common background knowledge. The question about repossession takes place in the context of a debate about a new law. The question about handguns takes place in the context of the debate about gun control and different state laws. The question about Muslim divorce takes place in the context of attitudes towards divorce in different types of society. The questioner and the questioned understand each other in each example. In the same way, the question to Jesus about divorce took place in the context of an ongoing debate about the meaning of "matter of indecency." There was no need for the long versions of the question or the answer because both sides understood the exceptions. They were concerned about the general principles, not the exceptions that were obvious.

Much has been made, by some commentators, of the complexity of **the grammatical construction** "whoever does D (divorces), except in the case of P *(porneia),* and does R (remarries) is guilty of A (adultery)." This construction has been interpreted in three main ways:

1. whoever does D and R, let alone P, is guilty of A;
2. whoever does D, which is impossible except in the case of P, and does R is guilty of A; and
3. whoever does D and R, and does not fit into the class of P, is guilty of A.

The first interpretation was suggested by Augustine and can be paraphrased as: "anyone who divorces his wife, setting aside the matter of *porneia,* which I am not discussing at present, and remarries, commits adultery." This was defended by Bruce Vawter,[45] though he later admitted that the Greek syntax does not support it.[46] The second interpretation is that of G. J. Wenham[47] and has the

45. Bruce Vawter, "The Divorce Clause of Mt 5,32 and 19,9," *Catholic Biblical Quarterly* 16 (1954): 155-67.

46. Bruce Vawter, "Divorce and the New Testament," *Catholic Biblical Quarterly* 39 (1977): 528-42.

47. G. J. Wenham, "The Syntax of Matthew 19.9," *Journal for the Study of the New Testament* 28 (1986): 17-23, and William A. Heth and Gordon J. Wenham, *Jesus and Divorce* (London: Hodder & Stoughton, 1984), pp. 113-16.

advantage of following the word order in Greek. However, Wenham was unable to find another example of this type of construction anywhere in the Gospels or other ancient literature. The third interpretation is the most common, and very similar constructions are found in rabbinic literature, for example:

> R. Eliezer said: "**If** a man divorced his wife, saying to her, You are hereby permitted to any man **except** So-and-so, **and** she went and married some other man and was widowed or divorced, **then** she is permitted to marry the man to whom she had been forbidden." (*b. Git.* 83a)[48]

The difference between the two exception formulae (παρεκτὸς in ME.5 and μὴ ἐπὶ in Mt.19) is not significant. Although there may be slight differences in the way that these two constructions are employed in Greek, they can both be seen as an attempt to translate the common Hebrew construction "**לא . . . אלא**" which literally means "not. . . but," and is best translated "except."

Much has been made by other commentators of the fact that the exception clause is not "except for valid grounds" but is **"except for indecency"** (**πορνείᾳ**). It has been assumed, understandably, that this means Jesus only recognized one ground for divorce, which he called πορνείᾳ (Matt. 19:9) or λόγου πορνείας, "matter of indecency" (Matt. 5:32). I will argue here that he used the term λόγου πορνείας because this was the best translation of the phrase **ערות דבר** in Deuteronomy 24:1, on which the Hillelites based their new rule. Therefore he used the exception "except for indecency" because he was replying to a question about the meaning of this phrase.

The meaning of πορνείᾳ is not nearly as clear-cut as μοιχεία, adultery.[49] It has a wider range of connotations throughout the area of sexual sin and impropriety, including the act of adultery. Its use in Hebrews 13:4 makes it very clear that it means more than just adultery, because it says: "let the marriage bed be undefiled; for God will judge the immoral (πόρνους) and adulterous (μοιχοὺς)." Some have claimed that it covers a much wider area, including physical abuse and even mental torture, so that Jesus specifically allowed divorce on these grounds too. However, there is no evidence for this.[50] Others

48. His sayings can be dated in the late first or early second century C.E., and they normally represent conservative views that differ from the innovations of his contemporaries. It might be argued that in this example there is a very clear link between the first "if a man divorce" and the "except" clauses, but this was also the case in Jesus' saying. Jesus was alluding to the rabbinic debate that was summarized as "A man should not divorce his wife except for a matter of indecency" (*m. Git.* 9.10).

49. Lövestam ("Divorce and Remarriage in the New Testament") gives a good summary of the situation. In his thesis he studied eleven different interpretations.

50. E.g., Ken Crispin, *Divorce, The Forgivable Sin?* (London: Hodder & Stoughton, 1988).

have suggested that it covers only the very narrow meaning of "incest." Although the philological evidence for this argument is weak, it has had much support, and so we need to examine it in more detail.

The LXX uses πορνείᾳ to translate the Hebrew זנות, *zenut,* which is used for immorality and also specifically for incestuous marriages and other illegitimate forms of marriage. If this were the meaning of πορνείᾳ in the exception clause, it would translate something like "except for illegitimate marriages." Joseph Bonsirven first suggested this possibility,[51] and many have been persuaded by his argument,[52] especially after J. A. Fitzmyer suggested that the Qumran documents appeared to add weight to it.[53] Other scholars pointed out that זנות is used for the full range of sexual immorality, including adultery, in the Old Testament,[54] intertestamental literature,[55] and Qumran scrolls.[56] The word πορνεία is used in the sense of "incestuous or illegitimate marriage" in some of its NT occurrences. Bonsirven listed 1 Corinthians 5:1; Acts 15:20, 29; 21:25; Hebrews 12:16, though not all of these are equally convincing. The 1 Corinthians 5 reference is convincing because its context speaks about a case of incest, though not of incestuous marriage. All the references in Acts refer to the Council of Jerusalem decree that included πορνεία as one of the things the Gentiles should avoid. Although it is likely to include "illegitimate marriages," there is no reason why it should not also refer to other forms of sexual immorality. Similarly, the

51. Joseph Bonsirven, *Le divorce dans le Nouveau Testament* (Paris: Société de S. Jean l'Evangéliste, Desclée & Die, 1948), esp. pp. 46-60.

52. E.g., James R. Mueller, "The Temple Scroll and the Gospel Divorce Texts," *Revue de Qumran* 10 (1980): 247-56; Tord Fornberg, *Jewish-Christian Dialogue and Biblical Exegesis,* Studia Missionalia Upsaliensia 47 (Uppsala: 1988), pp. 17-18; Augustine Stock, "Matthean Divorce Texts," *Biblical Theology Bulletin* 8 (1978): 24-33; G. J. Wenham, "Matthew and Divorce: An Old Crux Revisited," *Journal for the Study of the New Testament* 22 (1984): 95-107; Heth and Wenham, *Jesus and Divorce,* ch. 7.

53. J. A. Fitzmyer, "The Matthean Divorce Texts and Some New Palestinian Evidence," *Theological Studies* 37 (1976): 197-226.

54. Lövestam, "Divorce and Remarriage in the New Testament," esp. p. 57; Craig L. Blomberg, "Marriage, Divorce, Remarriage, and Celibacy: An Exegesis of Matthew 19.3-12," *Trinity Journal* n.s. 11 (1990): 161-96. Lövestam points out that *zenut* is used side by side with "adultery" (*na'af/moicheuein* and derivatives) in, e.g., Hos. 1:2; 2:4; Jer. 3:1-3; Ezek. 16:38-41; 23:37, 43-45; etc.

55. Lövestam ("Divorce and Remarriage in the New Testament") points to *T. Jos.* 3.8; 4.6; *T. Levi* 14.6; *T. Asher* 2.8.

56. J. Kampen, "The Matthean Divorce Texts Re-examined," in *New Qumran Texts and Studies: Proceedings of the First Meeting of the International Organization for Qumran Studies, Paris, 1992,* ed. George J. Brooke and Florentino Garcia Martinez, Studies on the Texts of the Desert of Judah 15 (Leiden: Brill, 1994), pp. 149-67, esp. pp. 157, 161. Kampen finds the term referring to sex in a state of impurity in 4QDe, with a parallel in 4QDb, and to harlotry in 4QpNah 3 ii 7.

reference in Hebrews 12:16 and all the other occurrences of πορνεία in the NT can include the meaning of "illegitimate marriage," but one would also expect it to include sexual immorality in general. The Qumran evidence that Fitzmyer pointed to in CD 4.19–5.11 shows **זנות** being used with the meaning of "illegitimate marriage" in a passage that had been thought to parallel Jesus' teaching on divorce. However, as pointed out in chapter four, the so-called "divorce" passages at Qumran are concerned solely with polygamy, not divorce. Therefore, although Bonsirven has demonstrated that πορνεία *can* mean "illegitimate marriage," this is only part of a wide range of meanings that includes all other forms of sexual sin and impropriety.

If the narrow meaning of πορνεία as "incest" were correct, which seems unlikely from the philological evidence above, it would not make good sense in the context of Jesus' teaching. Jesus was criticizing those who use a divorce certificate too freely. Matthew said that he allowed it to be used for the case of πορνεία. In the case of incest, however, there is no need for a divorce certificate because the marriage would be considered invalid from the start. The rabbis did not consider that any marriage had taken place.[57] A relatively early ruling in the Mishnah makes it clear that in this kind of situation "they are not betrothed."[58] If no betrothal took place, any marriage is equally invalid, and there is no need for a divorce.

The most likely reason for using the term πορνεία or λόγου πορνείας is that this is the most accurate **translation of ערות דבר** (Deuteronomy 24:1 "indecent matter"), especially in terms of the Hillelite-Shammaite debate. It is clearly not based on the Septuagint, which translated this phrase as ἄσχημον πρᾶγμα, "a shameful matter." The words λόγος and πρᾶγμα can probably be regarded as synonymous in this context, but ἄσχημον, which means "shameful" or "naked," has much wider connotations than πορνεία and does not always refer to sexual shame (e.g., Exod. 20:26; 22:27; 28:42; Deut. 23:13-14; 25:3; Ezra 4:14). The Septuagint translation is more accurate in a word-for-word sense because **ערוה** literally means "nakedness." However, in the context of the Hillelite-Shammaite debate, and in the context of Deuteronomy 24, the sexual implica-

57. This point is argued strongly by Philip Sigal, *The Halakah of Jesus of Nazareth according to the Gospel of Matthew* (New York, London, Lanham, Md.: University Press of America, 1986), pp. 100-101. It is a principle called *kiddushin einan tofsin*, "a valid betrothal is not transacted" (*m. Qidd.* 2.7; *b. Yebam.* 10b; 44b; 52b; 69a; 92b; *b. Ketub.* 29b; *b. Qidd.* 64a; 67b; 68a; *b. Soṭa* 18b; *b. Sanh.* 53a; *b. Tem.* 29b). It may be possible that a conscientious Jew would issue a *get* for the sake of public propriety, but this would not be necessary.

58. *m. Qidd.* 2.7. This ruling cannot be dated, but the anonymous nature of the story attached to it suggests that the event occurred at least one or two generations earlier than the final editing of the Mishnah in about 300 C.E.

tions of πορνείᾳ make much more sense. It is general enough to include any sexual immorality that might be implied by ערוה without forcing a decision about whether this means adultery (as the Shammaites argued) or more general sexual impropriety.

The order of the words λόγου πορνείας in Matthew 5:32 is the reverse of the natural order and is of particular significance. It is likely that this word order was deliberately intended to reflect the Shammaite interpretation because they reversed the order of the words in the biblical text in this same way, in order to emphasize their interpretation of Deuteronomy 24:1:

> The School of Shammai says: A man should not divorce his wife except he found in her a matter of indecency (דבר ערוה), as it is said: *For he finds in her an indecent matter* (ערות דבר). (*m. Git.* 9.10)

Therefore it is likely that the exception that occurs in Matthew is a literal translation of ערות דבר in Deuteronomy 24:1 in a way that summarizes the Shammaite interpretation. This fits in with the fact that the extra phrase in Matthew's version of the question is a summary of the Hillelite interpretation of the same words.

In conclusion, contemporary Jews would have mentally added something like this exception, whether it was present or not. They would either have added "except for valid grounds" (if they were thinking of divorce in general) or "except for indecency" (if they were thinking just about Deuteronomy 24:1). In Matthew the clause "except for indecency" was used because the whole incident, as he reported it, is concerned with the debate about Deuteronomy 24:1.

The Short Versions

Two short versions of the divorce teaching are found at Matthew 5:31-32 and Luke 16:18.

> Matt. 5:31-32: It was also said, "Whoever divorces his wife, let him give her a certificate of divorce." (32) But I say to you that every one who divorces his wife, **except for a matter of indecency, makes her an adulteress;** and whoever marries a divorced woman commits adultery.
>
> 31 Ἐρρέθη δέ: ὃς ἂν ἀπολύσῃ τὴν γυναῖκα αὐτοῦ, δότω αὐτῇ ἀποστάσιον. 32 ἐγὼ δὲ λέγω ὑμῖν ὅτι πᾶς ὁ ἀπολύων τὴν γυναῖκα αὐτοῦ **παρεκτὸς λόγου πορνείας ποιεῖ αὐτὴν μοιχευθῆναι,** καὶ ὃς ἐὰν ἀπολελυμένην γαμήσῃ, μοιχᾶται.

> Luke 16:18: Every one who divorces his wife **and marries a different one** commits adultery, and he who marries a woman divorced from her husband commits adultery.
>
> 18 Πᾶς ὁ ἀπολύων τὴν γυναῖκα αὐτοῦ **καὶ γαμῶν ἑτέραν** μοιχεύει, καὶ ὁ ἀπολελυμένην ἀπὸ ἀνδρὸς γαμῶν μοιχεύει.

These same phrases are also found in the longer versions, which were dealt with above. However, they present the teaching in such an abbreviated form that it would be difficult for a reader to understand them unless he were familiar with the longer versions. This is particularly difficult in Luke's Gospel, which does not contain the longer version and does not even have the exception clause. The clues in the context of the debate are missing in these short versions, and so there is nothing to tell the reader how to understand the text. If the texts might be misleading in this way, why were they included?

These words may have been directed at **Herod Antipas** as well as at the Pharisees.[59] This is seen in the context of the Matthean version and in the precise wording of the Lukan version. The context in Matthew is a section of three related sayings in the Sermon on the Mount, Matthew 5:21-32. They can be summarized as:

> Matt. 5:21-26: "You think that you are innocent of murder, because you only did it in your heart? You *are* guilty of murder."
>
> Matt. 5:27-30: "You think that you are innocent of adultery, because you only lusted in your heart? You *are* guilty of adultery."
>
> Matt. 5:31-32: "You think that you are innocent of adultery because you have a divorce certificate? You *are* guilty of adultery."

The three sayings can be applied to Herod Antipas. He desired Herodias, his brother Philip's wife (cf. 5:28 regarding lusting in your heart), then divorced his own wife without sufficient grounds (cf. 5:32a regarding divorce except for indecency), and then married Herodias who had divorced her husband (cf. 5:32b regarding marrying a divorced woman).

The precise wording of the Lukan version fits the actions of Herod Antipas particularly well. It describes the actions of Herod, who divorced his

59. This is well argued in William F. Luck, *Divorce and Remarriage: Recovering the Biblical View* (San Francisco: Harper and Row, 1987), pp. 88-90, 98, 111-29. It was perhaps first suggested by F. Crawford Burkitt (*The Gospel History and Its Transmission,* 2nd ed. [Edinburgh: T. & T. Clark, 1907]), though it is incipient in the comments of Tertullian, *Marcion* 4.34.

wife in order to marry Herodias, and Herodias, who divorced her husband Philip in order to marry Herod (Josephus, *Ant.* 18.110-12). The verb describing the woman as ἀπολελυμένην, "divorced," is usually translated as a passive, but it could also be a reflexive middle, which would fit Herodias better because she initiated the divorce herself. This makes sense in the context of Luke where the Gospel speaks about the ministry of John the Baptist (in v. 16). John was the only person who stood up against Herod and told him that he was acting sinfully.

The more serious problem with these shorter versions is the misunderstanding that they can produce in a reader. When Jesus' conclusion is removed from the context of the debate, it is impossible for a reader to understand the meaning. However, if we assume that the Early Church allowed divorce for adultery, and possibly for other Old Testament grounds (as argued in the next chapter), all readers of Luke's Gospel would be aware of divorces occurring. They would therefore realize that this highly abbreviated saying had further complexities behind it.

Abbreviating the Answer

Abbreviation was a common procedure in the ancient world, as it also is in the modern world. The subject of abbreviation was an area of academic study in the schools of rhetoric, although this is probably not the best place to learn about how abbreviation occurred in the New Testament. A better model for the New Testament is rabbinic literature, which has debates that are abbreviated in similar ways, and for similar reasons.

It is evident that even the longer accounts in Mark 10 and Matthew 19 were abbreviated because a verbatim account would be inappropriately long. However, the amount and style of abbreviation are important to recognize, because sometimes the argument has been obscured by the omission of important elements. In particular, the exegesis has been severely abbreviated. I have suggested above that a citation of Genesis 7:9 has been omitted, and that the quotation of Genesis 2:24 has been shortened. Fortunately we can fill in the gaps from the Damascus Document, which uses precisely the same argument, and from other rabbinic exegeses, which shorten texts in the same way. The omission of the exception clause and part of the question from some versions is not problematic because any contemporary Jewish reader would have inserted them, though this would have created problems very quickly when the Gospel texts were used with non-Jewish audiences.

To understand why and **how the texts were abbreviated,** it is instructive to look at rabbinic literature. None of the rabbinic literature that has survived is contemporary with the NT, and even the Mishnah was edited in the late second or early third century. Despite this, there are instructive parallels between these two sets of literature, as Birger Gerhardsson showed.[60] Both of them faced the problem of preserving a valuable oral tradition in a context where a written copy was not immediately appropriate. They both employed similar methods of abbreviation and memorization.

Rabbinic law was passed on from teacher to disciple in oral form, and before the Mishnah was written at the beginning of the third century it was never passed on in written form, though students might have used written notes to aid their memory. Rulings were therefore abbreviated down to their absolute minimum and were arranged in balanced phrases that were easy to remember. Anything that was implicit or obvious was omitted for the sake of brevity. This often makes individual rulings difficult to understand outside the context of the debate that prompted them.

An example of rabbinic abbreviation was seen in the last chapter with regard to the formula used in a divorce certificate. The actual certificate contained the words "And this shall be to you from me a writ of divorce and bill of release and *get* of dismissal that you may be married to any man you wish." The rabbinic abbreviation "Lo, you are permitted to any man" implied the whole of this written formula and also established links with other laws about emancipation that were relevant to the divorce certificate.

The accounts of the **Hillelite-Shammaite divorce dispute** that are preserved in rabbinic literature demonstrate the principles of abbreviation that they employed. In the main account in the **Mishnah** the dispute is recorded in an abbreviated but relatively full form:

> The School of Shammai says: A man should not divorce his wife except if he found a matter of indecency in her, since it says: *For he found in her an indecent matter.* And the School of Hillel says: Even if she spoiled his dish, since it says: *For he finds in her an indecent matter.* (*m. Git.* 9.10)

60. Birger Gerhardsson, *Memory and Manuscript,* Acta Seminarii Neotestamentici Upsaliensis 22 (Uppsala, 1961). Jacob Neusner originally criticized Gerhardsson severely for using rabbinic literature to illustrate methods of transmission in the NT. However, in his foreword to the edition republished by Eerdmans in 1998, he says that he had mistakenly overlooked the fact that Gerhardsson had recognized this problem and had merely tried to show that the two types of literature shared a common set of problems that they solved in a similar way.

The *Sifré* preserves what appears to be an older account[61] that contains fuller accounts of the exegesis used by both sides:

> The School of Shammai says: A man should not divorce his wife except if he found indecency in her, since it says: *For he found in her an indecent matter* [Deut. 24:1].
>
> And the School of Hillel said: Even if she spoiled his dish, since it says: *[Any] matter.*
>
> The School of Hillel said to the School of Shammai, Since it said *matter* [in Deut. 24:1] why did it [also] say *indecency,* and since it said *indecency,* why did it also say *matter?* Because if it said *matter* and it did not [also] say *indecency* I would say: She who is discharged because of a *matter* is permitted to remarry, but she who is discharged because of *indecency* may not be permitted to remarry.
>
> And do not be surprised [that she should be forbidden to remarry]. If she is forbidden [to marry] him [her first husband] who had been permitted to her, [why should she] not be forbidden from him who had been forbidden to her?
>
> As Scripture teaches: *Indecency . . . and she leaves his house and goes and becomes the wife of another* [Deut. 24:1-2].
>
> And if it said *indecency* and it did not [also] say *matter,* I would say: She may go because of *indecency* [but] she may not go because of a *matter.*
>
> As Scripture teaches: *A matter . . . and she leaves his house* [Deut. 24:1-2].[62]

Even in the longer *Sifré* account, the exegesis is highly abbreviated and difficult to follow. The exegesis in *Sifré* shows that the Shammaites argued that the word "indecency" was superfluous in the Hillelite interpretation. The Hillelites countered by saying that the word "indecency" was necessary in order

61. It is difficult to decide on the relative ages of the accounts of this debate. The *Sifré* account appears at first to be an amalgamation of *m. Git.* 9.10 and the *baraita* in *b. Git.* 90a. However, the Mishnah account appears to be more highly edited, with a more exact balancing of the Shammaite and Hillelite arguments, which also implies the fuller argument found in the *baraita.* The *Sifré* account is less highly edited, as is seen by the deficiency where Shammai's first reply is missing. The reply was presumably something like: If "matter" means "any matter," then "indecency" is redundant. This gap is made up in the *baraita.* The shorter version of the Shammaite account, as found in *Sifré,* is also the same as the one preserved in *y. Soṭa* 1.2. It therefore seems likely that the *Sifré* account is the older, and the Mishnah account is an abbreviation of it. The *baraita* preserves the rest of the *Sifré* account in an unabbreviated form but is edited to restore a balanced debate.

62. *Sifré Deut.* 269, ed. Finkelstein 288.

to show that even someone who was divorced for indecency was allowed to remarry.[63]

The Mishnah account is more highly edited than the *Sifré* account. It preserves only the opening exchanges of the debate, but it balances the weight of the Hillelite and Shammaite arguments. Most of the exegesis is omitted from the Mishnah account, but it is implied when the Mishnah extends the quotation of the Hillelites from the one word "matter" to "For he finds in her an indecent matter." The inclusion of the full quotation by the Hillelites reminded the scholar of the rest of the exegesis, so there was no need to record it in full, as in *Sifré*.

The account of this debate was further abbreviated in a later discussion that is preserved in the **Jerusalem Talmud**. In that discussion a later rabbi was trying to show that a particular halakah of R. Eliezer followed the Shammaites. To do so, he quoted only the Shammaite part of the debate:

> The School of Shammai says: A man should not divorce his wife except if he found indecency in her. (*y. Soṭa* 1.2, 16b)

In this extremely abbreviated account, we have only the reply of the Shammaites, without the question to put it into context or the exegesis to show what they based it on. It was assumed that the reader would already know the context and therefore would understand the meaning of this reply.

The aim of abbreviation was to produce an account that was easier to remember. Therefore the account was made shorter in such a way that what remained would remind the scholar of what had been omitted. The *Sifré* was already highly abbreviated, and so the only way that the Mishnah could make it shorter was to omit the exegesis. A reminder of the exegesis was inserted by extending the biblical quotation. What was lost completely was the Hillelite teaching on remarriage. In the *Sifré* version they accounted for the word "indecency" by saying that this shows that even those divorced for adultery have the right to remarry. This omission is of little importance because all sectors of Judaism allowed remarriage after divorce. It was necessary to retain only those details that demonstrated the differences between the Hillelites and Shammaites. This same principle was applied when the shortened version in the Mishnah was even further abbreviated in the Jerusalem Talmud. Here only the Shammaite point of view is preserved, without any exegesis. However, this highly abbreviated account was still sufficient for a scholar to be able to reconstruct the whole debate because he had knowledge of the background of the issue.

63. For a full analysis, see my *Techniques and Assumptions*, pp. 136-38.

If the only surviving record of the debate available to us were the highly abbreviated account in the Jerusalem Talmud, we would assume that the Shammaites allowed divorce only on the ground of indecency. If we also had the slightly longer account in the Mishnah, we would also see that this saying relates to their interpretation of Deuteronomy 24:1. Not even the fuller account in *Sifré* mentions the fact that the Shammaites also allowed divorce on the grounds named in Exodus 21:10-11[64] or that they allowed remarriage even after a Hillelite "any matter" divorce,[65] or that they allowed remarriage if the marriage ended by death. None of these details needed mentioning in the debate because they were not matters that made the Shammaites distinct from the Hillelites, or even from any other Jews.

The purpose of the abbreviated records is not to give us a complete summary of what the Shammaites believed about divorce but only the significant details that were noteworthy enough to be memorized and recorded. The only factors that were significant in the debate were the ways in which the two sides differed. Matters on which they agreed were not worth recording.

The types of abbreviation that have taken place in rabbinic literature help us to understand the process of **abbreviation in the Gospel accounts**. First, the exegesis was largely removed because the same exegesis was used regularly in the synagogue sermons and would be widely known. Only the unusual parts of the exegesis were left, together with a couple of pointers indicating the traditional method of exegesis that had been used. Second, commonly understood phrases were removed, most of which modern readers can add for themselves, such as the niceties of introduction and the transitional phrases that make the difference between a live meeting and a set of minutes. Some of these common phrases would include aspects of the debate that were well known, such as "What is your interpretation of the words 'indecent matter' in Deuteronomy 24:1?" Other phrases would be obvious to an ancient listener or reader but not so obvious to a modern one, such as the phrases that summarize the Hillelite position ("for any matter") and the corresponding summary of the Shammaite position ("except for indecency").

In one aspect the Gospel accounts are very different from records of rabbinic debates. In the Gospel accounts, Jesus was given a disproportionate

64. This is confirmed by *m. Ketub.* 5.6, which records a debate they had with the Hillelites. They debated about the length of time a man was allowed to withhold conjugal rights before he could be taken to court and sued for divorce on the grounds of Exod. 21:10. This is discussed in the previous chapter.

65. *t. Yebam.* 1.10. For pragmatic reasons, the Shammaites and Hillelites agreed to recognize each other's decisions concerning divorce and cleanliness, on which they differed in several regards. This is discussed in the previous chapter.

amount of space. In rabbinic debates the two sides are typically balanced, with roughly equal space given to both sides of the argument, though there are a vast number of exceptions to this general rule. In the Gospels, Jesus was allowed more space not only to expand on his opinion but also to introduce other matters relating to the subject. He introduced teaching on monogamy, on the lifelong nature of marriage, and possibly on stubbornness in the breaking of vows. In each of these areas he disagreed fundamentally with the teaching of all or most Jewish groups of the time.

The different versions of the same debate in rabbinic literature are similar to the different versions of the debate with Jesus on this subject, as recorded in the Gospels. The very short logia in Matthew 5:31-32 and Luke 16:18 are similar to the very abbreviated account in the Jerusalem Talmud, and the accounts of the debate in Matthew 19 and Mark 10 are similar to the account in the Mishnah. When we unpack the exegesis found in these Gospel accounts, we have something similar to the longer account in *Sifré.*

What is missing from these Gospel accounts, and from rabbinic records of debates, are the points of similarity between the two sides. Perhaps these similarities were not stated by either side because they would not have been relevant; or perhaps they did summarize their own positions on related matters at the start of the debate, in order to find their areas of agreement. Either way, one would not expect to find this common ground recorded in a summary of their debate. It would occupy a great deal of space and would be unimportant to the reader.

None of the Gospel accounts tells us about the teaching of Jesus on the grounds for divorce in Exodus 21:10-11, or remarriage after the death of a spouse. His silence on the former is assumed by most interpreters to imply that he allowed no other grounds for divorce, though his silence on the latter, by contrast, is usually taken to mean that he gave tacit approval to remarriage after a spouse has died. It would be more logical to say that he accepted or rejected both of them, and the most natural conclusion is that he agreed with the unanimous opinion of the rest of Judaism on these points. It is relatively clear that Paul believed one could remarry after the death of a former spouse (Rom. 7:2; 1 Cor. 7:39), and it will be argued in the next chapter that he also agreed with the rest of Judaism about the grounds for divorce in Exodus 21:10-11. Therefore it is likely that these matters were omitted from the abbreviated account of the debate because they did not represent differences between the two sides.

In contrast, accounts of the Hillelite-Shammaite debate omit a matter that is emphasized in the Gospels. It is not mentioned in any version of that debate that Shammaites allowed **remarriage** even after a Hillelite "any matter" divorce. They decided that if a legal court had granted a divorce, they would not countermand the court's decision even though it was counter to what they would have decided. Jesus, however, refused to recognize the validity of this type of divorce. He not only refused to allow "any matter" divorces but declared that they were invalid, so that anyone remarrying after an "any matter" divorce was committing adultery. In this opinion Jesus stood out from all other groups within Judaism. He sided with the Shammaites in their interpretation of "matter of indecency," and he sided with Qumran in their teaching on monogamy, but only Jesus declared that "any matter" divorces were invalid.

This is the one detail that remains even in the most highly abbreviated account of Jesus' teaching on divorce and remarriage. The fullest account is in Matthew 19, though even this omits anything about grounds for divorce in Exodus 21:10-11. Mark 10 removes a couple of phrases that any Jewish reader would have supplied; Matthew 5 removes all the exegesis and other reasoning but adds a reference to the divorce certificate in Deuteronomy 24:1 and the exception clause, which act as a reminder of the debate. The most highly abbreviated account is in Luke, which retains only the conclusion without any hint of the context; the only detail that remains is Jesus' assertion that remarriage after an invalid divorce is adulterous. The reason for this is now clear. This was the only point at which Jesus differed with everyone else in Judaism.

Marriage and Children Are Not Compulsory

> Matt. 19:10: The disciples said to him, If such is the case of a man with his wife, it is not expedient to marry. (11) But he said to them, Not all men can receive this saying, but only those to whom it is given. (12) For there are eunuchs who have been so from birth, and there are eunuchs who have been made eunuchs by men, and there are eunuchs who have made themselves eunuchs for the sake of the kingdom of heaven. He who is able to receive this, let him receive it.
>
> 10 Λέγουσιν αὐτῷ οἱ μαθηταὶ [αὐτοῦ]:[66] εἰ οὕτως ἐστὶν ἡ αἰτία τοῦ ἀνθρώπου μετὰ τῆς γυναικός, οὐ συμφέρει γαμῆσαι. 11 ὁ δὲ εἶπεν αὐτοῖς: οὐ πάντες χωροῦσιν τὸν λόγον [τοῦτον][67] ἀλλ' οἷς δέδοται. 12 εἰσὶν γὰρ εὐνοῦχοι οἵτινες ἐκ κοιλίας μητρὸς ἐγεννήθησαν οὕτως, καὶ εἰσὶν εὐνοῦχοι οἵτινες εὐνουχίσθησαν ὑπὸ τῶν ἀνθρώπων, καὶ εἰσὶν εὐνοῦχοι οἵτινες εὐνούχισαν ἑαυτοὺς διὰ τὴν βασιλείαν τῶν οὐρανῶν. ὁ δυνάμενος χωρεῖν χωρείτω.

66. The MS evidence for this is equivocal.
67. The MS evidence for this is equivocal.

In Matthew, though not in Mark, Jesus spoke further about abstinence from marriage. This was an answer to a question asked by the disciples, and the answer was directed to them. Thus, this teaching was away from the crowd. Mark also has this final section of teaching in private with his disciples "in the house," but for Mark this final section is the answer to the Pharisees' question. This difference will be discussed below, with regard to which version came first.

The disciples expressed their surprise at the limitations that Jesus put on divorce. This surprise may be directed at the fact that Jesus rejected the Hillelite "any matter" divorces, or that he implied that one should forgive an erring partner unless he or she stubbornly refuses to repent. The latter point was not made very explicitly in either Matthew or Mark, and so it is likely that the disciples were portrayed as expressing surprise at the removal of the Hillelite ground for divorce. The surprise indicates that they regarded the Hillelite "any matter" reason as a normal and perhaps even a necessary procedure. They probably regarded it as necessary in order to control their wives, or because they felt that they needed a way to get out of a marriage in which they had lost control. There is certainly a sense of fear or foreboding in their words "If this is the case of a man with his wife, it is not expedient to marry."[68]

Jesus now made his most surprising pronouncement: that **not all men are expected to marry**. This does not sound surprising to a modern reader, but Jews considered "go and multiply" as one of the 613 commands given by God in the Torah. It was the duty of every man to marry and have children.[69] In the section on monogamy, we have already seen the debate between the Hillelites and Shammaites about how many children one must have. Underlying this debate was the assumption that all men must "multiply."

This command to marry was so fundamental to Judaism that many commentators assume that Paul was married at one time, and some even assume that Jesus had been married.[70] The silence concerning his singleness is certainly

68. Jacques Dupont ("Mariage et divorce dans l'évangile: Matthieu 19.3-12 et parallèles," *Theological Studies* 22 [1961]: 466-67) argued that this teaching shows that Jesus rejected all remarriage, so that those who divorce "make themselves a eunuch." However, Jerome Kodell ("Celibacy logion in Matthew 19.12," *Biblical Theology Bulletin* 8 [1978]: 19-23) pointed out that this does not take into account that Jesus is speaking about those who "make themselves a eunuch for the sake of the Kingdom." This state of unmarriage is not just an inability to get married but a positive decision, like Paul's.

69. It was normally considered to be the duty of a man but not a woman. Women were not liable for positive commands that were limited by time (*m. Qidd.* 1.7), and this was traditionally numbered with time-limited commands. This may not have been the case in the first century.

70. William Phipps has addressed both of these in "Is Paul's Attitude toward Sexual Relations Contained in 1 Cor. 7.1?" *New Testament Studies* 28 (1982): 125-31, and *Was Jesus Married? The Distortion of Sexuality in the Christian Tradition* (New York: Harper & Row, 1970).

striking in the context of the belief that it was every man's religious duty to marry and have children. It is unlikely that people would assume that Jesus was planning to marry later, because marriage was expected to occur in one's teenage years.[71]

One possible reason why Jesus did not marry is that contemporary **Jews regarded his birth as illegitimate.** It was generally assumed in rabbinic literature that his birth was illegitimate, and some traditions name his father as a soldier called Pandera.[72] Although these traditions are late, it is likely that they circulated earlier. It is clear from the Gospels that he was not officially considered a *mamzer* or illegitimate because such individuals were not allowed in the temple courts and were not allowed to take an active part in synagogue worship. Presumably it would also have been very difficult for him to be recognized as a teacher.

Jesus' birth was not officially regarded as illegitimate, but this does not mean that people were not suspicious, especially within the small village where he grew up. Considerable proof was needed before deciding that someone was a *mamzer,* including two witnesses of illegitimacy, neither of whom could be the parents.[73] Even though the proof was lacking, there was probably widespread suspicion that Jesus was of questionable birth. This would have made it almost impossible for him to marry since no respectable family would want to give their daughter in marriage to him. One who was illegitimate could offer a large dowry to secure a wife, but there is no indication that Jesus' family was wealthy. He could not even marry a woman of illegitimate birth, because only a *mamzer* could marry a *mamzer.*

It is not surprising that we find some justification for remaining unmarried in the teaching of Jesus. However, this should not distract us from recognizing how shocking this teaching would seem to a first-century Jew.

Jesus introduced the subject of remaining single or celibate by speaking about the three possible reasons why a man might be a eunuch. The first two

71. Boys were also to be married at twelve (*Lam. Rab.* 1.2; cf. *y. Qidd.* 1.7, 61a). These texts are relatively late, but there is nothing to suggest that this teaching had changed.

72. The passages are dealt with well in Joseph Klausner, *Jesus of Nazareth: His Life, Times, & Teaching,* trans. Herbert Danby (New York: Menorah, 1979; London: Allen & Unwin, 1925), pp. 18-45. See also a more recent though less detailed analysis in Jane Schaberg, *The Illegitimacy of Jesus: A Feminist Theological Interpretation of the Infancy Narratives* (San Francisco: Harper and Row, 1987).

73. *m. Qidd.* 4.8. This restriction was presumably introduced in order to limit the number of *mamzerim.* The existence of *mamzerim* created considerable problems and formed a subclass of Jews. A *Mamzerim* and their descendants to the tenth generation were unable to join fully in worship, and they could not marry a non-*mamzer.*

possibilities (eunuchs by birth and eunuchs by the action of men) were unsurprising and were the same two categories that were recognized by the early rabbis.[74] It was recognized that men could be born defective and that they could be emasculated. Both of these states carried a stigma because, like the *mamzer*, they could not enter the temple to take part in leading worship.

The third category was a new one, which was not discussed by contemporary Jews. Jesus introduced a new reason for childlessness, which he described as "for the sake of the kingdom of heaven." This was a totally voluntary state that individuals inflicted on themselves; they "made themselves eunuchs." It is very unlikely that this referred to castration.[75] It is shocking enough that Jesus was **commending a life without marriage** and without children. Self-mutilation was never part of Judaism, even in aesthetic branches (though, admittedly, we know very little about these branches of Judaism). Mutilation of the body would have been regarded as marring the image of God, in which man was made.[76] Therefore, the phrase "made themselves eunuchs" probably means no more than celibacy, as suggested by the context regarding marriage. It forms the reply to the comment that it might be better not to marry at all.

The shocking nature of this teaching lay in the phrase "for the sake of the kingdom," which gives a pious motive to what most would have regarded as breaking a commandment. Such teaching was not unknown — there does seem to have been an ascetic movement within Judaism that remained celibate — though such a condition was officially frowned upon.[77] It seems likely too that some of the Essene communities practiced abstinence from marriage, but these kept the command to "multiply" by adopting children.[78] Among the rabbis, there is only one unmarried scholar, Ben Azzi, and even he had difficulty de-

74. *m. Yebam.* 8.4. This is a later discussion of teaching that is earlier than R. Eliezer (80-120 C.E.). Cf. *m. Yebam.* 8.4; *b. Yebam.* 75a, 79b, and the footnote in Davies and Allison, *Saint Matthew*, pp. 22-24.

75. See Davies and Allison, *Saint Matthew*, p. 24.

76. The early rabbis regarded man as made in the literal image of God (see Alon Goshen Gottstein, "The Body as Image of God in Rabbinic Literature," *Harvard Theological Review* 87 [1994]: 171-95). A story about Hillel says that he regarded bathing as a religious act because he was cleaning God's image (*Lev. Rab.* 34.3).

77. The evidence for this is summarized well in Brian S. Rosner, *Paul, Scripture and Ethics: A Study of 1 Corinthians 5–7*, Arbeiten zur Geschichte des antiken Judentums und des Urchristentums 22 (Leiden: Brill, 1994), pp. 155-59.

78. Though Isaksson has argued persuasively in *Marriage and Ministry in the New Temple* that they did marry for a few years, in order to fulfill this command, and then gave up their wives.

fending his position.[79] The potential scandal of this teaching may have been the reason why it was given in private to the disciples.

This teaching became increasingly important in the Church in the following centuries. It is difficult to read this passage without thinking about self-denial, which was glorified in the Early Church. The original readers would not have read it in this way. They would not have regarded this as a commendation of the single life but as permission to remain single. The whole emphasis regarding marriage in rabbinic and other Jewish teaching was about its necessity. Jesus' saying gave permission for Jews to remain unmarried, even with a good motive: "for the sake of the kingdom." There is absolutely no guilt associated with remaining single if this is done in order to work for God. However, this is an exceptional situation, as is indicated by the concluding encouragement addressed to "him who can receive it."

Which Version Came First?

The Synoptic problem is still a problem. The recent revival of Matthean primacy may prove to be a passing fad, and consensus certainly lies with Markan priority. Yet good arguments come from both sides, and any conclusion in the overall argument may not provide a definitive solution about every passage. For that reason, we must examine this pericope on its own merits.

Matthew 19:	*Mark 10:*
The Question (3)	*The Question (2)*
And Pharisees came up to him and tested him by asking, Is it lawful to divorce one's wife **for any matter**?	And Pharisees came up and in order to test him asked, Is it lawful for a man to divorce his wife?

79. He was betrothed to Aqiba's daughter and he preached against celibacy, but he put off marrying indefinitely, arguing that he was married to the Torah (*t. Yebam.* 8.4 and parallels). It is also possible that he *had* been married and that he was defending his decision to avoid remarriage.

Digression (4-6)
He answered, Have you not read that **he who created them from the beginning** *made them male and female* [Gen. 1:27], (5) and said, *"For this reason a man shall leave his father and mother and be joined to his wife, and the two shall become one flesh"* [Gen. 2:24]? (6) So they are no longer two but one flesh. What therefore God has joined together, let not man separate.

Moses' Teaching (3-5)
He answered them, What did Moses command you? (4) They said, Moses allowed a man to write a certificate of divorce, and to put her away. (5) But Jesus said to them, For your hardness of heart **he wrote you this commandment.**

Moses' Teaching (7-8)
They said to him, Why then did Moses command one to give a certificate of divorce, and to put her away? (8) He said to them, For your hardness of heart Moses allowed you to divorce your wives, **but from the beginning it was not so.**

Digression (6-9)
But **from the beginning of creation,** *"He made them male and female"* [Gen. 1:27]. (7) *"For this reason a man shall leave his father and mother and be joined to his wife,* (8) *and the two shall become one flesh"* [Gen. 2:24]. So they are no longer two but one flesh. (9) What therefore God has joined together, let not man separate.

Answering the Question (9)
And I say to you: whoever divorces his wife, **unless for indecency**, and marries another, commits adultery.

Answering the Question (10-12)
And in the house the disciples asked him again about this matter. (11) **And he said to them**, Whoever divorces his wife and marries another, commits adultery against her; (12) and if she divorces her husband and marries another, she commits adultery.

Marriage Is Optional (10-12)
The disciples said to him, If such is the case of a man with his wife, it is not expedient to marry. . . .

The two accounts of Jesus' teaching on divorce in Matthew and Mark are clearly related, but they have been edited for two different purposes or situations. They both share an overall structure, of Question, Digression, Moses' Teaching, and Jesus' Answer, though the middle two sections are reversed in the two versions.

Mark's version is more suitable for use in a **sermon**. The question-and-answer session at the beginning (2-4) summarizes the position of the Jews, and the latter three quarters (5-12) has the teaching of Jesus. The teaching of Jesus is directed first to the Jews (5-9) and then to the Church (10-12). The flow of the teaching is more natural than in Matthew. The question leads to "Moses' command necessitated by sin," which leads to teaching on monogamy based on the ideals of sinless Eden, which leads to the answer for a sinful society.

Matthew's version reflects a real rabbinic **debate**. The opening question frames the debate and leads into exegesis concerning a related point. A second question brings Jesus back to the area of the original question. The second question is answered, and then finally the opening question is answered. This is not a typical form for recording rabbinic debates. Normally a question would be followed by an answer, and then a further question from the original questioner, or a counter question from the person who was questioned. There was usually a degree of balance in the reporting of a debate, so that both sides were more or less equally represented. In this debate, the Pharisees' point of view is very poorly represented, though Matthew takes care to record a summary of the two main Pharisaic viewpoints in this debate.

From this structure, it could be argued that either of these accounts was the original and that the other developed from it. It could be argued that Matthew reconstructed the teaching into the form of a rabbinic debate in order to interact with the debate that was still going on in the Jewish world. It could be argued equally that Mark transformed a rabbinic debate, which was becoming increasingly irrelevant to the Church, into a form that lent itself to Christian teaching. A more detailed analysis also provides arguments for the originality of either version.

On the one hand, it has often been argued that Matthew's version is secondary because he has added the phrases summarizing the two schools of opinion, "for any matter" and "a matter of indecency." It is likely that these have been added by Matthew rather than omitted by Mark because both accounts in Matthew have such summaries but neither account in Mark or Luke has them. It is also likely that Matthew has changed "from the beginning of creation" in Mark 10:6 and witnessed to in CD 4.21 to "who created them from the beginning."

On the other hand, it could also be argued that Mark's version has lost the contrast where the Pharisees say "Moses commanded divorce" and Jesus says

"Moses allowed divorce." He has managed to retain the phrase "Moses allowed," but his editing has put this in the mouth of a Pharisee, and he has had to repeat "Moses commanded," once with the words of the Pharisees and once with the words of Jesus.

Another structure that can also be discerned is **public question, public answer; private question, private answer.** This is a structure that occurs in a few rabbinic debates at about 70 C.E.[80] In Matthew the private question concerns whether or not one should marry (10-12). In Mark the private question is a repeat of the original question ("And in the house the disciples asked him again about this matter"), and the private answer is Jesus' answer to the original question, which is given in public in Matthew. Both Matthew and Mark have retained this form, though they have employed it in different ways. Again, it is difficult to decide which version was adapted from which.

On the one hand, it could be argued that Mark's version is closer to the rabbinic form where the same question is always asked in both halves of the debate. Also, it could be said that Matthew has clumsily added the teaching on optional marriage into the debate by transforming it into a private question-and-answer session. On the other hand, the double question and answer in Matthew conform very closely to the rabbinic form of debates, and the extra question in private may simply be an extension of it. A rabbinic form including an extra question that is sometimes asked in private is found especially in the traditions of Yohanan ben Zakkai, who taught in Galilee at the same time as Jesus.[81] In addition, it seems unlikely that the Pharisees in Mark's version would consider

80. Five early debates of Yohanan ben Zakkai follow this form. In two debates with Angetos, a Gentile, he is asked a question, and he first gives a public answer that is well reasoned and acceptable. Then his disciples say to him in private that *they* cannot be dismissed with such an easy answer, and so he gives them an answer that is more difficult for the uncommitted Gentile to accept (see *y. Sanh.* 1.2, 19b; *Num. Rab.* 19.8; for a full analysis, see my *Techniques and Assumptions,* pp. 80-82). In his three debates with the Sadducees he uses a variant of this form, giving the same questioner first an obscure and clever reply and then a more closely argued reply. The second reply is prompted when the Sadducee, like his disciples, says that he cannot be dismissed with that answer (see *b. B. Bat.* 115b-16a; *b. Menaḥ.* 65ab; MegTaan. p. 338; for a full analysis and parallels, see my *Techniques and Assumptions,* pp. 96-100, 109-14).

81. Rabbinic chronologies are very difficult to reconstruct because the only biographical information we have about them is usually late. However, we do have early traditions that Yohanan ben Zakkai taught in Galilee (*m. Šabb.* 16.7; 22.3), and we have a credible tradition that he was there for eighteen years (*y. Šabb.* 16.7, 15d). We also know that after this he ruled in Jerusalem with Simeon ben Gamaliel, which was perhaps from 50 to 70 C.E. (see Jacob Neusner, *A Life of Rabban Yohanan Ben Zakkai, c. 1-80 CE* [Leiden: Brill, 1962], p. 17). So, it is likely that he taught in Galilee during the ministry of Jesus, or just after it.

that their question had been answered. It is likely that, as in Matthew's version, they would have attempted to pin Jesus down to a definite answer.[82]

It is unlikely that any definitive answer can be reached about which version developed from which. It is my personal view that both versions show signs of adaptation, though Matthew's version represents more aspects of the original debate. It is likely that Matthew did add the summaries of the Hillelite and Shammaite position, but that these correctly represented ideas that had already been abbreviated. He added them because he realized that his readers were not so easily able to supply them from their own knowledge of Jewish oral law. The original was already in the form of a debate, though Matthew has made this form clearer. Mark has edited the original in order to make it more usable in sermons and other Christian teaching, and has removed much of the debate structure. Both writers have adapted the original debate in order to help their own readers, but the original debate is still just as accessible to a reader today who is aware of the cultural background, as it was then.

Putting It All Together

We are now in a position to reconstruct the debate that Jesus had with the Pharisees. This debate was recorded in an abbreviated form by Mark, and Matthew (probably writing later) reinserted some of the details that had been abbreviated out. Using Mark's version as a basis and Matthew's helpful additions and rearrangement as a guideline, we can produce the following version of the debate. Matthew's additions are in square brackets. My additions are in curly brackets. Scripture citations are in italics.

> And Pharisees came up and in order to test him asked, "Is it lawful for a man to divorce his wife [for *'any matter'*] {Deut. 24:1, according to the Hillelite interpretation}?"
>
> [He answered, "Have you not read that] from the beginning of creation, *'He made them male and female'* {Gen. 1:27}, [and] *'For this reason a man shall leave his father and mother and be joined to his wife, and the two shall*

82. Matthew may be regarded as an amalgamation of the two varieties of this form, as is seen in the debates of Yohanan ben Zakkai. The first public debate with the Pharisees is very similar to Yohanan's debates with the Sadducees, where the original answer is dismissed as irrelevant, and they are finally satisfied with a clearer answer. The second question and answer in private is like the second half of Yohanan's debates with the Gentile, where he gives his disciples a more difficult teaching in private.

> *become one flesh'* {Gen. 2:24 LXX}? So they are no longer two but one flesh. What therefore God has joined together, let not man separate."
>
> [They said to him, "Why then did Moses command one to give *a certificate of divorce,* and to *put her away?"*] {Deut. 24:1}. He answered them, "What did Moses command you?" They said, "Moses [commanded] a man to *write a certificate of divorce,* and to *put her away*" {Deut. 24:1}. But Jesus said to them, "For your *hardness of heart* {Jer. 4:4 LXX} he wrote you this commandment. [Moses allowed you to divorce your wives, but from the beginning it was not so]."
>
> And in the house the disciples asked him again about this matter. And he said to them, "Whoever divorces his wife [except for *'a matter of indecency'*] {Deut. 24:1, according to the Shammaite interpretation} and marries another, commits adultery against her; and if she divorces her husband [except for *'indecency'*] and marries another, she commits adultery."

The resultant text is not the "original" in any sense. For example, adding Matthew's version in square brackets has resulted in some repetition in the third paragraph, and the text is still too abbreviated for a modern reader to grasp easily. The following **paraphrase** attempts to reconstruct the text further, to unpack it for a modern reader.

> And Pharisees came up and in order to test him asked, "Is it lawful for a man to divorce his wife on the grounds of *'any matter'* (Deut. 24:1) as the Hillelites say?"
>
> Jesus answered, "Have you not read that in the beginning of creation men could marry only one woman? Scripture says, *'He made them* (one) *male and* (one) *female'* (Gen. 1:27), and *'For this reason a man shall leave his father and mother and be joined to his wife, and the two shall become one flesh'* (Gen. 2:24 LXX). These verses also show that God made them, so it is God who joins them and makes them *one flesh.* Therefore if God has joined them together, neither of them should divorce the other."
>
> The Pharisees replied: "But if they should not divorce, then why did Moses command a husband to give *a certificate of divorce* to an adulteress and to *put her away?"* (Deut. 24:1). He answered them, "Moses did not command this, but he allowed it. He allowed it in the situation of stubborn *hardness of heart* (Jer. 4:4 — where God divorces Israel who stubbornly refuses to repent of her adulteries). But this is not what God wanted from the beginning."
>
> Later, in private, the disciples asked him again about this matter. And Jesus said to them, "If a man divorces his wife for *'any matter'* and not for *'a matter of indecency'* (the correct interpretation of Deut. 24:1), he does not

have a valid divorce. If he then marries another woman, he is committing adultery, because he is still married to his first wife. Similarly, if a woman forces her husband to divorce her for *'any matter'* and not for *'a matter of indecency,'* and she marries another, she is also committing adultery."

This paraphrase is still difficult to understand because it assumes a fairly good knowledge of the OT text. It assumes that the reader will know that "any matter" and "a matter of indecency" are competing interpretations of "indecent matter" in Deuteronomy 24:1, and that "hardness of heart" in Jeremiah 4:4 is a reference to the sin described in the previous chapter of Jeremiah (i.e., Israel's adultery).

The argument in the second paragraph is a little sloppy from a rabbinic point of view, but any rabbinic reader would add the other proof text from Genesis 7:9 ("they went in two by two, male and female"), which links the two texts quoted in the Gospels.[83] The LXX version of Genesis 2:24 is quoted by the Gospel because it inserts the word "two." It is unlikely that Jesus would have cited the LXX in a rabbinic debate, but there would have been no need if the missing proof text of Genesis 7:9 was present because it says "two by two." The Gospels had to cite the LXX because they omitted Genesis 7:9.

I have followed Mark's structure with regard to the final answer. Mark says that this was an answer to a private question by the disciples, while Matthew omits this detail and thereby implies that it was addressed to everyone. I am impressed by the similar structure in the debates of R. Yohanan ben Zakkai, who taught in Galilee during Jesus' ministry. He was known to give public answer to a question and then give a more straightforward answer to his disciples in private.[84]

The record of this debate in the Gospels is considerably less abbreviated than the equivalent rabbinic record of debates on this subject. Very little needs to be supplied, and we can be relatively certain that we have successfully understood each stage of the debate.

The Practical Consequences of Jesus' Teaching

The consequences of Jesus' teaching on divorce were very widespread. One gets the impression that Matthew regarded his teaching as impractical and anticipating a perfect world since he placed it alongside sayings such as:

83. As detailed above in the section "Digression on Monogamy."
84. As detailed above in the section "Which Version Came First?"

> Whoever insults his brother shall be liable to the council. (Matt. 5:22)

> Every one who looks at a woman lustfully has already committed adultery with her in his heart. (Matt. 5:28)

> If your right eye causes you to sin, pluck it out and throw it away. (Matt. 5:29)

Perhaps this is because Matthew, more than others, recognized the complete revolution that this teaching would bring to the Jewish world. If Jesus declared all the "any matter" divorces invalid, this would include almost all the divorces that had taken place during the previous generation, ever since the Hillelites had started offering divorce in this way.

There are several other consequences of this teaching, most of them due to other matters that Jesus taught during this debate. In the analysis of the passages above, we find that he taught six specific things, most of which are often overlooked:

1. Monogamy
   — an individual can be married to only one person at a time.
2. Marriage should be lifelong
   — and it is against God's will to break up a marriage.
3. Divorce is not compulsory
   — even in cases of adultery.
4. Divorce is allowable
   — if there is a stubborn refusal to stop committing adultery.
5. Marriage is not compulsory
   — so infertility is not a ground for divorce
6. Divorce for "any matter" is invalid
   — and so remarriage after this divorce is adulterous.

The consequences of each will be considered in turn.

1. Monogamy — an individual can be married to only one person at a time. Jesus' teaching on monogamy would have few practical consequences because polygamy was becoming rare except among the rich. Presumably Jesus would not recognize the validity of a second marriage, but he does not specifically say that this relationship would be illicit, as he did with remarriage after an invalid divorce.

The main consequence of Jesus' teaching on monogamy would be that

women gained the right to use adultery as a ground for divorce. In ancient Judaism, when polygamy was still permitted, a husband did not make a vow of sexual exclusiveness when he married. This meant that he could not be divorced for being sexually unfaithful. He could still be accused of adultery, but the offense was against the husband of the other woman and not against his wife. However, if polygamy was no longer permitted, it must be assumed that a husband owed sexual exclusivity to his wife, and therefore adultery became a ground for divorce that could be used equally by men and women.

One consequence for the Early Church was an increase in the number of **unmarried widows.** If the family of Babatha is typical (her family records have survived almost intact),[85] a second wife was often a widow. Marrying a widow was affordable even for men of the lower middle classes because the dowry was half and she often came with money of her own from the previous marriage that would help the family finances. However, without polygamy, a widow could marry only an unmarried man, of which there were far fewer. The Early Church appears to have met this problem very soon. The widows of Acts 6 may simply have been the equivalent of the poor in any Jewish community, but by the time of the Pastoral Epistles, the widows were starting to pose problems.[86] Unmarried widows had more freedom than married women, and they were causing problems by going from house to house and gossiping.[87] Therefore, the young widows were actively encouraged to marry,[88] and the older ones were organized into a special order of widows.[89] They were given tasks such as teaching the younger women.[90]

In the early centuries, widows were a significant burden on the Church.

85. The documents of the Babatha family dating from 93-132 C.E. have been found in a cave at Nahal Hever. These are edited in Hannah M. Cotton and Ada Yardeni, *Aramaic, Hebrew and Greek Documentary Texts from Nahal Hever and Other Sites: With an Appendix Containing Alleged Qumran Texts,* Discoveries in the Judaean Desert 27 (Oxford: Clarendon, 1997).

86. The whole subject of widows in the NT and the Early Church is covered in superb detail by Gustav Stählin, "χήρα," in *Theological Dictionary of the New Testament,* 10 vols., ed. Gerhard Kittel (Grand Rapids: Eerdmans, 1964-95), 9:440-65.

87. 1 Tim. 5:13; 2 Tim. 3:6. The latter text does not specifically mention widows, but the language used here normally refers to widows (see Stählin, "χήρα," p. 455, n. 140.

88. 1 Tim. 5:11, 14. In the Roman world widows were expected to remarry if of childbearing age (i.e., under fifty). Augustus even put this into law in 9 C.E. (see B. W. Winter, "Providentia for the Widows of 1 Timothy 5.3-16," *Tyndale Bulletin* 39 [1988]: 85).

89. 1 Tim. 5:9-12. It is not certain whether this was a recognized order in NT times (Stählin, "χήρα," p. 455, n. 144), but it became one soon after, and in some places the order came to hold a status almost akin to deaconesses (Stählin, "χήρα," pp. 459-65).

90. 1 Timothy 5 does not list any specific tasks because it is dealing with entrance requirements. Perhaps they had tasks similar to deaconesses in Titus 2:3-5, leading younger women to proper marriage and family life, and taking part in visitation of women.

There were over 1,500 widows and needy in the Roman church, and 3,000 widows and virgins in Antioch, who received daily support.[91] The orders of widows declined after a few hundred years, probably because they were replaced by convents.[92]

2. Marriage should be lifelong — and it is against God's will to break up a marriage. This teaching had little consequence because it is a statement of God's will in an ideal situation. However, it had a huge consequence when combined with the following aspects of Jesus' teachings, which severely limited the occasions when a divorce was allowed. Many rabbis were already teaching that marriage should be lifelong, but they also allowed divorce for "any matter." Jesus took the lifelong nature of marriage seriously and allowed divorce only when marriage vows were constantly being broken, so that the marriage was broken and irreparable.

3. Divorce is not compulsory — even in cases of adultery. The standard rabbinic teaching was that divorce was compulsory after a wife had been unfaithful, as was seen in the previous chapter. In theory one could, instead, subject one's wife to the rite of the suspected adulteress. However, this was extremely unpleasant for the wife, and embarrassing for the husband, and so it is unlikely that many would avoid divorce in this way. If a husband didn't love his wife, he would divorce her anyway (in case the rite absolved her), and if he did love her, he would not want to subject her to the rite.

The consequences of Jesus' teaching that divorce for adultery was optional were quite positive. For instance, it was no longer considered impious if one continued in marriage with someone who was a suspected adulteress. This would have been a great relief to many husbands who wanted to forgive their wives but who were not permitted to do so. Under Jesus' rule of monogamy, it also meant that women could forgive their adulterous husbands.

The consequences reached much further because this teaching affected the lifestyle of every married woman. In ancient Jewish society a woman became a suspected adulteress as soon as she spent a few minutes alone with a man. Even if there was another woman present, it was assumed that they would scheme to seduce the man (though if she was with two men it was assumed that the men would protect each other's virtue).[93] A woman could also become a

91. Stählin, "χήρα," p. 460.

92. Stählin, "χήρα," p. 465.

93. The blame for sexual lapses is placed on women. A woman may remain alone with two men, but not a man with two women (*m. Qidd.* 4.12).

suspected adulteress by speaking to a man in public on two occasions. If she was seen spending time speaking with a man to whom she was not related, it was assumed that they were planning a liaison, and her husband was required to warn her. If she was seen speaking to the same man a second time, after having been warned, it was assumed that they were having a sexual relationship.[94] Her husband would be expected to divorce her whether he wanted to or not.

These rules about suspected adultery dominated the everyday activities of every woman. Jesus' teaching would therefore allow women vastly more freedom than they had before. They could talk to men and even go and visit them, though they would nevertheless be advised to have a friend with them. They could do these things with the knowledge that their husbands would not be forced to divorce them.

4. Divorce is allowable — if there is a stubborn refusal to stop committing adultery. It is not certain that Jesus was teaching this. As was shown above, it is based on the assumption that "hardness of heart" is a reference to Jeremiah 4:4 and to chapter 3, for which 4:4 acts as a summary. This interpretation makes a lot of sense in the context of Jesus' other teachings as outlined here, but it should be treated with less certainty than those teachings.

The consequence of this teaching is that the followers of Jesus could divorce their unfaithful partners. Forgiveness could and should be offered, but it should follow repentance. An unrepentant and consistently adulterous partner could be divorced, although such action was still not compulsory.

If, as is suggested below, Jesus also recognized the other grounds in Exodus 21:10-11, then these would also apply. In other words, divorce would be allowable if there was a stubborn refusal to provide food, clothing, or love. There would be little need to state this because it was already the case in the rest of Judaism. If a husband neglected to provide food or clothing, a wife would have to prove this in a court, and this neglect would have to be shown over a period of time, though that time period is not defined in surviving rabbinic rulings.[95] The time period *is* defined when it comes to conjugal rights, and there was also a set regimen of fines that was designed to break down the

94. *m. Soṭa* 6.1: "[Concerning one] who warned his wife of his jealousy, and she [subsequently] secluded herself [with the man in question], even if [her husband] heard [about this] from a flying bird, he must divorce her [for suspected adultery]; but he must still deliver her marriage portion [i.e., because the bird is not a competent witness]. This is the opinion of R. Eliezer. But R. Joshua rules that [the husband is not forced to divorce her] until the women who spin by moonlight gossip about her [i.e., there is at least a plausible case against her]."

95. A husband presumably also had this right, but there were easier ways for a husband to get a divorce, and so there are no records of cases being brought by a husband.

resolve of a stubborn partner.[96] All those who stubbornly refused the pressure from the court to keep their marriage vows was forced to grant a divorce if their partner asked for it.

The fact that this principle of stubbornness was already present in contemporary Jewish divorce procedures for the three grounds from Exodus 21:10-11 gives weight to the suggestion that Jesus applied this same principle to the ground of adultery.

5. Marriage is not compulsory, and so infertility is not a ground for divorce. The command to "multiply" meant that infertility was a ground for divorce. Some later rabbis even considered it the duty of a couple to divorce if no children were born during the first ten years of marriage.[97] Jesus' teaching about the self-imposed state of a eunuch meant that marriage and childbearing were not compulsory. Although Jesus did not say so, this presumably meant that he did not regard the commandment to "multiply" as one that every man had to fulfill. One consequence of this was that infertility could no longer be regarded as a ground for divorce.

6. Divorce for "any matter" is invalid, and so remarriage after this divorce is adulterous. As stated above, this had huge consequences for the people whom Jesus was addressing. We do not know how common divorce was, but it appears to have been treated relatively lightly. It is likely that everyone was personally acquainted with at least one divorced person, and it is also likely that most, if not almost all of them, were the quick "any matter" divorces. Jesus was, in effect, calling them all adulterers and declaring that the children of the second marriages were illegitimate.

His listeners might have assumed that Jesus meant that he would not grant a divorce on these grounds, but that he recognized the validity of divorces granted in Hillelite courts, as the Shammaites did. The Shammaites and Hillelites were willing to live with each other's differences and recognize each other's divorces. This is similar to the way in which most denominations are willing to recognize the validity of a marriage or a baptism that has been performed in another church, even though it was performed using rites that are fundamentally different from their own. The Shammaites were willing to let even their daughters marry someone who had been through a Hillelite "any matter" divorce.

96. For details, see *m. Ketub.* 5.6-7 and the discussion in the previous chapter.

97. An infertile wife could be divorced without returning her *ketubah* (*m. Ketub.* 11.6). This was probably not regarded as a punishment for the wife but as incentive for the husband to find a fertile wife. See also the discussion in the previous chapter.

Jesus, however, was not willing to accept the validity of an "any matter" divorce. In order to emphasize this, he declared that all those who remarried after this type of divorce were committing adultery, because they were still married to their former partner.

There was a huge gulf between the teaching of Jesus and the rest of Jewish society. Not only did Jesus limit the grounds on which one could demand a divorce, but he also said that forgiveness should be offered before proceeding to divorce. For the followers of Jesus this had some good consequences and some difficult ones. We have seen that there were significant benefits in terms of additional freedom for women, as well as the benefits in saving marriages that would otherwise have ended in divorce. Yet this teaching also created problems, especially for those who had been divorced in a way that Jesus considered invalid.

Presumably those who became followers of Jesus after an invalid divorce had to recognize that their previous marriage was technically still legal. They could either return to their partner or remain single. If they had remarried, they would presumably have to free the woman and return her dowry, as a Jew did after committing technical adultery (as seen in the previous chapter). Similarly, if followers of Jesus became invalidly divorced against their will by partners who were not followers, they too had to try to return to their previous partner or remain single.

Jesus did not specifically say what should happen after an invalid divorce. I have assumed that his followers would feel that they had to be reconciled or remain single. In most cases reconciliation would be impossible, and so most of them would face a life of celibacy. This was very difficult in a culture that was suspicious of the morals of a single woman and was suspicious of the piety of a single man (unless he already had children from a previous marriage). This may be the reason that Matthew included the teaching about optional marriage at this point (Matt. 19:10-12). This teaching shows that celibacy can not only be a valid option, but a valuable one.

This presumed consequence for followers of Jesus who were divorced is very similar to the teaching of Paul in 1 Corinthians 7, though he had a slightly different view about the consequences for believers who were divorced against their will (as seen in the next chapter).

There is nothing to suggest that Jesus asked anyone to separate from the second husband or wife if one had remarried after an invalid divorce. Technically the marriage was adulterous, but if this was applied literally, then there would be huge confusion and disruption to people's lives and families. This is presumably why the divorce saying found its way into the Sermon on the Mount. Just as someone who hates his brother is not to be prosecuted for murder, so one who has remarried is not to be accused in court of committing adultery.

Other Grounds for Divorce

We cannot be certain from this debate whether Jesus did or did not approve of the other Old Testament grounds for divorce, as discussed in the previous chapter. However, his silence about them is more likely to indicate that he agreed with the rest of Judaism that these grounds were acceptable.

It has usually been assumed that Jesus named the single exception of πορνεία because this was the only ground for divorce that he recognized. It has been shown above that this assumption is faulty, because the same assumption would conclude that the Shammaites also allowed divorce only on the ground of adultery.

There are three factors that suggest that Jesus recognized the other Old Testament grounds for divorce. All **three** are **arguments from silence**, which have to be taken with very great caution.

The **first** factor is that **Jesus did not say anything about these other grounds** during this debate about divorce. This argument is not as weak as it initially seems, because Jesus did take the trouble to bring up several other matters relating to marriage and divorce in which he differed with general opinion.

Even though he had been asked about divorce, he first of all spoke about monogamy and gave two exegeses in support of this. Most Jews, though not all, believed that polygamy was allowed by Scripture, and so Jesus used Scripture to show that it was not in God's original plan. Then he spoke about the lifelong nature of marriage. Most Jews felt that this principle was unimportant because God had given a law of divorce, and they felt that this gave implicit permission to divorce. Jesus also addressed the issue of whether divorce was compulsory or optional when there had been sexual unfaithfulness. A growing number of Jews at the time felt that it was compulsory, and most felt that it was the morally correct thing to do, but Jesus said that Moses "allowed" divorce but did not "command" it. Jesus also indicated the circumstances in which divorce for unfaithfulness *was* appropriate by saying that the law had been given to cope with cases of stubborn hardness of heart, where there was a refusal to repent and change. He also taught, though only to his disciples, that marriage and childbearing were optional. Most Jews believed that procreation was a command of God that could be fulfilled only by marrying and having children, though there were a few ascetics among the Jews who did not get married. One important implication of this was that childlessness could no longer be used as a ground for divorce. This was counter to most Jews, though there were many who were uneasy about divorce on the grounds of infertility.

Jesus was not asked about any of these matters, but he was determined to speak about them, to the apparent annoyance of the Pharisees who had to bring him back to the point of the question. It would seem strange that Jesus would bring up all these issues, some of which were peripheral to the subject of divorce, and yet ignore an issue that was so central to the subject of the debate.

The **second** factor is that **everyone would assume that Jesus recognized that there were other Old Testament grounds for divorce** because this was a universally held view. None of the other areas that Jesus addressed were universally held in first-century Judaism. Among the many and disparate groups within Judaism one could find Jews who would agree with Jesus' teachings on monogamy, lifelong marriage, optional divorce, forgiveness for unfaithfulness except in cases of stubbornness, optional marriage, the invalidity of divorce for infertility, and, of course, the invalidity of the "any matter" divorce. In contrast, there was no group in first-century Judaism that rejected the grounds for divorce in Exodus 21:10-11. It would be strange if Jesus spent time on these various doctrines that were not unique in Judaism and neglected to mention a doctrine that was totally unique. If Jesus had wanted to teach a rejection of the grounds for divorce in Exodus 21:10-11, he would have had to say so very clearly, and if he said nothing about them, it would have been assumed that, like all other Jews, he accepted them.

If Jesus said nothing about a universally accepted belief, then it is assumed by most scholars that this indicated his agreement with it. He is never recorded as saying anything about the immorality of sexual acts before marriage (to the dismay of many youth leaders), but no one assumes that he approved of them. Similarly, everyone assumes that he believed in monotheism, but it would be difficult to demonstrate this from the Gospel accounts. Also, Jesus nowhere explicitly allowed or forbade remarriage after the death of a spouse, but we assume that he did allow this because all Jews, including Paul, clearly allowed it. In all these matters it is easy for us to assume that Jesus agreed with the universally held position because we too agree with it. However, in the matter of divorce on the grounds of Exodus 21:10-11, we find it harder to assume that Jesus accepted the universal position merely because we do not hold to it.

The **third** factor that indicates that Jesus accepted the grounds for divorce in Exodus 21:10-11 is the **almost perfect parallel between the wording of Jesus' exception clause and the Shammaite ruling** in the divorce debate. Most commentators have read Jesus' exception clause as a rejection of the other grounds for divorce, but the same exception clause is used by the Shammaites **who did recognize the other grounds for divorce**, as shown in the previous chapter. The Shammaite position was summarized in rabbinic literature in two very similar forms:

A man should not divorce his wife except he has found in her <u>indecency</u>. (*Sifré Deut.* 269; *y. Soṭa* 1.2 [16b])

לא יגרש אדם את־אשתו אלא אם כן מצא בה <u>ערוה</u>

A man should not divorce his wife except he has found in her <u>a matter of indecency</u>. (*m. Git.* 9.10)

לא יגרש אדם את־אשתו אלא אם כן מצא בה <u>דבר ערוה</u>

These are semantically identical to the two versions of the exception clause in Matthew, even as far as citing ערות דבר, "indecent matter" from Deuteronomy 24:1 in the reverse order of דבר ערוה, "matter of indecency."

Whoever divorces his wife, unless for <u>indecency</u> . . . (Matt. 19:9)

ὃς ἂν ἀπολύσῃ τὴν γυναῖκα αὐτοῦ μὴ ἐπὶ <u>πορνείᾳ</u>

Every one who divorces his wife, except for a <u>matter of indecency</u> . . . (Matt. 5:32)

πᾶς ὁ ἀπολύων τὴν γυναῖκα αὐτοῦ παρεκτὸς <u>λόγου πορνείας</u>

Jesus used the same terminology as the Shammaites, in the same context, at the same time period, and in a debate where Shammaites or their rivals the Hillelites were present. We may therefore confidently assume that he meant to convey the same meaning by these words that the Shammaites were trying to convey. When the Shammaites said "except . . . for a matter of indecency" in the context of this debate about "any matter" divorces, they meant that Deuteronomy 24:1 allows no type of divorce except that for indecency. They did not mean that Scripture allows no divorce except that for indecency because they allowed other divorces on the grounds in Exodus 21.

Therefore, when Jesus used this same phrase in this same debate, it would be extraordinary to conclude that he meant something different. If we concluded this, we would have to declare that Jesus spoke a different language than that of his contemporaries, where words and phrases can mean different things when Jesus uses them. We would then have no basis for working out the meaning of anything that he has said on any subject because he would be speaking a language that was totally unique, and any person's interpretation of his words would be as valid as anyone else's. However, if Jesus and the Gospel writers were trying to communicate eternal truths to their listeners and readers, they would presumably have used a language that was well known and understood, rather than a "sacred" language that had a secret interpretation. Therefore we must assume that when Jesus or the Gospel writers use the same phrase as their contemporaries, in the same context, they mean the same thing.

As I said at the beginning of this section, all these arguments suggesting that Jesus allowed other Old Testament grounds for divorce are arguments from silence, and so they must be treated with caution. However, it would be difficult to ignore them entirely, especially since Paul appeared to recognize these other OT grounds for divorce, as will be shown in the next chapter.

Conclusions

The two Gospel accounts, in Mark 10 and Matthew 19, both show signs of editing, and both originate from an abbreviated account of a debate between some Pharisees and Jesus about the interpretation of ערות דבר in Deuteronomy 24:1. Mark has edited the account to make it more suitable for preaching, and Matthew has edited it to help readers understand the debate and its consequences. The rabbinic accounts of the Hillelite-Shammaite debate provide an insight into the debate in which Jesus was asked to take part, and into the ways in which such debates were abbreviated. Matthew's addition of the Hillelite and Shammaite phrases was a correct reinsertion of well-known details that had been abbreviated out of the account in Mark, because without them the Pharisees' question makes no sense. These additions would have been self-evident to any contemporary Jew, who would have inserted them mentally if they were not present. When the exegeses and arguments are unpacked from their abbreviated form, we find that Jesus was teaching six separate matters:

- marriage should be monogamous,
- marriage should be lifelong,
- divorce is never compulsory,
- divorce should be avoided unless the erring partner stubbornly refuses to repent,
- marriage is optional,
- Hillelite "any matter" divorces are invalid.

All of these matters are contrary to what other first-century Jews taught, though Jesus expressed agreement with *some* of the things taught by *some* Jewish groups. He agreed with the Qumran community concerning monogamy and with the Shammaites concerning "any matter" divorces, and he indicated this agreement by using their terminology. The Gospels do not record Jesus' teaching on any matters where he might have agreed with all other Jews, such as the prohibition of sexual relations before marriage, or allowing divorce for the biblical grounds in Exodus 21.

7. Paul's Teaching

Biblical Grounds Include Neglect

Paul was aware of Jesus' teaching on divorce and agreed with it, though he was addressing a different problem. The Corinthians lived under Roman law where men and women could divorce their partners by separating from them — sending them away or moving out of the home. Paul told the Corinthians that Christians should not divorce in this way, and that they should never *cause* a divorce. However, if they were divorced by a non-Christian who refused to be reconciled, they were free to remarry, though they must marry a Christian. He also pointed out that their circumstances made it an inopportune time for them to marry, for practical reasons.

Most of Paul's teachings on marriage and divorce are found in 1 Corinthians 7, a large portion of which will be covered here. The sections of 1 Corinthians 7 are examined in the order they occur, except for verses 32-35, which are linked with verses 1-9. In this chapter Paul talked about the obligations within marriage, Jesus' teaching against divorce, the right to remarry if one is divorced against one's will, and delaying marriage for practical reasons. He nowhere dealt directly with the grounds for divorce, though he did deal with this indirectly throughout the chapter. He identified what the grounds for divorce were by emphasizing the obligations within marriage, the neglect of which formed the grounds for divorce in Jewish law. He also dealt with desertion, which he regarded as an improper means of divorce. Finally, he dealt with remarriage, which he regarded as a right for those who have been divorced against their will, even if the grounds for the divorce were not strictly those that are laid down in Scripture.

This chapter contains much that is unclear for the modern reader: whether Paul was speaking about divorce or simply separation, and whether Paul allowed a divorced person to remarry. Also, although Paul appeared to affirm the Jewish Old Testament marriage obligations, he did not specifically state that these could be used as grounds for divorce, as they were within Judaism. Yet Paul's original readers must have been as interested in such matters as modern readers are. We should conclude either that Paul was a very poor communicator (which is unlikely, given his track record for communicating the Gospel effectively) or that his original readers understood Paul's language and meaning better than do modern readers. Therefore we have to try to understand the Greco-Roman and Jewish language and society, so that we can understand Paul through the eyes of first-century believers, as far as that is possible. A study of Greco-Roman and Jewish marriage and divorce papyri from the fourth century B.C.E. to the fourth century C.E.[1] will help us understand Paul's remarks, though only the conclusions of that study can be presented here.

Divorce in the Greco-Roman World

In the Greco-Roman world men and women could **divorce** their partner **by unilateral separation**, as we already discussed in chapter four. To enact this divorce by separation, the owner of a house could simply tell his or her partner to leave, or the partner could move out of the house. Neither needed to give the partner any warning, and neither had the power to prevent the divorce. There was no need to name any grounds for this divorce, though in a few cases the reasons have been documented. One person divorced a partner who became blind in one eye, and another said that he was divorcing his wife because she had grown old and was not pretty any more.[2] It is difficult to know how many marriages ended in divorce, but anecdotal evidence suggests that the majority

1. These papyri have never been collected together before, though most of the Greek papyri were listed by Orsolina Montevecchi, "Ricerche di sociologia nei documenti dell' Egitto greco-romano," *Aegyptus* 16 (1936): 3-83, and *La papirologia,* Manuali universitari. 1: Per lo studio delle scienze dell'antichità (Torino: Società editrice internazionale, 1973). I collected together all the texts of these papyri and many others that she had missed and published them on the web site: http://www.tyndale.cam.ac.uk/Brewer/MarriagePapyri/Index.htm. See also my papers on these texts: "1 Corinthians 7 in the Light of the Graeco-Roman Marriage and Divorce Papyri," *Tyndale Bulletin* 52 (2001): 101-16, and "1 Corinthians 7 in the Light of the Jewish Greek and Aramaic Marriage and Divorce Papyri," *Tyndale Bulletin* 52 (2001): 225-43.

2. See Pieter Willem Pestman, *Marriage and Matrimonial Property in Ancient Egypt: A Contribution to Establishing the Legal Position of the Woman,* Papyrologica Lugduno-Batava 9 (Leiden: Brill, 1961), p. 75.

of marriages ended before the death of a partner.[3] Greco-Roman marriage certificates were worded as though they expected the marriage to end in divorce, not death. They contain far more details about what should happen in the event of divorce than about arrangements should one of the partners die.[4]

All this is in contrast with the Jewish law, as detailed in chapter five. **Jewish marriage was based on a concept of bondage** — both husband and wife were bound to keep the obligations outlined in their marriage contract, and a divorce required a certificate of freedom for the wife. A Jewish man or woman needed a specific ground for a divorce. One could get a divorce on the basis of the four biblical grounds, though from the time of Hillel a man could also get a divorce on the ground of "any matter." In some ways this was similar to the right under Greco-Roman law to get a divorce without any grounds, but there were two major differences. First, in Judaism this type of divorce was available only to men, and, second, the man still had to give his wife a divorce certificate. Jewish marriage certificates, unlike the Greco-Roman ones, were written with the assumption that the marriage would be ended by death; they had far less emphasis on what would happen in the event of a divorce. Nevertheless, the certificates laid out clearly the obligations within marriage, which implied the right to divorce if those obligations were neglected.[5]

3. A funeral inscription from the late first century B.C.E. says "Uncommon are marriages which last so long, brought to an end by death, not broken apart by divorce; for it was our happy lot that it should be prolonged to the 41st year without estrangement" (G. H. R. Horsley, ed., *New Documents Illustrating Early Christianity,* vol. 3 [North Ryde: The Ancient History Documentary Research Centre, Macquarie University, 1983], pp. 33-36). Also, in a famous comment, Seneca complains that there are women who do not number the years by consuls but by husbands — they divorce to marry and they marry to divorce (*De beneficiis* 3.16.2).

4. See my "1 Corinthians 7 in the Light of the Graeco-Roman Marriage and Divorce Papyri."

5. See my "1 Corinthians 7 in the Light of the Jewish Greek and Aramaic Marriage and Divorce Papyri."

The Emotional Obligations in Marriage

> 1 Cor. 7:1 Now, concerning the things which you wrote to me: It is
> good for a man not to touch a woman. 2 But, because of fornication,
> each man ought to have his own wife, and each woman ought to have
> her own husband. 3 The husband ought to render to the wife her due:
> and likewise also the wife to the husband. 4 The wife does not have au-
> thority over her own body, but the husband does: and likewise also the
> husband does not have authority over his own body, but the wife does.
> 5 Do not defraud each other, except by agreement for a time, so that
> you may have leisure for prayer. And then come together again, that
> Satan may not tempt you through lack of self-control. 6 But this I say
> as a concession, not a command. 7 For I wish that all men were even as
> I myself, but each has their own gift from God, one this and another
> that. 8 However, I say to the unmarried and to widows, It is good for
> them if they remain like me. 9 But if they do not have self-control,
> they should marry: for it is better to be married than to be inflamed.

> 7:1 περὶ δὲ ὧν ἐγράψατε, καλὸν ἀνθρώπῳ γυναικὸς μὴ ἅπτεσθαι: 2 διὰ
> δὲ τὰς πορνείας ἕκαστος τὴν ἑαυτοῦ γυναῖκα ἐχέτω, καὶ ἑκάστη τὸν
> ἴδιον ἄνδρα ἐχέτω. 3 τῇ γυναικὶ ὁ ἀνὴρ τὴν ὀφειλὴν ἀποδιδότω, ὁμοίως
> δὲ καὶ ἡ γυνὴ τῷ ἀνδρί. 4 ἡ γυνὴ τοῦ ἰδίου σώματος οὐκ ἐξουσιάζει
> ἀλλὰ ὁ ἀνήρ: ὁμοίως δὲ καὶ ὁ ἀνὴρ τοῦ ἰδίου σώματος οὐκ ἐξουσιάζει
> ἀλλὰ ἡ γυνή. 5 μὴ ἀποστερεῖτε ἀλλήλους, εἰ μήτι ἂν ἐκ συμφώνου πρὸς
> καιρόν, ἵνα σχολάσητε τῇ προσευχῇ καὶ πάλιν ἐπὶ τὸ αὐτὸ ἦτε, ἵνα μὴ
> πειράζῃ ὑμᾶς ὁ σατανᾶς διὰ τὴν ἀκρασίαν ὑμῶν. 6 τοῦτο δὲ λέγω κατὰ
> συγγνώμην, οὐ κατ' ἐπιταγήν. 7 θέλω δὲ πάντας ἀνθρώπους εἶναι ὡς
> καὶ ἐμαυτόν: ἀλλὰ ἕκαστος ἴδιον ἔχει χάρισμα ἐκ Θεοῦ, ὁ μὲν οὕτως, ὁ
> δὲ οὕτως. 8 λέγω δὲ τοῖς ἀγάμοις καὶ ταῖς χήραις, καλὸν αὐτοῖς ἐὰν
> μείνωσιν ὡς κἀγώ: 9 εἰ δὲ οὐκ ἐγκρατεύονται γαμησάτωσαν, κρεῖττον
> γάρ ἐστιν γαμῆσαι ἢ πυροῦσθαι.

The meaning of this passage hangs on the phrase **"It is good for a man not to touch a woman."** This is either the start of Paul's teaching or a slogan used by the Corinthians. Some commentators regard it as Paul's phrase, but there are clear indications that it is a phrase that he sets out to refute. The chapter opens with περὶ δὲ like the new sections at 7:25; 8:1; 12:1; 16:1; 16:12, which all mark the beginning of a new subject. It is likely that these were the subjects that the Corinthians asked him about in the letter that he referred to here. At 8:1 he also appears to cite a phrase from the Corinthians: "we all have knowledge." In 7:1 he cites their phrase: "It is good for a man not to touch a woman." This sounds like something from pre-Gnostic or ascetic Jewish philosophy. The NIV translation, "It is good for a man not to marry," is very unfortunate. It is certainly wrong in a literal sense, and it also fails to convey the meaning of the phrase. The phrase is a slogan of someone who is anti-sex, not anti-marriage.

Paul replied by stating the opposite. Paul said that married men and women are obligated to take part in sexual love with their partners. He stated this in very strong language. He spoke of the obligation in terms of a debt or robbery (ἀποστερέω) and submission to authority (ἐξουσιάζω). They had this authority over their "body," which is not the authority of a leader or an employer but the authority of a master who owns the body of his slave. **Paul's reply is based on the law of Exodus 21:10-11**, concerning the rights of the slave wife. This passage said that even a slave wife had the right to expect love from her husband, and so the rabbis (and Paul) deduced that a free wife and a husband also had the right to expect this. This explains why the language is so strong, and why he used the imagery of slavery.

However, it should be noted that Paul did not give either partner permission to demand his or her rights, though he told both sides that they *owe* these rights. He expressed this as an obligation to give love, not as an obligation to demand love. Paul also stated that both the man and the woman have equal rights and obligations. Paul taught these things, not merely as his own opinion, but as the command of the Law.

Paul then gave his own opinion on something that the Law does not cover: a period of sexual abstinence. Paul allowed couples to have periods of abstinence on three conditions: it should be of limited duration, it should be for spending time in prayer, and it should be by mutual consent. The written Law did not cover this, though rabbinic traditional law did deal with it. The schools of Hillel and Shammai both assumed that one could have a period of abstinence, though they disagreed about the maximum time permitted. The school of Shammai said two weeks, while the school of Hillel said one week (*m. Ketub.* 5.6; see ch. five). This gives us an idea of the length of time that Paul was considering, and it also shows that Paul was not interested in defining legal details to the same degree as were the rabbis.

There is a tension in this passage between the scriptural norm and Paul's own preference. From these verses it is clear that Paul regarded marriage as necessary but undesirable, though it is not clear what his reason was. Later we will see that he considered the times in which he lived to be dangerous and difficult for children and families, and that this was presumably the reason he discouraged marriage. Paul recognized that the scriptural norm is for men and women to marry. He also recognized that there are good pragmatic reasons for marriage, particularly to avoid sexual temptation. His reasons for avoiding marriage have nothing to do with sexual activity, as one might expect if Paul had agreed with the opening phrase. On the contrary, he regarded nonmarriage as a doorway to sexual sin. Some Corinthians, however, wished to avoid sexual activity, and this led them to separate from their marriage partners.

Paul referred to the Jewish law when he taught Christian sexual morals to the Corinthians. Perhaps he did this because many of the Christians in Corinth came from a Jewish background, but it is more probable that he did it because he based all his moral teachings on the Old Testament.[6] Although many commentators have missed the reference to Exodus 21:10-11 in this passage, others have noticed it.[7] As was seen in chapter five, the rabbis found three grounds for divorce in this passage, based on the three obligations of providing love, food, and clothing. They divided these into two groups: emotional obligations and material obligations. Paul has dealt with the emotional obligations in these verses. In verses 32-35 Paul deals with the material obligations.

6. This has been argued convincingly in Brian S. Rosner, *Paul, Scripture and Ethics: A Study of 1 Corinthians 5–7*, Arbeiten zur Geschichte des antiken Judentums und des Urchristentums 22 (Leiden: Brill, 1994).

7. It is noted in the excellent reference system prepared for the Revised Version (Cambridge University Press, 1912) and in a few publications including: R. J. Rushdoony, *The Institutes of Biblical Law* (Phillipsburg, N.J.: Presbyterian and Reformed Publishing Co., 1973), p. 403; William F. Luck, *Divorce and Remarriage: Recovering the Biblical View* (San Francisco: Harper and Row, 1987), pp. 34-35; Otto A. Piper, *The Biblical View of Sex and Marriage* (London: James Nisbit & Co. Ltd., 1960), pp. 31-32; Rosner, *Paul, Scripture and Ethics*, p. 159; Peter J. Tomson, *Paul and the Jewish Law: Halakha in the Letters of the Apostle to the Gentiles*, Compendia Rerum Iudaicarum ad Novum Testamentum III.1 (Minneapolis: Fortress, 1990), p. 107; David Daube, *The New Testament and Rabbinic Judaism* (London: Athlone, 1956), p. 365. The connection was shown convincingly more than a century ago in N. Herz, "A Hebrew Word in Greek Disguise: 1 Cor. vii.3," *Expository Times* 7 (1895): 48. He pointed out that ὀφειλὴν, *debt*, has a difficult variant ὀφειλομένην εὔνοιαν, *debt of goodwill*. This phrase never occurs in the sense of conjugal rights, and he suggested that εὔνοιαν may be a transliteration of the word interpreted by the rabbis as conjugal rights in Exod. 21:10, עונתה. He noted that such transliteration occurs often in LXX proper names or doubtful words, e.g., 1 Chron. 4:22. However, it is also possible that *debt of goodwill* is one of the "ascetic" glosses that are found throughout this chapter.

The Material Obligations in Marriage

32 But I wish you to be without concerns. The unmarried is concerned
for the things of the Lord, how to please the Lord: 33 but the married
is concerned about the things of the world, how he will please his wife.
34 He is divided. Similarly the unmarried woman and the virgin is
concerned for the things of the Lord, to be holy in both body and
spirit, but the married is concerned about the things of the world, how
she will please her husband. 35 And this I say for your own benefit; not
that I may cast a snare upon you, but for decency and devotion to the
Lord without distraction.

32 θέλω δὲ ὑμᾶς ἀμερίμνους εἶναι. ὁ ἄγαμος μεριμνᾷ τὰ τοῦ Κυρίου,
πῶς ἀρέσῃ τῷ Κυρίῳ: 33 ὁ δὲ γαμήσας μεριμνᾷ τὰ τοῦ κόσμου, πῶς
ἀρέσῃ τῇ γυναικί, 34 καὶ μεμέρισται. καὶ ἡ γυνὴ ἡ ἄγαμος καὶ ἡ
παρθένος[8] μεριμνᾷ τὰ τοῦ Κυρίου, ἵνα ᾖ ἁγία καὶ τῷ σώματι καὶ τῷ
πνεύματι: ἡ δὲ γαμήσασα μεριμνᾷ τὰ τοῦ κόσμου, πῶς ἀρέσῃ τῷ ἀνδρί.
35 τοῦτο δὲ πρὸς τὸ ὑμῶν αὐτῶν σύμφορον λέγω, οὐχ ἵνα βρόχον ὑμῖν
ἐπιβάλω, ἀλλὰ πρὸς τὸ εὔσχημον καὶ εὐπάρεδρον τῷ Κυρίῳ
ἀπερισπάστως.

Paul's motive for discouraging marriage was to save people from the accompanying material obligations during the time of "present distress" and "tribulation in the flesh" (vv. 26, 28) that the Corinthians were experiencing. It is likely that this referred to the famines that were afflicting Corinth at this time,[9] which were probably the cause of illness and death within the congregation (see 11:30). Being married and looking after a family was a full-time occupation at that difficult time. Paul wished them to realize that this would interfere with their service for the Lord. This does not mean that marriage was generally regarded as incompatible with Christian service. Peter had a wife who accompanied him on at least some missionary journeys, and Paul spoke very highly of Aquila and Priscilla. However, marriage meant children, and children needed food, which was scarce at that time.

8. There is some confusion in the variants for this difficult phrase. The various versions make little difference to the argument presented here. The differences are discussed helpfully in Gordon D. Fee, *The First Epistle to the Corinthians,* The New International Commentary on the New Testament (Grand Rapids: Eerdmans, 1987), pp. 334-35.

9. Bruce Winter ("Secular and Christian Responses to Corinthian Famines," *Tyndale Bulletin* 40 [1989]: 86-87) has suggested that the distress may be due to the grain shortages and attendant social unrest from 40 to 60 C.E., for which evidence is found in Eusebius, Pliny, Suetonius, and nonliterary sources.

Paul described the material obligations, like the emotional obligations, in terms of exact equality of men and women. This equality is emphasized almost to the point of repetitiveness. The rabbis also taught that the obligation of material provision applied to both men and women, even though it applied only to the man in the original legislation of Exodus 21:10-11. Presumably they felt that if a slave wife had a right to food and clothes, then so did the free wife, and so did a man. As seen in chapter five, the rabbis carefully defined both the amount of food and clothing that the husband had to provide, and the tasks that the wife had to perform in preparing the meals and clothes. Paul did not speak in such legalistic terms. He referred to the husband and wife who wished to "please" each other. He said nothing negative about these material concerns, even though they are "of the world." This is an obligation within marriage that he recognized in the Law.

Paul did not discuss the use of these obligations with regard to divorce. In this chapter he tried to discourage the Corinthians from divorcing their partners. Therefore we would not expect him to add "By the way, you can use these obligations as grounds for divorce if your partner does not fulfill them." This would give completely the wrong emphasis. Paul's message was that Christians should not cause divorce. They should not separate from their partners, and they should fulfill their marriage obligations so that they do not create an occasion for divorce. He certainly recognized that these obligations could give grounds for divorce; he was clearly familiar with the normal Jewish understanding of Exodus 21:10-11 because he applied it in exactly the same way in which all sections of Judaism applied it: he divided up the three obligations into emotional and material support; he applied them to both male and female equally; and he interpreted the third obligation, which is difficult to translate, as sexual love. Paul assumed that his readers would know about the normal Jewish application of these obligations (his argument in verse 15 seems to depend on this knowledge; see below). Yet as far as Paul was concerned, he wanted to stress that divorce could be avoided if these obligations were kept.

The rabbis similarly tried to discourage divorce on these grounds by encouraging compliance with marital obligations. In contrast to divorce on the ground of unfaithfulness, divorce on the grounds of emotional or material neglect would be delayed while the court tried to persuade the negligent party to change one's ways. If the husband were negligent in emotional support, the court would fine him by increasing the dowry; if the wife were negligent, they would fine her by decreasing the dowry (*m. Ketub.* 5.7; see ch. five). This would continue until the unobliging partner relented or until that person's money was spent. There are no records of courts persuading someone who neglected material support, but the fact that the woman's clothing is defined in monetary terms (*m. Ketub.* 5.8; see ch. five) probably means that a court once imposed a fine to this value when a husband neglected to clothe his wife.

Therefore Paul, like the rabbis, tried to avoid divorces based on the neglect of marital obligations. Paul did not even mention the use of these obligations as grounds for divorce. Instead, he was keen to emphasize the duty of each partner to fulfill these obligations that had been promised in the marriage vows.

Desertion Is Not a Valid Means of Divorce

> 10 And to the married I command (not I, but the Lord): A wife ought
> not to separate herself from her husband 11 (and even if she separates
> herself, she ought to remain unmarried, or she ought to be reconciled
> to her husband); and a husband ought not dismiss his wife. 12 But
> concerning other matters I say, not the Lord: If any brother has an un-
> believing wife, and she is content to live with him, he ought not dis-
> miss her. 13 And a woman who has an unbelieving husband, and he is
> content to live with her, she ought not dismiss her husband. 14 For the
> unbelieving husband is sanctified in the wife, and the unbelieving wife
> is sanctified in the brother: otherwise your children would be unclean;
> but as it is they are holy. 15 But if the unbeliever separates themself,[10]
> let them separate themself: the brother or the sister is not bound in
> such [cases]: for God has called us in peace. 16 For how do you know,
> wife, whether you will save your husband? Or how do you know, hus-
> band, whether you will save your wife?
>
> 10 τοῖς δὲ γεγαμηκόσιν παραγγέλλω, οὐκ ἐγὼ ἀλλὰ ὁ Κύριος, γυναῖκα
> ἀπὸ ἀνδρὸς μὴ χωρισθῆναι[11] 11 — ἐὰν δὲ καὶ χωρισθῇ, μενέτω ἄγαμος
> ἢ τῷ ἀνδρὶ καταλλαγήτω — καὶ ἄνδρα γυναῖκα μὴ ἀφιέναι. 12 τοῖς δὲ
> λοιποῖς λέγω ἐγώ, οὐχ ὁ Κύριος: εἴ τις ἀδελφὸς γυναῖκα ἔχει ἄπιστον,
> καὶ αὕτη συνευδοκεῖ οἰκεῖν μετ' αὐτοῦ, μὴ ἀφιέτω αὐτήν: 13 καὶ γυνὴ εἴ
> τις ἔχει ἄνδρα ἄπιστον, καὶ οὗτος συνευδοκεῖ οἰκεῖν μετ' αὐτῆς, μὴ
> ἀφιέτω τὸν ἄνδρα.[12] 14 ἡγίασται γὰρ ὁ ἀνὴρ ὁ ἄπιστος ἐν τῇ γυναικί,

10. I have used here the ugly form "themself" for a singular person who may be either male or female.

11. This aorist is passive but can be read in a middle reflexive mood. The Greek is as ambiguous as the English "let her not be separated." A few manuscripts make it unambiguously reflexive, using χωρίζεσθαι (present middle infinitive, "to separate oneself," in A D F G 1505 1881) or χωριζέσθω (third person singular, present imperative middle, "let her separate herself," in P^{46}, 614).

12. Most MSS read αὐτόν, "him." Nestle-Aland (*Novum Testamentum Graece,* ed. Kurt Aland et al. [Stuttgart: Deutsche Bibelstiftung, 1979]) follows א A B C D* etc. Probably the

καὶ ἡγίασται ἡ γυνὴ ἡ ἄπιστος ἐν τῷ ἀδελφῷ: ἐπεὶ ἄρα τὰ τέκνα ὑμῶν
ἀκάθαρτά ἐστιν, νῦν δὲ ἅγιά ἐστιν. 15 εἰ δὲ ὁ ἄπιστος χωρίζεται,
χωριζέσθω: οὐ δεδούλωται ὁ ἀδελφὸς ἢ ἡ ἀδελφὴ ἐν τοῖς τοιούτοις: ἐν
δὲ εἰρήνῃ κέκληκεν ὑμᾶς ὁ θεός. 16 τί γὰρ οἶδας, γύναι, εἰ τὸν ἄνδρα
σώσεις; ἢ τί οἶδας, ἄνερ, εἰ τὴν γυναῖκα σώσεις;

Before discussing the meaning of the passage there are **a few matters of translation** to consider. In the above translation I have used "ought" to indicate the imperative mood, except for the "permissive" imperative in verse 15, for which I have used the normal "let." The normal way to translate the imperative is "let . . .," but this is usually misleading because the imperative normally carries the sense of an order, or at least a request.[13] The other translation difficulty lies with the use of the passive/middle mood for the verb χωρίζω "to separate." The verb occurs regularly in this passage in a form that could be either passive ("to be separated") or middle (i.e., reflexive, "to separate oneself"). In the context of this passage one can not use the passive throughout, especially in verse 15 where the unbeliever separates himself or herself against the wishes of the believer. The reflexive mood makes good sense throughout this passage.[14]

Both the verbs χωρίζω and ἀφίημι have the sense of "to divorce" although they have been translated here by "to separate" and "to dismiss," respectively. Differences between these words should not be exaggerated. There may be no

---

shorter "him" is correct because Paul has been very careful throughout this chapter to balance the phrases relating to male and female roles, even to the point of needlessly repeating himself. The less ambiguous "her husband" may have been written to confirm the surprising conclusion that a woman can divorce her husband.

13. The so-called "permissive imperative" is a misnomer. Daniel B. Wallace (*Greek Grammar beyond the Basics: An Exegetical Syntax of the New Testament* [Grand Rapids: Zondervan, 1996]) suggests it should be called "an imperative of resignation" because it is used when there is a *fait accompli*. Two of the few occurrences of this type of imperative are seen in this chapter, at vv. 15, 36.

14. J. A. Fitzmyer ("The Matthean Divorce Texts and Some New Palestinian Evidence," *Theological Studies* 37 [1976]: 197-226) said that χωρίζω can bear only the middle (reflexive) mood in the present tense, and that most manuscripts have the aorist tense in v. 10, which always has a passive mood. This assertion has been repeated by other authors who depend on it for their argument, especially Jerome Murphy-O'Conner, "The Divorced Woman in 1 Cor. 7.10-11," *Journal of Biblical Literature* 100 (1981): 601-6. However, it is not possible to maintain this fine distinction between tenses. We find an example in a papyrus dated 13 B.C.E. where the aorist tense is used in a reflexive, not passive, mood. *BGU* IV.1101 (i.e., GM-13 in my *Marriage and Divorce Papyri*, http://www.tyndale.cam.ac.uk/brewer/MarriagePapyri/TableGM-1.htm [2000]) reads ἐχωρίσθημεν ἀπ' ἀλλή(λων) "separated from each other." It is not possible they could *both* be passively separated by the other, though they could both separate *themselves* from each other. It therefore makes more sense to translate "separate" reflexively throughout 1 Cor. 7:10-15.

significance in their use other than stylistic variation. In English one might use both "divorce" and "dissolution" in the same paragraph without intending any difference in meaning. There were more than fifty words used for "divorce" in Greek marriage and divorce contracts, and it was common to use several in a single document.[15] It is certainly not possible to say that ἀφίημι is a legal divorce and χωρίζω is just a separation.[16] In Greco-Roman society separation *was* a legal divorce, and χωρίζω is the most common of the words used for divorce. Nor can one say that Paul was distinguishing between the passive "being divorced" (represented by "to be separated") and the active "divorcing" (represented by "dismiss him/her").[17] The passive "to be separated" should be read as reflexive because it is used in verse 15 even of someone who has decided to be separated against the will of the partner. Therefore, both verbs, as used in this passage, portray the actions of someone who has chosen to divorce the partner.

The type of divorce that Paul referred to here is the **Greco-Roman divorce by separation.** The verbs used for divorce in this passage are particularly apt for divorce by separation. The house owner would "dismiss" (ἀφίημι) his or her partner from the house, whereas the nonowner would "separate" (χωρίζω) himself or herself from the household. Paul mostly spoke of "separation" as the wife's action and "dismissal" as the husband's, which reflects the normal situation where the man owns the house.[18]

Paul's message here is in two parts, the first "from the Lord" and the second from himself, and at first sight the two parts contradict each other.[19] The first part in **verses 10-11** is simply stated as authoritative and is presumably based on what the Corinthians knew of the Gospel traditions. It states that a husband or wife "ought not separate himself or herself" (χωρισθῆναι). One could translate "divorce" instead of "separate" because Paul is using χωρίζω, which is a standard term for the Greco-Roman "divorce by separation."

Paul added that if divorce by separation had occurred, believers must do everything they can to reverse it. They should try to be reconciled, and they

15. See my "1 Corinthians 7 in the Light of the Graeco-Roman Marriage and Divorce Papyri." One of the contracts analyzed there, p.Ryl. 154 of 66 C.E., uses six different words for divorce in the single papyrus.

16. As in J. K. Elliott, "Paul's Teaching on Marriage in 1 Corinthians: Some Problems Reconsidered," *New Testament Studies* 19 (1972-73): 219-25, esp. p. 224.

17. As attempted in Murphy-O'Conner, "The Divorced Woman in 1 Cor. 7.10-11," esp. p. 601. He relies on Fitzmyer (see n. 14 above).

18. Paul did not adhere strictly to this distinction because in v. 13 the woman is told not to dismiss her husband. Although a woman would not normally own a house, a rich widow or a daughter of a rich man may own a house in which the couple choose to live.

19. Murphy-O'Connor ("The Divorced Woman in 1 Cor. 7.10-11") says that Paul is clearly contradictory at this point.

should remain single so that they remain available for reconciliation. Paul applied this to the woman ("if she separates herself . . ."), but it is presumably meant to apply equally to the man. This caveat makes sense only if Paul was talking about divorce by separation in a Greco-Roman context. If he was referring to simple separation, as in a Jewish context, the woman would not have the right to remarry, and neither of them could be called "unmarried" (ἄγαμος)

This **appears to contradict verse 15**, which allows this same "divorce by separation": "if the unbeliever separates themself, let them separate themself: the brother or the sister is not bound." As we will see below, there have been attempts to interpret verse 15 as allowing separation without divorce, but such interpretations would not be understood by a first-century reader.

Many commentators assert that verses 10-11 and verses 12-15 are addressed to two slightly different groups. They would say that the first section is addressed only to believers who are married to believers, while the second section is addressed to believers who are married to nonbelievers. This may be indicated by the opening words of verse 12: "To the rest I say . . ." (τοῖς δὲ λοιποῖς λέγω), though this should probably be translated as "But concerning other matters I say. . . ." Although the latter section speaks about mixed marriages, there is nothing in the first section to indicate that it applied only to nonmixed marriages.

This apparent contradiction is similar to the contradiction that some see in the Gospels. If Jesus condemned all divorce, how could he allow divorce for adultery? However, the contradictions are solved if both Jesus and Paul condemned only a particular type of divorce. As seen in the previous chapter, Jesus condemned the Hillelite no-fault divorce called "any matter" divorce. In the same way, Paul condemned the Greco-Roman "divorce by separation," which was also a no-fault type of divorce. Both Jesus and Paul allowed divorce for a valid grounds, such as adultery (specifically mentioned by Jesus) or desertion (which I will argue is the subject of v. 15).

Paul's message in **verses 12-15** was, as he admitted, based on his own opinion and not divine revelation. Therefore, instead of just stating it, he buttressed it throughout with reason. Paul commanded the believer to remain married, even if the partner was an unbeliever, as long as the unbeliever was willing to stay married. The question that naturally arises is, What does one do if an unbelieving partner is not willing? This is answered in verse 15: if the unbeliever wishes to separate himself or herself (i.e., divorce the believer), then let him or her do so. The believer should want to continue the marriage, and so the believer should not be the one who carries out the divorce by separation. The next question that arises is, Should the believer remain single and try to be reconciled, as commanded in verse 11? This is answered with the words "the brother or the sister is not bound in such [cases]: for God has called us in peace." The most straightforward reading of these words is that Paul allowed the believer in this situation to remarry. However, these words have been the subject of huge debates, and thus this interpretation will be examined at greater length in the next section.

Paul, therefore, did not allow any Christian to use the Greco-Roman procedure of divorce by separation. He based this both on Jesus' teaching and on his own understanding of marriage. Jesus taught that one cannot get divorced on the Hillelite ground of "any matter," which was very similar to the Greco-Roman divorce by separation. Paul added that one could not use this procedure even if one was married to a non-Christian. However, if a non-Christian used this procedure, there was nothing that the Christian could do to prevent it. Is this Christian free to remarry? The next section discusses the meaning of Paul's answer to this implied question.

"Not Bound"

> 15 But if the unbeliever separates themself, let them separate themself: the brother or the sister is not bound in such [cases]; for God has called us in peace.
>
> 15 εἰ δὲ ὁ ἄπιστος χωρίζεται, χωριζέσθω· οὐ δεδούλωται ὁ ἀδελφὸς ἢ ἡ ἀδελφὴ ἐν τοῖς τοιούτοις· ἐν δὲ εἰρήνῃ κέκληκεν ὑμᾶς[20] ὁ θεός.

Many different meanings have been suggested for the phrases "is not bound" and "God has called us in peace." The significant question to ask is, In what way is the person now free? Proposals have included: free to separate or remain separate (i.e., not required to seek reconciliation), free to divorce, and free to remarry. Of these, only the last one makes sense in the context of the passage and of the first-century Greco-Roman world. It would be meaningless to declare the person free to remain separate because there was nothing one could do about reversing the separation, other than pestering one's former partner to return.

Paul has already said that believers should attempt to remain with their spouses and that they should not employ divorce by separation themselves. If

20. The United Bible Society text has ὑμᾶς even though the MSS evidence is poor. Bruce Metzger (*A Textual Commentary on the Greek New Testament: A Companion Volume to the United Bible Societies Greek New Testament,* 2nd ed. [Stuttgart: Deutsche Bibelgesellschaft, 1994]) explains that scribes tend to "make modifications in the interest of generalising the reference of aphorisms."

the unbeliever has nevertheless walked out or asked the believer to leave (depending on who owns the house), there is nothing that the believing partner can do. Of course, if it is the believer who has initiated the separation, the Church can exert pressure to be reconciled, or at least to remain single while other problems can be tackled. Yet if a nonbelieving partner has initiated the separation, it is meaningless to say that the believer is free to remain separated. It is also meaningless to say that the believer is free to divorce because if separation has taken place, the couple have already completed the divorce procedure, according to Greco-Roman law. Even if the dowry was not returned, they were still considered legally divorced, and the wife would have to take her ex-husband to court for the return of the dowry.[21] No rite or document was needed to complete the divorce, so there was nothing more that they needed do to complete a divorce other than separate.

The only situation where separation would not necessarily be equivalent to divorce was where the unbeliever was a Jewish man. A Jewish man might separate from his Christian wife without giving her a divorce certificate. In this situation Paul's words might mean that the Christian was free to pursue a Jewish divorce through a Jewish court, citing the grounds of material and emotional neglect. This would, however, be entirely unnecessary unless the Christian was planning to marry another non-Christian Jew, which Paul would forbid in any case.

The only freedom that makes any sense in this context is the **freedom to remarry**. We do not have to rely on a process of elimination to decide what this phrase means, because the language that Paul used would have been very plain to any first-century reader. We find similar phraseology in a large number of ancient divorce certificates. As seen in chapter five, all Jewish divorce certificates and most Greco-Roman ones contained the words "you are free to marry any man you wish," or something very similar. These words were so important that the rabbis concluded that they were the only words that were essential in a Jewish divorce certificate. These words can be found in Jewish divorce certificates in rabbinic sources from the first-century C.E. and back to the Aramaic contracts from the Elephantine community of the fifth century B.C.E. They can be traced in non-Jewish sources in Greco-Roman and Demotic papyri from the

21. We have examples of such law cases, e.g.: "Serapion, having squandered my dowry as he pleased, continually ill-treated me and insulted me, using violence towards me, and depriving me of the necessaries of life. I therefore beg you to order him to be brought before you in order that he may be compelled perforce to pay back my dowry increased by half its amount" (P.Oxy. II.281 = GR35; 20-50 C.E., Egypt). We also have a petition from a husband whose wife left with some of his property: "she became dissatisfied with our union, and finally left (the house) carrying off property belonging to me" (P.Oxy. II.281 = GR35; 30-35 C.E., Egypt).

fourth century C.E. to 548 B.C.E.,[22] to divorce stipulations in marriage contracts of Babylon in the seventh to the third century B.C.E., to the laws of Charondas in sixth century B.C.E. Rhegium,[23] and possibly to the Middle Assyrian laws of 1400 B.C.E.[24]

To first-century readers, whether they were Jewish or Greco-Roman, Paul's words would immediately remind them of the freedom to remarry. This is also the meaning that fits best in the context of the passage. Paul has just spoken about a believer who has been divorced against his or her will, and so the natural question is whether or not this person was allowed to remarry. The words "the brother or sister is not bound in this situation" answers that question.

"For God Has Called Us in Peace"

The phrase "for God has called us in peace" is more difficult, but Gordon Fee has pointed us in the right direction. He made a comparison with the phrase "for the sake of peace," which occurs in early rabbinic writings. It was used in pre–70 C.E. rabbinic Judaism to indicate that **a pragmatic solution** was necessary that did not necessarily conform with the legalistically correct procedure. Sometimes the solution suggested by a strict interpretation of the Law did not have the desired effect. Strictly speaking, an imbecile could not be prosecuted for stealing, but, nevertheless, stolen goods were confiscated from him and returned to their owner "for the sake of peace."[25] Sometimes pragmatism has to rule over the strict application of law, for the sake of a peaceful society and in order that God's will be done.

22. See my "1 Corinthians 7 in the Light of the Graeco-Roman Marriage and Divorce Papyri."

23. Diodorus of Sicily wrote about the laws of Charondas in the sixth century B.C.E. Rhegium. These laws allowed a man to "dismiss a wife" (ἐκβάλλω γυναῖκα) and allowed a wife to "be free from the husband" (ἀπολύειν τὸν ἄνδρα) and "marry whomever she chose" (D.S. 12.17-18).

24. See my "Deuteronomy 24.1-4 and the Origin of the Jewish Divorce Certificate," *Journal of Jewish Studies* 49 (1998): 230-43, and details in ch. two.

25. According to *m. Git.* 5.8, the non-Jewish poor were not strictly allowed to take the gleanings, but they were allowed "for the sake of peace," and mental defectives were held partly responsible for theft "for the sake of peace" (*m. Git.* 5.8). Fee (*First Epistle to the Corinthians*, pp. 304-5) regarded it as meaning "in order to make a good impression on Gentiles," but I have shown elsewhere that it was rabbinic legal terminology for what we might now call "pragmatism" (*Techniques and Assumptions in Jewish Exegesis before 70 CE*, Texte und Studien zum antiken Judentum 30 [Tübingen: J. C. B. Mohr, 1992], pp. 21, 37, 82, 144-45).

Strictly speaking, deserted believers were not free to remarry under the laws of Scripture. They were free to remarry only if they had a valid divorce based on one of the four grounds named in Scripture. Desertion was not one of the grounds, though most Jews would have said that there was no problem for a man who had been deserted because he could simply write out a divorce certificate citing "any matter" as the ground. A woman, however, was stuck unless she could persuade her ex-husband to write a divorce certificate for her. This type of situation still occurs today, and such women are called *agunot* or "chained women." They cannot remarry without a divorce certificate, and their husbands refuse, out of spite, to write one. There are many calls for changes to the Jewish law to release such women.

Paul cut through this legal problem by declaring "God has called us in peace." The pragmatic solution that he proposed is that all those who have been divorced against their will, and who therefore can do nothing to reverse it, should be regarded as validly divorced; they are no longer bound by their marriage contract and are free to remarry.

Paul could have argued for this in a slightly more legalistic way. He could have said that anyone who deserted a partner (i.e., turned that partner out of the house, or walked out of the house) was neglecting to supply food, clothing, and love from that point in time. Therefore, the neglected partner could divorce on these biblical grounds. Yet this neglect would take months to prove, and perhaps years. It is significant that Paul did not apply the law in this legally correct way but instead simply applied a pragmatic solution. It probably indicates that Paul was not too concerned with the exact grounds for divorce when a man or woman is divorced against his or her will in a society that is governed by nonbiblical laws.

Paul's general principle is therefore that a man or woman who has been divorced against his or her will should be free to remarry. Usually one would be able to demonstrate that the partner who forced the divorce had provided sufficient grounds for a divorce, but there is no need to demonstrate this. The fact that the partner considered the divorce to be legal and final was sufficient. This does not mean, of course, that believers can also divorce their partners for any cause. Paul told the believers that they may not use the Greco-Roman divorce by separation, and Jesus told them that they cannot use the Hillelite divorce for "any matter," which is the Jewish equivalent. Paul also said that believers who had deserted their partners should attempt to be reconciled (vv. 10-11).

Marriage Is Good, and Lifelong, but Difficult at Present

25 Now concerning virgins I have no commandment of the Lord: but I
give my opinion, as one that has obtained mercy of the Lord to be
trustworthy. 26 I think therefore that this is good in view of the present
distress, that it is good for a man to remain as he is. 27 Are you bound
to a wife? Do not seek release. Are you released from a wife? Do not
seek a wife. 28 But if you do marry, you have not sinned; and if a virgin marries, she has not sinned. Yet such will have physical tribulation,
and I would spare you that. 29 But I mean, brothers, that the time is
short, and from now both those who have wives will be like those who
had none; 30 and those who weep, like those who wept not; and those
that rejoice, like those who rejoiced not; and those who buy, like those
who owned nothing; 31 and those who use the world, as those not using it to the full: for the form of this world is passing away. . . .

36 But if any man thinks that he is behaving wrongly to his virgin,
if [she is] past marriageable age,[26] and if necessity arises, he ought to
do what he wishes; he does not sin; let them marry. 37 But he who
stands firm in his heart, having no necessity, but is firm with regard to
his own desires, and has decided in his own heart to keep his own virgin, will do well. 38 So then both he who marries his own virgin does
well; and he that does not marry her shall do better.

25 περὶ δὲ τῶν παρθένων ἐπιταγὴν Κυρίου οὐκ ἔχω, γνώμην δὲ δίδωμι
ὡς ἠλεημένος ὑπὸ Κυρίου πιστὸς εἶναι. 26 νομίζω οὖν τοῦτο καλὸν
ὑπάρχειν διὰ τὴν ἐνεστῶσαν ἀνάγκην, ὅτι καλὸν ἀνθρώπῳ τὸ οὕτως
εἶναι. 27 δέδεσαι γυναικί; μὴ ζήτει λύσιν: λέλυσαι ἀπὸ γυναικός; μὴ
ζήτει γυναῖκα. 28 ἐὰν δὲ καὶ γαμήσῃς, οὐχ ἥμαρτες: καὶ ἐὰν γήμῃ ἡ
παρθένος, οὐχ ἥμαρτεν. θλῖψιν δὲ τῇ σαρκὶ ἕξουσιν οἱ τοιοῦτοι, ἐγὼ δὲ
ὑμῶν φείδομαι. 29 τοῦτο δέ φημι, ἀδελφοί, ὁ καιρὸς συνεσταλμένος
ἐστίν: τὸ λοιπὸν ἵνα καὶ οἱ ἔχοντες γυναῖκας ὡς μὴ ἔχοντες ὦσιν, 30 καὶ
οἱ κλαίοντες ὡς μὴ κλαίοντες, καὶ οἱ χαίροντες ὡς μὴ χαίροντες, καὶ οἱ
ἀγοράζοντες ὡς μὴ κατέχοντες, 31 καὶ οἱ χρώμενοι τὸν κόσμον ὡς μὴ
καταχρώμενοι: παράγει γὰρ τὸ σχῆμα τοῦ κόσμου τούτου. . . .

36 εἰ δέ τις ἀσχημονεῖν ἐπὶ τὴν παρθένον αὐτοῦ νομίζει, ἐὰν ᾖ
ὑπέρακμος, καὶ οὕτως ὀφείλει γίνεσθαι, ὃ θέλει ποιείτω: οὐχ ἁμαρτάνει:
γαμείτωσαν. 37 ὃς δὲ ἕστηκεν ἐν τῇ καρδίᾳ αὐτοῦ ἑδραῖος, μὴ ἔχων
ἀνάγκην, ἐξουσίαν δὲ ἔχει περὶ τοῦ ἰδίου θελήματος, καὶ τοῦτο κέκρικεν
ἐν τῇ ἰδίᾳ καρδίᾳ, τηρεῖν τὴν ἑαυτοῦ παρθένον, καλῶς ποιήσει: 38 ὥστε

26. Or, "if [his] passions are strong."

> καὶ ὁ γαμίζων τὴν ἑαυτοῦ παρθένον καλῶς ποιεῖ, καὶ ὁ μὴ γαμίζων κρεῖσσον ποιήσει.

The meaning of these verses is difficult to determine because we do not know what Paul meant by παρθένος, "virgins" or "unmarried." He appears to address males who are responsible for a female virgin, advising them not to marry the virgin because of the "present distress." **There are three possible interpretations** of what Paul said:

a. he was advising an unmarried man not to marry his betrothed;
b. he was advising a father not to marry his daughter to her betrothed; or
c. he was advising an ascetic couple in a sex-free marriage not to start normal marital relations.

The third interpretation is a recent suggestion that is included here for completeness. There is little to commend it, and it contradicts Paul's teaching that sexual relations are an integral part of marriage (vv. 3-5). The second, where Paul addressed a virgin's father, is the traditional interpretation. It is based on the variant in verse 36 — γαμείτωσαν *let them marry* instead of γαμείτω *let him marry*[27] — and the use of the different verb γαμίζων in verse 38. This difference, a subtle one, is based on a distinction that is not often maintained in contemporary Greek, and so it is not safe to build a case around it.[28] The first possible interpretation is most likely: that is, Paul was addressing a man who was wondering about whether or not to marry his betrothed.[29]

It makes little difference which interpretation is correct, as far as the argument of this book is concerned. What is important, with regard to the question of divorce and remarriage, is the meaning of verse 27. It appears to advise those who have been released from their marriages that they should not seek to marry again because of the present distress. The question is whether this is addressed to someone who was betrothed or someone who was married and divorced. If it is the latter, then Paul was very clearly allowing remarriage. Although he advised against marriage, he also said that it would not be sinful to marry (v. 28).

I have already concluded above that Paul allowed those who were divorced against their will or who had divorced on the basis of biblical grounds to

27. The majority of texts support the former, and the latter is found in D* F G and a few other sources.

28. In classical Greek, there is sometimes a distinction between γαμέω "to marry" and γαμίζω "to give in marriage." However, this distinction had broken down in the *koine* Greek of the New Testament period (see Fee, *First Epistle to the Corinthians*, p. 354).

29. Fee (*First Epistle to the Corinthians*, pp. 325-54) makes a very strong case for this.

remarry. Therefore, it is possible that Paul was addressing divorced persons in verse 27, advising them not to remarry but allowing them to do so if they so desired. However, those who wish to argue that Paul did not allow remarriage after divorce would say that Paul meant to give this permission only to those who were released from a betrothal agreement. This limited application is possible, though unlikely. Although verse 27 occurs in the context of a passage speaking mainly about betrothal, it is quite possible that Paul should also direct his advice to those who had divorced, and there is nothing in the context to rule this out. The term "released," λύσιν, is used generally for release from any type of contract, including a marriage contract.[30] However, it would be unsafe to base a firm conclusion either way on this verse.

Remarriage after Widowhood (or Divorce)

> 39 A wife is bound for so long a time as her husband lives; but if the husband should fall asleep, she is free to be married to whom she wishes; only in the Lord. 40 But she is happier if she remains as she is, in my judgment: and I think that I also have the Spirit of God.
>
> 39 γυνὴ δέδεται ἐφ' ὅσον χρόνον ζῇ ὁ ἀνὴρ αὐτῆς· ἐὰν δὲ κοιμηθῇ ὁ ἀνήρ, ἐλευθέρα ἐστὶν ᾧ θέλει γαμηθῆναι, μόνον ἐν Κυρίῳ.
> 40 μακαριωτέρα δέ ἐστιν ἐὰν οὕτως μείνῃ, κατὰ τὴν ἐμὴν γνώμην, δοκῶ δὲ κἀγὼ πνεῦμα Θεοῦ ἔχειν.

This section is almost certainly addressed to widows, though some have argued that it is addressed to women whose betrothed have died.[31] The reason for this seemingly improbable interpretation is that the structure of the chapter suggests it. The chapter starts by addressing the married and unmarried (vv. 1-16), then it addresses betrothed men (vv. 25-38), and so one might expect it to end by addressing betrothed women (vv. 39-40). The only merit of this interpretation is its tidiness. On the surface these verses are addressed to women whose husbands have died. Even if betrothed widows were in Paul's mind at this point, he was certainly also addressing unbetrothed widows.

30. It occurs in P.Oxy. XII.1473 = GM201, a marriage contract that starts with a reference to a previous marriage that is a "discharged contract" (συγγραφὴ ἐλύθη). It is commonly used to refer to discharge from financial or social contracts (see James Hope Moulton and George Milligan, *The Vocabulary of the Greek Testament: Illustrated from the Papyri and Other Non-literary Sources* [London: Hodder and Stoughton, 1930]).

31. E.g., Stephen Clark, *Putting Asunder: Divorce and Remarriage in Biblical and Pastoral Perspective* (Bridgend, Wales: Brynterion, 1999).

As Fee and others have suggested, the obvious message of these verses is that a Christian widow was not subject to the Jewish custom of **levirate marriage.** This Old Testament law said that a Jewish woman whose husband died childless had to marry her brother-in-law until she had a child. This was still practiced in the first century, though it was becoming less common.[32] Paul stated that it was unnecessary for a Christian widow. She could marry (or not marry) whomever she wished.

Paul presumably realized that levirate marriage was no longer necessary now that property was bought and sold for permanent ownership. Land used to be returned periodically to the original family line to which it had been allocated by Joshua. This would happen every fiftieth year, the Jubilee year. However, this redistribution of land probably did not take place very often in practice, and it is very unlikely that it ever happened after the Exile. It was certainly impossible after the Roman occupation. Without this Jubilee redistribution, it was not necessary for every family line to have a descendant who could receive back their parcel of land. So, levirate marriage became an unnecessary suffering borne by a widow. For Christians it was doubly unnecessary because they were for the most part outside the inheritance of Israel. Thus, this Old Testament law was irrelevant to them, and Paul said so.

The most interesting aspect of these verses is Paul's **quotation from a standard Jewish divorce certificate.** According to the Mishnah, which is confirmed by a surviving papyrus, first-century divorce certificates contained a line stating:

> You are free to marry any Jewish man you wish.[33]

The only difference in Paul's version is the stipulation that she must marry a man who is "in the Lord" instead of a "Jewish man." The words that Paul quoted were the most important part of the divorce certificate and were the only words that were necessary on the certificate. Greco-Roman divorce certificates often contained similar words, but there was never any reference to the religion of the man she should marry. Paul was therefore quoting the standard Jewish divorce certificate, but why? The explanation can be found in a very similar passage in later rabbinic writings. Later, when R. Ashi similarly wanted to argue that levirate marriage was unnecessary, he used almost exactly the same reasoning that Paul used here.

32. Hillel started this trend in the first century B.C.E., as evidenced by the school debate in *m. Yebam.* 13.1.

33. As in the Mishnah at *m. Git.* 9.3 and in the certificate found at Masada, dated 72 C.E. (Pierre Benoit, Jozef T. Milik, and Roland de Vaux, *Discoveries in the Judaean Desert, II: Les grottes de Murabba'at* [Oxford: Clarendon, 1961], p. 19).

Rabbi Ashi (died 427 C.E.) set out to prove that a widow was free to marry whomever she wanted, even if she was childless. He reasoned that if a divorce gave a woman complete freedom to marry whomever she wished, then widowhood would give her the same freedom. If Ashi had stating his reasoning in full (which he did not need to do because he was speaking to fellow rabbis), he would have linked the widow and divorcée by an *a fortiori* statement, which is called *gezerah shavah* in rabbinic exegesis, that is, a statement like "if this major point is true, then this other minor one is certainly true."[34] He would have said: "If a divorcée is free from the obligations of her marriage contract when her husband is still alive, a widow is certainly free from these same obligations."

Paul said almost exactly the same thing. To paraphrase Paul slightly, he said:

> A woman is bound to her husband by a marriage contract so long as he lives. If her husband dies, she is free. She certainly has as much freedom as a divorcée who may "marry any man she wishes," though she should only marry in the Lord.

It is interesting to see that, for Paul and for his contemporary Jews, it was more obvious that a divorcée could marry anyone she wished than that a widow had this freedom. In order to prove that a widow had this freedom too, Paul pointed out that a divorcée had this freedom, and not the other way round.

Many commentators have misunderstood what Paul was trying to say here and have concluded that Paul thought a marriage could end only with death. This is an understandable mistake, especially when one compares this verse with Romans 7:2, which we must now consider.

Romans 7:1-4: Married to the Law or Christ

> 7:1-4: Do you not know, brethren — for I am speaking to those who know the law — that the law is binding on a person only during his life? (2) Thus a married woman is bound by law to her husband as long as he lives; but if her husband dies she is discharged from the law concerning the husband. (3) Accordingly, she will be called an adulteress if she lives with another man while her husband is alive. But if her husband dies she is free from that law, and if she marries another man she is not an adulteress. (4) Likewise, my brethren, you have died to the law through the body of Christ, so that

34. See my *Techniques and Assumptions,* pp. 17-18.

> you may belong to another, to him who has been raised from the dead in order that we may bear fruit for God.

Paul was speaking here about a woman who was freed from her marriage contract through the death of her husband. For a Jewish woman who was desperately unhappy with her marriage, or who wanted to marry someone else, this was often the only hope she had. She could not initiate a divorce unless her husband neglected one of the obligations of Exodus 21:10-11, and she could not simply walk out because her husband had the legal right to use all her property while they were married. Even if she had parents to support her, so that she could live separately from her husband, she could certainly not marry another man unless her husband divorced her. She could, of course, go and live with another man whom she wished to marry, and her husband would feel obliged to divorce her for adultery; but rabbinic law forbade a divorced woman from marrying anyone with whom she had committed adultery (*m. Soṭa* 5.1; *m. Yebam.* 2.8). So, her only hope was that her husband would die and leave her free to marry the man she loved.

In Romans 7 Paul is demonstrating that we were servants of the Law before Christ rescued us. He begins with an illustration in which we are married to the Law but we want to be married to Christ instead. The only way we can be released from our marriage to the Law is if the Law divorces us (which he will not do) or if the Law breaks the marriage contract so that we can force a divorce. The Law is law-abiding by nature, so he is not likely to give us cause for a divorce, and our only hope is that the marriage will end by death, though of course the Law will not die. Paul says that Christ releases us by *his* death, which we share. Our marriage to the Law ends when we die in Christ and are raised with him, so we are alive and able to marry Christ, our beloved. Therefore, the whole passage is an illustration by which Paul describes how Christ has released us from the Law.

This illustration is not meant to teach us about divorce or remarriage. It is meant to teach us about the way we have died to the Law and been raised to new life in Christ. Nevertheless, many commentators have also tried to use this illustration to learn about remarriage. They have concluded that remarriage is possible only after death because Paul says here that "a married woman is bound by law to her husband as long as he lives" (v. 2).

The fact that Romans 7:2 and 1 Corinthians 7:39 both speak about death ending a marriage, without any mention of divorce, should not lead us to the conclusion that divorce for a valid cause does not also end a marriage. We have seen from the context of both verses that there were good reasons for omitting a reference to divorce. In 1 Corinthians 7:39-40 Paul was teaching specifically about remarriage after widowhood, and in Romans 7:1-4 Paul is using marriage as a metaphor for the dissolution of the Law through Christ's death.

Even without the above arguments, it would also be wrong to conclude a rejection of remarriage after divorce simply from Paul's silence in these verses. The following example shows that **divorce could similarly be omitted in a carefully crafted Greco-Roman legal document**, without implying that the right of divorce and remarriage was being denied.

> And it shall not be lawful for Philiscus to bring in any other wife but Apollonia, nor to keep a concubine or boy, nor to have children by another woman while Apollonia lives.[35]

One might conclude from this marriage contract that the husband was not allowed to remarry during the lifetime of his wife. However, this would be totally contrary to everything we know about Greco-Roman marriage contracts. In Greco-Roman law either partner had the right to divorce the other partner at any time and remarry. It would be inconceivable that the absence of any reference to divorce could be interpreted as a denial of this right. The right to remarriage was embedded so deeply in Greco-Roman marriage law that there was no need to mention it. It was, however, necessary to state that a husband may not maintain a mistress or have children by another woman. Although adultery was an offense, sexual relations with slaves were generally permitted. This contract was making clear at the outset of the marriage that the wife would not tolerate this type of behavior while she was alive and while she was his wife. She could, of course, still be divorced, and then this stipulation about having children by other women would end, because the marriage contract had ended.

The right to remarry after divorce was the fundamental right that was communicated by the Jewish divorce certificate. It was also seen as an undeniable right in Greco-Roman marriage and divorce law. Technically it was actually illegal for a divorced Roman woman to remain single for more than eighteen months, though this law was rarely enforced.[36] It would therefore have been very difficult for Paul to convince his readers that they no longer had the right to remarriage after a valid divorce, and it is inconceivable that he could

35. Marriage certificate, 92 B.C.E., Tebtunis, Egypt; P.Tebt. I.104, lines 19-20 = GM92.

36. Augustine's laws, the *lex Julia de maritandis ordinibus* (18 B.C.E.) and *lex Papia Poaea nuptialis* (9 B.C.E.), which were later merged into a single text *(lex Iulia et Papia)*, made it a duty of all Roman men age twenty-five to sixty and Roman women age twenty to fifty to be married. Widows could remain unmarried for two years, and divorcées for eighteen months, but then they were expected to remarry.

have expected his readers to conclude, simply by his silence when discussing the issue of widowhood or illustrating the end of the believer's marriage to the Law, that remarriage of a divorcée was unacceptable.

Conclusions

Paul addressed several problems faced by believers who were living in the Greco-Roman world, where anyone could employ divorce by separation. He reminded them that Jesus forbade this type of separation when he condemned the very similar Hillelite "any matter" divorce. Paul also reminded them about their marital obligations of material and emotional support because he did not want any believer to be the cause of a divorce.

Paul had to face the problem of those who had been divorced against their will and could do nothing to reverse it. He decided to apply a pragmatic solution and declare that such divorces are valid, so that the believer is free to remarry. A widow can also remarry without worrying about levirate marriage. However, Paul advised all who were unmarried to remain single during the "present crisis" (probably a famine), presumably because it would be difficult to support a family.

By reminding believers about their obligations of material and emotional support, it is clear that Paul regarded these obligations as part of their marriage vows, in the way that all other Jews also did, and therefore he regarded their neglect as grounds for divorce. Spouses whose partners deserted them against their will had a right to a divorce because of the neglect of the marital obligations. However, it is clear that Paul would have counseled caution in the use of these grounds for divorce, as contemporary Jews also did. In the end, however, when believers tried reconciliation and failed, Paul said that they were free to accept that the marriage had ended, and (by implication) they were free to remarry.

Paul's lack of unambiguous teaching about remarriage is not surprising. He implied the right to remarry in verse 15 and perhaps in verse 27 and verse 39. The meaning of the words "not bound" in verse 15 is not immediately obvious to a modern reader, though any first-century reader would have understood them to mean "free to remarry." There was no need to emphasize the right to remarry because it was a firmly established right of a divorced person in both Jewish and Greco-Roman culture.

The main message of this chapter is that a believer should never cause a divorce, either by separating from his or her partner or by neglecting marital obligations, but if the marriage ends despite the best efforts, he or she is entitled to a divorce and is free to remarry.

8. Marriage Vows

Vows Inherited from the Bible and Judaism

Jewish marriage contracts and Christian marriage services both contain vows or promises made by the couple to each other. Similar vows are found in Jewish marriage contracts from the early centuries B.C.E. through to the Middle Ages and to the modern day. The earlier examples show that these vows are based on the three obligations of Exodus 21:10-11. Christian marriage services are based on the same vows using the language of Ephesians 5. The language of these vows has become dignified and less direct over the years, and an examination of their origin helps us to understand the meaning of the promises that are made in modern weddings.

Marriage vows were the basis of Jewish divorce. If a marriage vow was broken, it became a ground for divorce by the injured party. These marriage vows were found in the marriage contract, though it was not necessary to state them all — some were present by implication only. Greco-Roman marriage contracts contain similar vows, but they are more concerned with financial penalties and other arrangements that will take place after a divorce than with the grounds for divorce.

The vow of sexual faithfulness is missing from almost all ancient contracts, both Jewish and non-Jewish. This is probably because the whole point of the contract *was* a vow of faithfulness. Adultery was an automatic ground for divorce in Judaism and all ancient cultures, and divorce was often regarded as compulsory in these circumstances. In the English-language marriage service (which we will discuss in the second half of this chapter), the same marriage vows occur, and they are all stated clearly — including the vow of sexual faithfulness.

Jewish Marriage Vows

As we noticed in chapter five, the Jewish marriage vows and grounds for divorce were based on the two OT texts, Deuteronomy 24:1-4 and Exodus 21:10-11. The Deuteronomic text allowed divorce for sexual indecency, which was generally interpreted as adultery, and therefore implied the vow of faithfulness. The law of Exodus 21:10-11 was the basis of the other three vows, to feed, clothe, and love, which became the other grounds for divorce.

The way in which these vows were expressed varied over time and in different branches of Judaism. The use of Exodus 21:10-11 is implied in early marriage contracts, but it is seen more clearly in later contracts that emphasize the biblical basis of their wording. By the time the traditional rabbinic marriage contract became fixed, these vows had changed greatly. The language tended to become more dignified and euphemistic, especially with regard to conjugal rights, though they still followed the same model found in the early centuries.

Early Judaism (First to Fourth Centuries C.E.*)*

Early Jewish marriage contracts were fashioned partly on the teachings of the Scriptures and partly on the style of contemporary Greco-Roman contracts. They were probably also influenced by earlier Neo-Babylonian and Demotic contracts, which contained stipulations that the groom had to provide food and clothing.[1] Jewish marriage contracts, unlike all other marriage contracts, made these stipulations apply to both husband and wife and added the third stipulation: that they must provide love. These particularly Jewish features are usually missing from early contracts, which tend to emulate contemporary Greco-Roman contracts. They are not seen clearly until the fifth century, when Judaism had gained some independence in the way it administered its marriage laws. However, it is possible to find early evidence for these specifically Jewish features in some first-century case law preserved in the Mishnah, as seen in chapter five.

1. Cf. the threefold "food, clothing, and oil" in ancient Near Eastern contracts of support, discussed in chapter one. Most Demotic contracts mention only "necessities and clothing," as in Greco-Roman contracts, but some have a threefold phrase such as "necessaries, clothing, and whatever else is proper for a wedded wife" (P.Tebt. 104). Jacob J. Rabinowitz ("Marriage Contracts in Ancient Egypt in the Light of Jewish Sources," *Harvard Theological Review* 46 [1953]: esp. pp. 95-97) thought that the last term in this trio was euphemistic and that Demotic contracts were themselves influenced by LXX Exod. 21:10, though this seems unlikely. It is more likely that this type of trio occurred elsewhere.

Only a small number of Jewish marriage certificates have survived from the first few centuries — five in Greek and four in Aramaic, all from the early second century. All of them contain a phrase referring to the obligation to clothe and feed.[2] Like Greco-Roman contracts, these obligations are incumbent only on the man, and there is no mention of conjugal rights, except in one of the Aramaic contracts:

> . . . [you will be] my wife [according to the la]w of Moses and the Judaeans and I will [feed you] and [clothe] you and I will bring you (into my house) by means of your *ketubah,* and I owe you the sum of four hundred denarii *(zuzin)* which equal one hundred tetradrachms *(ṣōr īn)* whichever you wish to take and to [. . .] . . . together with the due amount of your food and your clothes and your bed(?).[3]

This contract contains two different **euphemistic references to conjugal rights** — "I will bring you into my house" and "your bed."[4] Both are listed as a third item along with food and clothing. It is not surprising that this stipulation is missing from the other contracts. It was not normal to state this in Greco-Roman contracts, and it might be said to be implied by the fact that the couple were getting married. The euphemistic language suggests there was a certain coyness about this subject. Probably the contract was read aloud at the wedding, and so they tried to find fine language that would be suitable for a public reading. The same reasons explain why the contract says nothing about a vow of sexual fidelity. Getting married might be said to imply faithfulness, and one might not wish to mention the possibility of infidelity at a wedding.

There are two possible reasons why these contracts mention only the man's responsibility to provide food, clothing, and love and say nothing about the woman's equal responsibilities to prepare this food and clothing and to reciprocate love. First, they may have wished to conform as closely as possible to Greco-Roman norms, because they were still subject to Greco-Roman courts for

2. This phrase does not actually occur in one (DJD.XXVII.11 = AM100 in my *Marriage and Divorce Papyri*), www.tyndale.cam.ac.uk/brewer/MarriagePapyri/TableAM.htm (2000), but it is extremely fragmentary. The words that have survived suggest that it is similar to the other contracts.

3. P.Yadin.10 = AM126 in my *Marriage and Divorce Papyri.*

4. The translation of this latter term is debatable but is likely to be correct. Yigael Yadin says the word פרש may be פרס "to spread out, cover," which is euphemistic for conjugal relations, or it may be a loanword from Arabic *farš,* "bed," which is also a euphemism (Yigael Yadin, Jonas C. Greenfield, and Ada Yardeni, "Babatha's *Ketubba,*" *Israel Exploration Journal* 44 [1994]: 88-89).

most areas of justice.[5] Second, the contract is written, like Greco-Roman marriage contracts, from the point of view of the man, as if it were a statement made by him. Therefore, there is no reference to what the bride promises or wishes.

Early traditions in the Mishnah confirm that these vows were incumbent on both bride and groom, and that the vow of conjugal relations and sexual faithfulness was regarded as part of these vows. In chapter five we have already seen that there was a school dispute concerning the amount of time one could abstain from marital relations, and the punishments that were imposed if either side refused to fulfill the vow of "love." We also saw that the rabbis defined carefully the amount of food or cooking and cloth or weaving that the partners had to give each other in order to fulfill their vows to "feed and clothe." Furthermore, of course, sexual unfaithfulness was regarded as a compulsory ground for divorce.

It appears therefore that first-century Jewish law recognized the vows to "feed, clothe, and love" as incumbent on both bride and groom, but the early marriage certificates did not reflect that law. A clear statement of mutual responsibilities of bride and groom does not occur until the fifth century, in the first Jewish marriage contract that survived after the second century.[6]

P.Colon. 12, Aramaic *ketubah* of 417 C.E., Antinoopolis:

5 [בעיר] [א֯]נטינו לפרוטאטי דתיבאיס אנה שׂ[מ֯ואל בר֯ ס֯]מפט[י֯]
6 [מן —]סוס ושׂרי באנטינו אמר[ת֯ ו֯]בעית מן דעתי מן [צ֯ב֯י֯ו֯ני]
7 [נפשי֯] למסב לי יאת מיטרא ברת לעזר מן אלכסנדריא ושׂ֯[ריה]
8 [באנט]ינו בתולתה לאתה כנימוס [כל֯ ב֯נ֯ת֯] ישׂראל ו[א֯נ֯ה֯ א֯מ֯ר֯ת]
9 [שׂמוא֯]ל֯ בר סמפטי חתנה דאנה [זן ומפרנס . . .]

5. The Mishnah records that rabbinic divorce courts sometimes had to take into account the rulings of Gentile courts (*m. Git.* 9.8), and some Jewish marriage contracts were specifically "in accordance with the laws of the Greeks" (ἑλληνικῷ νόμῳ), a phrase used in P.Yadin.18 = JM128 and P.Yadin. 37 = DJD.XXVII.65. = JM131 in my *Marriage and Divorce Papyri.* The influence of Greek law was still felt even in the fifth century B.C.E., as seen in the phrase in papyrus Colon. 12: "according to the *nomos* [כנימוס] of . . . Israel." This transliterated Greek νόμος, "law," is only one of more than two dozen similar transliterations in this papyrus. Hannah M. Cotton concludes: "The use of Greek in my opinion is to be explained by the desire to make the deed of gift valid and enforceable in a Greek-speaking court, such as that of the governor of the province." She points out that some Greek marriage contracts have very poor Greek and read as though they were woodenly translated from Aramaic (see Hannah M. Cotton, "The Rabbis and the Documents," in *Jews in a Graeco-Roman World,* ed. Martin Goodman [Oxford: Clarendon; New York: Oxford University Press, 1998], pp. 167-79).

6. See Colette Sirat, P. Cauderlier, M. Dukan, and C. Friedman, eds., *La Ketouba de Cologne: un contrat de mariage juif à Antinoopolis,* Papyrologica Coloniensia 12 (Opladen: Westdeutscher Verlag, 1986) for the text and translation into French. There is no other English translation in print.

10 — בתו[ל֯]ת[ה] כ[לתה]
11 בקוש[ט֯ה] — [ק֯בלת֯ למ֯הו֯י מ֯ו֯קרה ית֯ה֯]
12 לשמואל ברת בר סמפטי בדכו ו֯ב[קדו]שה וב
13 ישראל [צ֯נ֯י֯]עתה והכדין אפרן י[ת֯ה] <לעזר> אסת֯ר֯ אמ֯[ה֯]

5 . . . . I, Samuel son of Sampati, [of
6 . . .]sos and resident at Antinoopolis, declare and ask, of my own decision and [my wish],
7 to take to me Metra, daughter of Leazar of Alexandria and re[sident]
8 [in Ant]inou, a virgin, to be a wife according to the law [*nomos*] of [all the daughters of] Israel. And [I declare that] I,
9 Samuel son of Sampati, agree[7] that I [will provide this . . . . . .]
10 [. . . . .] the virgin, the bride [. . . . .]
11 truth. [On her side, she will] honor
12 Samuel daughter of [*sic*] son of Sampati in purity, and [holiness . . . according to the custom of the daughters]
13 of Israel, [who are] modest. This is the dowry that his mother provides for him. . . .

The details of the vows occur in damaged portions of this contract, and although the editor has attempted reconstructions, these should be treated with care. However, it is clear that both bride and groom make promises. The details of these promises are not clear, but very similar wording is found in later, less fragmentary marriage contracts. There is an indirect reference to Exodus 21:10-11 in the phrase "according to the custom of the daughters of Israel," which is a clear allusion to Exodus 21:9 "the custom of the daughters." This phrase is seen first in an Edomite contract from 176 B.C.E., and it is often seen in later marriage contracts.[8]

7. Sirat read this as **התנה** but it makes more sense as **חתנה**, "agree."

8. This phrase is almost completely missing in this fragmentary contract, but the length of the gaps and the widespread use of this phrase in other contracts make the reconstruction likely. It is possible that this phrase in line 12 should be reconstructed as "according to the law [*nomos*] of the daughters of Israel," as it is in line 8. The use of this Greek word is seen in exactly the same form in an Edomite marriage certificate on a pottery shard, dating from 176 B.C.E.: "according to the *nomos* of the daughters of [Edom]" (see Esther Eshel and Amos Kloner, "An Aramaic Ostracon of an Edomite Marriage Contract from Maresha, Dated 176 B.C.E.," *Israel Exploration Journal* 46 [1996]: 1-22). It is also seen in one of the Geniza marriage contracts (e.g., Mordechai Friedman, *Jewish Marriage in Palestine: A Cairo Geniza Study,* 2 vols. [Tel Aviv: Tel-Aviv University, Chaim Rosenberg School of Jewish Studies; New York: Jewish Theological Seminary of America, 1980-81], #4), while others use **הלכת** "halakah" or "traditional law" (e.g., Friedman, *Jewish Marriage in Palestine,* #8, 10, 13, 15, 16, 17, 18, 19, 31, 56).

Traditional Judaism (Talmud to Geniza)

By the time of the Talmuds the wording of marriage contracts had become relatively fixed, with slightly different versions in the Babylonian and Palestinian traditions. These two traditions are reflected in contracts that were preserved in the Cairo Geniza, which come mainly from the mid-eleventh century. These contracts have been analyzed by J. Olszowy-Schlanger,[9] who has examined all the Karaite contracts (which are dealt with in the next section), and M. A. Friedman,[10] who looked mainly at the non-Karaite contracts. In general, the Karaite contracts followed the lead set by the Babylonian Talmud and the non-Karaite contracts followed the Palestinian Talmud.[11]

The Talmuds do not contain the text of a marriage contract, but they make several references to it. The vows made by the bride and groom are mentioned on a few occasions in relation to levirate marriages, where the obligation to clothe and feed may be limited by the fact that she already has financial support from the *ketubah* of her deceased husband (*t. Yebam.* 2.1; *b. Yebam.* 52a). There is also a discussion about whether a man can state in his marriage contract that he will forgo his obligation to provide food, clothing, and conjugal rights (*t. Ketub.* 4.7; *y. Git.* 9.10, 50d; *b. Ketub.* 77a, 63a). The Talmuds also contain evidence of the change of language used for these obligations, preferring to speak of "maintain" or "provide for" instead of "clothe," and of "honor," "esteem," or "support" instead of "feed,"[12] sometimes using **language that is reminiscent of Ephesians 5.**[13]

This terminology is also found in the Geniza contracts, though there was still considerable variation in the phraseology that is used in different contracts even from the same era and place. Variations may have been due to different local or scribal traditions, or more probably to the personal preferences of the groom and bride, or of the two families. Some grooms still write out their own marriage contract today, which makes it into a very personal statement, though they tend to follow traditional formulations.

The Geniza contracts contain many examples of these vows:

> I desire of my own will to marry <wife's name> that I might bring her into my house so that she will be [my wife on condition that I hon]our her, feed

9. Judith Olszowy-Schlanger, *Karaite Marriage Contracts from the Cairo Geniza: Legal Training and Community Life in Mediaeval Egypt and Palestine* (Leiden: Brill, 1998).

10. Friedman, *Jewish Marriage in Palestine.*

11. This is the conclusion of Olszowy-Schlanger, *Karaite Marriage Contracts,* p. 190.

12 See the summary in Friedman, *Jewish Marriage in Palestine,* 1:170.

13. E.g., "He who loves his wife as himself and honours her more than himself" (*b. Yebam.* 62b). This is a *baraita,* and so it is likely to be first or second century C.E.

> her, sustain her, esteem [her] as all [. . . in the man]ner of dece[nt Jewish] men [who honour, feed, sustain and esteem their wives fa]ithfully.
>
> And she undertook to honour, esteem, attend and [serve him . . . in the manner of dece]nt [women], the daughters of Israel, who attend and serve ["stand before"] their husbands in purity and san[ctity . . .][14]

A few contracts simply use the plain language of "food" and "clothing":

> I will supply you with your food and your clothing, as other Jewish husbands who maintain their wives faithfully.[15]

Others use a variety of terms, which have the effect of making the bare biblical stipulations into flowing elegant language:

> He undertook to esteem, honour, nourish, provide for and clothe her, in the manner of Jewish men who esteem, honour, nourish, provide for, and clothe their wives faithfully. Similarly <the wife> accepted and undertook to esteem, honour, attend and serve her husband in purity, in the manner of respectable women, the daughters of Israel, who esteem, honour, attend and serve their husbands in purity and cleanness.[16]

Most of these terms can be regarded as elaborations on the twin themes of feeding and clothing. The concept of feeding encompasses the ideas of sustaining and providing for, while the concept of clothing includes the ideas of honoring and esteeming. The rabbis commented that the clothing spoken about was not just ordinary clothing but festival clothing, which brings honor and esteem to the woman.[17]

The term **"serving"** is introduced in two of the above examples. It is a translation of a phrase that means literally "work before."[18] This type of promise occurs in many contracts and is usually made only by the bride,[19] though a

14. Friedman, *Jewish Marriage in Palestine,* #2 (Tyre 1023). Very similar phraseology is found in #4, 6, 9, 10, 11, 14, 15, 17, 22, 29, 31, 33, 34, 44, 50, 56, 59, 60.

15. Friedman, *Jewish Marriage in Palestine,* #7 (Aleppo 1027), using מזוניך for "your food" and תכשיטיך as a misspelling of תכסיתיך for "your clothing."

16. Friedman, *Jewish Marriage in Palestine,* #8 (place and date missing). Very similar phraseology is found in #13, 16, 18, 19.

17. Friedman, *Jewish Marriage in Palestine,* 1:175. This is probably a very early concept because the early Mishnah also speaks about festival clothing (see *m. Ketub.* 5.8).

18. The normal phrase is "and she serves her husband" (ופלחה קידם בעלה). The verb פלח means "dig," "work," "serve," or "worship."

19. E.g., Friedman, *Jewish Marriage in Palestine,* #2, 6, 7, 8, 10, 11, 12, 15, 16, 18, 19, 22, 29, 31, 33, 36, 41, 60.

significant number of grooms make a complementary promise to "serve" their brides.[20] Although it is possible that this term was regarded as a summary of the service of feeding and clothing, this seems unlikely. It is more likely a reference to submission, or a reference to conjugal rights. It is significant that Paul uses the language of servitude when he reminds the Corinthians about conjugal rights: "the wife does not rule over her own body, but the husband does; likewise the husband does not rule over his own body but the wife does" (1 Cor. 7:4).

Another phrase that probably refers to sexual activity is "in purity and cleanness," which usually ends the section concerning the bride's promise. The sexual connotation of these words is made explicit in one unusually worded contract that says:

> And you shall strive to do with me all that proper women do wi[th] their husbands, in purity and cleanness.[21]

In a few contracts, these obligations are summarized as the "three needs":

> If he fulfils her three needs, [she] has no [right . . .][22]

Although the fragment of this contract ends with this phrase, the contract would probably have gone on to state that the wife had no right to her *ketubah* because her husband had fulfilled her three needs, as defined by Exodus 21:10-11.[23] One contract spells this out in unusual detail:

> She has no right to claim of them one *peruṭa* as long as he is alive and she is under his jurisdiction and he fulfils her three needs. But if he hates her [i.e., divorces her] without any misconduct (on her part) and does not fulfil her three needs, he shall pay them to her, viz. the balance of her *mohar,* of 12 *dinars,* and release her with a bill of divorce.[24]

20. E.g., Friedman, *Jewish Marriage in Palestine,* #4, 9, 27, 44, 56.

21. Friedman, *Jewish Marriage in Palestine,* #9.

22. Friedman, *Jewish Marriage in Palestine,* #36 (Tyre 1089-99). Other references to these "needs" (סיפוקה) are found in #20, 27, 30, 38, 53b, 53c, 54.

23. This is the conclusion of Friedman (*Jewish Marriage in Palestine,* 1:174, 342). The term "needs" may be related to the term "necessities" (δέοντα) that occurs in the phrase "her clothing and necessities" in many Greek contracts (see my "1 Corinthians 7 in the Light of the Jewish, Greek, and Aramaic Marriage and Divorce Papyri," *Tyndale Bulletin* 52 [2001]: 225-43). The LXX use of δέοντα for "food" in Exod. 21:10 makes it likely that the term would find its way into Jewish marriage contracts. However, the occasional reference to "three needs" suggests that it can also be a summary statement for the "food, clothing, and love" of Exod. 21:10-11.

24. Friedman, *Jewish Marriage in Palestine,* #11.

These marriage contracts preserved in the Geniza collection were among the last to display such a wide diversity of phraseology. The traditional formulation, as recorded or defined by Maimonides, was gradually accepted, and the variations diminished as a result. In this standard contract, the groom vows:

> Be my wife according to the law of Moses and Israel, and I will work for you, honour, support, and maintain you in accordance with the custom of Jewish husbands who work for their wives, honour, support, and maintain them in truth. And I will set aside for you 200 *zuz* in lieu of your virginity, which belong to you (according to the law of Moses), and your food, clothing, and necessaries, and live with you in conjugal relations according to universal custom.[25]

Many marriage contracts also use the traditional formula recommended by Hai Gaon:

> I am obligated to provide your food, clothing and needs and to come to you as the way of all the world.[26]

Therefore, in almost all cases traditional Jewish marriage contracts contain references to food and clothing, and sometimes they also refer to conjugal relations, though without any explicit citation of Exodus 21:10-11.

Karaite Judaism

The Karaites were a back-to-Scripture movement that started in the seventh century, though most of its literature dates from the tenth to thirteenth centuries. Their discussions of law are often based on the Talmuds, even though they aimed to reject postbiblical traditions. As a result, they often preserve the biblical basis for rabbinic thinking, though one must always bear in mind that their biblical justification may not be the same as the rationale behind rabbinic traditions. They discuss the obligations to provide food and clothing in terms that are very similar to rabbinic discussion (*t. Ketub.* 4.7; *y. Git.* 9.10, 50d; *b. Ketub.* 77a, 63a), though they relate them to **Exodus 21:10-11** in a clearer way than is found in the rabbinic writings. For example, a ninth-century theological treatise on marriage reads:

25. Maimonides, "Yad" Yabim 4.33
26. As cited in Friedman, *Jewish Marriage in Palestine,* 1:178.

> He who says, "I refuse to feed and support my wife," must be compelled to divorce her and pay her the full amount of her marriage contract, as it is written: *He shall not diminish her food, raiment, and cohabitation. And if he do not fulfil these three for her, she shall go free* [Exod. 21:10-11].[27]

The marriage service in the book of Karaite liturgy has the groom state the following promise:

> I have betrothed and sanctified unto myself the lady so-and-so, daughter of so-and-so, the virgin maiden, to be my wife, in purity and holiness, by way of bridal gift, marriage writ and marital intercourse, according to the Law of Moses, the man of God, and according to the statutes of Israel, the pure and holy ones. I will clothe and cover and hold dear and support and feed her, and I will work for her to supply all her proper needs and desires, according to my strength and to the extent that I can afford. I will not oppress or despise her, nor will I betray her, and I will not diminish her food, clothing and marital intercourse, as prescribed in the Law. And I will conduct myself toward her with truth, pity, and mercy, and I will treat her in the manner of the sons of Israel, who feed, honour, hold dear, and clothe their virtuous wives, and do all that is proper for them in faithfulness and uprightness.[28]

Several Karaite marriage contracts have survived from the eleventh century in the Geniza collection. J. Olszowy-Schlanger, who translated and analyzed them, has pointed out that the section concerning the promises by bride and groom is based on Exodus 21:10-11, though the terminology has been highly elaborated.[29] The most common wording is:

> I will dress, clothe, support, respect and esteem her and I will fulfil her needs and desires to the best of my strength and possibilities. And I will be with her in truth, justice, love, and affection and I will not afflict her, act against her or oppress her and I will not diminish her food, clothes and sexual intercourse, like the children of Israel who feed, support, dress, clothe and esteem their pure wives, and do all they owe them in faithfulness and honesty.[30]

27. Benjamin al-Nahawandi, mid-ninth century C.E., *The Book of Rules*, section VI.2 ("Marriage"), cited in Leon Nemoy, *Karaite Anthology: Excerpts from the Early Literature* (New Haven and London: Yale University Press, 1952), p. 27.

28. From the Karaite Prayer Book, based on the work of Aaron ben Joseph in the late thirteenth century C.E., cited in Nemoy, *Karaite Anthology*, p. 283.

29. Olszowy-Schlanger, *Karaite Marriage Contracts*, pp. 186-90.

30. Olszowy-Schlanger, *Karaite Marriage Contracts*, pp. 186-87. This wording, or very similar, is found in twenty-one of the forty-three contracts that have been preserved.

The Karaite bride promises:

> . . . to be his wife and companion in purity, holiness and awe, to obey, esteem, respect and help him, and to do in his house all that the pure daughters of Israel do in the house of their husbands, and to behave towards him in truth, justice, love, compassion, honesty and faith, to be under his dominion, and to have her desire directed towards him.

Each of these witnesses to the Karaite marriage vows demonstrates a clear dependence on the three obligations of Exodus 21:10-11, including references to conjugal rights that mainstream Jewish contracts avoided. The bride's promise also appears to refer to sexual faithfulness in the closing phrase, "and to have her desire directed towards him."

Samaritan Judaism

Samaritan theology is, potentially, much older than rabbinic theology. It stems from the time of the exile, when the only inspired Scriptures were the books of Moses. However, the earliest surviving Samaritan documents date from the eleventh century, and most Samaritan texts are from the eighteenth century. It is often impossible to tell how much development has taken place in the intervening centuries, though modern-day Samaritans claim that their traditions have remained unchanged.

The study of Samaritan marriage contracts has expanded considerably in recent years. John Bowman, writing in 1977,[31] said that only two Samaritan marriage contracts had survived, from the eighteenth and nineteenth centuries, but Reinhard Pummer was able to say in 1993 that he had found 114 contracts from as early as 1510, though most come from the eighteenth century.[32] They share many features found in the rest of early Judaism, including references to the marriage vows. They mostly follow very similar terminology:

> And he married her, and *she became his wife* (Gen. 24.67), excluded and withheld from every man apart from him. And he shall be her husband and shall treat her according to the manner with which women (are treated), as the Lord said through his servant Moses: *He shall not diminish her food, her*

31. John Bowman, trans. and ed., *Samaritan Documents Relating to Their History, Religion and Life*, Pittsburgh Original Texts and Translations (Pittsburgh: Pickwick, 1977), p. 310.

32. They are all published in Reinhard Pummer, *Samaritan Marriage Contracts and Deeds of Divorce*, 2 vols. (Wiesbaden: Harrassowitz, 1993, 1997).

> *clothing or her marital rights* (Exod. 21.10). And he upholds her vows and her abstentions, or dissolves them. And towards him she is obliged to marital love; she shall listen to his words and not contradict him; *and she shall be a fitting help for him* (Gen. 2.18). . . . But he should cleave to her as the Lord said: *Therefore a man leaves his father and his mother and cleaves to his wife, and from the two of them there becomes one flesh.* (Gen. 2.24 Sam. Pent.)

This contains a very explicit reference to **Exodus 21:10**, though the quotation of other verses suggests that the contract has been written to reflect as much Scripture as possible. It is impossible to know whether this quotation is an accurate reflection of the original basis for phrases about food and clothing, or whether the Samaritans have consciously striven to return to Scriptures for their source of theology. In general the latter is probably true, because although the contract shares a similar structure to early rabbinic contracts, there is very little shared terminology other than that which is found in Scripture and in marriage contracts from a wide variety of ancient nations.

There is also a significant addition with regard to the wife's submission. She must "listen to his words and not contradict him." This may be similar to the phrase "serve him" in the Geniza marriage contracts, though it clearly goes much further. This concept was expanded in the treatise on marriage in a twelfth-century Samaritan work:

> . . . he should be in charge of her and should rule over her, according to the saying of the Lawgiver: "And he shall rule over thee" [Gen. 3:16]. And this cannot be reversed.[33]

The concept of submission as a possible marriage vow is treated in more detail at the end of this chapter.

Development of Jewish Marriage Vows

In conclusion, Jewish marriage contracts have contained references to marriage vows based on the three obligations of Exodus 21:10-11 from at least the second century C.E. We do not have any earlier marriage contracts, but it is likely that they would have been very similar because the language had already become stylized and traditional. This reflects the fact that the first-century case law that is preserved in mishnaic passages depended on this text. However, these mar-

33. From a work known as "Kitāb al-Kāfī," for which there is no printed edition or translation. This section is translated in Pummer, *Samaritan Marriage Contracts*, 1:37.

riage contracts did not allude directly to the biblical text. The earliest Jewish marriage contracts were styled after Greco-Roman contracts and contained only promises made by the groom. These usually consisted of the promise to feed and clothe, though one contract included a reference to conjugal rights. By the fifth century the bride also made promises, though the fragmentary text does not tell us what these were. By the tenth and eleventh centuries (for which we have the most evidence) the language had become formal and elaborate, but references to the three promises are still discernible, especially when they were called "the three needs" in some contracts. The only contracts that contained clear quotations from Exodus 21:10-11 are those of the Karaites and Samaritans, who both wanted, for different reasons, to show that their marriage contracts were based on Scripture. It is almost certain that these later Jews who referred to Exodus 21:10-11 were accurately reflecting the scriptural origins of the Jewish marriage promises.

Christian Marriage Vows

The same marriage vows that are named in early Jewish marriage contracts are also found in the NT, though they have been rarely recognized. In 1 Corinthians 7, as we discussed in the previous chapter, Paul reminds married couples about their responsibilities for providing material and emotional support to each other. In Ephesians 5, the trio of "food, clothing, and love" are found with reference to Christ's love for his Church. Also, the NT contains clear references to the vow of faithfulness. We will look at each of these in turn, beginning with the last, which is missing from Jewish marriage contracts. These vows will then be traced in the development of the English-language marriage service.

Faithfulness

The clearest reference to the vow of faithfulness is in Matthew's use of *porneia*, which we discussed in chapter six. Jesus did not agree with contemporary Jews who regarded adultery as a ground for divorce only if it was committed by the woman. If the man committed adultery, he could not be said to break a marriage vow because in a polygamous society the man could not make a vow to be sexually faithful to only one woman. Adultery was sinful for a Jewish male, but it could not be a ground for divorce because no marriage vow was broken. Jesus taught monogamy, however, so that the vow of faithfulness was implicit for both the groom and the bride.

The rest of the NT contains many calls to a high standard of sexual morality. These were necessary in the context of the contemporary Greco-Roman society. Although adultery was illegal, it was only a civil offense, and so one could be prosecuted only by an offended husband or wife. It was more likely that one would suffer the inconvenience of divorce by one's own spouse. Sexual relations with prostitutes, boys, or slaves were not illegal and were considered a part of normal life. A host who invited friends to a meal would be expected to provide the "after food" entertainment of prostitutes. In the first century, women were starting to accompany their husbands to meals. This did not result in a rise in the moral behavior of men, but it was part of the declining standards of women.[34]

Very occasionally one finds a Greco-Roman marriage contract in which such behavior is specifically ruled out, probably under the influence of a rich bride or an influential bride's father. For example, a contract from Egypt in 92 B.C.E. states:

> It shall not be lawful for <the husband> to bring in any other woman but <the wife>, nor to keep a concubine or boy, nor to have children by another woman. . . . In the same way it shall not be lawful for <the wife> to spend the night or day away from the house of <the husband> without his consent or to have intercourse with another man.[35]

This exception confirms the rule that such behavior was normally accepted though not universally practiced. Occasionally one finds a marriage where the partners were faithful to each other, though it is not certain that they would have regarded relationships with a boy, a prostitute, or even a mistress as constituting unfaithfulness. A term found on tombstones describing a faithful wife is *univira*, "a woman of one (husband)," and occasionally one finds the Greek equivalent μόνανδρος on Greek and Jewish funeral inscriptions.[36] Being

34. "No Roman thinks it shameful to take his wife to a dinner party. At home the wife, as mistress of the household, takes first place in it and is the centre of its entertaining. Things are very different in Greece, where the wife is never present at dinner, except for a family party, and spends all her time in the Women's Quarter, separated from the rest of the house — an area broached only by close male relatives" (Cornelius Nepos, preface to De Vit. III, cited in Suzanne Dixon, *The Roman Family* [Baltimore and London: The Johns Hopkins University Press, 1992], p. 83).

35. P.Tebt. I.104 = GM92 in my *Marriage and Divorce Papyri* — a marriage certificate from Tebtunis, Egypt, in 92 B.C.E.

36. See references in Craig S. Keener, . . . *And Marries Another: Divorce and Remarriage in the Teaching of the New Testament* (Peabody, Mass.: Hendrickson, 1991), pp. 92-93.

faithful was regarded as a high ideal, but it was an ideal that was only recognized in a few marriages.

"Husband of One Wife"

In 1 Timothy we find a similar Greek term that is usually translated as "wife of one husband" (5:9), and the equivalent for a man, "husband of one wife" (3:2). These terms have often been misunderstood as meaning "not remarried," which is technically possible but unlikely. Remarriage of divorcées and widows was technically mandatory under Roman law,[37] and the Pastorals specifically allow it (1 Tim. 5:14; cf. 1 Cor. 7:27, 39; see chapter seven above). It is much more likely that this phrase meant that the leaders of the Church were expected to have high moral standards.

The Early Church could not escape the effect of the surrounding culture. The epistles show that even among Christians, loose sexual morals were not unknown. The frequent exhortations about sexual morality suggest that this was a pressing concern in the Early Church and a practical problem for many individuals. Jesus had very little to say about sexual misconduct, other than immorality committed "in the heart," because the vast proportion of Jewish society already had very high sexual morals. Yet believers from a non-Jewish background came from a very different culture, and it is clear that they sometimes found it difficult to leave behind their Greco-Roman lifestyle.

In this context it was necessary to make sure that the leaders of the Church were people who were known to be faithful to their partners. It was not enough that they were technically faithful — in the Greco-Roman world one could have a mistress without being guilty of adultery — they had to be known as someone who "has eyes for only one woman" (as we would say in modern English), that is, as a "husband of one wife."

Various **other interpretations** of the phrase "husband of one wife" have been put forward. Some suggested it meant that a Church leader must not be polygamous, or even that a Church leader must be married. Although these are possible readings, they do not work with the accompanying phrase "wife of one husband" in 5:9. This similar phrase must presumably mean the same, though for women instead of men. It could not refer to women who simultaneously had more than one husband because that was unknown anywhere in the NT

37. The *Lex Julia de maritandis ordinibus* of 18 B.C.E. permitted a private prosecution of any fertile woman who did not remarry within eighteen months (if she was divorced) or two years (if she was widowed).

world. Also it could not mean that the women had to be married, because the phrase is used in 5:9 to describe widows. It therefore seems likely that this phrase is related to the similar Latin *univira* and refers to sexual faithfulness. Therefore this phrase teaches that a Christian leader should be known as "a man of one woman," which is equivalent to our phrase "having eyes for only one woman."

Feed and Clothe

The vow to feed and clothe each other has been part of traditional Jewish marriage certificates as far back as the earliest evidence goes: back to Exodus 21:10-11, and back to the wording of laws originating at the time of Hammurabi or perhaps even earlier, as we saw in chapter two. The Jews took these vows very seriously and allowed women to use them as grounds for divorce, as we saw in chapter five. Therefore it is not surprising that one can find evidence for these vows elsewhere in Scripture even though the wording of a marriage certificate is not preserved for us anywhere in the OT or NT.

We have already seen in chapter three the references to these vows for feeding and clothing in passages relating to God's divorce from Israel. For instance, they are cited as some of the grounds for divorce in **Ezekiel 16** because Israel used the food and cloth, which was provided for her by God, to feed and clothe idols:

> 16 You took some of your garments, and made for yourself gaily decked
> shrines, and on them played the harlot; the like has never been, nor ever
> shall be. 17 You also took your fair jewels of my gold and of my silver, which
> I had given you, and made for yourself images of men, and with them
> played the harlot; 18 and you took your embroidered garments to cover
> them, and set my oil and my incense before them. 19 Also my bread which I
> gave you — I fed you with fine flour and oil and honey — you set before
> them for a pleasing odour, says the Lord God. (Ezek. 16:16-19)

A more incidental reference to these vows occurs in **Psalm 132** where God speaks of Zion as his bride, on whom he will lavish food, clothing, and love:

> 13 For the Lord has chosen Zion;
> he has desired it for his habitation:
> 14 This is my resting place for ever;
> here I will dwell, for I have desired it.
> 15 I will abundantly bless her provisions;

I will satisfy her poor with bread.
16 Her priests I will clothe with salvation,
and her saints will shout for joy.

The most interesting reference to these vows is in **Ephesians 5**, where the Church is described as a bride and Christ is portrayed as a groom who does everything a Jewish groom was expected to do.

> 25 Husbands, love your wives, as Christ loved the church and gave himself
> up for her, 26 that he might sanctify her, having cleansed her by the washing
> of water with the word, 27 that he might present the church to himself in
> splendour, without spot or wrinkle or any such thing, that she might be
> holy and without blemish.
>
> 28 Even so husbands should love their wives as their own bodies. He
> who loves his wife loves himself. 29 For no man ever hates his own flesh, but
> nourishes and cherishes it, as Christ does the church, 30 because we are
> members of his body.
>
> 31 For this reason a man shall leave his father and mother and be joined
> to his wife, and the two shall become one flesh. 32 This mystery is a pro-
> found one, and I am saying that it refers to Christ and the church. (Eph.
> 5:25-32, RSV)

Christ is seen here partly as a groom and partly as a parent. He organizes the prenuptial preparations that were spoken of symbolically and literally as "washing," which, in Ephesians, becomes a picture of sanctification.[38] He also gives away the bride, like a father. Then, as groom, he promises to love her, feed her, and clothe her, and finally he is joined as one with her, in love.

The English translations usually obscure the references to feeding and clothing that occur in verse 29 because they are trying to convey a fuller nuance of the words. The words often translated **"nourish" and "cherish"** or something similar are words for "feeding" and "warming" a small child.[39] The choice of these words has perhaps been influenced by the twin role of Christ as parent and groom, or perhaps the terms "feed" and "clothe" were considered to be too

38. This probably represents a play on words. The Hebrew *kiddushin* can mean both betrothal and sanctification.

39. ἐκτρέφω means "to nourish, to rear, to bring up from childhood," or is even used of sperm that are "animalcules that are invisible for smallness and . . . *are nourished* to a great size within the womb" (*Timaeus* 91d). θάλπω means "to keep warm, cherish" and is used even of birds warming their young (as in LXX Deut. 22:6). This was recognized as long ago as Bengel in *Gnomon*, 2:653, who says they mean "feed" and "clothe." The Vulgate recognizes this, translating the terms as *nutrit et fovet*.

bland and cold for describing the warmth of a marriage relationship, and so more caring and endearing terms were used. This same tendency appears in Jewish and English marriage terminology. Jewish contracts, as seen above, continue to use more and more elaborate terms, especially in later centuries, and English marriage services follow the same type of pattern.

Vows in Modern Marriage Services

A modern marriage service fulfills a similar function to a Jewish marriage contract. The contract was originally written as a record of a verbal agreement that was spoken at the wedding. Later, the contract became a written document that was designed to be read aloud at the wedding either by the groom or on his behalf. This is still practiced by some Jews today. The wording of a modern wedding service fulfills the joint function of providing words to be spoken by the leader and words to be spoken by the couple who are getting married. It should therefore contain all the promises and warnings of a marriage contract, setting them in a theological and liturgical context, as well as giving the couple opportunity to express their vows to each other. The traditional Christian marriage services fulfill these functions very well.

The **earliest English marriage vows** date from the *Use of Sarum,* the most complete and influential of the early versions of the English liturgy that was drawn up about 1085 by Osmund, Bishop of Salisbury and Chancellor of England.[40] The marriage service can be seen to be a merging of (1) the old Roman ceremony of Espousal, followed by (2) the Benediction and (3) the nuptial Mass. It is partly in Latin and partly in vernacular English:

> N. Vis habere hanc mulierem in sponsam, eam diligere, honorare, tenere, et custodire sanam et infirmam, sicut sponsus debet sponsam; et omnes alias propter eam dimittere, et illi soli adhaerere quamdiu vita utriusque vestrum duraverit?
>
> Volo.
>
> N. Vis habere hunc virum in sponsum, et ei obedire et servire; et eum diligere, honorare, et custodire sanum et infirmum sicut sponsa debet sponsum; et omnes alios propter eum dimittere, et illi soli adhaerere quamdiu vita utriusque vestrum duraverit?
>
> Volo.

40. Francis Procter, *A History of the Book of Common Prayer: With a Rationale of Its Offices,* 4th ed. (London: Macmillan, 1860), p. 4.

> I N take the N to my wedded wyf to have and to holde fro this day forwarde for better: for wors: for richere: for poorer: in sykenesse and in hele: tyl dethe us departe, if holy chyrche it woll ordeyne, and therto I plight the my trouthe.
>
> I N take the N to my wedded housbonder to have and to holde fro this day forwarde for better: for wors: for richere: for poorer: in sykenesse and in hele: to be bonere and buxum in bedde and at the borde tyll dethe us departe, if holy chyrche it woll ordeyne, and therto I plight the my trouthe.
>
> . . . With this rynge I the wed, and this gold and silver I the geve, and with my body I the worshipe, and with all my worldely cathel I the endowe.[41]

The 1549 version is very similar, though now the wonderfully alliterative phrase "bonny and buxom in bed and at board" is omitted. This was probably because "bonny and buxom," which originally meant "good and obedient," was already starting to change its meaning. After 1549 there was almost no change until the modern day — the changes are marked in square brackets:

> N. Wilt thou have this woman to thy wedded wife, to live together after God's ordinance, in the holy estate of matrimony? Wilt thou love her, comfort her, honour, and keep her in sickness and in health? And forsaking all other keep thee only to her, so long as you [1662: ye] both shall live?
>
> I will.
>
> N. Wilt thou have this man to thy wedded husband, to live together after God's ordinance, in the holy estate of matrimony? Wilt thou obey him, and serve him, love, honour, and keep him in sickness and in health? And forsaking all other keep thee only to him, so long as you [1662: ye] both shall live?
>
> I will.
>
> I N take thee N to my wedded wife, to have and to hold from this day forward, for better, for worse, for richer, for poorer, in sickness and in health, to love and to cherish, till death us depart [1662: death us do part]: according to God's holy ordinance: And thereto I plight thee my troth.
>
> I N take thee N to my wedded husband, to have and to hold from this day forward, for better, for worse, for richer, for poorer, in sickness and in health, to love, cherish and to obey, till death us depart [1662: death us do part]: according to God's holy ordinance: And thereto I give thee my troth.
>
> With this ring I thee wed: [1549 only: This gold and silver I thee give]:

41. Procter, *A History of the Book of Common Prayer*, pp. 401-3.

> with my body I thee worship: and with all my worldly goods I thee endow: In the name of the Father, and of the Son, and of the Holy Ghost. Amen.[42]

In the ancient Latin version the man vows to "esteem, honour, keep, and protect" while the woman vows to "obey, serve, esteem, honour, and protect." These are very similar to the terms used to elaborate the concepts of "feed and clothe" in the Jewish marriage contracts and the English translations of Ephesians 5. It is difficult to know whether these similarities are due to parallel developments or whether the Jewish and Christian communities influenced each other. There was a surprising amount of contact between Christian theologians and Jewish scholars in the centuries before the growth in Hebrew literacy among Christian scholars. However, it is likely that the Christian liturgy was influenced mainly by Ephesians 5, and that both communities changed the language in similar ways to make it more elegant for public reading.

Unlike Jewish marriage contracts, the early Christian marriage vows make clear reference to the vows of "love" and sexual faithfulness. In the ancient English version the bride promises to be "bonny and buxom in bed," and the groom says, while giving the ring, "with my body I thee worship." The term "worship" is Old English for "serve," and thus this is similar to the Pauline admonition in 1 Corinthians 7:4 that each partner must serve the other in marital relations. This is perhaps also reflected in the vow to "serve," which was sometimes made by grooms as well as brides in Jewish marriage contracts, as we saw above. By 1549 the reference to "bed" has disappeared, but both bride and groom promise to "love" as well as honor, keep, and so forth. There is also a clear reference to the vow of sexual faithfulness in the words "forsaking all others," which is translated from the ancient Latin version.

Therefore the English marriage service specifically refers to all four of the biblical marriage vows. They are clearly expressed as vows, and in this service the bride and groom are keenly aware that their marriage is based on life-long promises made to each other before God and many witnesses.

Obey Is Not a NT Marriage Vow

The vow of obedience has been added to some Christian marriage services, though it is now usually missing or optional. It differs from the other vows in

42. *The First Prayer Book of Edward VI: Compared with the Successive Revisions of The Book of Common Prayer: Also a Concordance to the Rubricks in the Several Editions* (Oxford: Parker, 1877), pp. 336-38.

two ways: (1) it is one-sided in that only the wife makes this promise; and (2) it is difficult to argue that it is a biblical marriage vow.

The concept of women submitting to their husbands was an accepted norm during the centuries before the NT and, to a lesser extent, in Christian and Jewish culture during the centuries after the NT. However, during the first century, the submission of wives was a hotly contested subject that divided society into, very approximately, the moral and the immoral.

In Roman society the oldest form of marriage was based on a "with *manus*" contract. This contract reflected the ancient concept that marriage involved a transfer of ownership of a woman from her father into the "hand" *(manus)* of her husband. In this form of marriage, the woman owed obedience to her husband, whom she addressed as "lord" *(kurios).*

In Jewish society the concept of marriage as a transfer of ownership had already disappeared by the first century. The OT word for betrothal, *erubin,* suggested that a wife was "acquired," and so the word *kiddushin,* "sanctified," was used instead, which suggests that the bride and groom set themselves apart, or sanctified themselves, for each other.[43] This is probably the reason why "sanctification" is part of the role of Christ as the groom in Ephesians 5:26-27. In Samaritan marriage contracts, where the concept of submission was greatly emphasized, the word *erubin* continued to be used.[44]

By the first century, the Roman "with *manus*" type of marriage had also disappeared and had been replaced by "free" marriage or marriage "without *manus.*" In "free marriage" the woman had the freedom to control her own property and the freedom to divorce her husband. At first, the loss of *manus* or ownership simply meant theoretical freedoms for the wife and changes in the laws of inheritance. Women could still not legally conduct business or appear in court on their own behalf, and they had to rely on their "guardian" (also called their *kurios*) to do these things for them. Originally their guardian was their husband, and then later it was another male relative chosen by her husband or father, such as her brother-in-law. By the first century B.C.E., however, most women were able to choose their own guardian, which meant, in practice, that they could choose someone who they knew would do whatever they wanted. During the reign of Claudius, just before most of the NT was written, a

43. See Leone J. Archer, *Her Price Is beyond Rubies: The Jewish Woman in Greco-Roman Palestine,* Journal for the Study of the Old Testament Supplement 60 (Sheffield: Sheffield Academic Press), p. 158.

44. Samaritan marriage contracts continue to use the OT word *erubin,* and they do not recognize the rabbinic concept of *kiddushin* (see Pummer, *Samaritan Marriage Contracts,* 1:27, 29.

law was passed allowing women to act without a guardian for the first time. **The first century C.E.** was therefore **a revolutionary time for Greco-Roman women.**

Gradually women exercised more and more freedom in the disposal of their own money, in business, and in marriage. One unforeseen by-product of this social revolution was women's self-proclaimed sexual freedom. This resulted in a minority of women who took their freedom to an excessive extreme of licentiousness and arrogance. Rich women also used their wealth to dominate and even persecute their husbands who depended on them for money. These trends resulted in many men reacting against such changes and longing for the old days of submissive and sexually moral wives.[45]

The NT has two responses to this nostalgia. On the one hand, it affirmed the traditional morals that structured society before this social revolution because these were seen as a bulwark against the rise in sexual immorality and other forms of social rebellion. On the other hand, it added a Christian call to mutual support and fundamental equality despite differences of rank in human society. To do this, the NT writers utilized a widely accepted **threefold structure of submission** and added a Christian commentary to it. This same teaching about submission was also used by Greek, Jewish, and Egyptian moralists.[46] It consisted of the three sets of relationships of the *pater familias,* the head of a household, to the members of his household:

1. submission of the wife to her husband,
2. submission of children to their father, and
3. submission of slaves to their master.

This moral code is quoted and given a Christian commentary in Ephesians 5:22–6:9; Colossians 3:18–4:1; 1 Peter 2:18–3:7 (wife and slaves only); and 1 Timothy 2:9-15, 6:1-2 (wife and slaves only). This non-Christian moral code is transmitted faithfully in these different parts of the NT, though in each case the author adds Christian caveats and comments. 1 Peter discusses why one should submit to unworthy masters and husbands (2:19; 3:1) and concludes that it was necessary to aid evangelism, following the example of Christ (3:1). 1 Timothy

45. For more details see Elaine Fantham, ed., *Women in the Classical World: Image and Text* (New York: Oxford University Press, 1995), esp. pp. 264-80; Bruce Winter, "The 'New' Roman Wife and 1 Timothy 2.9-15: The Search for a Sitz im Leben," *Tyndale Bulletin* 51 (2000): 283-92.

46. See summary and references in Craig S. Keener, *Paul, Women & Wives: Marriage and Women's Ministry in the Letters of Paul* (Peabody, Mass.: Hendrickson, 1992), pp. 145-46. For Jewish sources, see W. D. Davies, *Paul and Rabbinic Judaism: Some Rabbinic Elements in Pauline Theology,* 2nd ed. (London: SPCK, 1955), pp. 130-33.

discusses why one should submit to fellow believers and concludes that otherwise the faith would be slandered (6:1). Some of them comment that submission should be honest and not just for show, and that one should submit in the same way that Christ submitted (1 Pet. 2:20-23; Eph. 6:6-8; Col. 3:22-24). Colossians and Ephesians add a series of caveats addressed to the *pater familias;* these caveats emphasize that submission does not mean denigration: wives should be honored and loved (Eph. 5:25-33; Col. 3:19); children should not be frustrated (Eph. 6:4; Col. 3:21); slaves should be treated with respect (Eph. 6:9; Col. 4:1); and all Christians (including, presumably, the *pater familias*) should submit to each other (Eph. 5:21).

Taking these passages as a whole, it would appear that the main reason for following this submission code was to conform with the normal expectation of what morality meant in the first century. Yet the aim was to move beyond mere conformity and submit willingly, in true service, as though to the Lord. However, the Christian *paterfamilias* had to give respect to those who were submitting to him. The motive for all this was the proclamation of the gospel because if this social structure were not followed, the faith would be slandered. This is stated clearly in 1 Timothy 6:1, though perhaps it is even clearer in Titus 2:4-5:

> Train the young women to love their husbands, to love their children, be sober-minded, chaste, workers at home, kind, being in subjection to their own husbands, so that the word of God be not blasphemed.

Part of the Christian commentary on the first section in Ephesians consists of a plea that Christian husbands should love their wives more than their own lives, just as Christ did. The description in this passage, of Christ as the loving husband of the Church, is part of this exhortation. This means that there is now an inextricable link between the teaching of the submission of wives and the description of Christian marriage. However, this does not mean that submission has become an extra marriage vow, in addition to the four OT vows of sexual faithfulness, and the provision of food, clothing, and love.

It may be argued that we live in a time that is very similar to the first century, and so the NT teaching about submission of wives should be equally important to us. The previous century has witnessed an emancipation of women, including a growth in the legal rights to their own property within marriage, the ability to initiate divorce, and equal employment opportunities. Alongside these changes there has also been a sexual revolution that has provided safe birth control and a removal of the normal restraints on woman's sexual behavior, so that women have become as sexually liberated as men have traditionally been.

All this is similar to what transpired in the first century and in **the "first family" of the Emperor Augustus.** Augustus saw the growth of women's freedom as a danger to the state and passed laws making it illegal to remain deliberately unmarried or childless. Even widows had to remarry within two years, and divorcées within eighteen months if they were of childbearing age.[47] Augustus promoted his own family as the ideal to be followed by the whole empire. Pictures of his wife Livia and his children accompanied him on coins and plaques everywhere, and numerous statues were made of Livia as a stern and upright matron. However, his own daughter, Julia, rebelled against her father's restrictions and pursued a modern lifestyle, eventually falling into the extremes of sexual libertarianism. She was known to attend wild parties and roam the streets looking for lovers, even waiting by the statue of Marsyas where the prostitutes plied their trade (Seneca, *De beneficiis* 6.32.1). When her father made her an example by exiling her, she complained that she was simply following in his footsteps, enjoying the same freedom that he had enjoyed during his youth. Indeed, Augustus was known for his extramarital relationships throughout his life, and when he was too old to find women for himself, his wife supplied them for him (Suetonius, *Augustus* 71.1), but none of this was considered improper for a man.[48] The new laws of Augustus failed to restrain the liberation movement of women. Large portions of the female population started to emulate the lifestyle of Julia, while the men longed nostalgically for the days when all women were like Livia.

The answer of the NT was to emphasize "proper" family relationships of **submission** that were **tied inextricably to sexual morality.** Many would argue that today's Christian moralists should emphasize these same two subjects: sexual morality and the submission of wives and children. Others (including me) would say that there is no longer any need to teach submission because this is not considered part of normal morality, and it is no longer linked to sexual morality. In NT days it would cause a scandal if the submission of wives were omitted from moral instruction, but now it is likely to cause an equal scandal if it is included. The threefold teaching of submission did not have a Christian origin, and the number of caveats and explanations added to this teaching by NT au-

47. The *Lex Julia de maritandis ordinibus* and *Lex Julia de adulteriis* (both 18 B.C.E.) and the *Lex Papia Poppaea nuptialis* (9 B.C.E.) were later merged into a single text, the *Lex Iulia et Papia.* Useful discussions of these laws are found in Jane F. Gardner, *Women in Roman Law & Society* (London: Croom Helm, 1987), pp. 20, 52-54, 85-90, 103-4, 121-27; Judith Evans Grubbs, "'Pagan' and 'Christian' Marriage: The State of the Question," *Journal of Early Christian Studies* 2 (1994): 378-79; Alfredo M. Rabello, "Divorce of Jews in the Roman Empire," in *The Jewish Law Annual,* ed. B. S. Jackson (Leiden: Brill, 1981), 4:83; Dixon, *The Roman Family,* pp. 79-80.

48. Fantham, *Women in the Classical World,* pp. 292, 295, 313-15.

thors suggests that they were somewhat uncomfortable with it. They attempted to Christianize it by adding that the head of the household should show respect for those submitting to him, and perhaps submit to them in return.

Whatever one concludes about the reasons why the NT taught submission of wives to their husbands, it is undeniably part of many marriage vows. In my opinion, any Christian bride should be allowed to make a vow of submission, but no bride should be forced to do so. If a bride chooses to make that vow, the groom should be encouraged to make the same vow of submission to his bride. This is in line with the Christian introduction to the submission code in Ephesians, which says that we should all submit to each other (Eph. 5:21). The ancient Jewish and Greco-Roman marriage contracts contained many additions to the standard vows, which individual couples decided to make to each other, and a vow of submission has often been added to Jewish and Christian marriages. However, the vow of submission is not a biblical marriage vow and should never be mandatory.

Conclusions

In Jewish marriage contracts, both the bride and groom promised to feed, clothe, and love each other, and some contracts specifically related this to Exodus 21:10-11, while Greco-Roman contracts contained a promise by only the groom to feed and clothe his wife. Neither Jewish nor non-Jewish contracts contained a vow of sexual faithfulness, but this was part of Greco-Roman law, so it was not necessary. Although the OT and NT do not record the wording of a marriage contract, the three vows of food, clothing, and love do occur occasionally. In Ephesians 5 Christ is pictured as a groom who feeds, clothes, and loves the Church. The language of these vows in traditional Christian marriage services is probably based on this passage. There is therefore no doubt that the origins of the Christian marriage vows lie in Exodus 21:10-11, as mediated by Ephesians 5:29. The vow of obedience was added later, probably because this same subject is addressed in Ephesians 5.

9. History of Divorce

Interpretations in Church History

The traditional view is that Jesus forbade all divorce except in the case of adultery, and that he forbade all remarriage. This view can be traced through the Church Fathers, Church canon law, and the writings of the Reformers. It was developed in two different directions in the Catholic and Reformed churches, one moving towards easier annulment and the other towards easier divorce. In general, however, divorce was possible only for the very rich or influential.

The Loss of Jewish Teaching in 70 C.E.

The Early Church lost touch with its Jewish roots in or before 70 C.E. Various passages in the NT suggest that Christians were excommunicated from the synagogue before the NT canon was completed, and certainly before 70 C.E. This marked the beginning of the loss of Jewish culture within the Church. A few Christian groups such as the Nazarenes and Ebionites continued to follow Jewish customs, but these soon died out. The Church very quickly forgot its Jewish roots, and thereby lost contact with much of the Jewish background of the NT writings.

The date of 70 C.E. was also very significant for Jews because the destruction of Jerusalem at this time marked a complete break with many aspects of Jewish culture. Post-70 Judaism contained almost no Sadducees or Shammaites, and their teachings became a historical curiosity. The academy of rabbis that was set up at Yamnia became the authoritative voice in Judaism for all matters of law and custom. This academy and the Babylonian academy both followed Hillelite teaching and developed it into the Amoraic teaching represented today by the Palestinian and Babylonian Talmuds, respectively. Although the Talmuds contain many traditions about the Sadducees and Shammaites, they are seen almost completely from the point of view of the Hillelite Pharisees. Virtually all that we know about these groups is represented as debates that they had with Hillelites, in which they almost always lost, according to these Hillelite sources.

The interpretation of "a matter of indecency" in Deuteronomy 24:1 is one of these debates. After 70 C.E. this debate was still of scholarly interest, but it was no longer of interest to ordinary Jews. They could no longer choose between a Shammaite or a Hillelite court, and so the only type of divorce available to them was a Hillelite divorce. Thus, there was no longer any need for people to know the differences between Hillelite and Shammaite grounds for divorce. The ground of "any matter" was established as suitable for every divorce, and any man could write out a divorce certificate without stating the grounds. There was not even a need to state that the ground was "any matter," and thus even this phrase disappeared from common usage. The phrases "any matter" and "matter of indecency" were still known to the scholars, but not to the ordinary Jews.

Jesus' teaching about divorce was now utterly incomprehensible to Christians, as well as to most Jews. Christians were no longer familiar with the terms "any matter" and "matter of indecency" that formed the basis of Jesus' debate with the Pharisees. Christians were ignorant of these phrases both because of their separation from Judaism in general and because most Jews were themselves now ignorant of these terms. Mark's account, which did not mention these phrases because they were so well known, could not be understood at all after 70 C.E. Matthew, writing a little later than Mark, reinserted these phrases, presumably because he thought that the ordinary Christian might not immediately recognize that they were the subject of the debate. Yet even Matthew's account became incomprehensible once the meaning of these phrases was forgotten by Christians.

The Church's struggle to understand Jesus' teaching is seen in the large number of variants in the Gospel texts and in the wide variety of interpretations in the Early Church.

Interpretations by the Church Fathers

The Church Fathers generally approached the Gospel traditions about divorce in a straightforward way. Without any information about the Jewish background, the text appeared to say that it is wrong to divorce, except in the case of adultery, and that it is wrong to remarry for any reason. This concurred with the views of the ascetic movement in the Early Church, and so there was little cause to question this interpretation. However, this still left plenty of room for uncertainty about details.

Hermas

Hermas is our earliest witness, writing in Rome between 100 and 150 C.E. In one vision he asked a guide called the Shepherd what one should do if a believing wife commits adultery. The answer was that the husband should separate; otherwise he shares her guilt. This was presumably based on the Gospel exception clause:

> "Sir, if any one has a wife who trusts in the Lord, and if he detect her in adultery, does the man sin if he continue to live with her?" And he said to me, "As long as he remains ignorant of her sin, the husband commits no transgression in living with her. But if the husband know that his wife has gone astray, and if the woman does not repent, but persists in her fornication, and yet the husband continues to live with her, he also is guilty of her crime, and a sharer in her adultery."[1]

Hermas then asked if one should forgive the sin of adultery if she repents. The Shepherd answered that one should forgive, but not repeatedly, because Christians have only one chance of repentance.

> He ought to take back the sinner who has repented. But not frequently. For there is but one repentance to the servants of God. In case, therefore, that the divorced wife may repent, the husband ought not to marry another, when his wife has been put away.[2]

The Shepherd said that a man should not remarry after divorce in case the wife repents. This might perhaps imply that a man would normally be allowed to remarry if repentance was no longer possible (i.e., if she had married someone else), because if remarriage was not permitted at all, it would have been superfluous to give a reason why remarriage was not allowed in this case.

1. Hermas, *Command.* 4.1.6. This and many of the following translations of the Fathers are taken from Philip Schaff, ed., *A Select Library of the Nicene and Post-Nicene Fathers of the Christian Church,* 38 vols. (New York: Christian Literature Co., 1886-90); reprint, Philip Schaff and Henry Wace, eds., *Nicene and Post-Nicene Fathers,* 2nd series (Grand Rapids: Eerdmans, 1979). They are freely available at http://www.ccel.org/. They are noted as "(Schaff)."

2. Hermas, *Command.* 4.1.8 (Schaff).

However, it is more likely that remarriage was completely forbidden unless the spouse died (which is allowed in *Command.* 4.4), and that the apparently superfluous reason was given to bolster the argument.

The teaching about "one repentance" in this passage was elaborated by Hermas in section III of Mandate 4.

> There is no other repentance than that which takes place, when we descended into the water and received remission of our former sins.[3]

Hermas believed, like most of the Church Fathers, that one could repent only once, and any **sin committed after baptism** would be **unforgivable**. This teaching was based on Hebrews 6:4-8; 10:26-31 and was very widespread in this period. It was the reason why many Christians were baptized on their deathbed.

Most people who use the Fathers to justify their interpretation of the divorce texts would, however, reject their teaching on "no forgiveness after baptism." This position is illogical, because the Fathers are far more likely to be aware of the original meaning of Hebrews than of the Gospels. Hebrews was written to Jews living outside Palestine in a largely Greco-Roman culture, while the Gospels are full of references to Jewish practices and vocabulary that would have been obscure to someone from outside Palestine. If one were to argue that the Fathers knew the social and linguistic background of the divorce texts better than do modern scholars, then one would certainly have to accept their interpretation of the passages in Hebrews for the same reasons. However, as explained above, the Gospel divorce texts would have been obscure even to Jews in this period.

Justin Martyr

Justin Martyr, writing about 139 C.E., had a very similar viewpoint to that of Hermas. He quoted a series of sayings by Jesus and concluded that it is sinful to remarry:

> Concerning chastity, He uttered such sentiments as these: "Whosoever looketh upon a woman to lust after her, hath committed adultery with her already in his heart before God." . . . And, "Whosoever shall marry her that is divorced from another husband, committeth adultery." . . . So that all who, by human law, are twice married, are in the eye of our Master sinners, and those who look upon a woman to lust after her.[4]

3. Hermas, *Command.* 4.3.1 (Schaff).
4. Justin, *Apol.* 1.15.1-4 (Schaff).

Justin also recorded a case where **the Church was divided** about whether or not a converted woman should leave her unbelieving and adulterous husband. Some advised that she should stay in the hope of converting him, while others said that she was being defiled by his sin. Eventually she sent him a *repudium,* a Latin divorce certificate, while he was away:

> A certain woman lived with an intemperate husband; . . . when she came to the knowledge of the teachings of Christ she . . . endeavoured to persuade her husband likewise. . . . But he, continuing in the same excesses, alienated his wife from him by his actions. For she, considering it wicked to live any longer as a wife with a husband who sought in every way means of indulging in pleasure contrary to the law of nature, and in violation of what is right, wished to be divorced from him. And when she was over-persuaded by her friends, who advised her still to continue with him, in the idea that some time or other her husband might give hope of amendment, she did violence to her own feeling and remained with him. But when her husband had gone into Alexandria, and was reported to be conducting himself worse than ever, she — that she might not, by continuing in matrimonial connection with him, and by sharing his table and his bed, become a partaker also in his wickednesses and impieties — gave him what you call a bill of divorce, and was separated from him.[5]

The significance of this case for Justin was not the teaching on divorce but the persecution that followed. In his anger, the divorced man denounced her and those Christian leaders who had taught her. A local official arrested those leaders and some other followers and then started arresting anyone who professed the faith. The significance for us is the uncertainty in the story. When she became a Christian, she was taught that she should divorce her adulterous husband, even though some of her friends thought she should not in the hope that he might convert. Eventually she divorced him with a *repudium,* which would allow her to remarry, though we are not told whether the Church would have allowed such a remarriage.

Athenagoras

Athenagoras, a converted Athenian philosopher writing in 177 C.E., boasted that Christians avoided sexual activity, except for childbearing, and said that many Christians were celibate.

5. Justin, *Apol.* 2.2.1-8 (Schaff).

> A person should either remain as he was born, or be content with one marriage; for a second marriage is only a specious adultery. "For whosoever puts away his wife," says He, "and marries another, commits adultery;" not permitting a man to send her away whose virginity he has brought to an end, nor to marry again. For he who deprives himself of his first wife, even though she be dead, is a cloaked adulterer, resisting the hand of God, . . . and dissolving the strictest union of flesh with flesh.[6]

Athenagoras appears to **forbid remarriage even after the death of a partner.** This was perhaps based on a concept of an unbreakable "one flesh" marriage, though it was not spelled out. He went beyond the teaching of the NT, mainly because he was keen to show that Christians should avoid sexual activity unless it is necessary.

Theophilus

Theophilus, who was Bishop of Antioch in approximately 171-188 C.E., quoted Jesus' words along with Proverbs to emphasize the biblical teaching on chastity:

> And concerning chastity . . . Solomon . . . said: "Let thine eyes look right on, and let thine eyelids look straight before thee: make straight paths for your feet." And the voice of the Gospel teaches still more urgently concerning chastity, saying: "Whosoever looketh on a woman who is not his own wife, to lust after her, hath committed adultery with her already in his heart." "And he that marrieth," says [the Gospel], "her that is divorced from her husband, committeth adultery; and whosoever putteth away his wife, saving for the cause of fornication, causeth her to commit adultery." Because Solomon says: "Can a man take fire in his bosom, and his clothes not be burned? Or can one walk upon hot coals, and his feet not be burned? So he that goeth in to a married woman shall not be innocent."[7]

It is difficult to know if Theophilus implied that marriage is unbreakable. His conclusion — "he that goeth in to a married woman shall not be innocent" — may relate to the saying of Jesus about marrying a divorcée, or it may relate to the warnings of Solomon and the Gospel about adultery. Probably it was simply a general conclusion to the whole subject of chastity. He cited the exception "saving for the cause of fornication" without comment, and thus

6. Athenagoras, *Plea for the Christians* 33 (Schaff).

7. Theophilus, *To Autolycus* III.13 (Schaff).

presumably he allowed divorce on this ground, but he did not comment on remarriage.

Clement of Alexandria

Clement of Alexandria, writing at about 192 C.E., stated his position much more fully. He struggled between his personal ascetic feelings and the need for the production of children. He concluded that marriage is necessary, but **passions should be restrained** within marriage, and the punishment for adultery should be most severe:

> Now that the Scripture counsels marriage, and allows no release from the union, is expressly contained in the law, "Thou shalt not put away thy wife, except for the cause of fornication"; and it regards as fornication, the marriage of those separated while the other is alive. . . . "He that taketh a woman that has been put away," it is said, "committeth adultery; and if one puts away his wife, he makes her an adulteress," that is, compels her to commit adultery. And not only is he who puts her away guilty of this, but he who takes her, by giving to the woman the opportunity of sinning; for did he not take her, she would return to her husband. What, then, is the law? In order to check the impetuosity of the passions, it commands the adulteress to be put to death, on being convicted of this; and if of priestly family, to be committed to the flames. And the adulterer also is stoned to death, but not in the same place, that not even their death may be in common. And the law is not at variance with the Gospel, but agrees with it. How should it be otherwise, one Lord being the author of both? She who has committed fornication liveth in sin, and is dead to the commandments; but she who has repented, being as it were born again by the change in her life, has a regeneration of life; the old harlot being dead, and she who has been regenerated by repentance having come back again to life.[8]

Clement, like Hermas, said that remarriage should be avoided in order to allow reconciliation, but he did not state whether or not remarriage was allowed after reconciliation became impossible. From the tenor of his ascetic thoughts, one may assume that he would have been against all remarriage, but this is not stated. Clement contained the seeds of the Reformers' position that the adulterous partner should be regarded as dead, and he appeared to believe that this penalty is reversed in case of repentance. It is not clear if he believed

8. Clement, *Miscellanies* II.23 (Schaff).

that remarriage is allowed after this type of "death," as the Reformers did. Probably this was not in Clement's mind.

Tertullian

Tertullian, writing from about 193 to 220 C.E., changed his views when he became a Montanist. He always followed ascetic principles, but these became more and more rigid. Before he became a Montanist he wrote for his wife, in 200-206 C.E.:

> Therefore when, through the will of God, the husband is deceased, the marriage likewise, by the will of God, deceases. Why should *you* restore what God has put an end to? . . . For even if you do not *"sin"* in re-marrying, still he says "pressure of the flesh ensues." Wherefore, so far as we can, let us love the opportunity of continence.[9]

He was permitting his wife to remarry after his death, though he urged her not to do so. This is in line with an ascetic reading of 1 Corinthians 7:39-40. In 206-212 C.E., when he had become sympathetic to Montanism, he wrote *An Exhortation to Chastity* that contains roughly the same kinds of opinions, but by 211-215, when he wrote *On Monogamy,* he had come to believe that **remarriage, even after the death of a partner, is sinful:**

> "What God hath conjoined, man shall not separate," — for fear, namely, that he contravene the Lord: for He alone shall "separate" who has "conjoined" (separate, moreover, not through the harshness of divorce, which [harshness] He censures and restrains, but through the debt of death). . . . Therefore if those whom God has conjoined man shall not separate by divorce, it is equally congruous that those whom God has separated by death man is not to conjoin by marriage; the joining of the separation will be just as contrary to God's will as would have been the separation of the conjunction.[10]

This is clearly contrary to 1 Corinthians 7, but Tertullian justified it by basing it on the revelations given by the Paraclete to the Montanists:

> "Hardness of heart" reigned till Christ's time; let "infirmity of the flesh" (be content to) have reigned till the time of the Paraclete. The New Law abro-

9. Tertullian, *Wife* I.7 (Schaff).
10. Tertullian, *Monogamy* 9 (Schaff).

gated divorce — it had (somewhat) to abrogate; the New Prophecy (abrogates) second marriage, (which is) no less a divorce of the former (marriage).[11]

However, in a debate with Marcion in 207 C.E., Tertullian appeared to allow remarriage after a valid divorce for adultery. Marcion pointed out that Moses allowed divorce, and Tertullian replied that Jesus also allowed divorce, but only for adultery, and that he forbade remarriage after an invalid divorce:

> His words are: "Whosoever putteth away his wife, and marrieth another, committeth adultery; and whosoever marrieth her that is put away from her husband, also committeth adultery," — "put away," that is, for the reason wherefore a woman ought not to be dismissed, that another wife may be obtained. For he who marries a woman who is unlawfully put away is as much of an adulterer as the man who marries one who is un-divorced. Permanent is the marriage which is not rightly dissolved; to marry, therefore, whilst matrimony is undissolved, is to commit adultery.[12]

The implication of this argument is that Jesus would allow remarriage after a divorce for adultery because this would be a valid divorce. However, it is possible that this was simply an apologetic that was presented for the sake of argument. We cannot be certain what Tertullian's position would have been outside the cut and thrust of a debate. He was giving a justification for Jesus' teaching that remarriage is adulterous and tried to show that Moses and Jesus did not completely disagree. Although the argument presented here would imply that he allowed remarriage after a valid divorce, it is not clear that Tertullian actually permitted this in practice.

Origen

Origen (185-254 C.E.) asked himself (and his congregation) many difficult questions. He courageously explored some nonstandard replies and even left a few questions unanswered. Like Tertullian, he had to combat the Marcion tendency to dismiss the Old Testament. He therefore had to grapple with the reason why the New Testament appeared to have a fundamentally different teaching about divorce. He took the risky route of saying that **Moses got it wrong** because he was simply stating his own opinion:

11. Tertullian, *Monogamy* 14 (Schaff).
12. Tertullian, *Marcion* IV.34 (Schaff).

> God spake many things though Moses, but some things Moses ordained on his own authority, as the Lord most clearly distinguishes. You see then that God did not command divorce, nor will it to be done; but Moses in consequence of the hard-heartedness of the Jews wrote that divorce should be given.[13]

Origen took the rest of the Old Testament seriously, including the fact that God is portrayed as a divorcé. He applied this to Christ divorcing Jerusalem, who demonstrated her adultery when she asked for Barabbas to be freed:

> Now, keeping in mind what we said above in regard to the passage from Isaiah about the bill of divorcement, we will say that the mother of the people separated herself from Christ, her husband, without having received the bill of divorcement, but afterwards when there was found in her an unseemly thing, and she did not find favour in his sight, the bill of divorcement was written out for her; . . . And a sign that she has received the bill of divorcement is this, that Jerusalem was destroyed. . . . There was found in her an unseemly thing; for what was more unseemly than the circumstance that, when it was proposed to them to release one at the feast, they asked for the release of Barabbas the robber, and the condemnation of Jesus? . . . The first wife, accordingly, not having found favour before her husband, because in her had been found an unseemly thing, went out from the dwelling of her husband, and, going away, has become joined to another man, to whom she has subjected herself, whether we should call the husband Barabbas the robber, who is figuratively the devil, or some evil power.[14]

When Christ marries the Church, this would presumably be a remarriage after a divorce. However, Origen did not conclude that humans can remarry because he regarded Christ as being above the Law. He then discussed whether **Christ can remarry Israel** when "all Israel are saved." He concluded that just as Christ is Lord of the Sabbath, **he is** also **above the law** of Deuteronomy 24:1-4. He made it plain that a divorced person cannot remarry when he discussed an actual case where certain Church leaders allowed this to happen. Origen allowed remarriage only after the death of a former spouse:

> But now contrary to what was written, some even of the rulers of the church have permitted a woman to marry, even when her husband was liv-

13. Origen, *Numbers, Hom.* 16.4.330; translated in Harold Smith, *Ante-Nicene Exegesis of the Gospels,* Translations of Christian Literature Series 6 (London: The Society for Promoting Christian Knowledge; New York and Toronto: Macmillan, 1925-29), 4:216.

14. Origen, *Matthew,* II.14.19 from the translation provided in the New Advent collection at http://newadvent.org/. Translations from this source are noted as "(NA)."

> ing, doing contrary to what was written, where it is said, "A wife is bound for so long time as her husband liveth," and "So then if while her husband liveth, she shall be joined to another man she shall be called an adulteress," not indeed altogether without reason, for it is probable this concession was permitted in comparison with worse things, contrary to what was from the beginning ordained by law, and written.[15]

This is a remarkable passage because Origen concluded that the leaders had good reasons to rule as they did. Origen was often willing to consider ideas that were contrary to Scripture, though he concluded that Scripture was correct, even where it appeared to be illogical. He discussed, for example, the reasons why adultery was the only ground for divorce, and he **expressed surprise that other seemingly more serious matters were not valid grounds**:

> But it might be a subject for inquiry if on this account He hinders any one putting away a wife . . . for any other reason, as for example for poisoning, or for the destruction during the absence of her husband from home of an infant born to them, or for any form of murder whatsoever. And further, if she were found despoiling and pillaging the house of her husband, . . . for to endure sins of such heinousness which seem to be worse than adultery or fornication, will appear to be irrational; but again on the other hand to act contrary to the design of the teaching of the Saviour, every one would acknowledge to be impious.[16]

He also pointed out that adultery by a wife may be partially caused by the husband, and he wondered why the husband should be blameless:

> For the husband can . . . cause his own wife to commit adultery; as, for example, allowing her to do what she wishes beyond what is fitting, and stooping to friendship with what men she wishes, . . . but whether there is a ground of defence or not for such husbands in the case of such false steps, you will inquire carefully, and deliver your opinion also in regard to the difficult questions raised by us on the passage. And even he who withholds himself from his wife makes her oftentimes to be an adulteress when he does not satisfy her desires.[17]

These question went unanswered, but Origen remained committed to the teaching that divorce was only on the ground of adultery and remarriage was not

15. Origen, *Matthew,* II.14.23 (NA).
16. Origen, *Matthew,* II.14.24 (NA).
17. Origen, *Matthew,* II.14.24 (NA).

permitted before the death of a spouse. However, he was happy to leave others to come to their own conclusions: "you will inquire carefully, and deliver your opinion also in regard to the difficult questions raised by us on the passage."

Irenaeus and Ptolemaeus

Irenaeus and Ptolemaeus, both from the late second century, argued that **Moses' law was inferior to Christ's.** They did not want to fall into the Marcion heresy of abandoning the Old Testament, and so they either blamed Moses or the Jews. Ptolemaeus said that the fault lay with Moses who expressed his own opinion that was contrary to God's law:

> For since they were unable to observe God's mind, which made it not lawful to put away their wives, with whom some of them were living without pleasure, and were from this likely to turn away further into unrighteousness and so to destruction, Moses, seeking to remove this displeasure, enacted (a less evil instead of the greater). This was his idea, by which he is found legislating contrary to God; but that the Law of Moses is here shown to be other than the Law of God, is indisputable.[18]

Irenaeus suggested that the law was different in the OT and in the NT because the situations were different and, in particular, because the Jews were so difficult to rule:

> The Lord also showed that certain precepts were enacted for them by Moses, on account of their hardness [of heart], and because of their unwillingness to be obedient, when, on their saying to Him, "Why then did Moses command to give a writing of divorcement, and to send away a wife?" He said to them, "Because of the hardness of your hearts he permitted these things to you; but from the beginning it was not so;" thus exculpating Moses as a faithful servant, but acknowledging one God, who from the beginning made male and female, and reproving them as hard-hearted and disobedient. And therefore it was that they received from Moses this law of divorcement, adapted to their hard nature.[19]

These statements show how difficult the Fathers found the teaching of the

18. Ptolemaeus, *To Flora* 2.4 = Epiphanius *Contra Haereses* 33. Translated in Smith, *Ante-Nicene Exegesis of the Gospels,* 4:215-16.

19. Irenaeus, *Against Heresies* 4.15.2 (Schaff).

Old Testament. They said that the Jews forced Moses' hand by being hard-hearted and by threatening to abandon their wives. Moses enacted a law that was not within God's ideal but that was a lesser evil. The greater evil was, presumably, that the wives would be abandoned without a divorce certificate. They did not say why it was better for the wives to have Moses' law of the divorce certificate. Perhaps they felt that this provided a legal framework for the divorce so that the wives were not simply abandoned. Yet what did this mean in practice? The only significance of a divorce certificate in Judaism or the Greco-Roman world was the permission that it gave to the woman to remarry. Did Irenaeus and Ptolemaeus imply that Moses wanted to allow divorced women to remarry? Was this a lesser evil than being abandoned? If they had thought through the implications of what they had written, this must be so.

More probably, they linked the divorce certificate with the woman's dowry. This means that they confused Moses' law of the divorce certificate with the Jewish custom of a dowry receipt that was given by the bride to the groom in Jewish and Greco-Roman society. Allowing the man to divorce the woman and return her dowry was a lesser evil than abandoning her without means of support.

Ambrosiaster

Ambrosiaster is a relatively unimportant Church Father who cannot be identified with certainty but probably wrote at the end of the fourth century. He is important in this survey because he is the first Father who specifically said that **remarriage was allowed after an unbeliever separates.** His commentary on 1 Corinthians 7 argues that Paul allowed the deserted believer to remarry in the same way that Ezra did. Ezra 9–10 says that the Israelites separated from foreign wives, but it does not say that they were allowed to remarry. However, it is generally assumed that they were allowed to remarry, and many scholars regard Malachi 2:14-16 as a reference to remarriages in Ezra's day that were enacted in order to produce a "holy seed." Ambrosiaster said that if Ezra allowed remarriage after a believer initiated a divorce, it is obvious that remarriage is permitted if an unbeliever initiates it.

> Marriage which is without devotion towards God is not valid, and therefore it is not a sin for a person who is divorced on account of God to marry someone else. For the unbeliever, in departing, is seen to sin both against God and against the marriage, because he has not been willing to have a marriage ruled by reverence for God. Therefore marital fidelity need not be

> maintained in the case of someone who has departed so as not to accept that the God of the Christians is the author of the marriage. For if Ezra brought about the divorce of believing husbands or wives in order that God might become propitious, and not angered, should they take other wives from their own race — for they were not instructed that, having divorced these wives, they absolutely must not marry others — how much more, if an unbeliever has deserted (her), will (a woman) have the free option to marry, if she wishes, a husband of her own law; for what has been done outside the law of God ought not to be considered matrimony.[20]

It is clear that Ambrosiaster considered marriage to an unbeliever who is "without devotion to God" as invalid. Therefore he did not really allow remarriage because the first marriage had not existed legally. If the marriage had continued, he would probably have regarded it as valid, but when the unbeliever left, he showed that he did not "accept that the God of the Christians is the author of the marriage." This meant that the marriage vows had been performed "outside the law of God," and that the relationship "ought not to be considered matrimony." Ambrosiaster was therefore arguing that Paul recognized a ground for annulment followed by a true marriage. This passage does not argue for divorce followed by remarriage.

Earlier in his commentary Ambrosiaster did allow remarriage after a divorce, but only for a man. He argued that a man was allowed to remarry after divorcing a sexually sinful wife, but not vice versa. He understood *porneia* to include both unfaithfulness and unnamed sexual deviations within marriage:

> For a woman is not allowed to marry, if she has sent away her husband because of his fornication or apostasy or if, impelled by lust, he is seeking enjoyment of his wife in an illicit way, because the inferior party certainly does not have the same right by this law as the stronger party. . . . *And a man is not to send his wife away.* There is the implication, *"except on the ground of fornication"*; the reason why he does not add, as he does in the case of the woman, "But if she departs, he should remain as he is," is that the man is allowed to marry, for he has divorced a sinful wife, because the husband is not restricted by the law as the woman is, *For the head of a woman is her husband.*

Ambrosiaster used an argument from silence in a curiously illogical way. Paul said "A wife is not to separate, and if she does, she should remain unmar-

20. Ambrosiaster, *Commentary on 1 Corinthians,* on 1 Cor. 7:15. Translation by Janet Fairweather (private communication).

ried," but when he says "And a man is not to send his wife away," Paul does not add "and if he does, he should remain unmarried." From this omission, Ambrosiaster inferred that the man is allowed to remarry. However, Paul is also silent about the grounds on which the man or woman breaks up the marriage, and here Ambrosiaster is quite happy to supply the ground from the Gospel: "except on the ground of fornication." His conclusion was therefore based on emphasizing one place where Paul was silent (concerning the man's right to remarry) while filling in the silence at another place (concerning the grounds for divorce).

Although Ambrosiaster was expressing a view that was not preserved earlier, he did not defend himself against detractors. He appeared to believe that this was a perfectly normal exegesis that the reader would accept without much persuasion. The rest of his commentary is marked by straightforward exposition without the flights of fancy and allegory that characterized many other commentaries, and he presumably felt that this too was a straightforward interpretation. Although he was not in the mainstream of the Church Fathers, he appeared to expect others to agree with him, and so he perhaps represented a sizable minority.

Jerome and Chrysostom

Most of the Church Fathers taught that a marriage could be ended only by the death of one partner. Some Fathers, such as Jerome and Chrysostom (both about 350-410 C.E.), upheld this orthodox position even when they were presented with very **difficult pastoral circumstances.**

Jerome was asked by a priest if a good woman in his parish could be allowed to take communion. She had been abandoned by her wicked husband and had been forced by her family to remarry. Jerome was uncompromising in his reply:

> A husband may be an adulterer or a sodomite, he may be stained with every crime and may have been left by his wife because of his sins; yet he is still her husband and, so long as he lives, she may not marry another. . . . Therefore if your sister, who, as she says, has been forced into a second union, wishes to receive the body of Christ and not to be accounted an adulteress, let her do penance; so far at least as from the time she begins to repent to have no further intercourse with that second husband who ought to be called not a husband but an adulterer.[21]

Chrysostom used language that was almost as blunt when he compared a divorced woman with a runaway slave:

21. Jerome, *Letters*, LV: *To Amandus* 3-4 (Schaff).

> If then a man wishes to dismiss his wife or the wife wishes to leave her husband, let her remember this saying and that it represents Paul as present and pursuing her, crying out and saying: "The wife is bound by the law." Just as escaped slaves, even if they have left the house of their master, still carry their chain, so wives, even if they have left their husbands, have the law in the form of a chain which condemns them, accusing them of adultery, accusing those who take them, and saying: "Your husband is still living and what you have done is adultery."[22]

Epiphanius

Epiphanius, bishop of Cyprus in the early fifth century, **allowed remarriage after divorce for fornication**, though he made clear that this was not ideal and was possibly the lesser sin.

> He who cannot keep continence after the death of his first wife, or who has separated from his wife for a valid motive, as fornication, or some other misdeed, if he takes another wife, or the wife takes another husband, the divine word does not condemn him nor exclude him from the Church or the life; but she tolerates it rather on account of his weakness.[23]

Augustine

Augustine was already writing on remarriage in 390 C.E. and wrote a two-volume work in 419 C.E., *To Pollentius — On Adulterous Marriages.* He established the theological basis for the teaching that adultery is the only ground for divorce and that such a divorce does not permit remarriage because the marriage bond can be broken only by death. He taught that the **indestructible** or ontological **nature of the marriage bond is due to the sacramental nature of marriage.**[24] Like baptism, which is our marriage to Christ, human marriage is irreversible.

22. Chrysostom, *Second Homily on Marriage, "De libello repudii,"* in J.-P. Migne, *Patrologia Graeca* (Paris: Migne, 1857-66), 51:218-19; translation by Alex R. G. Deasley, *Marriage and Divorce in the Bible and the Church* (Kansas City, Mo.: Beacon Hill, 2000), p. 203.

23. Epiphanius, *Against Heresies* 69.

24. David Atkinson (*To Have and To Hold: The Marriage Covenant and the Discipline of Divorce* [London: Collins, 1979], p. 42) argued that *sacramentum* in Augustine had the same meaning as in the Roman army, where it was a soldier's oath. This meant that although it was a moral obligation, it was still humanly possible to break the bond. However, this passage suggests that *sacramentum* meant something that continued even if a person changed his mind.

> There is also a certain sacramental bond in marriage which is recommended to believers in wedlock. Accordingly it is en-joined by the apostle: "Husbands, love your wives, even as Christ also loved the Church." Of this bond the substance undoubtedly is this, that the man and the woman who are joined together in matrimony should remain inseparable as long as they live; and that it should be unlawful for one consort to be parted from the other, except for the cause of fornication. . . . Thus between the conjugal pair, as long as they live, the nuptial bond has a permanent obligation, and can be cancelled neither by separation nor by union with another. But this permanence avails, in such cases, only for injury from the sin, not for a bond of the covenant. In like manner the soul of an apostate, which renounces as it were its marriage union with Christ, does not, even though it has cast its faith away, lose the sacrament of its faith, which it received in the laver of regeneration. It would undoubtedly be given back to him if he were to return, although he lost it on his departure from Christ. He retains, however, the sacrament after his apostasy, to the aggravation of his punishment, not for meriting the reward.[25]

Augustine's logic seemed impeccable to his contemporaries, who were willing to make harsh pastoral decisions on the basis of them, as we saw with Jerome above. Augustine himself, however, was not entirely convinced. In his *Retractations* he expressed **doubts about the type of sin that is referred to by the exception clause:**

> But the following question should be considered and examined again and again: what immorality the Lord means to be understood as that for which one may put away his wife? — that which is condemned in licentious acts or that about which the following is said: "Thou destroyest everyone who is unfaithful to Thee," in which, certainly, the former is included? . . . But what is to be understood by immorality and how it is to be limited, and whether, because of it, one may put away his wife is an almost obscure question. Yet there is no doubt that this is permitted because of the immorality committed in licentious acts.[26]

What grounds for divorce did Augustine want to include? Did he mean that all types of licentious acts, such as "unnatural" sex, should be included? Did he want to include apostates who are "unfaithful to Thee"? Perhaps his

25. Augustine, *On Marriage and Concupiscence* I.11 [X] (Schaff).

26. Augustine, *Retractations* I 18, as cited in Deasley, *Marriage and Divorce in the Bible,* p. 205.

scope was even wider because he said that those who are unfaithful include those who are licentious. The phrase "licentious acts" may include any number of serious sins that fall short of apostasy. This passage appears to be the first instance of someone arguing that the term *porneia* includes a wide range of sinfulness, which is much more than just sexual sin.

Augustine was also uncertain about the sinfulness of the innocent divorcé who remarried:

> The man who leaves his wife because of adultery and marries another is not, it seems, as blameworthy as the man who for no reason leaves his wife and marries another. Nor is it clear from Scripture whether a man who has left his wife because of adultery, which he is certainly permitted to do, is himself an adulterer, if he marries again. And if he should, I do not think that he would commit a grave sin.[27]

Augustine's uncertainty is very significant. He did not go so far as to doubt the ontological nature of marriage, but he did doubt that it was a *grievous* sin for the nonadulterous divorcé to remarry. This suggests that the concept of ontological marriage was, for Augustine, a purely theoretical construct. The marriage bond had to be theoretically indestructible in order to explain why remarriage would be adulterous. Yet this adultery was theoretical only, and it was not nearly as blameworthy as the adultery that split up the first marriage. This more nuanced and balanced approach was not the one that became Catholic canon law. Laws have to be black and white, defining right and wrong, without room for doubt.

Aquinas and Subsequent Canon Law

Roman Catholic canon law was based on Augustine, as systematized by Thomas Aquinas in the thirteenth century. Although he faithfully summarized the teaching of Augustine on divorce and remarriage, he did not always share the same emphases, and he did not take into account the more subtle nuances that were hinted at in Augustine's later rethinking.

Aquinas built on Augustine's view of marriage as a sacrament. This view was aided by the Vulgate translation of μυστήριον in Ephesians 5:32 as *sacramentum*. Before Aquinas, marriage was not considered a cause of grace, like the other sacraments, but Aquinas **confirmed the full sacramental character of**

27. Augustine, *On Faith and Works* (Acw. No. 48), as cited in Deasley, *Marriage and Divorce in the Bible,* p. 205.

marriage. This was the final foundation for understanding marriage to be ontologically indissoluble. From this basis it was possible to state conclusively that any reference to divorce in the NT referred only to separation, and that the freedom of 1 Corinthians 7:15 did not include the freedom to remarry. Separation was "from bed and board" *(a mensa et thoro)* but not the end of the marriage.

Aquinas's teaching held sway until the Reformation and beyond. The twenty-fourth session of the Council of Trent in November 1563 confirmed the official Roman Catholic position on divorce and remarriage in the aftermath of the Reformation. It reaffirmed that marriage was indissoluble and sacramental and confirmed that "the bond of matrimony cannot be dissolved on account of the adultery of one of the married parties," and that "neither spouse may contract a second marriage during the lifetime of another without committing adultery."[28]

While canon law was strengthened with regard to the indissolubility of marriage, there was a parallel development in the use of annulment to end marriages. A growing number of "impediments" to marriage were identified that could be applied retroactively. If it could be shown that the vows were made improperly, they could be declared invalid, so that the **marriage could be "annulled."** This meant that the marriage, in effect, had never happened. Marriage was allowable after annulment because, legally speaking, this was not remarriage.[29]

Summarizing the Fathers

It has often been assumed too glibly that the Fathers spoke with one voice. They were certainly relatively united in understanding the text in its seemingly plain sense, but they also expressed individual doubts about the difficulties of their position.

When the NT texts on divorce are read outside the context of the first century, they appear to teach that divorce is allowed only for adultery and for

28. *Council of Trent* Session 24 Canon 7 from *The Canons and Decrees of the Sacred and Ecumenical Council of Trent,* ed. J. Waterworth (London: Dolman, 1848).

29. For a modern Catholic view on annulment, see Oliver Stewart, *Divorce Vatican Style* (London: Olifants, 1971), or, for an American Catholic view, see Philip J., Grib, S.J., *Divorce Laws and Morality — A New Catholic Jurisprudence* (New York: Lanham, 1985). For a more critical view see Morris West and Robert Francis, *Scandal in the Assembly: A Bill of Complaints and a Proposal for Reform on the Matrimonial Laws and Tribunals of the Roman Catholic Church* (London: Pan, 1970) or Bernard Haring, *No Way Out? — Pastoral Care of the Divorced and Remarried* (Boston: St. Paul Publications, 1989).

desertion by a nonbeliever, and that remarriage before the death of a former partner involves sin. Ascetic beliefs, which characterize almost all the Fathers, minimized the problems with this "plain" meaning of the texts. Many of the Fathers regarded singleness or celibacy as preferable to the married state, though they acknowledged that marriage did not involve sin. The Fathers had little incentive to seek ways to help divorcés remarry, and they were happy to recommend the separation of marriage partners rather than divorce. Some, like Athenagoras and Tertullian, even used Jesus' teaching on remarriage to encourage celibacy.

They **did not give much discussion to the ground of desertion by an unbeliever** because they were writing for believers. They were concerned to discover the grounds by which a believer could decide to separate. If a believer was deserted, the separation did not give the believer a right to remarry, any more than a believer who divorced an adulterous partner had a right to remarry. Thus, there was little point in discussing the issue of desertion. The Council of Trent did, however, establish that a marriage that was broken by an unbeliever may be dissolved because it was not sacramental.

There were **a few dissenting voices**. The clearest of these is Ambrosiaster, who said that Paul allowed remarriage of a man who had divorced an adulterous partner. Although he was the only Father to specifically teach this, we know from incidental references to remarriages that this practice was fairly widespread. Justin Martyr recorded the case of a woman who sent her husband a *repudium* (which implied the right of remarriage) rather than simply separating from her husband. Origen had to address the case of a woman who had been allowed to remarry by the leaders of a church, and Jerome was asked his opinion on this issue by a priest who clearly wanted to allow a remarried woman to take communion. Epiphanius grudgingly allowed remarriage of one who divorced an adulterer, as a lesser sin than unchastity. It is likely that there were others who taught like Ambrosiaster, but their writings were not selected by monks for copying, and so they were not preserved for later historians.

It is possible that Tertullian recognized the right of a validly divorced person to remarry, but he may have stated this merely as a debating point, in order to make his position more logical. Origen regarded Christ's marriage to the Church as remarriage, but he said that Christ is above the Law. Clement said that adulterers were spiritually dead, but, unlike some Reformers, he did not take the next logical step and let their former partners remarry.

Some of the Fathers expressed **unease about the sinfulness of an innocent divorcé who remarried.** Although only Ambrosiaster is recorded as specifically allowing such remarriage, other Fathers considered it a lesser sin. This is especially clear in Augustine, but it is also seen in some early canon law enacted in 305-306 at the Council of Elvira in Spain. Canons 8 and 9 condemned a woman who divorced and remarried, but the woman who divorced on the ground of adultery received slightly less punishment than the woman who had no grounds for divorce.[30]

Some Fathers even discussed the possibility of **other grounds for divorce.** Origen pointed out that there were other offenses that were more serious than adultery, such as the attempted poisoning of a partner or killing of a child while the partner was absent. He also pointed out that a man may cause a divorce by sexual neglect of his wife. He did not, however, suggest that these should be additional grounds for divorce. He made the surprising decision to leave it to the individual's conscience. Augustine also suggested that Matthew's exception might mean sexual sin in general or might perhaps even include apostasy and other sins.

The **reasons given for denying remarriage** changed considerably over the centuries. Originally the divorced person was asked not to remarry in order to allow repentance and reconciliation. Hermas and Clement stated this clearly, though it is not clear whether they allowed remarriage when reconciliation was impossible. It is likely that this reason was simply a justification for a difficult teaching, and that remarriage was not allowed until after the death of the former partner. By the time of Augustine, marriage had become a sacrament, though it did not become a "cause of grace" until Aquinas. This meant that it had become irreversible, like the sacrament of priesthood or baptism.

Many of the Fathers had to combat the Marcionite tendency within the Church, and so they were keen to explain the reason why the OT appeared to be so contrary to the NT in this area. Some (e.g., Origen and Ptolemaeus) said that Moses simply expressed his own opinion, while others (e.g., Irenaeus) said that the Jews got the message that their hard-heartedness deserved.

The **general consensus** is that marriage is indissoluble except by death, though husband and wife can separate "from bed and hearth" if either commits adultery. It is ironic that this resultant teaching is precisely what Moses and Paul forbade. Moses stopped Israelite men from abandoning their wives without giving them a certificate of divorce, and thereby he allowed them to remarry. Paul stopped Christians from abandoning their husbands or wives and told them to attempt reconciliation. He reminded them that husbands and

30. The woman who divorces an adulterous partner may receive communion after the death of her first husband or on her deathbed, whereas the other is barred from communion even at death. See Deasley, *Marriage and Divorce in the Bible*, p. 200. Pierre Nautin ("Divorce et remariage dans la tradition de l'église latine," *Recherches de science religieuse* 62 [1974]: 7-54) suggested that many Fathers in the second-fourth centuries allowed a man to remarry after divorcing an adulteress wife.

wives owed each other emotional and material support. Aquinas's concept of separation from "bed and board" is an almost exact negation of what Paul commands in 1 Corinthians 7:10-14.

Interpretations after the Reformation

The Reformation was based on a fresh examination of Scripture and a break with traditional authority, and it sparked a great deal of reappraisal of Christian doctrines. In the area of divorce and remarriage this reappraisal resulted in a wide diversity of interpretations, all of which were considered to be biblically based. It was clear to most theologians that there was something wrong with the traditional approach. The doubts that had been expressed by Origen and Augustine could now be explored without the straitjacket of orthodoxy. However, the knowledge of the first-century background was still not available, and so it is not surprising that none of the ingenious solutions rang true.

Erasmus was one of the clearest thinkers among the new biblical scholars, and the publication of his Greek New Testament in 1516 was an important impetus to others. He pointed out that the Roman Catholic concept of marriage as a sacrament was based on the Vulgate translation of μυστήριον in Ephesians 5:32 as *sacramentum.* This translation made sense in the early centuries, when *sacramentum* had the broader sense of "symbol" or "mystery," but by the Middle Ages the meaning had narrowed to the technical theological meaning of an immutable means of grace.

Erasmus also took a new look at the divorce texts and tried to interpret them in the context in which they occurred. He suggested that the divorce saying of Matthew 5:32 should be **interpreted less legalistically**, in line with the rest of the Sermon on the Mount. He suggested that the sayings in Matthew 19 and Mark 10 were addressed to disciples who represented truly committed members of the kingdom, rather than to ordinary, imperfect ones. At the time of the Reformation virtually every member of the country was counted as a member of the kingdom, and it was difficult to apply these ideal regulations to a very imperfect society. He also pointed out that neither of the proof texts that were used for demonstrating that marriage ended only with death (i.e., Rom. 7:2-3; 1 Cor. 7:39) were actually dealing with divorce. He concluded that Paul allowed divorce with remarriage after desertion by an unbeliever, and that Jesus' exception allowed remarriage after divorce for adultery.[31]

31. Erasmus's contribution is summarized well in David L. Smith, "Divorce and Remarriage from the Early Church to John Wesley," *Trinity Journal* n.s. 11 (1990): 134, and V. Norskov

Luther

Luther normally followed the Fathers in matters of theology, but he departed from their almost universal teaching by allowing remarriage during the lifetime of a former spouse. In order to be faithful to the Fathers, who said that only death could truly end a marriage, Luther argued that **the adulterer or unbeliever was spiritually dead.** Adultery deserved the death penalty in the OT, and so an adulterer could be considered dead in God's eyes, as was also the unbeliever.

> Since it is only death that can dissolve a marriage and set you free, an adulterer has already been divorced, not by men but by God himself, and separated not only from his wife but from this very life. . . . He is already dead even though the judge may not have him executed. Because it is God that is doing the divorcing here, the other partner is set completely free and is not obliged, unless he chooses to do so, to keep the spouse that has broken the marriage vow. We neither commend nor forbid such divorces, but leave it to the government to act here; and we submit to whatever the secular law prescribes in this matter.[32]

This was part of his teaching on the two kingdoms, of the Church and the State. The Church could only excommunicate, while the State could carry out the death penalty if it wished. The State could also let an unbeliever or a non-Evangelical (nonreformed believer) divorce. Luther accepted this as a valid divorce.

> An additional cause for divorce is this: when one spouse deserts the other, that is, when he runs away out of sheer peevishness. For example, if a pagan woman were married to a Christian man, or as happens sometimes nowadays, if one spouse is an Evangelical and the other is not, is divorce legitimate in such a case? Paul discusses the matter in 1 Corinthians 7.13-15 and comes to this conclusion: If the one partner consents to remain, the other partner should keep him. . . . If it happens that the other partner simply refuses to remain. . . . If he refuses to return after a summons and a decent interval of waiting, the other partner should be set completely free. Such a person is much worse than a heathen and an unbeliever (1 Tim. 5.8); he is less tolerable than a wicked adulterer.[33]

Olsen, *The New Testament Logia on Divorce — A Study of Their Interpretation from Erasmus to Milton* (Tübingen: J. C. B. Mohr [Paul Siebeck], 1971).

32. Luther, *The Sermon on the Mount,* regarding Matt. 5:31-32, *Luther's Works* 21:96 from Jaroslav Pelikan, ed., *Luther's Works,* 55 vols. (St. Louis: Concordia Publishing House, 1955-86).

33. Luther, *The Sermon on the Mount,* regarding Matt. 5:31-32, *Luther's Works* 21:97.

Luther therefore allowed divorce with remarriage for the same two grounds as Erasmus — adultery and desertion by an unbeliever — and like Erasmus he regarded this as true **divorce** that **could be followed by remarriage.**

Luther named some **other grounds for divorce** in his sermon "The Estate of Marriage." Here he spoke about three grounds, which did not include desertion by a nonbeliever. Presumably he neglected to speak about desertion because he was speaking to believers about grounds that they might have. His first two grounds are unexceptional:

> The first, which has just been mentioned and was discussed above, is the situation in which the husband or wife is not equipped for marriage because of bodily or natural deficiencies of any sort. . . . The second ground is adultery.[34]

The first ground is a reference to the various impediments, such as the fact that husband and wife have the same mother. This would normally be regarded as a ground for annulment, but Luther despised the papal use of annulment, and so he probably preferred to avoid this term.

The third ground is the refusal of conjugal rights. He only discussed refusal by a wife, but presumably, like Paul whom he quotes, he would have said the same about a husband who refused:

> The third case for divorce is that in which one of the parties deprives and avoids the other, refusing to fulfil the conjugal duty or to live with the other person. For example, one finds many a stubborn wife like that who will not give in, and who cares not a whit whether her husband falls into the sin of unchastity ten times over. Here it is time for the husband to say, "If you will not, another will; the maid will come if the wife will not." Only first the husband should admonish and warn his wife two or three times, and let the situation be known to others so that her stubbornness becomes a matter of common knowledge and is rebuked before the congregation. If she still refuses, get rid of her; take an Esther and let Vashti go, as King Ahasuerus did [Esth. 1:1-17].
>
> Here you should be guided by the words of St. Paul, I Corinthians 7[:4-5], "The husband does not rule over his own body, but the wife does; likewise the wife does not rule over her own body, but the husband does. Do not deprive each other, except by agreement," etc. Notice that St. Paul forbids either party to deprive the other, for by the marriage vow each submits his body to the other in conjugal duty. When one resists the other and re-

34. Luther, "The Estate of Marriage," Part 2, *Luther's Works* 45:30.

> fuses the conjugal duty she is robbing the other of the body she had bestowed upon him. This is really contrary to marriage, and dissolves the marriage. For this reason the civil government must compel the wife, or put her to death. If the government fails to act, the husband must reason that his wife has been stolen away and slain by robbers; he must seek another. We would certainly have to accept it if someone's life were taken from him. Why then should we not also accept it if a wife steals herself away from her husband, or is stolen away by others? . . .
>
> What about a situation where one's wife is an invalid and has therefore become incapable of fulfilling the conjugal duty? May he not take another to wife? By no means. Let him serve the Lord in the person of the invalid and await His good pleasure.[35]

Luther argued, from Paul, that conjugal activity was a necessary part of marriage, and that refusal was a ground for divorce. He regarded this refusal as equivalent to a dissolution of the marriage. In the process of arguing this, he also showed that he allowed remarriage in the case of a wife who has been kidnapped, without hope of return but without proof of death.

Zurich and Geneva Reformers

Zwingli and Bullinger in Zurich also **allowed divorce for reasons other than adultery**, saying that Christ did not exclude other grounds when he asserted that one. Bucer, on the basis of Bullinger, even allowed divorce for mental incompatibility and by mutual consent. In contrast, Calvin and Beza in Geneva allowed only the standard two exceptions.[36]

Calvin, like Luther, said that the OT death penalty should ideally be applied but "the wicked forbearance of magistrates makes it necessary for husbands to put away unchaste wives, because adulterers are not punished."[37] Calvin also allowed remarriage after a nonbeliever divorced a believer. He justified this by saying that "the unbelieving party makes a divorce with God rather than with her partner."[38]

35. Luther, "The Estate of Marriage," Part 2, *Luther's Works* 45:33-35.

36. Olsen, *The New Testament Logia on Divorce*, pp. 146-47.

37. John Calvin, *Commentary on a Harmony of the Evangelists, Matthew, Mark and Luke*, trans. and collated William Pringle (Edinburgh: Calvin Translation Society, 1845-46), 2:384, regarding Matt. 19:9.

38. John Calvin, *Commentary on the Epistles of Paul the Apostle to the Corinthians*, trans. and collated William Pringle (Edinburgh: Calvin Translation Society, 1848-49), 1:244, regarding 1 Cor. 7:15.

Despite this insistence that the NT has only two grounds for divorce, the exigencies of governing Geneva led him to allow three others. In his "Ecclesiastical Ordinances" he allowed impotence, extreme religious incompatibility, and abandonment.[39]

English Reformers

Divorce law in England became tied up with politics, especially in the light of the marriages of Henry VIII. **William Tyndale** agreed with Luther that marriage was not a sacrament and allowed remarriage after divorce for adultery or desertion. However, he did not agree that the divorce of King Henry VIII from Catherine of Aragon was valid.[40] Thomas Cranmer supported Henry's divorce and was made Archbishop of Canterbury in 1533.

Cranmer, who was responsible for much of Anglican theology, wanted to avoid both the "Pope's Law" of annulment and also some of the reformers' more extreme developments. His views were expressed in the *Reformatio legum ecclesiasticarum,* which he hoped would become the basis for English church law. This abolished separation *a mensa et thoro* and allowed divorce with remarriage for adultery, desertion, prolonged absence, mortal hatred, and cruelty.[41] This reform was never instituted due to opposition in Edward's reign and the conservatism of Elizabeth's.[42]

The Anglican Church was therefore left with the strictures of the Catholic Church (separation for adultery only, and no remarriage until after the death of the former spouse) but without the standard annulment procedure that allowed Catholics to remarry. The Anglican ecclesiastical courts did occasionally allow an annulment, though this required a private act of parliament in each case. Divorce was therefore extremely expensive, and there were only 317 such annulments between 1697 and 1855.

Modern England and USA

In the nineteenth century when the middle classes became more vociferous,

39. John Calvin, *Ecclesiastical Ordinances, Corpus Reformatorum,* x.10-14, cited by Olsen, *The New Testament Logia on Divorce,* p. 99.

40. Smith, "Divorce and Remarriage," p. 138.

41. *Reformatio legum ecclesiasticarum,* Cardwell's Edition (Oxford, 1850), chs. 5, 8, 9, 10, 11, cited in Charles Gore, *The Question of Divorce* (London: John Murray, 1911), p. 7.

42. Olsen, *The New Testament Logia on Divorce,* p. 148.

there was growing pressure for a cheaper route to divorce. There was also pressure for grounds other than adultery, such as cruelty, desertion, insanity, or a long term of imprisonment. These grounds were introduced in **The Matrimonial Causes Act 1937**, where they were listed as "matrimonial offenses" on the basis of which the innocent partner could sue for divorce.

The ground of adultery was still the commonest, though when both partners wanted a divorce but neither had committed an "offense," adultery was often manufactured. The husband would hire a hotel room, a woman, and a private detective with a camera who would "discover" the "adulterer" and provide evidence for the court. This brought the law into disrepute, and so the Anglican Church report *Putting Asunder* recommended that the principle of "irretrievable breakdown" of marriage should supplant the concept of "matrimonial offenses." This was implemented in the **Divorce Reform Act 1969**, which said that "irretrievable breakdown" should be demonstrated by adultery, intolerable behavior, desertion for two years, separation for two years, or separation for five years if one party contests the divorce. **The Family Law Act of 1996** still recognized "irretrievable breakdown" as the sole ground for divorce but removed the need to prove it in an effort to make divorce less litigious. It also introduced compulsory counseling and additional cooling-off periods. However, this reform was found to be unworkable, and the act was withdrawn before it was fully implemented.

In the United States the trend went in the opposite direction until 1969. Instead of fewer grounds there were a bewildering number of possible grounds for divorce because each state had its own laws. Donald W. Shaner estimated that there were more than thirty different grounds that were recognized in one or more states.[43] This was in 1969 when Ronald Reagan, then governor of California, signed the first **no-fault divorce law**, which has since **spread throughout the United States**. With this change in the law, the divorce rate jumped dramatically.

The Growth in Divorces

Similar evolutions of the law have taken place in most other countries in the world, making divorce less expensive and less complicated. As a result there has been a huge growth in the number of divorces. This increase has often been interpreted as a sign of modern immorality, or lack of determination to make marriages work. History suggests that **men and women have always had**

43. Donald W. Shaner, *A Christian View of Divorce* (Leiden: Brill, 1969), p. 8.

difficulties living together, and it was only legal difficulties or religious barriers that prevented them from divorcing. **Jesus** found it necessary to tell his followers not to be "hard-hearted," which implied that they should forgive their spouses rather than divorce them. **Paul** found it necessary to command those who had separated from their partners for no good cause to return. Both Jesus and Paul referred to the concept of "grounds" for divorce, and they both condemned the no-fault divorces that were popular in Jewish and Greco-Roman cultures.

The historical documents of the Church show that marriage was often tempestuous. **Calvin** had a very high view of marriage, yet even he said "marriage is the source and occasion of many miseries," though he immediately followed this with a warning against using "profane jests which are commonly in vogue . . . such as the following: that a wife is a necessary evil, and that a wife is one of the greatest evils."[44] **Luther** criticized society in a way that sounds very contemporary. He decried the individualism that makes people look for divorce as soon as anything gets in the way of their personal fulfillment:

> God has given every man his spouse, to keep her and for His sake to put up with the difficulties involved in married life. . . . They tire of it so quickly; and if it does not go the way they would like, they immediately want a divorce and a change. . . . Daily there have to be many troubles and trials in every house, city, and country. No station of life is free of suffering and pain, both from your own, like your wife or children or household help or subjects, and from the outside, from your neighbours and all sorts of accidental trouble. When a person sees and feels all this, he quickly becomes dissatisfied, and he tires of his way of life. . . . This is what the Jews found out too, as they divorced and changed their marriage partners.[45]

> The best way to prevent divorce and other discord is for everyone to learn patience in putting up with the common faults and troubles of his station in life and put up with them in his wife as well, knowing that we can never have everything just right, the way we would like to have it.[46]

One of the official **Homilies** that were prepared for clergy to read aloud during the reign of Elizabeth I describes marriage in terms that the common people were supposed to recognize and immediately agree with:

44. Calvin, *Commentary on the Epistles of Paul the Apostle to the Corinthians,* 1:224, regarding 1 Cor. 7:1.

45. Luther, *The Sermon on the Mount,* regarding Matt. 5:31-32, *Luther's Works* 21:95.

46. Luther, *The Sermon on the Mount,* regarding Matt. 5:31-32, *Luther's Works* 21:98.

> We see . . . how few matrimonies there be without chidings, brawlings, tauntings, repentings, bitter cursings, and fightings.[47]

It is surprising how many **Christian leaders** have had poor marriages. Thomas Dollin has listed William and Dorothy Carey, John and Molly Wesley, William and Catherine Booth, and others.[48] Sometimes it is necessary to read between the lines of the official biographies, which hide such difficulties. On other occasions the breakdown of the marriages of famous Christians is obvious to everyone. Indeed, their lamentable home life was sometimes the spur that kept them working for the Gospel. It is tempting to wonder how much less John Wesley would have achieved if he had been happily married like his brother Charles. While Charles sat at home and wrote hymns, John traveled all over England, setting up churches and schools everywhere and reading and writing while he rode on his horse.

It is no doubt true that many divorces today are preventable, and that many marriages would be saved if people worked harder at them, but this does not mean that society is any more corrupt today than it has been in previous ages.

Conclusions

The Fathers were ignorant of the Jewish background to Jesus' divorce debate with the Pharisees. As a result, they were almost universal in their teaching that adultery was the only ground for separation and that remarriage could take place only after the death of a former spouse. They gradually developed the idea that marriage is indissoluble, and the Catholic Church carried on this view right up to the present, though it has developed a flexible, easy approach to annulment.

The Reformers rejected indissolubility as a doctrine that was based on the Vulgate translation *sacramentum* in Ephesians 5:32. They therefore allowed remarriage after a divorce for adultery or desertion by an unbeliever. They had a variety of ways to show that such divorces do not involve breaking up a marriage. Luther and others said that adultery was punishable by death, and thus

47. "On the State of Matrimony" in the *Book of Homilies* 1571, cited in the Anglican Synod, *Marriage Matters: A Consultative Document by the Working Party on Marriage Guidance* (London: HMSO, 1979), p. 1.

48. Private communication. He wished to point out that the fact that these Christian leaders did not get divorced showed they were committed to teaching that Christians should not divorce.

the marriage had already ended in God's eyes. Calvin said that the desertion by a nonbeliever had already caused a divorce with God, and so the marriage had already ended when the believer carried out the divorce.

Various teachers looked for solutions to the pragmatic problems associated with these limitations on divorce. They proposed other grounds, such as refusal of conjugal rights and physical abuse, but these grounds did not become widespread until modern, secular reforms. Divorce is now widespread because it is easy, but this does not necessarily indicate a decline in moral standards. Imperfect and intolerable marriages have always been commonplace, as is evidenced by Church history and secular records.

10. Modern Reinterpretations

Different Ways to Understand the Biblical Text

Modern interpreters have tried to find biblical support for divorce and remarriage on grounds such as physical and emotional abuse. Some have tried to widen the two standard grounds, while others have created new grounds based on biblical principles of love and justice. Many have decided that the traditional two grounds are the only possible interpretation. A few have said that even these grounds are invalid, and that the NT does not allow believers to divorce their partners.

The apparent absurdity of refusing divorce to an abused partner or refusing remarriage to an innocent victim has resulted in many new interpretations. There is a wide consensus that some marriages should end in divorce even when adultery or desertion has not occurred. Physical and emotional abuse, or physical and emotional neglect, are generally seen as permissible grounds for divorce, but the biblical basis for these has been hard to find. Most of the new interpretations try to broaden the extent of the exceptions or apply biblical "principles" from which these grounds can be inferred. This can result in a free-for-all, in which almost any ground can be justified.

A reaction in the opposite direction has also occurred. Several interpreters have suggested that Jesus did not allow divorce on any grounds at all. This conclusion has been reached either by saying that the NT exceptions applied only to the first-century context or by saying that the exceptions were added later by the NT Church.

The result of all this is a confusing multitude of interpretations. A recent search on the American Theology Library Association bibliographic database of academic publications in the area of Religion found more than one thousand articles and book reviews since 1970 that contained the word "divorce" or "remarriage" in the title. I cannot hope to summarize all their views here or even read them all. However, most of them do not contain original ideas and instead try to make a novel mix out of old ideas and present them for different situations.

I have attempted here to collect all the possible biblical interpretations and present them in summary form, except for some of the farfetched ones. They are collected as **opinions on a series of questions:**

1. How many grounds for divorce apply today?
2. What does the *porneia* exception mean today?
3. What does Paul's exception mean today?
4. When is remarriage allowed today?
5. How much does the NT agree with the OT and first-century Judaism?
6. What is the main message of the NT about divorce?

The advantage of this method is that virtually all possible interpretations can be covered in a relatively short space. The disadvantage is that individual interpreters cannot be represented as fully as I might wish, and the issues are often simplified. For a historical survey of modern developments I would recommend Donald Shaner's *A Christian View of Divorce,*[1] and for a survey of recent academic work I would recommend Craig Blomberg's "Marriage, Divorce, Remarriage, and Celibacy."[2] The most complete general overview of the important interpretations is probably found in William A. Heth and Gordon J. Wenham, *Jesus and Divorce.*[3]

1. How many grounds for divorce apply today? The number of grounds varies from zero to infinity, though the wide variety of views can be fitted into four camps.

a. Two Grounds. This is the traditional view, as followed by the Fathers and most later interpreters in the established churches. The two grounds are, of course, **adultery and desertion by a nonbeliever**. The actual meaning of these

1. Donald W. Shaner, *A Christian View of Divorce* (Leiden: Brill, 1969).

2. Craig L. Blomberg, "Marriage, Divorce, Remarriage, and Celibacy: An Exegesis of Matthew 19.3-12," *Trinity Journal* n.s. 11 (1990): 161-96.

3. William A. Heth and Gordon J. Wenham, *Jesus and Divorce* (London: Hodder & Stoughton, 1984).

two grounds is the subject of much debate, which will be dealt with in Questions 2 and 3 below.

The Fathers generally discussed only the one ground of adultery, and it might be said that **Erasmus** was the first to speak about two grounds. In a broad sense this is correct, but it is likely that the Fathers simply ignored the second ground as irrelevant. Although they realized that Paul spoke about the unbeliever who deserts a marriage, they argued that this situation did not supply the believer with a means of divorce. They generally believed that remarriage was allowed only after the death of a spouse, and so "divorce" simply meant separation. If an unbeliever separated from a believer, the "divorce" (i.e., separation) had already occurred. One could not remarry until the spouse died, and thus Paul's exception had no effect except to state that one did not have to keep striving for reconciliation.

When Erasmus allowed remarriage after divorce, even before the spouse had died, this second exception finally had value. This view was followed by most Protestants and was popularized in modern times by **John Murray**.[4]

b. No Grounds. Two different approaches have resulted in the conclusion that Jesus did not intend to teach any grounds for divorce. One approach suggests that the early NT church added grounds for pragmatic reasons, and a second suggests that the exceptions represent divorces that were unavoidable in NT times. A third approach redefines *porneia* so that Jesus' exception was not really an exception; this approach will be examined under Question 2.

The first approach is best represented by the ingenious attempt of **R. H. Charles**[5] to make the NT speak with one voice. He tried to solve the differences between Mark, Matthew, and Paul by considering the situation of the time. He pointed out that the **death penalty for adultery** and other offenses may have been in use **in Jesus' day** but that it went out of use very soon afterwards. He based this on rabbinic traditions that date the loss of the death penalty at "forty years before the destruction of the temple," that is, about 30 C.E. (*b. Sanh.* 41a; *y. Sanh.* 18a, 24b). He proposed that Mark recorded Jesus accurately, and that Jesus said nothing about an exception for adultery — he did not need to because an adulterer would suffer the death penalty. Matthew, however, was written after Mark, when it was clear that the death penalty would never be practiced again. He felt it was in the spirit of Jesus' teaching to add this exception. Paul agreed with this, saying that a prostitute breaks the one-flesh relationship (1 Cor. 6:16), and therefore allowed divorce on this ground. In order to deal with

4. John Murray, *Divorce* (Philadelphia: Presbyterian and Reformed Publishing Co., 1961).

5. R. H. Charles, *The Teaching of the New Testament on Divorce* (London: Williams & Norgate, 1921).

1 Corinthians 7:11, which appears to forbid divorce without mentioning this exception, Charles concluded that verse 11a was a later interpolation.

This interpretation is marred by a lack of knowledge of the Jewish background, which became much better understood after Charles's death. The rabbinic dating of the end of the death penalty is almost certainly idealized. The rabbis were reluctant as well as unable to employ the death penalty even during Jesus' life. The proposed stoning of the adulteress in John 8 was an example of mob rule,[6] and the whole of the passion narrative is determined by the fact that the Jews were unable to execute Jesus. Charles's thesis depends on the assumption that the power to execute was lost some time between Jesus' teaching on divorce and his arrest. We have no evidence, apart from rather late rabbinic traditions, that there was a transition of this kind. It is much more likely that the Jews lost the power to execute criminals when Judea became a Roman province in 7 C.E. and the governor was given the right to execute.[7]

Charles was a good scholar who came very close to seeing the underlying Jewish background. He identified "for any matter" as "a catchword of the day" because he found the same phrase in Josephus and Philo.[8] It is unfortunate that he did not pursue this clue.

Other scholars followed a completely different course towards the same conclusion — that Jesus ruled against divorce without exception. **I. Abrahams,**[9] **Evald Lövestam,**[10] and more recently **Marcus Bockmuehl**[11] have pointed to rabbinic sources and suggested that **adultery was a compulsory ground for divorce** in Jesus' day. **Heth**[12] and **Andrew Cornes**[13] have argued that Jesus' exception referred to compulsory divorces that could not be prevented. In other words, Jesus told his followers: "Do not divorce for any matter, except adultery, for which divorce is unavoidable." Jesus did not want to allow divorce for adultery, but there was no choice within Judaism. For those outside the constraints of Jewish rulers,

6. See Roger David Aus, *"Caught in the Act,"* in *Walking on the Sea, and the Release of Barabbas Revisited,* South Florida Studies in the History of Judaism 157 (Atlanta: Scholars Press, 1997), pp. 1-50.

7. Josephus, *J.W.* 2.117. See the discussion in Lester L. Grabbe, *Judaism from Cyrus to Hadrian* (Minneapolis: Fortress, 1992), 2:392-95.

8. Charles, *The Teaching of the New Testament on Divorce,* p. 5.

9. I. Abrahams, *Studies in Pharisaism and the Gospels* (London: Macmillan, 1917).

10. Evald Lövestam, "Divorce and Remarriage in the New Testament," in *The Jewish Law Annual,* ed. B. S. Jackson (Leiden: Brill, 1981), 4:47-65.

11. Marcus Bockmuehl, "Matthew 5.32; 19.9 in the Light of Pre-Rabbinic Halakhah," *New Testament Studies* 35 (1989): 291-95.

12. Heth and Wenham, *Jesus and Divorce.*

13. Andrew Cornes, *Divorce and Remarriage: Biblical Principles and Pastoral Practice* (London: Hodder & Stoughton, 1993).

like Paul's Gentile churches, there was no need to have this exception. That is why neither Paul nor Mark (who wrote for Gentiles) mentioned it.

A similar argument might be put forward to explain why the Pauline exception applied only to the early centuries. In the Greco-Roman world separation was equivalent to divorce, and so, if an unbelieving partner left, the marriage was effectively over. One might argue that Paul's exception applied only to this type of involuntary divorce.[14] In other words, neither Jesus nor Paul wanted to allow divorce on any grounds at all, but they accepted that adultery and desertion resulted in *de facto* divorce, and so they stated these as exceptions in the Jewish and Greco-Roman contexts, respectively.

I find the logic of this position very sound. It makes Jesus into a truly revolutionary teacher on the subject of divorce, and it provides an interpretation that fits into the historical context.

However, the suggestion that adultery made divorce compulsory, even for the followers of a dissenting rabbi like Jesus, suggests a homogenous Jewish society where moral laws could be imposed even on conscientious objectors. This is very different from the Judaism that is portrayed in other sources. Groups like the Essenes followed a completely different calendar and perhaps even ignored the command to procreate. Syncretistic Jewish groups used pagan curses and probably went to sacrificial meals in temples. The *am haeretz* ("people of the land") were portrayed by the Pharisees as willfully ignorant of the laws of tithing and cleanliness. There is no evidence that the moral rules of one Jewish group could be imposed on any others.

This theory that Jesus allowed no grounds for divorce is also dependent on the idea that divorce for adultery was compulsory for faithful Pharisaic Jews in the time of Jesus. I have argued in chapter five that divorce for adultery did not become compulsory, even among the rabbis, till after 70 C.E. when the rite of the suspected adulteress fell into disuse. Jesus' family itself is proof that divorce was not compulsory for adultery. It would have been evident to anyone who could count, that Jesus was conceived outside marriage, and Christian tradition makes it clear that Joseph did not claim to be the father. Mary and Joseph may have experienced pressure to get divorced, but they were evidently able to resist such pressure.

The biggest problem with the interpretation that the NT has no grounds for divorce is that it is totally impractical. It makes no provision for divorce or even separation from adulterous or abusive partners. One may argue that it is no more impractical than "turn the other cheek," but in a non-ideal world we

14. I cannot recall reading this argument anywhere, but I include it for completeness. Heth and Wenham *(Jesus and Divorce)* and Cornes *(Divorce and Remarriage)* do not require it because they do not think that Paul is referring to divorce at all.

still need protection from muggers and abusive spouses. Cornes[15] has attempted to make this interpretation "pastorally sensitive" by allowing separation (though not divorce) in circumstances of extreme abuse, but he warns that this should apply only if the abuse is sufficiently continuous and dangerous so that a life is in danger. It is difficult to believe that the Bible can be as impractical as this interpretation implies.

c. There Are Other Grounds in the Bible. A few scholars have found other grounds for divorce in the Old Testament. Some have also found other grounds in the NT by widening the meanings of the two exceptions. These will be examined under Questions 2 and 3.

William F. Luck[16] and **R. J. Rushdoony**[17] have attempted to **apply the whole of OT moral legislation** to the believer. Luck has dealt only with the legislation with regard to marriage and divorce, but for Rushdoony this is only part of his program of rehabilitating the OT into the Church. This approach is an interesting one, but it produces some strange results. Some OT laws are very difficult to apply to the modern Church context. Luck attempted to apply them by looking for the principles behind them. He even dealt with difficult laws such as a false charge of nonvirginity (Deut. 22:19)[18] and marriage to a war slave (Deut. 21:10-14).[19]

Luck, like myself, examined Exodus 21:10-11, which was a key ground for divorce in rabbinic Judaism. However, he did not realize the importance of this text, because he did not know enough about the rabbinic background of the NT. He says:

> The question may now arise as to why this passage was not more explicitly discussed as a divorce passage by the rabbis in the days of Jesus. Two suggestions present themselves. First, the text may well have been thought not to apply to marriage per se, insofar as it deals, prima facie, only with concubinage. Second, the chief concern in the day of Jesus was to find a passage giving the husband a right to divorce the wife; in this text, the right of the wife to force a divorce from her husband is the prime concern.

Both of these approaches depend on the words of Jesus that he did not come to abrogate the Law but to fulfill it. However, the NT writers did not in-

15. Cornes, *Divorce and Remarriage.*

16. William F. Luck, *Divorce and Remarriage: Recovering the Biblical View* (San Francisco: Harper and Row, 1987).

17. R. J. Rushdoony, *The Institutes of Biblical Law* (Phillipsburg, N.J.: Presbyterian and Reformed Publishing Co., 1973).

18. Luck, *Divorce and Remarriage,* pp. 36, 54-55.

19. Luck, *Divorce and Remarriage,* p. 53.

tend to imply that all OT moral laws apply to Christian believers. As discussed under Question 5, the traditional approach is to follow only those OT laws that are affirmed in the NT.

d. The Grounds Vary with Society. Several scholars have argued that the grounds for divorce are not fixed for all time. The moral laws in the Bible change from one period to another, and one should not expect the same exceptions that apply in Jesus' day and society to be in force in Paul's day or ours.

L. H. Oppenheimer[20] pointed out that **Jesus wanted to move away from legalism**, and thus one should not read a new set of legislation into his words. A Christian should not ask, "How little need I give?" or "How much retribution can I exact?" and neither should he ask, "On what grounds can I get divorced?" The Christian is ruled by principles of love and justice and by the ideals of never-ending forgiveness and lifelong marriage.

Blomberg suggested that **the NT itself shows variation in teaching on divorce.** Jesus speaks about a single exception, and Paul speaks about a different exception. Both of them were necessitated by the different social contexts that Jesus and Paul addressed. Blomberg pointed out that Paul, even under the guidance of the Spirit, would not feel free to introduce a new exception unless he realized that Jesus' pronouncement was not absolute.[21]

Craig S. Keener[22] also emphasized the different social contexts of Jesus and Paul. He dealt especially with the problem of **desertion**, which **was equivalent to divorce in Greco-Roman culture** but which was punishable in Judaism by the loss of the dowry.

I have great sympathy with this approach, but it presents many new problems. Although it is true that rules about moral problems vary throughout Scripture, it is still important to look for absolutes whenever possible, and look for principles only when absolutes are not possible. We also need to ask whether the morals need to change or whether society needs to change. Otherwise, we may conclude that in today's sexually liberated society we should ignore all concepts of sexual restraint such as adultery, fornication, and bestiality. However, it is undoubtedly necessary sometimes to apply scriptural principles rather than rules. An example might be our rules about covering the head (1 Cor. 11:10-15) or single women (1 Tim. 5:14), neither of which should be applied in the same way today because the cultural reasons for those rules have disappeared. However, we should always try to apply the rules of Scripture

20. L. H. Oppenheimer, "Divorce and Christian Teaching," *Theology* 60 (1957): 311-19.

21. Blomberg, "Marriage, Divorce, Remarriage, and Celibacy," p. 187.

22. Craig S. Keener, . . . *And Marries Another: Divorce and Remarriage in the Teaching of the New Testament* (Peabody, Mass.: Hendrickson, 1991).

without change whenever possible and revert to principles only when the application of these rules result in absurdity.

My Position: Four Grounds Are Affirmed in the NT. In this book I agree with the two traditional grounds of adultery and desertion by an unbeliever, and two other OT grounds that are alluded to by Paul and Church tradition. These two are emotional neglect and material neglect and are alluded to in 1 Corinthians 7:3-5, 32-34. These two grounds were derived from Exodus 21:10-11, which states that a husband must give a wife food, clothing, and love. The rabbis and Paul applied these equally to the wife and husband, and they became the basis of the vows in Jewish marriage contracts and in Christian marriage services via the reference to them in Ephesians 5:28-29.

2. What does *porneia* mean today? Matthew recorded Jesus' single exception as μὴ ἐπὶ πορνείᾳ (Matt. 19:9) and παρεκτὸς λόγου πορνείας (Matt. 5:32). There has been a small debate about whether or not this is an exception, but the two forms of the exception (μὴ ἐπὶ and παρεκτὸς) remove uncertainty about that issue. Most of the debate has centered on the definition of πορνεία, *porneia*. It is generally accepted that *porneia* in the first century referred to sexual sins or deviations in general, but there has been much debate about its meaning in the NT and especially in this saying of Jesus. *Porneia* has been interpreted widely, from a very specific sexual fault to a variety of offenses, including matters that have nothing to do with sexuality.

a.* Porneia *Means Adultery. This is the traditional meaning of *porneia* in this passage according to the writings of **the Fathers** and later Church teachers. In other words, *porneia* is used as a synonym of μοιχεία, *moicheia*, which specifically means adultery. The use of two words to mean the same thing was a common rhetorical device in NT Greek and in many other languages, including most modern ones.

b.* Porneia *Has a Narrow Meaning. **Joseph Bonsirven**[23] pointed out that the LXX uses *porneia* to translate the Hebrew **זנות**, *zenut*. He also pointed out that one meaning of *zenut* is **"illegitimate marriage."** Jesus might therefore be saying: "no divorce except for illegitimate marriage." This would mean that Jesus was teaching annulment, not true divorce. An illegitimate marriage was not a legal marriage at all, and so Jesus allowed divorce (i.e., annulment) only for a marriage that was not really a marriage at all. J. A. Fitzmyer[24] gave this interpre-

23. Joseph Bonsirven, *Le divorce dans le Nouveau Testament* (Paris: Société de S. Jean L'Evangéliste, Desclée et Die, 1948).

24. J. A. Fitzmyer, "The Matthean Divorce Texts and Some New Palestinian Evidence," *Theological Studies* 37 (1976): 197-226.

tation additional weight when he pointed to a passage in the Dead Sea Scrolls that seemed to use *zenut* in the sense of "illegitimate marriage," and in the context of disallowing divorce (CD 4.19–5.11).

There are several problems with this theory. First, the Dead Sea Scroll passage is now generally understood as referring to polygamy and not divorce (see chapter four). Second, *zenut* has a much wider meaning and refers to sexual improprieties in general. Third, an illegitimate marriage does not require a divorce, and thus it would be meaningless to make it an exception to a ruling against divorce.[25]

A more convincing case was made by **Abel Isaksson**[26] who said that *porneia* refers to **premarital sex**. Evidence of premarital unfaithfulness was an OT ground for divorce. This evidence would normally be found on the wedding night, but one could also bring a charge before the wedding if the betrothed was found alone with someone. Even if the marriage did not take place, the separation would be regarded as a divorce and would require a divorce certificate because a betrothed couple were considered to be legally married. Jesus might have regarded them as not yet joined by God, so that a divorce was still possible.

This is a very plausible explanation, especially when Isaksson presents it as part of a larger picture. Isaksson argued that Jesus wanted his disciples to have the same purity as OT priests, who were not allowed to marry a divorcée nor a nonvirgin. Jesus used *porneia* to exclude the nonvirgin and also forbade the marriage of a divorcée. Isaksson was also able to point out that Joseph planned to divorce Mary for premarital unfaithfulness.

The main problem with these narrow definitions is that there is nothing to indicate that Jesus meant to limit the meaning of his exception in this way. While it is true that *porneia* can refer to illegitimate marriage and to premarital unfaithfulness, it can also refer to any number of other sexual offenses. Its meaning must be determined by the context, and in the context of the Jewish debate about legitimate grounds for divorce, *porneia* would mean adultery.

25. *b. Yebam.* 94b: "For it was taught: None of the women in incestuous marriages forbidden in the Torah require a letter of divorce, except a married woman who remarried in accordance with the decision of the Beth Din." This is pre-Aqiban, which dates it at the end of the first century C.E. There was a general principle that where there is no marriage, there is no need for a divorce — a principle called *kiddushin einan tofsin* "a valid betrothal is not transacted" (*m. Qidd.* 2.7; *b. Yebam.* 10b; 44b; 52b; 69a; 92b; *b. Ketub.* 29b; *b. Qidd.* 64a; 67b; 68a; *b. Soṭa* 18b; *b. Sanh.* 53a; *b. Tem.* 29b).

26. Abel Isaksson, *Marriage and Ministry in the New Temple: A Study with Special Reference to Mt.19.13*[sic]*-12 and 1.Cor.11.3-16,* trans. Neil Tomkinson and Jean Gray, Acta Seminarii Neotestamentici Upsaliensis 24 (Lund: Gleerup; Copenhagen: Munksgaard, 1965). This had already been proposed by E. G. Selwyn ("Christ's Teaching on Marriage and Divorce: A Reply to Dr. Charles," *Theology* 15 [1927]: 88-101), but the case was more soundly made by Isaksson.

This is confirmed by Jesus' use of *moicheia,* which has the narrow meaning of "adultery," in the same debate. Isaksson acknowledged that *porneia* and *moicheia* often occur together, but he denied that they are synonyms. He argued that, even when they are both used to describe the offense of adultery (as in *T. Joseph* 3.8; Sir. 23:23; Hermas, *Mand.* IV.1.3-8), they always represent different aspects of the offense. He suggested that *moicheia* represents the act of adultery, while *porneia* could have a different meaning such as the "sexual desire" that accompanies adultery. This argument is unconvincing. It is undeniable that *porneia* is sometimes used as a synonym for *moicheia,* and that this is the most natural meaning in the context of Jesus' debate with the Pharisees.

c. Porneia *Has a Wide Meaning.* Some scholars have suggested that Jesus referred to the full breadth of the meaning of *porneia* in the first century, and others have suggested that Jesus had a much wider definition than the one normally used in the first century.

Hugh Montefiore,[27] a first-class rabbinic scholar, suggested that Jesus could not have meant simply adultery because this was a customary ground for divorce, so he must have meant **a wider range of sexual offenses.** This is the opposite of the argument in 1b above that Jesus *did* mean adultery *because* this was a compulsory ground. Montefiore's argument is on a sounder footing than that in 1b because it does not depend on the idea that couples were *forced* to get divorced for adultery, which almost certainly did not happen. It only requires that there was a presumption that they would divorce. He backed up his argument by saying that the Shammaite interpretation of "a matter of indecency" was "general indecency," including even "indecent exposure," and that Jesus was agreeing with the Shammaites against the Hillelites.

It is difficult to see what made Montefiore interpret the Shammaite position in this way. Perhaps he based it on the tradition in the Jerusalem Talmud (*y. Soṭa* 1.2, 16b) where the later Amoraim appear to be vague about what the Shammaites believed. Although it is true that the Shammaites would have regarded "indecent exposure" as grounds for divorce, this is equally true of the Hillelites because both groups would have regarded this as an indication of adulterous behavior.[28] Both Hillelites and Shammaites regarded *porneia* as a

27. Hugh Montefiore, "Jesus on Divorce and Remarriage," appendix 1 in Anglican Synod, *Marriage, Divorce and the Church — the Report of a Commission Appointed by the Archbishop of Canterbury to Prepare a Statement on the Christian Doctrine of Marriage* (London: SPCK, 1971). His argument has been followed in varying degrees by B. Ward Powers, *Marriage and Divorce: The New Testament Teaching* (Concord, N.S.W.: Family Life Movement; Petersham, N.S.W: Jordan Books, 1987), and Blomberg, "Marriage, Divorce, Remarriage, and Celibacy."

28. In a relatively early portion of the Mishnah, they discuss the grounds for divorce, which include: "If she goes out with her hair unbound, or spins in public, or speaks with any

reference to adultery. Although they condemned a wide range of immodesty, such as being seen in public with loose hair or bare arms, these were considered dangerous because they were evidence of adultery or of behavior that led to adultery. All these related behaviors were condemned simply to prevent the one biblical offense of adultery.

The widest meaning of *porneia* has been proposed by **David Atkinson**,[29] who argued that Jesus is making a reference to the seventh commandment, "Do not commit adultery." He proposed that Jesus was making a general moral statement in the same tenor as the seventh commandment. The commandments can be seen as a generalized summary of the whole moral code, and so the seventh commandment condemns **anything that causes the breakdown of a marriage**. This could include anything from abuse or adultery to neglect or unpleasant habits. Similarly, Jesus' exception for "adultery" should be seen as a general catch-all reference to anything that breaks up marriage. By this saying, Jesus not only condemned all those activities that break up marriage, making a plea that no one should do so, but also allowed the victims of such activities to divorce their partners.

Although this view commends itself as the type of nonlegalistic and internalized saying that one might expect from Jesus, it is too vague. It says, in effect, that one can get divorced for anything that might break up a marriage. It is capable of becoming another version of the Hillelite "any matter."

My Position:* Porneia *Means Adultery. When we read the NT we must assume that it speaks with the language that would communicate itself successfully to original recipients of the text. The texts of the NT were letters, stories, and visions that were meant to communicate to first-century Jews and Gentiles. So, unless there is evidence to the contrary, we should assume that a word means the same thing in the NT as it would if it were spoken or written in a noncanonical story or letter. There are, of course, occasional words that are used in a special way in the NT, such as ἀγάπη, "loves," or perhaps πίστις, "faith," but these words are carefully defined in the NT as different, and their context leaves no confusion about their meaning.

There is no doubt that *porneia* carried the general meaning of sexual offense in first-century Greek. The context in the Gospels offers two clues to help

---

man" (*m. Ketub.* 7.6). The reference to "speaking with any man" indicates that they regard these as a list of indications that adultery has taken place. Spinning in public was shameful because her arms would be bare. Tosephta adds the following: "and she who goes out with both her sides (shoulders) bare . . . and bathes in a public bath with any man" (*t. Ketub.* 7.6). These portions are cited anonymously, and so they were approved by the Hillelites after 70 C.E.

29. David Atkinson, *To Have and To Hold: The Marriage Covenant and the Discipline of Divorce* (London: Collins, 1979).

define the meaning more clearly. First is the occurrence of *moicheia.* Although *moicheia* and *porneia* are not necessarily synonymous, the two are clearly related in some way in this passage, and there is no indication that they are used to contrast each other. These two words often occurred together in Greek referring to the same offense, and so one should assume that they are referring to the same offense in the Gospels unless the context indicates differently.

Second is the fact that *porneia* is being used to **allude to the OT phrase "indecent matter"** (Deut. 24:1). In Matthew 5:32 Jesus appears to cite the OT text in exactly the same way as the Shammaites, using their reverse word order: "matter of indecency" instead of "indecent matter" as in the OT text.[30] Both the Hillelites and Shammaites understood this very general word "indecency" as a reference to adultery. The LXX uses the vague phrase ἄσχημον πρᾶγμα, "a shameful matter," which is a more accurate translation but one that does not convey the meaning that the rabbis attributed to the Hebrew phrase; it is better represented by *porneia.*

In the context of the Jewish debate about divorce, *porneia* could have no meaning other than adultery. If Jesus had meant it to have a wider or narrower connotation, he would have had to state this very clearly. There is no indication in the Gospel passages that Jesus meant anything other than the normal, expected meaning of this word in this context.

3. What does Paul's exception mean today? In 1 Corinthians 7 Paul forbade the believers in Corinth to separate from marriage, except in one circumstance that he described in verse 15. Some scholars have regarded the freedom that is declared in verse 15 as a contradiction to verse 11, which says that a separated person should always seek to be reconciled. It is clear that verse 11 describes the norm and that verse 15 represents an exception. This exception has been defined in a wide variety of ways, from desertion by an unbeliever to anything that is nonconducive to continued marriage.

a. Desertion by an Unbeliever. This is the traditional explanation given by **the Reformers and Catholic** teachers, though they differ about the meaning of the freedom to which verse 15 refers. The Reformers generally regarded this as a freedom to remarry, while the Catholic Church regarded it as a freedom to remain separate without continually trying to promote reconciliation. This difference is dealt with in more detail under Question 4.

30. "The School of Shammai says: A man should not divorce his wife unless he found in her a matter of indecency (דבר ערוה), as it is said: *For he finds in her an indecent matter* (ערות דבר)" (*m. Git.* 9.10). They reversed the words in order to emphasize that this should be read as a construct phrase rather than a list of two offenses ("indecency" and "matter"), as the Hillelites read it. Jesus' phrase λόγου πορνείας appears to be directly equivalent to this Shammaite phrase.

It is likely that the Fathers understood this verse in the same way as the Catholic interpreters. There is little discussion of this exception by the Fathers, perhaps because it had no practical importance to believers in the early centuries. In the Roman Empire separation was equivalent to divorce, and so if an unbeliever deserted a believer, there was nothing that the believer could do about it. There was little point in trying to promote reconciliation when the unbeliever had already gone through the customary divorce procedure by walking out. Therefore, if the freedom spoken about here was merely the freedom to stop trying for a reconciliation, then this verse had almost no practical value.

This argument also suggests that the verse had a different meaning in Paul's day because there would be little point in Paul writing something that had no practical application for the Corinthians. The law of divorce by desertion was already in use in the Greco-Roman world of NT times, just as it was in the time of the Fathers. It makes little sense to tell believers that they are "no longer bound" to try to keep the marriage together when the unbeliever has already completed all the legal requirements of a divorce. Therefore, it is likely that it meant more than just a freedom to stop trying for reconciliation.

Since the Reformation, this interpretation became extremely useful and popular. The Reformers allowed remarriage after a valid divorce, and so "no longer bound" came to mean "free to remarry." This meant that a believer who was deserted by an unbeliever was released from that marriage and allowed to find a new spouse.

b. Desertion Also by an Unrepentant Believer. One limitation of the Reformers' teaching is that a believer who was deserted by another believer was unable to remarry. **Luther** suggested that unbelievers might include "nonevangelical" believers and even hinted that a believer who deserted his or her spouse was worse than an unbeliever.[31] **Jay E. Adams**[32] has developed this idea using Matthew 18:15-17, where Jesus says that **someone who refuses Church discipline should be treated as a Gentile**. Adams suggests that a believer who deserts his or her partner should be asked to return, first in private, then with a witness, and then by the Church (following the model laid down in Matt. 18:15-17). If he still refuses, he should be withdrawn from Church membership and be regarded as a nonbeliever. The situation then falls into the purview of 1 Corinthians 7:15, and the deserted believer can divorce the partner who is now regarded as an unbeliever.

31. He argued this on the basis of 1 Tim. 5:8. See Luther, *The Sermon on the Mount,* regarding Matt. 5:31-32, *Luther's Works* 21:96 from Jaroslav Pelikan, ed., *Luther's Works,* 55 vols. (St. Louis: Concordia Publishing House, 1955-86).

32. Jay E. Adams, *Marriage, Divorce & Remarriage in the Bible* (Phillipsburg, N.J.: Presbyterian and Reformed Publishing Co., 1980).

There is much to commend this ingenious solution, and I find Adams's writing refreshing in its clarity and originality of thought. He often cuts through centuries of debate and finds insights that had been missed before. However, his application of Matthew 18:15-17 seems more like casuistry than exegesis. He is using the NT as if it were a collection of laws that can be mixed and built upon as though they were a body of systematic legislation. In some ways this is similar to what lawyers do with the American Constitution or to the way in which they build upon case law. The NT, however, should not be treated as a collection of laws because this goes against the whole emphasis of Jesus and Paul who tried to distance themselves from the legalism of first-century Pharisaic Judaism.

c. Behavior Not Conducive to Continued Marriage. Adams's argument was taken further by **Stephen Clark.**[33] Paul told believers that they should not leave unbelievers who were willing to remain married. Clark said that this implied the converse, that believers were allowed to leave if the unbeliever did not wish the marriage to continue. He also said that any believer who acted in such a way as to cause the end of a marriage should be disciplined by the Church, and, if that believer did not repent, he or she should be regarded as an unbeliever. The believing partner can then obtain a divorce.

Clark applies this in a very generous way. He suggests that any behavior that is not conducive to a marriage **indicates that the person is not willing for the marriage to continue**. If that person does not change his or her ways, that individual can be regarded as a nonbeliever who wishes the marriage to end, and so the believer can obtain a divorce. The type of behavior that Clark envisages as nonconducive to continued marriage includes the watching of pornographic videos.

Clark himself was aware that this interpretation was open to misuse by believers who might be looking for a divorce on flimsy grounds. This by itself does not mean that the interpretation is wrong. However, this view of Scripture is even more legalistic than that of Adams. Clark is a lawyer by profession, and like a good lawyer he has found a loophole. Yet the discovery of a loophole is not good exegesis.

My Position: Desertion by a Believer or an Unbeliever. Although I have been very critical of Adams's theory, I have actually come to the same conclusion by a different route. Paul writes to believers in 1 Corinthians 7 and tells them that they should not desert their partners, even if those partners are nonbelievers. The "desertion" may include either walking out or throwing out —

33. Stephen Clark, *Putting Asunder: Divorce and Remarriage in Biblical and Pastoral Perspective* (Bridgend, Wales: Bryntrion, 1999).

Paul implies both in verses 10-11. This desertion was the recognized Greco-Roman method of divorce. Paul presents this command in the strongest terms, emphasizing that it is based directly on the teaching of Jesus. However, he cannot command nonbelievers in the same way. He can only hope that they will remain married to their believing partners.

Paul commands believers who have deserted their partners to remain unmarried and to seek reconciliation. He cannot, however, command nonbelievers who have deserted their partners to return to them. So, he tells deserted believers that there is nothing more that they can do, and that they are "no longer bound."

If believers are deserted by believing partners, Paul commands the deserters to return. There appears to be no doubt that the believers will obey this command. Paul says that it is not his own command, but that of Jesus (v. 10: "not I, but the Lord"). Paul therefore does not even discuss the possibility that believing deserters will not return to their partners. **If believers *did* refuse** to obey this command, and thereby refuse to obey the direct command of Jesus, the Church would presumably be forced to excommunicate them.

Therefore verse 15 applies not only to desertion by a nonbeliever, but to any desertion that cannot be reversed. Paul assumes that this will occur only if the deserter is a nonbeliever, but in a secular-minded church, even a so-called believer disobeys the direct command of Christ.

4. When is remarriage allowed?

a. Remarriage Only after a Former Partner Has Died. **The Fathers, followed by the Catholic Church and many others,**[34] said that a marriage ends only with death. This is based on **three strong arguments:**

1. Paul twice says that a marriage ends in death, without saying anything about divorce (1 Cor. 7:39; Rom. 7:2).
2. Jesus commanded, "those whom God has joined, let no one separate."
3. Jesus condemned remarriage as "adultery."

The **first** argument appears to be a strong one. Both texts state that a woman is bound to her husband as long as he lives, and Romans 7:3 says that if

34. E.g., J. K. Elliott, "Paul's Teaching on Marriage in 1 Corinthians: Some Problems Reconsidered," *New Testament Studies* 19 (1972-73): 219-25; Peter J. Tomson, *Paul and the Jewish Law: Halakha in the Letters of the Apostle to the Gentiles,* Compendia Rerum Iudaicarum ad Novum Testamentum III.1 (Minneapolis: Fortress, 1990); Cornes, *Divorce and Remarriage;* Heth and Wenham, *Jesus and Divorce;* Pierre Dulau, "The Pauline Privilege: Is It Promulgated in the First Epistle to the Corinthians? *Catholic Biblical Quarterly* 13 (1951): 146-52.

she married another man before he died, she would commit adultery. However, in neither context would one expect an exhaustive list of the ways in which a marriage can end, that is, death, divorce, or annulment. Furthermore, if either text *is* an exhaustive list, then marriage cannot end by annulment.

There are many sayings in Scripture where one has to supply a missing condition that is assumed to be obvious. A modern reader normally adds a condition to Matthew 5:28: "whoever lusts after a woman has committed adultery in his heart." We normally add: "unless she is his wife." Similarly, to the verse "a woman is bound to her husband as long as he lives" one should mentally add "unless she is his ex-wife." The addition of these conditions is, strictly speaking, unnecessary. One cannot conclude from the lack of these conditions that one may not have sexual thoughts about one's husband or wife. Similarly one cannot conclude that a marriage can end only in death.

The **second** argument assumes that "let no one separate" is a statement of fact rather than a command. It assumes that Jesus meant "no one *can* separate," rather than the imperative "*let* no one separate."[35] On this basis, Augustine likened marriage to the sacraments of ordination and baptism, which cannot be revoked or reversed, and Aquinas formally listed marriage as one of the seven sacraments. However, the use of the imperative suggests that Jesus is stating a command or making a plea. Jesus uses the same present active imperative in the sayings "let those in Judea flee to the mountains" (Matt. 24:16), "let your words be Yes or No" (Matt. 5:37), "let him be put to death" (Matt. 15:4), and so forth. None of these carry the suggestion that it is impossible to disobey the command or plea. Therefore, when Jesus said "let no one separate," Jesus was telling believers that they should not break up marriages, but he was not telling them that a breakup was impossible.

The **third** argument, like the first, is based on an assumption that an absolute saying cannot have unspoken conditions. Jesus said, "anyone who divorces and remarries, commits adultery"; the statement shows that divorce is invalid until after the former spouse has died. This argument is circular. Divorce is impossible, as proved by the fact that remarriage is called adultery; and remarriage is called adultery because divorce is impossible.

I have argued in this book that this saying makes sense when you take into account an **unspoken condition**. When Jesus said "anyone who divorces" he meant "anyone who divorces on the grounds of 'any matter.'" Matthew makes this clear, but Mark and Luke do not. Mark's and Luke's absolute saying was perfectly "true" before 70 C.E. when virtually all divorces were on the ground of "any matter."

35. This has been argued well in Blomberg, "Marriage, Divorce, Remarriage, and Celibacy."

Unspoken conditions are part of life, and part of Scripture, as pointed out above. Whatever your interpretation of Jesus' divorce saying, you have to add some kind of unspoken condition. I have added "assuming they were divorced on the ground of 'any matter.'" Someone who believes that remarriage is impossible until after the death of a spouse has to add "assuming that the spouse is still alive." If the spouse was dead, Jesus could not charge the person with adultery when that person remarried. Which assumption is easier to omit? It would be virtually unknown for a Jew to be divorced for anything other than "any matter," but death of a spouse before remarriage would have been relatively common. If the Gospel writers could be forgiven for leaving out the assumption about the spouse being alive, they can certainly be forgiven for leaving out the assumption that the divorce was on the grounds of "any matter."

b. Remarriage Also after Legal "Death." In OT law the penalty for adultery was death, but by NT times this penalty had fallen into disuse. The worst that an adulterer faced was divorce and the payment of the *ketubah,* which acted like a fine. **Luther** suggested that one might **consider an adulterer as dead in the eyes of God.**[36] If the state failed to carry out the sentence, the Church should nevertheless act as though the sentence has been carried out. Therefore, the marriage has ended, just as it would have if the adulterer had been executed. This reasoning has been followed by several modern scholars.[37]

A variation of this is seen in the **Orthodox** Church concept of the **death of a marriage.** Some Orthodox theologians have likened the end of marriage to an illness followed by death and finally burial. The burial is the divorce, which takes place after the marriage has been found to be truly and irreversibly dead. This view has the advantage of stepping back from an adversarial search for fault and also concentrating attention on the end of the marriage rather than the legal proceedings of the divorce.[38] Some non-Orthodox have adopted a similar viewpoint.[39]

36. Luther, *The Estate of Marriage,* Part 2, *Luther's Works* 45:32: "The temporal sword and government should therefore still put adulterers to death, for whoever commits adultery has in fact himself already departed and is considered as one dead. Therefore, the other [the innocent party] may remarry just as though his spouse had died." Origen also pointed out that the adulterer is theoretically dead, but he did not go on to say that the marriage is therefore ended (see ch. 9).

37. E.g., Charles, *The Teaching of the New Testament on Divorce;* Rushdoony, *The Institutes of Biblical Law;* Murray, *Divorce;* Derek Prince, *God Is a Matchmaker* (Eastbourne: Kingsway, 1986).

38. Bernard Haring, *No Way Out? — Pastoral Care of the Divorced and Remarried* (Boston, Mass.: St. Paul Publications, 1989), pp. 48-49.

39. E.g., Rev. Dr. Brian Haymes (a British Baptist) in *Marriage Requests: Ministerial Responses* (Department of Ministry, Baptist Union, 1982).

Both of these views are useful, but neither can be said to represent what the NT means by the death of a partner. The two texts that state that death ends a marriage are clearly speaking about physical death.[40] These views are useful ways of examining the ending of a marriage, but they cannot be said to clarify the meaning of Scripture.

c. Remarriage Also after Any Valid Divorce. **Erasmus** (see details in chapter nine) undermined the concept of indissoluble marriage and reintroduced the concept of remarriage after a valid divorce, as well as after the death of a spouse. He pointed out that if Jesus forbade breaking asunder a marriage, then this was possible. He also pointed out that the freedom that Paul grants after the desertion of an unbeliever makes much more sense if it refers to the freedom to remarry rather than the freedom to remain separate. The reason why Jesus said remarriage was adulterous, according to this view, is that **Jesus referred to remarriage after an invalid divorce.**

Much of this had already been explored by **Ambrosiaster** (see details in chapter nine), who was one of the less well known of the Church Fathers. This view has been popularized in the modern debate by **Murray,**[41] and many scholars have followed this line of reasoning.[42] The grounds by which a valid divorce is defined varies according to the grounds that various interpreters accept (as explored in Question 1). The general principle is that remarriage after a valid divorce is permissible, but remarriage after an invalid one is adultery.

This view is virtually the same as the one that I advocate, though its proponents have not sufficiently dealt with its main weakness: that it is **an argument from silence.** It says, in effect, that remarriage is not forbidden after a divorce (once certain texts are understood correctly), and so remarriage should be allowed. Yet there is no actual text in the NT that commends remarriage, except for a widow (1 Cor. 7:39; 1 Tim. 5:14). Some have tried to fill this silence by saying that 1 Corinthians 7:27 refers to remarriage ("Are you freed from a wife? — do not seek marriage") but it could refer to a release from betrothal instead.

An argument from silence is a two-edged sword that can help or hinder. One denomination[43] forbids the use of musical instruments during worship because none are mentioned in NT worship. Youth pastors are constantly seeking for a text that forbids sexual experience before marriage while their flocks

40. While it is true that the wider context of Rom. 7:2 is speaking about metaphorical death of an individual in Christ, it is using the picture of a real marriage as a metaphor of spiritual marriage.

41. Murray, *Divorce.*

42. E.g., Philip Sigal, *The Halakah of Jesus of Nazareth according to the Gospel of Matthew* (New York, London, Lanham: University Press of America, 1986); Luck, *Divorce and Remarriage.*

43. The traditional congregations of the Church of Christ.

argue for sexual freedom from the silence of Scripture. The need for a simple statement of the Trinity was so strong in the Early Church that someone inserted it into the Vulgate at 1 John 5:7-8, from where it found its way into a few Greek texts.

There are also several silences in Jesus' teaching; he does not teach anything about monotheism, protection of the fatherless, or other themes that are clearly taught in the OT and in first-century Judaism. He did not need to teach these things because they were already accepted by all of his hearers.

Therefore, silence can be both misused — when it is assumed to commend a nonexistent or a minority opinion — and legitimately used — when it commends a majority opinion. When the silence concerns an opinion that was universally held at the time of writing, and there is a suitable context where this subject has been discussed, it becomes increasingly safe to infer that the silence indicates agreement. Jesus was silent about allowing remarriage after a valid divorce, which was universally accepted by all his hearers. The fact that Jesus debated the topic of divorce with his contemporaries makes it very likely that his silence was deliberate, and that it indicated agreement with them on this matter.

d. No Remarriage for the Guilty Partner. I cannot recall reading a considered defense of this position, though I am sure that it exists somewhere. This view is commonly heard in debates on the topic, especially from those who have never had to deal with pastoral situations. In practice I have found it almost impossible to decide which one, if either one, of the parties is innocent. Even Origen realized that adultery can sometimes be blamed on the partner who refused conjugal rights rather than on the partner who was unfaithful.[44] Often a case that seems clear-cut becomes very difficult to decide when we hear the other side of the story, and often the one who has the least reason to feel guilty takes in all the blame.

Alex R. G. Deasley[45] has suggested that the only time spouses can be said to be truly innocent is when they have had nothing to do with the divorce. That is, they have been divorced against their will. However, in my experience it is more often the innocent (or relatively innocent) partner who finally decides that enough is enough and pushes for a divorce.

Forbidding divorce to the guilty party goes against one of the fundamental tenets of the Christian faith: that God is willing to forgive. **Ken Crispin**[46] en-

44. Origen, *Matthew,* II.14.24, from the translation provided in the New Advent collection at http://newadvent.org/.

45. Alex R. G. Deasley, *Marriage and Divorce in the Bible and the Church* (Kansas City, Mo.: Beacon Hill, 2000).

46. Ken Crispin, *Divorce, The Forgivable Sin?* (London: Hodder & Stoughton, 1988).

titled his book on divorce *The Forgivable Sin?* to emphasize this fact. If we deny divorce to the "guilty" party, we are suggesting that the breakup of marriage is like blasphemy against the Holy Spirit: it is not capable of reversal by God's grace. Crispin points out that this is even more serious when we deny remarriage to both partners because we suggest that even the inadvertent sinner here cannot find forgiveness. Unless we have a very strong belief in the indissoluble nature of marriage, it is wrong to deny remarriage to a "guilty" party because a guilty person can always ask for God's forgiveness.

e. No Remarriage to One's Adulterous Partner. The **rabbis in the NT times** said that divorced persons could marry anyone with whom they could contract a legal marriage, except the person with whom they had had a suspected adulterous affair.[47] This was not based on OT law but was a pragmatic solution to a difficult problem. If they allowed a divorced person to marry the person who caused the breakup of the marriage, they not only condoned the adultery but also might encourage people to commit adultery in order to cause a divorce. If a woman wanted to marry her adulterous lover, she might decide to make life very difficult for her husband so that he would be forced to divorce her. If he had managed to prove her adultery, she would have lost her *ketubah,* but if he had to divorce her on lesser grounds, she would be able to keep her *ketubah* and marry her lover.

Some interpreters have suggested that this rule should be followed in the Church. **M. Madan**[48] wrote a series of four volumes in the eighteenth century, in which he argued that the Church should **allow polygamy** as a solution to the large number of unmarried widows. Part of his argument rested on Deuteronomy 22:29, which said that a rapist must marry his victim. He said that the rapist was not told to divorce his first wife, and that this taught the principle that one may not divorce one wife in order to marry another. **Spiros Zodhiates**[49] is another unconventional author who says something similar, though he spoils his good points by making gross blunders.[50]

47. See *m. Soṭa* 5.1; and if they married they had to divorce (*m. Yebam.* 2.8).

48. M. Madan, *Thelyphthora; or, A Treatise on Female Ruin, on Its Causes, Effects, Consequences, Prevention and Remedy, Considered on the Basis of the Divine Law,* 3 vols. (London: J. Dodsley, 1780-81).

49. Spiros Zodhiates, *What about Divorce? An Exegetical Exposition from the Greek Text of Matthew 5.27-32; 19.3-12; Mark 10.2-12; Luke 16.18; Romans 7.1-3* (Chattanooga, Tenn.: AMG, 1992), and Spiros Zodhiates, *May I Divorce and Remarry? An Exegetical Commentary on 1 Corinthians 7* (Chattanooga, Tenn.: AMG, 1992).

50. For example, he argued that Jews did not give a divorce certificate in the case of adultery. He argued this from the "fact" that adultery was punished by death, and so the divorce certificate in Deut. 24:1 did not refer to divorces for adultery.

David Bivin[51] has argued this same point from a more scholarly perspective. He points out that the simple conjunction "and" in Hebrew or Aramaic (which Jesus spoke) can often mean "in order to." He thus argues that Jesus may have said: **"whoever divorces his wife in order to marry another is committing adultery."** Jesus is therefore highlighting the fact that many men were divorcing their wives, not because of a fault in their wives but because they wished to marry other women. This is an interesting interpretation, but a weak one.

Forbidding remarriage to an adulterous partner is a good rule of thumb, but it is difficult to apply. It would make a good exception to the principle that anyone with a valid divorce should be allowed to remarry, whether or not one is the "guilty party." However, it is very difficult to justify from Scripture, and it is even more difficult to implement. If a new couple had already known each other while one of them had been married before, one has to make a judgment about the type of relationship that they had. Were they acquaintances, good friends, intimate friends, or lovers? This puts the pastor in the role of a private investigator and judge, which should be avoided.

My Position: Remarriage after Any Valid Divorce. I have argued for a position very similar to that in section "c" above: that remarriage is allowed after any valid divorce. I pointed out that the inherent weakness of this position (that it relies on an argument from silence) does not necessarily make it less persuasive.

This silence is not as total as one might think because the whole purpose of a Jewish divorce certificate is to allow the woman to remarry, and the only necessary wording of the certificate is "You are allowed to marry any man you wish." Therefore, when the Pharisees mention divorce certificates to **Jesus**, his silence concerning them is deafening. Jesus spends most of his time in this debate with the Pharisees disagreeing with their laws on divorce. He disagreed with their teaching on polygamy, on compulsory divorce for adultery, with their lack of forgiveness of faults within marriage, and with their interpretation of the phrase "a matter of indecency" (see the end of chapter six). The fact that he did not forbid remarriage, even after a divorce certificate had been mentioned, is very significant.

Paul, similarly, did not specifically mention remarriage even though this was a fundamental right within Greco-Roman society. Many Greco-Roman marriage contracts included the right of a divorced person to remarry, and even when this is not mentioned, it is assumed (see details in chapter seven). There was nothing in the Jewish or pagan backgrounds of Paul's readers that would

51. David Bivin, "'And' or 'In order to' Remarry," *Jerusalem Perspective* 50 (1996): 10-17, 35-38.

even hint at the immorality of remarriage. Indeed the Roman law of Augustus made it illegal to remain unmarried for more than eighteen months after a divorce. If Paul had wished to teach Christians that remarriage was not permitted to them, he would have had to do so very clearly. Therefore, his silence on this matter speaks very loudly.

I have also argued that Paul's words "you are no longer enslaved" in 1 Corinthians 7:15 is a reference to the Jewish divorce certificate, which was often likened to a certificate of emancipation from slavery because of the similar wording and procedures for them both. Paul was certainly familiar with the wording of the Jewish divorce certificate because he cites the right to remarry that is found on the certificate with regard to widows, who shared this same right (1 Cor. 7:39). This citation suggests that Paul expects his readers to be familiar with this wording too, as they no doubt were. When Paul said "you are no longer enslaved" in verse 15, this was in the context of release from a marriage to an unbeliever who had deserted. Paul used wording that was reminiscent of the wording on both Greek and Jewish divorce certificates. There would have been no doubt in the minds of his readers that Paul was referring to the right of a divorcée to remarry.

5. How much does the NT agree with the OT and first-century Judaism? This question covers three areas:

- Our understanding of Jesus as a Jew. Some portraits of Jesus hardly recognize his Jewishness and suggest that he made a complete break with the OT. Others make Jesus so indistinguishable from a first-century rabbi that one wonders why he was crucified. This divergence is seen particularly with regard to his teaching on divorce, though most views are somewhere in between the two extremes.
- The continuity or discontinuity of NT teaching with that of the OT. Should we ignore the OT legal system, or should we adopt only the moral laws, or should we adopt only those that are affirmed by the NT?
- The use of Jewish background in understanding the NT. Can we be sure that we understand the Jewish background sufficiently, and how much knowledge should we assume that the original readers of the NT had?

These are all difficult questions, and they are rarely addressed properly by books on divorce or remarriage. Unfortunately they will not be addressed sufficiently here either, because these subjects are now so vast that they each need a book to themselves. This short section will merely use these questions to examine three major views about the Jewishness of NT teaching.

a. The NT Is Completely Different to the OT or Judaism. The OT allowed divorce, and Jesus appears (when read without the social context) to forbid divorce. His teaching on divorce appears therefore to provide the strongest possible contrast to the OT. This is the view of the **Early Church Fathers**, as well as many interpreters since, especially those who think that marriage is indissoluble.

The Early Church had to contend with a strong movement that tried to abolish the use of the OT for Christians. We now call this movement Marcionism after Marcion, who was famous for this teaching. It was soon condemned as a heresy, and several of the Fathers wrote against it, especially Tertullian, who later joined a similar group. However, it was a way of thinking that infected many branches of the Church and is still evident in the modern world. For example, Hitler's Nazi movement tried to reinvent Christian theology completely separate from its Jewish heritage. Walter Grundmann headed a project to produce a hymn book and Church liturgy without any use of the OT or Hebrew terms such as "Hallelujah" and "Amen." Even today, many modern churches avoid the OT except in compulsory lectionary readings, and many Christians would ignore the OT as a source of moral teaching. This is in contrast to the NT, which uses the OT freely as a moral basis for Christian living. Even 1 Corinthians 1–6, which hardly ever quotes the OT directly, is full of moral teaching that is based on the OT.[52]

The Early Church Fathers were very blunt in their rejection of the OT teaching about divorce. They regarded **Jesus' teaching as a complete rejection of the OT** on this matter. Yet they did not want to suggest, like Marcion, that the OT was not inspired or that God had changed his mind, and so they had to explain why Moses was so wrong. Some said that Moses wrote his own opinion and not God's law, while others said that Moses gave a rule that was suitable for the hard-hearted and sinful Jewish people (see details in chapter nine). There was a general feeling that Christians were morally superior to Jews because the indwelling Holy Spirit enabled them to live better lives, and that Jesus expected the Church to follow higher standards. Perhaps this was true for the Early Church, which lived under constant threat of persecution. However, with the growth of the Church, less committed individuals joined, and the moral superiority of the Church became very difficult to demonstrate.

In modern times those who think that Jesus forbade all divorce, in direct contrast to the OT, either represent highly committed Christian groups or regard Jesus' moral teaching as idealism that will find fulfillment in a future king-

52. Brian S. Rosner, *Paul, Scripture and Ethics: A Study of 1 Corinthians 5–7,* Arbeiten zur Geschichte des antiken Judentums und des Urchristentums 22 (Leiden: Brill, 1994).

dom. Writers like Heth come from mainstream churches, but their conclusions, that Jesus forbade all divorce, are generally accepted only by highly committed and exclusive Christian groups.[53] Writers like Deasley, Graham Stanton, and Blomberg[54] interpret the law of Jesus as a higher moral ideal designed for a future perfect kingdom. Christians may attempt to fulfill it, but they also expect to fail. The law forbidding divorce is like the law to offer the other cheek and to lend without expecting repayment. In this world these laws would result in mayhem and oppression, and so they are generally relegated to a future kingdom or to small communities of self-sacrificing individuals.

b. The NT Affirms the OT Law. The traditional approach to the OT is **to accept any laws that are affirmed by the NT and to cautiously accept any laws that appear to follow the spirit of the NT.** This rules out all of the OT ceremonial laws and the more primitive and retributive laws of the OT.

This approach is sometimes confused with the more straightforward approach that accepts the OT moral code but not the OT ceremonial code. This approach is almost impossible to apply consistently because the OT contains many moral laws that simply do not fit into a Christian ethos. If all the OT moral laws were accepted today, we would need to apply the severest penalty for a rebellious teenager (Deut. 21:18-21 — where the penalty is death) and stop charging interest on loans (Exod. 22:25). Rushdoony[55] has attempted to explore the possibilities of this approach, and it has been applied to the law of divorce to some limited degree by Luck and Madan.[56] The conclusions at which they have arrived, such as allowing polygamy and compulsory marriage in cases of rape, suggest that their approach is not a productive avenue to explore.

The NT affirms several aspects of OT divorce law. It affirms the allowance of divorce for adultery and the provision of a divorce certificate (both based on Deut. 24:1-4, alluded to in the Gospel divorce debates). It also affirms the principle that divorce should be avoided if at all possible (based on Gen. 2:24 as cited by Jesus). This present study and a few others have also pointed out the af-

53. Many have read Heth and Wenham *(Jesus and Divorce)* as though they allow divorce for the two traditional grounds, though without remarriage. Their book is vague about this, but their argument rules this out. They argue that Jesus' exception was due only to compulsory divorce for adultery in Jewish society, and that Paul did not have an exception. Cornes (*Divorce and Remarriage,* pp. 296-97), who claims to follow Heth and Wenham, appears to assume that divorce (i.e., separation) is possible on these two grounds.

54. Deasley, *Marriage and Divorce in the Bible,* pp. 81-88; Graham N. Stanton, *The Gospels and Jesus* (Oxford: Oxford University Press, 1989), p. 245; Blomberg, "Marriage, Divorce, Remarriage, and Celibacy."

55. Rushdoony, *The Institutes of Biblical Law.*

56. Luck, *Divorce and Remarriage;* Madan, *Thelyphthora.*

firmation of the grounds for divorce in Exodus 21:10-11 by the use of that text in 1 Corinthians 7:3.

Although this is the approach which I have used in this study, I should point out some weaknesses with it. First, this approach assumes that the NT cites or alludes to all the moral laws of the OT that should be applied in a Christian life. If this assumption were taken to its logical conclusion, one might argue that we can ignore the OT as a source of moral teaching because everything of value is reiterated in the NT.

Second, it assumes that the NT is something akin to a systematic moral theology, though in a rather jumbled order, containing every moral teaching necessary for a Christian. In reality, the NT presents itself as a summary of Jesus' teaching within a brief narrative structure, and a collection of letters that mostly answer specific issues faced by first-century churches. There is no reason to assume that every issue has been covered.

Even if we have a strong sense of inspiration and assume that the Holy Spirit has guided the collection of these writings in such a way as to include everything we need, we should recognize that the Holy Spirit also directs our attention to the OT. The NT constantly points to the OT as a source of authority and examples for moral teaching, and Jesus specifically claims that he has not come to abrogate the OT.

The question of how to decide which OT laws apply to the Christian Church has no simple solution, and biblical theologians are still struggling with this problem.

c. The NT Affirms the OT and Also Agrees with Some Jewish Traditions. **Jewish traditions might provide valuable insights** into ways of interpreting the OT for our own situations. The rabbis faced the same problems that the Early Church faced, particularly of applying seemingly archaic OT rules to their own situation. Modern rabbis have an even greater task, especially as they do not have an inspired text such as the NT to which to appeal. However, most modern scholars have not employed the Jewish traditions as an insight into their own problems. They have instead used them to build up a picture of life and law in the times of the NT, in order to give them a better understanding of the NT text through the eyes of its original recipients.

Understanding the Jewish background is not usually straightforward. **Fitzmyer**[57] placed great emphasis on a **Qumran** text (CD 4.20–5.2) that **appeared to outlaw divorce**; thus, Jesus apparently was not the only rabbi who outlawed divorce. Commentators had struggled over the meaning of the question in Mark's Gospel: "Is it lawful to divorce your wife?" This question made

57. Fitzmyer, "The Matthean Divorce Texts."

no sense without Matthew's addition "for any matter" because divorce is plainly taught in the Law. Fitzmyer pointed out that if there was a group of Jews who forbade divorce, such as those at Qumran, then this question made sense without Matthew's addition. However, since Fitzmyer's work, our understanding of Qumran texts has grown considerably. The text on which he relied is now generally understood to condemn polygamy, not divorce, and other texts that speak about divorce at Qumran have been discovered.[58]

Most commentators now recognize the **rabbinic background to the Gospel divorce debate.** It is generally agreed that Jesus was being invited to express his opinion concerning a debate between the Hillelite and Shammaite Pharisees in the first century. Virtually no one disputes that this is the background to Jesus' debate, though some suggest that Matthew has deliberately exaggerated the references to this debate in his version. Most commentators, except for a few scholars who have misunderstood what the Shammaite position was, point out that Jesus' reply reflects the Shammaite position.

A few scholars have departed from this consensus. **Belkin**, a normally careful and exceptional scholar, who is an expert in Philo, thought that "any matter" was the Shammaite, not Hillelite, position. He came to this conclusion because he realized that the Shammaites allowed divorce for emotional neglect, but he did not realize that all Jews allowed this on the basis of Exodus 21:10-11.[59] **Montefiore**[60] similarly misunderstood the Shammaites. He said that Jesus was significantly different to the Shammaites in that they allowed divorce for a much wider range of sexual offenses than adultery (as dealt with above in Question 2c). A few scholars have questioned whether Jesus could have presented the same position as the Shammaites, and they have argued that his disciples would not have expressed shock at Jesus' teaching if he simply repeated the known position of the Shammaites. Clark strenuously denies that Jesus should be attributed with any teaching that is Jewish.[61]

Apart from the few scholars just mentioned, it is generally accepted that

58. Adriel Schremer, "Qumran Polemic on Marital Law: CD 4.20–5.11 and Its Social Background," in *The Damascus Document, a Centennial of Discovery: Proceedings of the Third International Symposium of the Orion Center for the Study of the Dead Sea Scrolls and Associated Literature, 4-8 February, 1998,* ed. J. M. Baumgarten et al. (Leiden: Brill, 2000), pp. 147-60; and my "Nomological Exegesis in Qumran 'Divorce' Texts," *Revue de Qumran* 18 (1998): 561-79.

59. Samuel Belkin (*Philo and the Oral Law: The Philonic Interpretation of Biblical Law in Relation to the Palestinian Halakah,* Harvard Semitic Series 11 [Cambridge: Harvard University Press, 1940]) interpreted *Spec. Leg.* 3.30 in the light of *m. Ketub.* 5.6. This is accepted by Sigal, *The Halakah of Jesus of Nazareth,* p. 109.

60. Montefiore, "Jesus on Divorce and Remarriage."

61. Clark, *Putting Asunder.*

Jesus' divorce debate, as represented in Matthew and probably also in Mark, reflects the Hillelite-Shammaite debate about divorce. It is also generally accepted that Jesus sided with the Shammaites in this debate, though, as I summarized in Question 4 above, Jesus also disagreed with the Shammaites on many matters regarding marriage and divorce. Knowledge of the Jewish background to NT teaching is therefore invaluable, especially in the area of divorce and remarriage.

My Position: The NT Was Written for First-Century Readers. As already mentioned in sections b and c above, I regard the NT teaching on divorce as based on the OT and as in agreement with some rabbinic viewpoints. However, although Jesus agreed with the Shammaite interpretation of "indecent matter," he also disagreed with them on several other matters. This viewpoint is based on the following **three principles of hermeneutics.**

First, Scripture speaks to a particular culture in order to change it, and it thereby addresses future generations as well. In order to do this, it uses language and concepts that could be easily understood by the original readers. Later readers must acquaint themselves with the language and culture of the time in which the text was written in order to attempt an understanding of the author's intent. I reject the modern pessimism about the impossibility of understanding authorial intent, though I acknowledge the many difficulties that have been highlighted in linguistic studies. Therefore:

> (1) *Scripture should be read through the filters of the language and culture to which it was first addressed.*

My **second** principle of interpretation is that Scripture does not present a systematic legal code or a systematic theology. Systematic presentations may perhaps be derived from Scripture, but we should not expect Scripture to address every aspect of law and morals that is of importance to us. Scripture presents the will of God as revealed through specific events, which are preserved in prophecy, letters, and other writings related to those events. There are a few exceptions where writings are not related to specific events, such as the wisdom in generalized Proverbs and the worship in generalized Psalms. Yet there are no generalized works of theology or generalized legal systems other than brief summaries such as the Ten Commandments.

Many aspects of law and morals are missing from Scripture because they were self-evident in the societies that Scripture addressed. Scripture contains no detailed description of a marriage ceremony, but this does not mean that Jews or Christians should not use marriage ceremonies. There was no occasion in Scripture when a marriage ceremony needed to be promoted because every culture addressed by Scripture recognized the need for such ceremonies. In contrast, the concept of monotheism is discussed at length in Scripture, though never by Jesus because first-century Palestinian Jews were fully convinced of that doctrine. Silence on a subject may indicate agreement with the prevailing culture, or it may indicate that the subject was irrelevant to that culture. Therefore:

> (2) *The morals and laws of Scripture should be compared with those of the cultures for which Scripture was written.*

My **third** principle is that Scripture is inspired by the Holy Spirit who used mortals with limited intellect and limited experience to convey a message in limited human language. Readers are expected to use the help of the Holy Spirit, as well as their limited intelligence and limited experience, to understand that message. The Bible is not like the Qur'an, which claims to be dictated by God. Each book of Scripture displays the style, viewpoint, and culture of its author, and each book needs to be read, as much as possible, through the eyes of that author. Scripture was addressed primarily to ordinary people, and only secondarily to lawyers, systematic theologians, and modern scholars. Therefore:

> (3) *The primary meaning of Scripture is the plain sense, as it would be understood by an ordinary person in the culture for which it was written.*

These principles are particularly important when looking at the subject of divorce. The particular cultures addressed by the Scripture texts dealing with divorce vary hugely. The Mosaic code of divorce is addressed to a nomadic people influenced by ancient Near Eastern cultures (as I showed in chapters one and two). In these cultures it was almost impossible for women to remarry, and so Moses instituted the divorce certificate, which gave them that right. The Law also provided protection from abuse and neglect for slave wives (and any other wives); this protection was not found in ancient Near Eastern law codes. The prophetic literature is addressed to people experimenting with the idolatrous religions of surrounding nations, and it is this spiritual adultery for which God divorced Israel. The Gospels summarize the arguments presented by Jesus when he took part in a rabbinic debate that divided Jewish society in the early first century. He sided with the Shammaites on one matter, though he disagreed with all the Jews on several other matters. Paul's first letter to the Corinthians tells those with ascetic tendencies in Greco-Roman society that they should not end their marriages or their conjugal relations, though single people should perhaps avoid marriage during the "present crisis."

In all these cases, our understanding of the text is greatly enhanced by an understanding of the background culture. In some cases we will completely misunderstand the text if we do not know the background.

It seems **unlikely that we will be able to produce systematic teaching on divorce simply from the scriptural passages.** Even if we assume that the Holy Spirit preserved exactly those texts that would, through careful interpretation, yield every detail that we need, it is still unlikely that we will come to a simple consensus about how to reconstruct those clues. The two case laws about divorce in the OT do not add up to a systematic legal code. The two disputes about divorce in the NT, in the Jewish and Greco-Roman contexts, do not add up to a systematic theology. The best we can do is create a set of principles that are based on Scripture.

In the light of all this it is perhaps surprising to find that Scripture contains enough data to produce a fairly complete and self-consistent theology of divorce. The OT and NT contain four grounds for divorce, which cover most of the circumstances that mark the end of a marriage. Perhaps this is surprising, or perhaps it is a sign of the Holy Spirit's guidance over the writing and compilation of Scripture. It is also remarkable that these four grounds have found their way into the vows that make up the majority of Christian marriage services because they have based their language on Ephesians 5:28-29. Perhaps this is another sign of the activity of the Holy Spirit, inspiring the leaders of the Church when they compiled the liturgies.

The Church has therefore included the OT grounds for divorce in Christian marriage vows. When we marry, we make promises that we will do all those things that become a ground for divorce if neglected. We promise to love, feed (cherish), clothe (honor), and be faithful to each other, as listed in Exodus 21:10-11 and Deuteronomy 24:1. One might conclude that the Holy Spirit believes in continuity with the OT.

6. What is the main message of the NT about divorce? Trying to identify a "main" message does not imply that there is only one message about divorce in the New Testament. It is clear that there are many important messages, but different interpretations result in a different emphasis or emphases. The following are the common messages that have been identified as the "main" NT teaching about divorce.

a. Christians Can Never Divorce. This position is based on simple and clear logic, but it is difficult to apply in a world of fallible humans. Many who have sought to follow it have suffered long-term abuse within marriages that they believe that they must not leave. Others, who have been divorced or separated against their will, live without any hope of remarriage in Church because they believe that a valid divorce is impossible.

This is the traditional emphasis of the **Roman Catholic Church and** of **some evangelical churches.** Although separation is allowed for adultery or desertion by an unbeliever, this is not real divorce. Many believe that marriage is indissoluble — a characteristic that is variously called "ontological," "one-flesh," or "sacramental." The Catholic Church ameliorates the problems of this position by allowing the "annulment" of marriages.

b. Divorce Is Allowed in Only Two Circumstances. This regards the exceptions of Jesus and of Paul as the most significant contributions to the issue of divorce, though most proponents of this position would also say that these exceptions emphasize that divorce should be a rare and exceptional occurrence.

This is the traditional emphasis of **most Reformation churches**, which allow divorce for adultery or desertion by an unbeliever. The Catholic Church allows separation in these circumstances but not divorce. Some Reformers of the past also allowed divorce for a handful of other grounds (see chapter nine).

c. Christians Should Not Cause a Divorce. This emphasizes that Jesus and Paul were addressing believers when they taught against divorce. Believers should therefore not be unfaithful or desert their partners or do anything else that breaks up a marriage. If believers are a victim of any of these things, the end of the marriage can be recognized by a divorce, which frees them for remarriage.

This is **a moderate position** that is taken by many who have despaired of finding sensible grounds for divorce in the Bible. They have made a pragmatic decision to allow divorces for grounds such as abuse and adultery, basing it on scriptural principles of love and justice, while admitting that specific scriptural support is difficult to find.

My Position: Divorce Should Be Avoided and Restricted to Biblical Grounds. There are two equally important emphases in the New Testament's teaching on divorce. First, both Jesus and Paul emphasized that **believers should hold marriages together, even at great cost to themselves**. Even if there is unfaithfulness, the Christian should attempt to forgive. Jesus disagreed with the rabbis who said that divorce was commanded in the case of adultery. Jesus said that divorce was merely *permitted* and that it should be used only if the adulterer is "hard-hearted." Jeremiah used the term "hard-hearted" to describe Judah's stubborn refusal to repent of her adultery against Yahweh (Jer. 4:4). Jesus taught that we should forgive seven times seven times, though this is dependent on repentance (Luke 17:4). Jesus permitted divorce only if someone hard-heartedly refused to repent.

Paul similarly emphasized that the believer should try to maintain a marriage even if the spouse was not a believer. He was writing when some believers had already separated from (i.e., divorced) their unbelieving partners, and he told them to seek reconciliation. It was only when their unbelieving partners divorced them against their will that Paul allowed them to regard the marriage as ended in divorce.

The second emphasis is that **divorce should be based on biblical grounds.** The NT does not emphasize that divorce is allowed. It merely implies that it is, by alluding to the Old Testament grounds for divorce. The OT allowed divorce if any of the four marriage vows were broken, while the New Testament emphasized that these vows should be kept by the believer, and that the believer should attempt to forgive the spouse if he or she does not keep these vows. Ultimately, however, if someone continually breaks the vows without repentance, both Jesus and Paul allowed divorce, but only on the basis of these Old Testament grounds.

Jesus criticized the rabbis who allowed divorce for "any matter," and Paul criticized those who were willing to use divorce by desertion in the Greco-Roman fashion. They can both, therefore, be said to criticize divorces that were not based on biblical grounds. Both Jesus and Paul referred to the various grounds for divorce, albeit in a sideways manner. Jesus referred to adultery, and Paul referred to the lack of emotional and material support. Even when Paul allowed divorce for desertion, this can be seen as a reference to lack of material and emotional support. There is therefore an emphasis in the NT on divorce for specific grounds.

The overall emphasis of the NT calls believers to a very high view of marriage. The believer is called to commit himself or herself totally to marriage, even to the point of putting up with repeated breaking of marriage vows by a weak partner. If, however, the partner is "hard-hearted" and does not genuinely repent and struggle to change one's ways, the biblical remedy is divorce. Jesus did not naively assume that everyone in the kingdom would be perfect, and Paul realized there were special problems when a believer was married to an unbeliever, or to someone who *acted* like an unbeliever. Christians are called to suffer in marriage, if necessary, but they are also given a solution, if necessary.

Conclusions

The NT teaching on divorce and remarriage has been interpreted in a wide variety of ways. The traditional view says that there are only two grounds for divorce and that remarriage is not allowed during the lifetime of the former spouse, though this view does not make sense when it is viewed through the eyes of a first-century Jew or Gentile. Also, it is internally inconsistent because it appears to allow divorce for some grounds but not for other more serious grounds such as physical abuse. Some scholars have attempted to broaden these grounds by novel interpretations of *porneia* or of Paul's exception, but these interpretations are contrary to the way the original readers of the New Testament would have understood the text.

The New Testament teaching on remarriage after a valid divorce is, admittedly, ambiguous and unclear. However, remarriage after divorce was a fundamental right in the first-century world, and it was often regarded as an obligation. Thus, the New Testament writers knew that they would have to enunciate their teaching extremely clearly and unambiguously if they wanted to teach the opposite of this universally held view.

Of all the interpretations that have been described in this chapter, there are two that are both internally consistent and consistent with the cultural context of the New Testament. The first is the view that Jesus condemned all divorce, and that the exceptions were not part of his intended teaching. According to this interpretation, the exceptions were either pragmatic additions by the Church, situations where divorce was unavoidably compulsory in the first century, or situations where marriage had not really taken place, such as an illegitimate marriage.

The second view that I regard as consistent with all the facts is, of course, my own: that Jesus and Paul affirmed all four OT grounds for divorce and remarriage while emphasizing that divorce should be avoided whenever possible and that believers should go the extra mile in trying to maintain a marriage. They allowed divorce on specific grounds from the Old Testament and rejected the no-fault divorces of the Hillelites and of Greco-Roman culture.

11. Pastoral Conclusions

Reversing Institutionalized Misunderstandings

An overview of this book reveals that the emphasis of the NT is against divorce unless it is truly necessary. Jesus and Paul teach against the no-fault divorce procedures of Jewish and Greco-Roman societies, respectively. Christians should never cause a divorce by breaking marriage vows and are encouraged to forgive their partners as long as they repent. These conclusions depend on reading the NT text through the eyes of a first-century believer. The modern church minister should concentrate on keeping marriages together but also should support those who have gone through the pain of divorce, enabling them to remarry after finding forgiveness.

An Overview

In this book I have attempted to read the Scriptures through the eyes of the original recipients of the text. I have attempted to contrast the teaching of Scripture with the cultural norm of the society to which the different texts were written. This provides an important clue about the emphasis of the text and the reason why it was originally written.

In the **first two chapters** I looked at the **ancient Near Eastern background** to the Mosaic material. Although the Pentateuch was probably edited at several stages over a period of many hundreds of years, much of the material shows itself to be very ancient. The teaching on divorce and remarriage shows literary and cultural links with ancient Near Eastern texts dating back to 1400 B.C.E., though a similar culture was prevalent for several centuries later. In this culture it was almost impossible for women to remarry even if they had been abandoned for many months or even several years. The former husband could always return and reclaim his wife and children from her new husband. This meant that the new husband could end up paying for the upbringing of children without benefiting from them when they were old enough to work. The Mosaic law decreed that the husband had to give a wife a divorce certificate if he ceased to care for her. This released her from the former marriage and enabled her to remarry. The Mosaic law also defined the ways in which a husband had to care for his wife. He had to supply her with food, clothing, and love, and none of these must diminish even if he marries a second wife.

In **chapter three** we saw that the **Prophets and Writings of the OT** speak about marriage as a contract. This was the same way that all ancient Near Eastern cultures regarded marriage, as I pointed out in chapter one. The Mosaic model defined the terms of the contract (i.e., to supply food, clothing, and love, and be faithful) and defined the way to end the contract (i.e., write a certificate of divorce). Several prophets pictured Israel as married to God and divorced by him for breach of the marriage contract. They regarded God as the innocent partner who reluctantly made the decision to divorce his wife. Most of the prophets point out that Israel had been unfaithful to God, while Ezekiel adds that she also refused to return his love and refused to prepare meals and clothes for him from the food and cloth that he supplied. The Prophets regarded the terms of the marriage contract as grounds for divorce, and they regarded them as incumbent on the wife as well as on the husband. Malachi contains the most severe criticism of divorce in Scripture, expressing the hurt of God's first-hand experience: "I hate divorce" (Mal. 2:16).[1] Divorce is defined in this Malachi passage as the breaking of marriage covenant vows: "dealing treacherously against your companion, your covenant wife" (Mal. 2:14).

Chapters four and five detailed the huge cultural changes that took place **between the OT and NT**, particularly in the development of a **rabbinic theology** of divorce. The rabbis continued to regard marriage as a contract, and they continued to recognize OT terms of this contract: faithfulness, food, clothing, and love. They classified the latter three in the two categories of material support and emotional support, and they regarded abuse as a negation of such support.

There was an increasing tendency in rabbinic teaching to ignore the binding nature of the marriage contract. In general contract law, a contract could be declared void only if one party failed to keep one's side of the contract and the other party decided that the contract should be ended as a result. In the rab-

1. This is one possible translation. There are many problems with the translation of this verse, which I dealt with in chapter three.

binic development of divorce law, only the man could decide to end the marriage contract (irrespective of who had broken the contract). This was based on the fact that the man wrote the divorce certificate. However, a wife could also force a husband to divorce her if she could prove to a rabbinic court that he had broken the marriage contract.

Some rabbinic courts also allowed huge leniency to men who claimed that their wife had broken the marriage contract. The Hillelites said that they could literally cite "any matter." The ground "any matter" was based on their own interpretation of the phrase "matter of nakedness" in Deuteronomy 24:1 as "any matter, or indecency." There was no need to prove this ground in court, and so divorce became a very simple procedure. These groundless divorces based on "any matter" became the basis of almost all divorces, except where adultery could be proved.

Jesus' response to these rabbinic developments was detailed in **chapter six**. He was asked if he accepted the Hillelite groundless divorce based on "any matter." He replied that such divorces were completely invalid and that any remarriage after such a divorce was equivalent to adultery. The true interpretation of the phrase in Deuteronomy 24:1 was "a matter of indecency," as the Shammaites said. The Shammaites understood the phrase to mean "adultery," and presumably Jesus did also. Jesus probably also allowed divorce on other biblical grounds, namely, neglect of food, clothing, and love, as the Shammaites and all other Jews did. The main emphasis of Jesus' teaching, when he was asked about the ground of "any matter," was that divorce should not happen. Neither partner should break up the marriage by breaking the marriage vows. Even if someone is unfaithful, the law does not command a divorce; it only allows one. Furthermore, it should take place only if the person is "hard-hearted" (i.e., stubbornly refusing to repent, like Israel when God divorced her).

The world of **Paul**, described in **chapter seven**, was completely different. In the Greco-Roman world anyone could divorce simply by separating from one's spouse. Paul forbade Christians from using this divorce by separation. He based this on the teaching of Jesus, presumably because divorce by separation was another example of a groundless divorce. Like Jesus, he emphasized ways to remain married rather than ways to divorce. He reminded the Corinthians of their marriage contracts, which said that they should provide emotional support (including physical love, where appropriate) and material support (food and clothing). If a believer was divorced against his or her will, and there was no means of reconciling the marriage, Paul allowed the person to regard it as a valid divorce and to remarry. Perhaps this was because divorce by separation is equivalent to both physical neglect and emotional neglect, but Paul said that he was simply following the rule of pragmatism.

The **marriage vows** in Judaism and Christianity were dealt with in **chapter eight**. They can both be traced back to the terms of the OT marriage contract. The Christian wording of "cherish, honor, and love" can be traced back to Exodus 21:10-11 via Ephesians 5:29, which can be translated literally as "feed," "keep warm," and "love." These, together with the vow to be "faithful," are the four obligations of an OT marriage contract. The Christian marriage service can therefore be regarded as a version of the biblical marriage contract. The rule that a Church leader should be "a man of one woman" or "a woman of one man" refers to the vow of sexual faithfulness, and not to compulsory marriage, or to divorce and remarriage.

Chapter nine traced the **history of interpretation** of these difficult texts. The knowledge of the Jewish background of the divorce debate was lost to the Church from a very early date. Even within Judaism, the debate in which Jesus participated became no more than a historical curiosity after 70 C.E. when virtually all non-Hillelite teaching was lost. The question about divorces on the basis of the "any matter" interpretation was understood as a question about "any divorce." Interpreters could not see the invisible quotation marks around the phrases "any matter" and "a matter of indecency." So, when Jesus condemned divorces for "any matter," he appeared to condemn all divorces. When he affirmed the interpretation "a matter of indecency," he appeared to make an exception just for adultery. The only logical way to understand this condemnation of divorce was to conclude that marriage was an indissoluble sacrament, like entering the priesthood. Therefore remarriage was not allowed until God performed a separation through the death of one of the partners.

The **modern struggle** with these texts is outlined in **chapter ten**. The pastoral problems of physical and emotional abuse forced many exegetes to look for biblical means of divorce in these cases. The Catholic Church found it in annulment, and many Protestant churches found it by ingenious interpretations of the biblical text. A few sections of the Church decided to maintain the position that Jesus appeared to state that there should be no divorce whatsoever.

How Should We Read Scripture?

My personal view is, of course, that the position adopted in this book has a stronger historical and exegetical basis than others, but I recognize that this depends on the way one reads the text. My view is the result of reading the text in a culturally sensitive way, through the eyes of a Christian living at the time that the texts were written. The traditional view is based on reading the text through the eyes of someone in the second century or beyond, when specific details of first-century culture had been forgotten. The approach adopted in this book, of reading Scripture in the context of its culture, is based on the three principles of hermeneutics that were discussed in chapter ten:

1. Scripture should be read through the filters of the language and culture to which it was first addressed.
2. The morals and laws of Scripture should be compared with those of the cultures it was written for.
3. The primary meaning of Scripture is the plain sense, as it would be understood by an ordinary person in the culture for which it was written.

A Jewish Christian before 70 C.E. would assume that divorce and remarriage was allowed for all four biblical grounds because these grounds were accepted by all branches of Judaism. He would recognize that Jesus forbade the use of the new Hillelite ground of "any matter," and that Jesus also criticized polygamy and compulsory divorce for adultery. He would assume that Jesus allowed divorce on biblical grounds because Jesus did not criticize them and Jesus affirmed other aspects of OT moral law. Both a Jewish and a Greco-Roman Christian would assume that Paul allowed remarriage when he said that someone who was divorced against one's will was "no longer bound."

Other views have a stronger basis than mine if the NT is read through the eyes of Church tradition or through the eyes of a modern reader. The traditional Church interpretation is almost uniformly that of indissoluble marriage, with separation allowed only on the grounds of adultery. This is based on a "plain" reading of the text without any pre-70 C.E. insight into the Jewish background of the Gospel passages. The modern reader is likely to come to the same conclusion about the "plain" meaning of the text.

The deciding factor might be **our view of inspiration**. Did the Holy Spirit inspire the writers of the NT to communicate primarily to the original recipients of the texts, or did he also make sure that future generations would be able to understand it? On the one hand, it might be argued that the Holy Spirit would not have allowed the Church to be confused about such an important matter for so many centuries just because the scholars had not yet rediscovered the cultural context in NT times. On the other hand, the Bible is not dictated, as the Quran is claimed to be. Inspiration is mediated through real people and real history, and so we have to read the Bible through the eyes of the original recipients as much as possible.

It is generally accepted that we need some knowledge of ancient culture in order to understand certain texts. It is impossible to understand many of Jesus' criticisms of the Pharisees in Matthew 23 without knowing about their rules on vows, tithing, and cleanliness. These rules remained common knowledge well beyond the first century, and thus the Church had little difficulty in understanding these texts. Some commands, such as those about head coverings and making images of animals, are generally regarded as culturally determined. Few churches exclude women without hats or ban depictions of animals within their walls. The cultural background to these rules has been common knowledge, though covering the head remained compulsory in churches for a long time.

The Church has also been beset by theological problems and misunderstandings that are more serious than the matter of divorce and remarriage. Some problems have divided the Church or caused mass excommunications, or even mass executions. The doctrines of the Trinity, the Mass, and apostolic succession have caused much pain in the past, and today the Church has new divisions based on the gifts of the Holy Spirit, women in leadership, and the nature of scriptural inspiration. If one argues that the Holy Spirit would not have allowed the Church to be confused about the doctrine of divorce and remarriage, one would surely expect Scripture to be less ambiguous about these other subjects as well.

Actually, much of **the Jewish background to the divorce debate** has been well understood by scholars for many decades. It was one of the important discoveries after the revival of Jewish studies in the mid-1800s. After about 1850 all good commentaries mentioned the Hillelite-Shammaite debate as an explanation of the Gospel material.[2] The only significant new factor that has not been properly noted before was the acceptance of the other three biblical grounds for

2. There is no mention of Hillel and Shammai with regard to divorce in H. Hammond's *Paraphrase and Annotations upon All the Books of the New Testament: Briefly Explaining All the Difficult Places Thereof,* 5th ed., corrected (London: J. Macock and M. Flesher, 1681) or John Albert Bengel's *Gnomon of the New Testament,* 4th ed., rev. and ed. Rev. Andrew R. Fausset (Edinburgh: T. & T. Clark, 1860 [1742]), even though both cite the Talmud, sometimes even in Hebrew. Henry Alford's *The Greek Testament: With a Critically Revised Text, a Digest of Various Readings, Marginal References to Verbal and Idiomatic Usage, Prolegomena, and a Critical and Exegetical Commentary: For the Use of Theological Students and Ministers,* new ed. (London: Rivingtons, 1880-81 [1849]) says: "This was a question of dispute between the rival Rabbinical schools of Hillel and Shammai; the former asserting the right of arbitrary divorce, from Deut. 24:1, the other denying it except in cases of adultery," and he notes the use of the phrase "any matter" in Josephus, *Ant.* 4.253. John Lightfoot (*A Commentary on the New Testament from the Talmud and Hebraica,* vol. 2: *Matthew — 1 Corinthians* [Peabody, Mass.: Hendrickson, 1989]) made rabbinic parallels to the NT easily available. He said that "the school of Shammai permitted not divorces, but only in the case of adultery; the school of Hillel otherwise" (p. 260). This insight became firmly established through the widely read commentaries of Heinrich August Wilhelm Meyer (*Critical and Exegetical Handbook to the Gospel of Matthew* [Edinburgh: T. & T. Clark, 1879]) and Charles John Ellicott (*A New Testament Commentary for English Readers* [London, 1884]).

divorce by all Jews, including the Shammaites. Once the debate behind the Gospel account is recognized, it becomes clear that Jesus is giving his opinion about the Hillelite interpretation "any matter," and so he is not condemning "every divorce." Although this is obvious, very few scholars have either recognized it or written about it clearly because the traditional teaching about indissoluble marriage was so firmly entrenched in Christian theology.

Even before the rediscovery of this Jewish background by the Christian Church, the knowledge was never far away. Most Christian communities contained Jews and Jewish scholars, any of whom could have pointed out this parallel. Perhaps the Church has suffered from its own anti-Semitism, which stopped it from learning from Jewish scholars until relatively recently.

The Holy Spirit can perhaps be seen at work in preserving the biblical marriage vows in the Christian wedding service. The same OT vows of faithfulness, food, clothing, and love have come into our wedding services via Ephesians 5:29. This means that, when Christians marry, they make the same promises that were made by Jews in the OT and NT, promises which became the basis of a divorce if they were broken.

Modern Church Practice

The established churches have attempted to remain faithful to the traditional interpretations. For the Catholic Church this means that marriage is a sacrament and therefore indissoluble. Even the Anglican Church, which separated from Rome because of the issue of divorce, has a fundamentally identical view. Only the **Orthodox Church** has allowed divorce and remarriage on a wide variety of grounds from an early date, especially on the grounds of unfaithfulness and abandonment.[3] Although Orthodox theology regards marriage as lifelong, it also recognizes the power of the Church to end marriages that it considers to have died.

In recent years, the **Catholic Church** has made the process of annulment much easier. Impediments include the making of vows when one is too young or immature to understand the consequences, or making vows under duress or fear. Vows can even be declared invalid if one partner did not give due delibera-

3. The first recorded canon allowing divorce and remarriage dates from Alexius of Constantinople (1025-43 C.E.), which allowed it only for adultery. However, it is widely assumed that the Orthodox Church recognized the right of secular law to grant divorces from the time of Justinian's Novels XXII and CXVII in 536 C.E. and 542 C.E. Over the centuries, Byzantine canon law grew in complexity until now there are twenty-one distinct grounds for divorce.

tion to the matter, or later claimed to have only pretended to give consent. This wide flexibility can amount virtually to divorce on demand.

The absurd situations created by this position were highlighted by Bernard Haring, a Catholic priest and lecturer in moral theology who wrote a frank book *No Way Out?* while dying of cancer. He presented the example of a Catholic man whose wife went off with a lover, leaving him with five children. He wanted to remarry but did not want an annulment because he regarded a denial of his former marriage as a dishonor to his children. Another example involved a woman who fled when her husband attacked her with a knife, but who could not get an annulment because her husband couldn't be found to give evidence.[4]

In the **Anglican Church** the situation varies greatly from one area to another. Depending on the view of the local bishop and clergy, a church may allow a divorcé to marry or offer a service of blessing after a civil remarriage, or refuse either.

In the **nonestablished churches** there is a wide variety of views that depend only partly on the denomination of the church. Denominations such as Baptists, which value the independence of member churches, do not prescribe on this issue. Each local congregation decides whether or not they will remarry divorcés or whether they will allow divorcés and remarried persons to take communion or to serve as leaders. Often the position will change with the minister in charge of the congregation, or whenever a difficult situation is brought to a vote at a church meeting.

The New Testament's Message to the Modern World

Applying the NT texts in today's context is sometimes seen as the greatest difficulty. Actually, today's context is not so different from that of the NT. The social conditions of the first-century Greco-Roman world are very similar to those of the modern Western world, though the first-century Jewish world was more like the Western world two centuries ago.

Two centuries ago, a man could get a divorce if he was wealthy enough, but a woman had great difficulties. The religious authorities were in charge of moral issues, and the vast majority of the population assented to their leadership and followed high sexual morals. This is very similar to the world that Jesus addressed, where a man could get divorced easily although it cost him the

4. Bernard Haring, *No Way Out? — Pastoral Care of the Divorced and Remarried* (Boston, Mass.: St. Paul Publications, 1989), pp. 14, 17.

price of the *ketubah,* which was often quite high. Marital infidelity was very rare, and so divorces for adultery were almost unknown.

Today's society is more like the Greco-Roman society of Paul's day. Marriage was popular, but infidelity was rife and divorce was common and easy, with affordable financial arrangements. Religious guidance was completely separate from secular law, and it was largely ineffective at guiding public morals.

The trend in modern society is to make divorce easier, as was the case in both Jewish and Greco-Roman societies. The new Hillelite divorce for "any matter" had already transformed Jewish society, and divorces on other grounds were extremely rare. This meant that divorce was no longer a matter for the courts, and it had become merely a financial transaction. In the first-century Greco-Roman world the "free marriage" had almost completely replaced the *manus* marriage, and so divorce had become simply a matter of separation. In modern societies the number of grounds for divorce steadily increased up to the end of the 1960s, when the concept of the no-fault divorce was introduced in both the United States and the United Kingdom, as well as in other countries.

The message of the NT to believers living in both Jewish and Greco-Roman social contexts was the same. Both Jesus and Paul criticized the groundless no-fault divorces. Jesus condemned the divorce for "any matter" and Paul told believers that this also applied to the Greco-Roman divorce by separation. There is no reason to believe that their message to modern society would be any different. Believers should not break their marriage vows, and they should not divorce unless their partner breaks those vows.

Christian Grounds for Divorce

The biblical grounds for divorce are all failures to keep the marriage vows — that is, promises of faithfulness and provision of food, clothing, and love. The latter three may be generalized as material and emotional support. Physical and emotional abuse are extreme failures of material and emotional support.

How should these grounds for divorce be applied by Christians today? We should not apply them in the same way that the rabbis of NT times applied them. Their error, which Jesus and Paul criticized on many occasions, was legalism. They applied the law according to its letter, even when this went against all normal concepts of justice and good sense. They also added extra laws that provided a "fence" around the law. This fence added strictures and additional warnings to make sure that they did not even get close to transgressing a biblical law. Their application of the law in this way was a mark of their respect for

God as a law maker. Yet Jesus and Paul criticized this approach and said that they should rather follow the spirit of the Law.

In the matter of divorce and remarriage, **the rabbis were legalistic** in two ways. First, they carefully defined exactly how much food, clothing, and love had to be provided before the marriage vow was broken. These definitions included the weights of different types of food that the man had to give to his wife, the money that he had to spend on clothing, and the occupations that the wife had to perform with regard to making meals and making clothing (*m. Ketub.* 5.5, 8-9). They even included the number of times the man must make love to his wife, which varied greatly according to his profession (*m. Ketub.* 5.6).

The second way in which the rabbis were legalistic was their response to "technical" adultery. If a husband or his scribe had filled out a divorce certificate wrongly, with a wrong place-name or a wrong date, the divorce certificate was invalid. If the man or woman had remarried before the mistake was discovered, then this remarriage was technically adulterous. The rabbis said that in this situation the couple must separate and they could not marry each other because one may not marry one's adulterous partner. Any children that they had were declared "illegitimate," and thus they couldn't enter the temple or marry a legitimate Jew. In other words, they treated this "technical" adultery as though the couple had deliberately committed adultery.

Jesus and Paul did not comment on these legalistic rabbinic interpretations of the biblical law of divorce, though they both condemned similar interpretations in other areas. Paul applied the grounds for divorce in the opposite direction. Instead of being more specific than the biblical text, by defining quantities and frequency, he was *less* specific. He summed up the three grounds of "food, clothing, and love" as just the two issues of "love" and "material support." A similar generalization is probably behind the words "nourish" and "keep warm" ("cherish") in Ephesians 5:29.

The legalistic response to "technical" adultery is also very different in the NT. Jesus pointed out that virtually every remarried divorcé was committing technical adultery because divorce based on "any matter" was invalid. Yet there is no indication that Jesus expected them all to leave their partners and declare their children to be "illegitimate." If he had done so, the disciples would have expressed far more surprise at this ruling than the fact that marriage was meant to be life-long.

Paul, in particular, emphasized a pragmatic rather than a legalistic approach. When he addressed the issue of believers who had been divorced against their will by a nonbeliever, he could have given a legalistic response. He could have said: "You have been abandoned, so you have a ground for divorce because they are neglecting your food, clothing, and love." Instead he simply told them that they were no longer bound, and he referred to the rabbinic formula for a pragmatic decision: "For the sake of peace."

Jesus also criticized the rabbis who said that divorce was compulsory in the event of adultery. He said that Moses did not *command* divorce in this situation but *allowed* it, and he allowed it only in cases of stubborn hard-heartedness. This was presumably a reference to the lack of repentance by adulterous Israel whom God divorced in Jeremiah 4:4 (the only place where "hard-hearted" occurs in this context is the LXX). If one's partner is repentant and asks for forgiveness, a believer should forgive. It was a general principle of Jesus that a believer should always forgive someone who repents and asks for forgiveness. If, of course, there is no sign of repentance (as in the case of hard-hearted Israel), then Moses' law allows divorce.

Christians should not, therefore, be tempted to apply the biblical grounds for divorce in a legalistic way. The OT allowed divorce for broken marriage vows, but both Jesus and Paul refused to apply these in a legalistic manner. Jesus emphasized that these grounds *allowed* divorce, but a believer should go on striving to maintain the marriage as long as possible.

What the Church Should Do

The following is a personal view, based on pastoral experience. It is not based on Scripture, and it will not fit into every church structure. But it has worked for me.

The main role in the Church is before marriage. **Any couple who wants to get married in a church should** be asked to **attend the church** for at least a month before the wedding. This is so that they will make friends among the congregation, before some of whom they will be making their vows. If they are not Christians, it is to be hoped that they will learn something of the gospel, and that they will come to realize that the church is not just a beautiful building that will look good in their wedding photos.

The couple should also **attend a premarriage course.** In my parish the churches worked together to produce and run premarriage group sessions. The clergy from the different churches put together a course that was based on the excellent material that the Catholic Church produces, though other good material is widely available. The aim is to get the couple talking to each other about all matters of family life. This includes everything from future aspirations and whether or not they want children, to expectations about who should do the housework and the gardening. These issues are approached in a light-hearted way, using the types of questionnaires that are popular in women's magazines. Each partner fills in the questionnaire and then swaps results with the other. There is then a group discussion based on any issues that come up. There are five sessions covering "nonreligious" topics; these are led by lay couples trained for the task. The sixth session is led by the minister who will marry them, and it covers "religious" topics.

The couple should understand that marriage vows are the most important aspect of the **wedding service.** If possible, the couple should be involved in writing their own marriage service. I am a Baptist, and so there is no set liturgy that I am required to use. Therefore I can give couples a copy of three or four marriage services and ask them to put together their own. Mostly they simply pick one of them, and in that case I go through it carefully, making sure that they agree with every part. The vows are especially important, and most couples realize this because it is the part of the service during which they have to speak. I would not allow them to omit the biblical vows of "faithfulness, food, clothing, and love" (or their modern equivalents such as "keep," "cherish," etc.), but I have never had to insist on this. When a couple is getting married, both people usually have stars in their eyes and are willing to promise anything. I allow them to include "obey" if they both agree, but I would always suggest that both partners promise the same submission, as in Ephesians 5:21.

When a marriage is going wrong, the role of the minister is to encourage the couple to rescue the marriage, if at all possible. In my opinion, a minister should rarely, if ever, advise a divorce, even if there are clear grounds for it. The only exception would be when one of the couple is in danger, but even in that situation the minister should suggest separation and counseling, not divorce. The minister might be asked to discuss whether or not the marriage vows have been broken, which would give the wronged partner a right to divorce, but encouragement to divorce should not come from the minister. The minister's role is to suggest ways to heal the marriage, and to encourage repentance and forgiveness.

If the minister is trained in **counseling**, this can be offered, but a minister is rarely the best type of counselor. The role of a counselor is to listen and to explore options without telling the couple what they should do. The couple need to be encouraged to talk to each other and to listen to each other, not to the counselor. They should be enabled to come to informed decisions based on their own choices and their own determination. It is often difficult for a minister to be nondirective, and it is difficult for a couple to make decisions of which they feel the minister may disapprove. If the minister is a good counselor, he will not be able to be a good minister, because a minister *should* be direct.

If the couple finally **decide to get divorced**, the minister has to support them. This is difficult when there are no clear biblical grounds for the divorce, and this should be pointed out. It is difficult if the minister feels that they have not made sufficient effort to repent and reform, or to forgive. It is especially difficult if the person who makes the decision to divorce is not the injured party. The person who breaks the marriage vows should not be the person who decides that the marriage is over, because the vow breaker has no grounds. The decision should be made by the partner who has been betrayed, neglected, or abused. In the end, however, each person must live before God and with one's own conscience. The role of the minister is to point out the right way, as he sees it, and then to support the individual, even if that person makes a morally wrong choice. If we threw all sinners out of the church, the pews would be empty, and so would the pulpit.

The most difficult issue is **remarriage**. When divorcés come to ask to be married, I have made the personal decision to ask no questions about their former marriages. Nevertheless, they usually wish to tell me about either their guilt or their innocence. I have come to the reluctant conclusion that the reality is often the opposite of what they express. It is impossible to decide the rights or wrongs of former marriages without being intimately involved with both sides during the actual breakups. In any case, the past is past, and sins can be forgiven. I would not forbid a repentant murderer from joining the church, and so I cannot forbid a repentant adulterer from marrying in the church.

The case of **remarriage to the adulterous lover** is perhaps different. The church may decide to refuse such a marriage, and conducting this marriage could be said to condone the sin. If such marriages were known to be allowed, then someone could blatantly take a lover in the confidence that the partner will seek a divorce and the church will legitimize the new relationship by performing a marriage. Personally I have not faced this decision. I have probably conducted such marriages in ignorance because I do not inquire into the reasons for a past divorce. Yet if the couple admitted to me that their affair had broken up the marriage, I would refuse to marry them. In other words, I would act like a defense lawyer who dismisses a client when he pleads not guilty after plainly admitting to the lawyer that he is guilty.

If either one of the couple has been divorced, I insist on **a service of "repentance for broken promises"** before the wedding. This normally takes place in the church on the evening before the wedding, just after the final rehearsal. This is an ideal time and venue because both are thinking very clearly about their vows, having just rehearsed them, and they are in the building where they are about to take those vows for a second time. The service is very short and can be informal or formal depending on the couple and on the traditions of the church. It is basically a prayer shared by all three of us, confessing that we have each made promises that we have not kept, and asking forgiveness. The following form can be used:

> **All:** Heavenly father, who has cared for me from my birth, and who has promised to love me unconditionally, I come to you in confession. I confess that I have made promises to you and to others that I have not kept. I have promised to pray for and promised to love and promised to care for others, and I have not kept these promises as I should. Please forgive me for my sin and give comfort to those whom I have let down and hurt. Please give me strength for the future, to be able to keep the promises I make. Amen.
>
> **Minister:** (A prayer for the couple's wedding and future life.)

When a church leader becomes divorced, this is always a serious matter. There is always the suspicion that he or she may not be trustworthy and that, "if he cannot run his own household, how can he care for the household of the church?" (1 Tim. 3:4 — though this refers mainly to unruly children). Even if a marital breakup proceeds to divorce, the church should not simply dismiss their minister. The sin of divorce lies in the breaking of marriage vows, not in divorce, and the minister may be entirely innocent. In this situation it is right that the church should ask who was to blame for the marriage breakup, even though this might normally be regarded as an entirely private matter. This kind of question is usually best asked by an outsider with authority, such as a bishop or a minister of another church, who can then report his findings to the church. If the minister is a guilty party in the divorce (and it is rare that anyone is entirely innocent), the church has a right to expect a public apology for the disgrace brought upon the church. The church will then have to decide whether to dismiss the minister, though in practice, the minister is usually best advised to move to another church in any case.

Should any church employ a divorcé as a minister? There is no biblical prohibition of divorce or remarriage for church leaders. The description of a church leader as "man of one woman" or "woman of one man" (1 Tim. 3:2; 5:9) is sometimes regarded as a prohibition of remarriage, though we have found that it meant someone who was faithful to one partner (i.e., had high sexual morals, in contrast to the norm of the Greco-Roman empire).

Sexual sins have always engendered a special abhorrence in the church environment, as well as undue fascination. A church might be proud that their minister was a former member of a violent gang, or a repented murderer, but they are equally likely to be embarrassed that their minister is a divorcé. Marriage breakup should be treated like any other sin in the past. It should be repented of and then treated as forgiven by God. It should also be remembered that divorce itself is not the sin, but the breaking of marriage vows, of which the minister may not be guilty. What an individual church decides is, ultimately, a matter for the congregation, which will have to respect and follow the leadership of that minister, but there is no biblical reason to forbid a divorced minister from leading a church. After all, the OT prophets portray God himself as a reluctant divorcé.

Conclusions

The message of the NT is that divorce is allowed but should be avoided whenever possible. Divorce is allowed only on the grounds of broken marriage vows, and the decision to divorce can be made only by the injured party. A believer should never break the marriage vows, and should try to forgive a repentant partner who has done so. If divorce does happen, remarriage is permitted. All this would be obvious to a first-century believer, but the meaning of the text was obscured at a very early date due to ignorance about the Jewish background after 70 C.E. Modern Church practice can be easily adapted to this insight because our marriage services still preserve the four biblical grounds for divorce in the marriage vows.

The Church should now be humble and admit that a great mistake has been made. Too many generations of husbands and wives have been forced to remain with their abusing or neglectful partners and have not been allowed to divorce even after suffering repeated unfaithfulness. The Church should not continue in a false teaching because Church tradition should not be regarded as superior to the teaching of Jesus and Paul.

Bibliography

Abrahams, I. *Studies in Pharisaism and the Gospels.* London: Macmillan, 1917.

Adams, Jay E. *Marriage, Divorce and Remarriage in the Bible.* Phillipsburg, N.J.: Presbyterian and Reformed Publishing Co., 1980.

Alford, Henry. *The Greek Testament: With a Critically Revised Text, a Digest of Various Readings, Marginal References to Verbal and Idiomatic Usage, Prolegomena, and a Critical and Exegetical Commentary: For the Use of Theological Students and Ministers.* New ed. London: Rivingtons, 1880-81.

Amram, D. W. "Divorce." In *Jewish Encyclopedia,* ed. Isidore Singer, vol. 4, pp. 624-28. New York and London: Funk & Wagnalls Co., 1905.

———. *The Jewish Law of Divorce according to Bible and Talmud.* Reprint of undated original. New York: Sepher-Hermon, 1975.

Anglican Synod. *Marriage Matters: A Consultative Document by the Working Party on Marriage Guidance.* London: HMSO, 1979.

———. *Marriage and the Church's Task.* Report of the General Synod Marriage Commission. London: CIO Publishing, Church House, 1978.

———. *Marriage, Divorce and the Church — the Report of a Commission Appointed by the Archbishop of Canterbury to Prepare a Statement on the Christian Doctrine of Marriage.* London: SPCK, 1971.

———. *Putting Assunder — A Divorce Law for Contemporary Society.* The Report of a Group Appointed by the Archbishop of Canterbury in January 1964. London: SPCK, 1966.

Anonymous. "The Excepting Clause in St. Matthew." *Theology* 36 (1938): 27-36.

Anonymous. "The Law of Divorce and the Problem for the Church — by A Student." *Theology* 34 (1937): 272-81.

Archer, Leone J. *Her Price Is beyond Rubies: The Jewish Woman in Greco-Roman Palestine.* Journal for the Study of the Old Testament, Supplement 60. Sheffield: Sheffield Academic Press, 1990.

Atkinson, David. *To Have and To Hold: The Marriage Covenant and the Discipline of Divorce.* London: Collins, 1979.

Aus, Roger David. *"Caught in the Act," Walking on the Sea, and the Release of Barabbas Revisited.* South Florida Studies in the History of Judaism 157. Atlanta: Scholars Press, 1997.

Bammel, Ernst. "Markus 10.11f. und das jüdische Eherecht." *Zeitschrift für die neutestamentliche Wissenschaft* 61 (1970): 95-101.

Baptist Union. *Marriage Requests: Ministerial Responses.* Department of Ministry, Baptist Union, 1982.

Barrett, C. K. *A Commentary on the First Epistle to the Corinthians.* London: A. & C. Black, 1968.

Baumgarten, Joseph M. "The Qumran-Essene Restraints on Marriage." In *Archaeology and History in the Dead Sea Scrolls,* ed. L. H. Schiffman, pp. 13-24. Journal for the Study of the Pseudepigrapha, Supplement 8. Sheffield: JSOT Press, 1990.

———. *Studies in Qumran Law.* Leiden: Brill, 1977.

Belkin, Samuel. *Philo and the Oral Law: The Philonic Interpretation of Biblical Law in Relation to the Palestinian Halakah.* Harvard Semitic Series 11. Cambridge, Mass.: Harvard University Press, 1940.

Ben-Barak, Zafrira. "The Legal Background to the Restoration of Michal to David." In *Telling Queen Michal's Story: An Experiment in Comparative Interpretation,* ed. David J. A. Clines and Tamara C. Eskenazi, pp. 74-93. Journal for the Study of the Old Testament, Supplement 119. Sheffield: Sheffield Academic Press, 1991. Originally published in *Studies in the Historical Books,* ed. J. A. Emerton, pp. 15-29. Leiden: Brill, 1979.

Bengel, John Albert. *Gnomon of the New Testament.* Rev. and ed. Rev. Andrew R. Fausset. 4th ed. Edinburgh: T. & T. Clark, 1860-67.

Benoit, Pierre, Jozef T. Milik, and Roland de Vaux. *Discoveries in the Judaean Desert,* vol. 2: *Les grottes de Murabba'at.* Oxford: Clarendon, 1961.

Bickerman, E. J. "Two Legal Interpretations of the Septuagint." In *Studies in Jewish and Christian History,* vol. 1, pp. 201-24. Arbeiten zur Geschichte des antiken Judentums und des Urchristentums; vol. 9, pts. 1-3. Leiden: Brill, 1976-86.

Bivin, David. "'And' or 'In order to' Remarry." *Jerusalem Perspective* 50 (1996): 10-17, 35-38.

Blomberg, Craig L. "Marriage, Divorce, Remarriage, and Celibacy: An Exegesis of Matthew 19.3-12." *Trinity Journal* n.s. 11 (1990): 161-96.

Bockmuehl, Marcus. "Matthew 5.32; 19.9 in the Light of Pre-Rabbinic Halakhah." *New Testament Studies* 35 (1989): 291-95.

Bonsirven, Joseph. *Le divorce dans le Nouveau Testament.* Paris: Société de S. Jean l'Evangéliste, Desclée et Die, 1948.

Boring, M. Eugene. *Hellenistic Commentary to the New Testament.* Nashville: Abingdon, 1995.

Bowman, John, trans. and ed. *Samaritan Documents Relating to Their History, Religion and Life.* Pittsburgh Original Texts and Translations. Pittsburgh: The Pickwick Press, 1977.

Bradley, K. R. "Remarriage and the Structure of the Upper-Class Roman Family." In *Marriage, Divorce and Children in Ancient Rome,* ed. Beryl Rawson, pp. 79-93. Oxford: Clarendon, 1991.

British Museum. *Cuneiform Texts from Babylonian Tablets in the British Museum.* London: British Museum, 1898-1977.

Brooten, Bernadette J. "Zur Debatte über das Scheidungsrecht der jüdischen Frau." *Evangelische Theologie* 43 (1983): 466-78.

———. "Könnten Frauen im alten Judentum die Scheidung betreiben? Überlegung zu Mk 10,11-12 und 1 Kor 7,10-11." *Evangelische Theologie* 42 (1982): 65-80.

Broshi, Magen. *The Damascus Document Reconsidered.* Jerusalem: Israel Exploration Society, 1992.

Brownlee, William H. *Ezekiel 1–19.* Word Biblical Commentary 28. Waco: Word Books, 1986.

Bruce, F. F. "Biblical Exposition at Qumran." In *Gospel Perspectives,* vol. 3: *Studies in Midrash and Historiography,* ed. R. T. France and D. Wenham, pp. 77-98. Sheffield: JSOT Press, 1983.

———. *Biblical Exegesis in the Qumran Texts.* London: Tyndale, 1959.

Bullimore, John W. *Pushing Asunder?* Grove Booklet No. 41. Bramcote: Grove, 1981.

Burkitt, F. Crawford. *The Gospel History and Its Transmission.* 2nd ed. Edinburgh: T. & T. Clark, 1907.

Calvin, John. *Commentary on the Epistles of Paul the Apostle to the Corinthians.* Trans. and collated William Pringle. Edinburgh: Calvin Translation Society, 1848-49.

———. *Commentary on a Harmony of the Evangelists, Matthew, Mark and Luke.* Trans. and collated William Pringle. Edinburgh: Calvin Translation Society, 1845-46.

Cardascia, Guillaume. *Les Lois Assyriennes.* Paris: Cerf, 1969.

Carmichael, Calum M. *The Laws of Deuteronomy.* London and Ithaca: Cornell University Press, 1974.

Carroll, Robert P. *Jeremiah.* London: SCM, 1986.

Carson, Don A. "Matthew." In *The Expositor's Bible Commentary with NIV,* vol. 8: *Matthew, Mark, Luke,* ed. Frank E. Gaebelein. Grand Rapids: Zondervan, 1984.

Casey, Maurice. *Aramaic Sources of Mark's Gospel.* Society for New Testament Studies, Monograph Series 102. Cambridge: Cambridge University Press, 1998.

Cassuto, U. *A Commentary on the Book of Exodus.* Jerusalem: Magnes, 1967.

Charles, R. H. *The Teaching of the New Testament on Divorce.* London: Williams & Norgate, 1921.

Charlesworth, James H. *The Dead Sea Scrolls: Hebrew, Aramaic, and Greek Texts with English Translations.* 2 vols. Tübingen: Mohr, 1995.

Clark, Stephen. *Putting Asunder: Divorce and Remarriage in Biblical and Pastoral Perspective.* Bridgend, Wales: Brynterion, 1999.

Clifford, Paula. *Divorced Christians and the Love of God.* London: SPCK, 1987.

Cohen, Boaz. *Jewish and Roman Law: A Comparative Study.* 2 vols. New York: Jewish Theological Seminary of America, 1966.

———. "Concerning Divorce in Jewish and Roman Law." *Proceedings of the American Academy for Jewish Research* 21 (1952): 3-34.

———. "On the Theme of Betrothal in Jewish and Roman Law." *Proceedings of the American Academy for Jewish Research* 18 (1948): 67-135.

Cohen, Shaye. *The Family in Antiquity.* Atlanta: Scholars Press, 1993.

Collins, John J. "Marriage, Divorce and Family in Second Temple Judaism." In *Families in Ancient Israel,* ed. Leo G. Perdue et al., pp. 104-62. Louisville: Westminster/John Knox, 1997.

Corbier, Mireille. "Divorce and Adoption as Roman Familial Strategies." In *Marriage, Divorce and Children in Ancient Rome,* ed. Beryl Rawson, pp. 47-78. Oxford: Clarendon, 1991.

Cornes, Andrew. *Divorce and Remarriage: Biblical Principles and Pastoral Practice.* London: Hodder & Stoughton, 1993.

Cotton, Hannah M. "The Rabbis and the Documents." In *Jews in a Graeco-Roman World,* ed. Martin Goodman, pp. 167-79. Oxford: Clarendon; New York: Oxford University Press, 1998.

———. "A Cancelled Marriage Contract from the Judaean Desert *(XHev/Se Gr. 2).*" *Journal of Roman Studies* 84 (1994): 64-86.

Cotton, Hannah M., and Ada Yardeni. *Aramaic, Hebrew and Greek Documentary Texts from Nahal Hever and Other Sites: With an Appendix Containing Alleged Qumran Texts.* Discoveries in the Judaean Desert 27. Oxford: Clarendon, 1997.

Cowley, A. E. *Aramaic Papyri of the Fifth Century* B.C. Oxford: Clarendon, 1923.

Crispin, Ken. *Divorce, The Forgivable Sin?* London: Hodder & Stoughton, 1988.

Daube, David. *The New Testament and Rabbinic Judaism.* London: Athlone, 1956.

———. "The New Testament Terms for Divorce." *Theology* 47 (1944): 65-67.

Davies, Philip R. *Behind the Essenes: History and Ideology in the Dead Sea Scrolls.* Brown Judaic Studies 94. Atlanta: Scholars Press, 1987.

———. *The Damascus Document: An Interpretation of the "Damascus Document."* Journal for the Study of the Old Testament, Supplement 25. Sheffield: Sheffield Academic Press, 1983.

Davies, W. D. *Paul and Rabbinic Judaism: Some Rabbinic Elements in Pauline Theology.* 2nd ed. London: SPCK, 1955.

Davies, W. D., and Dale C. Allison. *A Critical and Exegetical Commentary on the Gospel according to Saint Matthew.* 3 vols. Edinburgh: T. & T. Clark, 1988-97.

Deasley, Alex R. G. *Marriage and Divorce in the Bible and the Church.* Kansas City, Mo.: Beacon Hill, 2000.

Deissmann, G. Adolf. *Bible Studies: Contributions Chiefly from Papyri and Inscriptions to the History of the Language, the Literature, and the Religion of Hellenistic Judaism and Primitive Christianity.* Trans. Alexander Grieve. Peabody, Mass.: Hendrickson, 1988. Original published Edinburgh: T. & T. Clark, 1901.

Deming, Will. *Paul on Marriage and Celibacy: The Hellenistic Background of 1 Corinthians 7.* Cambridge: Cambridge University Press, 1995.

Dixon, Suzanne. *The Roman Family.* Baltimore and London: Johns Hopkins University Press, 1992.

Dorff, E. N., and A. Rosett. *A Living Tree: The Roots and Growth of Jewish Law.* New York: Jewish Theological Seminary of America, State University of New York Press, 1988.

Driver, S. R. *A Critical and Exegetical Commentary on Deuteronomy.* 3rd ed. Edinburgh: T. & T. Clark, 1902.

Dulau, Pierre. "The Pauline Privilege: Is It Promulgated in the First Epistle to the Corinthians?" *Catholic Biblical Quarterly* 13 (1951): 146-52.

Dupont, Jacques. "Mariage et divorce dans l'évangile: Matthieu 19.3-12 et parallèles." *Theological Studies* 22 (1961): 466-67.

Durham, John I. *Exodus.* Word Biblical Commentary. Waco: Word Books, 1987.

Ellicott, Charles John. *A New Testament Commentary for English Readers.* London: 1884.

Elliott, J. K. "Paul's Teaching on Marriage in 1 Corinthians: Some Problems Reconsidered." *New Testament Studies* 19 (1972-73): 219-25.

Elon, Menachem. *Jewish Law: History, Sources, Principles.* 4 vols. Philadelphia: Jewish Publication Society, 1994.

Epp, Theodore H. *Marriage, Divorce and Remarriage.* Doncaster: Good News Broadcasting Association, Bawtry, 1954. Reprint Doncaster: Good News Broadcasting Association, Bawtry, 1991.

Epstein, Louis M. *The Jewish Marriage Contract: A Study in the Status of the Woman in Jewish Law.* New York: Johnson Reprint Corp., 1968 (original 1942).

———. *Sex Laws and Customs in Judaism.* American Academy of Jewish Research. New York: Ktav, 1967 (original 1948).

———. *Marriage Laws in the Bible and Talmud.* The Harvard Semitic Series 12. Cambridge, Mass.: Harvard University Press, 1942.

Erlandsson, S. "Bāghadh." In *Theological Dictionary of the Old Testament,* vol. 1, ed. Johannes G. Botterweck, Helmer Ringgren, and Heinz-Josef Fabry, pp. 470-73. Grand Rapids: Eerdmans, 1974.

Eshel, Esther, and Amos Kloner. "An Aramaic Ostracon of an Edomite Marriage Contract from Maresha, Dated 176 B.C.E." *Israel Exploration Journal* 46 (1996): 1-22.

Falk, Ze'ev W. *Introduction to Jewish Law of the Second Commonwealth.* 2 vols. Leiden: Brill, 1972, 1978.

Family Action Group Order of Christian Unity. *Torn Lives? The Effects of Divorce and of the Law of Divorce on Children: A Child-centred Approach to Divorce.* Unity Press, Becket Publications, 1979.

Fantham, Elaine, ed. *Women in the Classical World: Image and Text.* New York: Oxford University Press, 1995.

Fee, Gordon D. *The First Epistle to the Corinthians.* The New International Commentary on the New Testament. Grand Rapids: Eerdmans, 1987.

Fekkes, Jan III. "'His Bride Has Prepared Herself': Revelation 19–21 and Isaian Nuptial Imagery." *Journal of Biblical Literature* 109 (1990): 269-87.

The First Prayer-Book of Edward VI: Compared with the Successive Revisions of the Book of Common Prayer: Also a Concordance to the Rubricks in the Several Editions. Oxford: Parker, 1877.

Fishbane, Michael. *Biblical Interpretation in Ancient Israel.* Oxford: Clarendon, 1985.

Fitzmyer, J. A. *Wandering Aramean: Collected Aramaic Essays.* Missoula, Mont.: Scholars Press, 1979.

———. "Divorce Among First-Century Palestinian Jews." *Eretz-Israel* 14 (1978): 103-10.

———. "The Matthean Divorce Texts and Some New Palestinian Evidence." *Theological Studies* 37 (1976): 197-226.

———. "The Use of Explicit Old Testament Quotations in Qumran Literature and in the New Testament." In *Essays on the Semitic Background of the New Testament,* pp. 3-58. London: Geoffrey Chapman, 1971. Originally in *New Testament Studies* 7 (1960-61): 297-333.

Ford, Josephine M. "Levirate Marriage in St. Paul (1 Cor. VII)." *New Testament Studies* 10 (1963-64): 361-65.

Fornberg, Tord. *Jewish-Christian Dialogue and Biblical Exegesis.* Studia Missionalia Upsaliensia 47. Uppsala: Svenska Institutet for Missionsforskning, 1988.

Foster, Richard. *Money, Sex and Power: The Challenge of the Disciplined Life.* London: Hodder & Stoughton, 1985.

Friedman, Mordechai A. "Divorce upon the Wife's Demand as Reflected in MSS from Cairo Geniza." In *The Jewish Law Annual,* vol. 4, ed. B. S. Jackson, pp. 103-26. Leiden: Brill, 1981.

———. "Israel's Response in Hosea 2.17b: 'You Are My Husband.'" *Journal of Biblical Literature* 99 (1980): 199-204.

———. *Jewish Marriage in Palestine: A Cairo Geniza Study.* 2 vols.: *The Ketubba Traditions of Eretz Israel* and *The Ketubba Texts.* Tel-Aviv: Tel-Aviv University, Chaim Rosenberg School of Jewish Studies; New York: Jewish Theological Seminary of America, 1980-81.

———. "Termination of the Marriage upon the Wife's Request: A Palestinian Ketubba Stipulation." *Proceedings of the American Academy for Jewish Research* 37 (1969): 29-55.

Fugette, J. Preston. *Marriage a Covenant — Not Indissoluble; or The Revelation of Scripture and History.* Baltimore: Cushing & Co., 1895.

Gaca, Kathy L. "The Early Christian Adaption of Ancient Greek Philosophical and Biblical Principles of Human Sexual Conduct." Ph.D. thesis, University of Toronto, 1996.

Gadd, C. J. "Tablets from Kirkuk." *Revue d'Assyriologie et d'Archéologie Orientale* 23 (1926): 49-161.

Gagper, J. G. *Curse Tablets and Binding Spells from the Ancient World.* Oxford and New York: Oxford University Press, 1992.

Galambush, Julie. *Jerusalem in the Book of Ezekiel: The City as Yahweh's Wife*. Society for Biblical Literature Dissertation Series 130. Atlanta: Scholars Press, 1992.

Gardner, Jane F. *Women in Roman Law and Society*. London: Croom Helm, 1987.

Geller, Markham J. "New Sources for the Origins of the Rabbinic Ketubah." *Hebrew Union College Annual* 49 (1978): 227-45.

———. "The Elephantine Papyri and Hosea 2.3: Evidence for the Form of the Early Jewish Divorce Writ." *Journal for the Study of Judaism* 8 (1977): 139-48.

Gerhardsson, Birger. *Memory and Manuscript*. Acta Seminarii Neotestamentici Upsaliensis 22. Uppsala, 1961. Reprinted Grand Rapids: Eerdmans, 1998, with "Tradition and Transmission in Early Christianity" and a Foreword by Jacob Neusner.

Gibson, J. C. L. *Canaanite Myths and Legends*. 2nd ed. Edinburgh: T. & T. Clark, 1978.

Ginzberg, Louis. *An Unknown Jewish Sect*. New York: Jewish Theological Seminary of America, 1978.

———. *The Legends of the Jews*. Trans. Henrietta Szold. Philadelphia: Jewish Publication Society of America, 1913-67.

Gordon, Edmund I. *Sumerian Proverbs: Glimpses of Everyday Life in Ancient Mesopotamia*. Philadelphia: University of Pennsylvania, 1959.

Gordon, J. Dorcas. *Sister or Wife? 1 Corinthians 7 and Cultural Anthropology*. Sheffield: Sheffield Academic Press, 1997.

Gore, Charles. *The Question of Divorce*. London: John Murray, 1911.

Gottstein, Alon Goshen. "The Body as Image of God in Rabbinic Literature." *Harvard Theological Review* 87 (1994): 171-95.

Grabbe, Lester L. *Judaism from Cyrus to Hadrian*. Minneapolis: Fortress, 1992.

Graf, K. H. *Der Prophet Jeremia*. Leipzig: T. O. Weigel, 1862.

Greenberg, Blu. "Marriage in the Jewish Tradition." *Journal of Ecumenical Studies* 22 (1992): 3-20.

Greenberg, M. *Ezekiel 1–20*. Anchor Bible 22. Garden City, N.Y.: Doubleday, 1983.

Greengus, Samuel. "The Old Babylonian Marriage Contract." *Journal of the American Oriental Society* 89 (1969): 505-32.

———. "Old Babylonian Marriage Ceremonies and Rites." *Journal of Cuneiform Studies* 20 (1966): 55-72.

Grether, Herbert G. "Translating the Questions in Isaiah 50." *Bible Translator* 24 (1973): 240-43.

Grib, Philip J., S.J. *Divorce Laws and Morality — A New Catholic Jurisprudence*. New York: Lanham, 1985.

Gribble, Francis. *The Fight for Divorce*. London: Hurst & Blackett Ltd., 1932.

Griffith, F. L. *Catalogue of the Demotic Papyri in the John Rylands Library, Manchester: With Facsimiles and Complete Transcriptions*, vol. 3: *Key-list, Translations, Commentaries and Indices*. Manchester: Manchester University Press, 1909.

Grubbs, Judith Evans. "'Pagan' and 'Christian' Marriage: The State of the Question." *Journal of Early Christian Studies* 2 (1994): 361-412.

Gundry, Robert H. *Matthew: A Commentary on His Handbook for a Mixed Church under Persecution.* Grand Rapids: Eerdmans, 1994.

Hagner, Donald A. *Matthew 14–28.* Word Biblical Commentary 33b. Dallas: Word Books, 1995.

Hallo, William W., and K. Lawson Younger. *The Context of Scripture,* vol. 1: *Canonical Compositions from the Biblical World.* Leiden: Brill, 1997.

Hammond, H. *A Paraphrase and Annotations upon All the Books of the New Testament: Briefly Explaining All the Difficult Places Thereof.* 5th ed. corrected. London: J. Macock and M. Flesher, 1681.

Haring, Bernard. *No Way Out? — Pastoral Care of the Divorced and Remarried.* Boston, Mass.: St. Paul Publications, 1989.

Hauck, F. "μοιχάω." In *Theological Dictionary of the New Testament,* vol. 4, ed. Gerhard Kittel, pp. 729-35. Grand Rapids: Eerdmans, 1964-95.

Haut, Irwin H. *Divorce in Jewish Law and Life.* Studies in Jewish Jurisprudence 5. New York: Sepher-Hermon, 1983.

Hayes, Christine. "Intermarriage and Impurity in Ancient Jewish Sources." *Harvard Theological Review* 92 (1999): 3-36.

Herz, N. "A Hebrew Word in Greek Disguise: 1 Cor. vii.3." *Expository Times* 7 (1895): 48.

Heth, William A., and Gordon J. Wenham. *Jesus and Divorce.* London: Hodder & Stoughton, 1984.

Hill, David. "A Note on Matthew 1.19." *Expository Times* 76 (1964-65): 133-34.

Holladay, William L. *A Commentary on the Book of the Prophet Jeremiah.* 2 vols. Philadelphia: Fortress, 1986.

Holmén, Tom. "Divorce in CD 4.20–5.2 and in 11Q 57.17-18: Some Remarks on the Pertinence of the Question." *Revue de Qumran* 18 (1998): 397-408.

Horsley, G. H. R., ed. *New Documents Illustrating Early Christianity.* Vol. 3. North Ryde: The Ancient History Documentary Research Centre, Macquarie University, 1983.

Hugenberger, G. P. *Marriage as a Covenant: A Study of Biblical Law and Ethics Governing Marriage, Developed from the Perspective of Malachi.* Vetus Testamentum Supplement 52. Leiden and New York: Brill, 1994.

Hunt, A. S., and C. C. Edgar, eds. *Select Papyri,* vol. 1: *Non-literary Papyri: Private Affairs.* The Loeb Classical Library 266. Cambridge, Mass.: Harvard University Press; London: Heinemann, 1959.

Ide, Arthur Frederick. *Marriage, Divorce, Remarriage, Women and the Bible.* Tangelwüld: Garland, 1995.

Ihinger-Tallman, Marilyn, and Kay Pasley. *Remarriage.* Family Studies Text Series. Newbury Park, Calif.: Sage, 1987.

Ilan, Tal. *Mine and Yours Are Hers: Retrieving Women's History from Rabbinic Literature.* Leiden: Brill, 1997.

———. "Notes and Observations on a Newly Published Divorce Bill from the Judean Desert." *Harvard Theological Review* 89 (1996): 195-202.

———. *Jewish Women in Greco-Roman Palestine: An Inquiry into Image and Status.* Peabody, Mass.: Hendrickson, 1996.

Instone-Brewer, David. "1 Corinthians 7 in the Light of the Jewish, Greek, and Aramaic Marriage and Divorce Papyri." *Tyndale Bulletin* 52 (2001): 225-43.

———. "1 Corinthians 7 in the Light of the Graeco-Roman Marriage and Divorce Papyri." *Tyndale Bulletin* 52 (2001): 101-16.

———. "Jewish Women Divorcing Their Husbands in Early Judaism: The Background to Papyrus Ṣe'elim 13." *Harvard Theological Review* 92 (1999): 349-57.

———. "Deuteronomy 24.1-4 and the Origin of the Jewish Divorce Certificate." *Journal of Jewish Studies* 49 (1998): 230-43.

———. *Marriage and Divorce Papyri of the Ancient Greek, Roman, and Jewish World.* Web publication: http://www.tyndale.cam.ac.uk/brewer/MarriagePapyri/ (2000).

———. "Nomological Exegesis in Qumran 'Divorce' Texts." *Revue de Qumran* 18 (1998): 561-79.

———. *Techniques and Assumptions in Jewish Exegesis before 70 CE.* Texte und Studien zum antiken Judentum 30. Tübingen: Mohr, 1992.

Isaksson, Abel. *Marriage and Ministry in the New Temple: A Study with Special Reference to Mt. 19.13*[sic]*-12 and 1. Cor. 11.3-16.* Trans. Neil Tomkinson and Jean Gray. Acta Seminarii Neotestamentici Upsaliensis 24. Lund: Gleerup; Copenhagen: Munksgaard, 1965.

Jacob, Benno. *The Second Book of the Bible, Exodus.* Trans. with an introduction by Walter Jacob. Hoboken: Ktav, 1992.

Japhet, Sara. "The Relationship between the Legal Corpora in the Pentateuch in Light of Manumission Laws." In *Studies in Bible 1986,* ed. S. Japhet, pp. 63-89. Scripta Hierosolymitana 31. Jerusalem: Magnes, 1986.

Jastrow, Marcus. *A Dictionary of the Targumim, the Talmud Babli and Yerushalmi, and the Midrashic Literature.* New York: Pardes, 1950.

Jeremias, Joachim. *Jerusalem in the Time of Jesus.* London: SCM, 1969.

Joubert, Stephen, and Jan Willem van Henten. "Two A-typical Jewish Families in the Greco-Roman Period." *Neotestamentica* 30 (1996): 121-40.

Kahana, K. *The Theory of Marriage in Jewish Law.* Leiden: Brill, 1966.

Kalluveettil, P. *Declaration and Covenant: A Comprehensive Review of Covenant Formulae from the Old Testament and the Ancient Near East.* Rome: Biblical Institute Press, 1982.

Kampen, John. "The Matthean Divorce Texts Reexamined." In *New Qumran Texts and Studies: Proceedings of the First Meeting of the International Organization for Qumran Studies, Paris, 1992,* ed. George J. Brooke and Florentino Garcia Martinez, pp. 149-67. Studies on the Texts of the Desert of Judah 15. Leiden: Brill, 1994.

———. "A Fresh Look at the Masculine Plural Suffix in CD iv, 21." *Revue de Qumran* 16 (1993): 91-97.

Keener, Craig S. *Paul, Women and Wives: Marriage and Women's Ministry in the Letters of Paul.* Peabody, Mass.: Hendrickson, 1992.

———. *. . . And Marries Another: Divorce and Remarriage in the Teaching of the New Testament.* Peabody, Mass.: Hendrickson, 1991.

Klausner, Joseph. *Jesus of Nazareth: His Life, Times, and Teaching.* Trans. Herbert Danby. London: Allen & Unwin, 1925. Reprinted New York: Menorah, 1979.

Kodell, Jerome. "Celibacy logion in Matthew 19.12." *Biblical Theology Bulletin* 8 (1978): 19-23.

Korpel, Marjo Christina Annette. *A Rift in the Clouds: Ugaritic and Hebrew Descriptions of the Divine.* Münster: Ugarit-Verlag, 1990.

Kraeling, Emil G. *The Brooklyn Museum Aramaic Papyri: New Documents of the Fifth Century B.C. from the Jewish Colony at Elephantine.* New Haven: Yale University Press, 1953.

Lauterbach, J. Z. "Ketubah." In *Jewish Encyclopedia,* ed. Isidore Singer, vol. 7, pp. 472-76. New York and London: Funk & Wagnalls Co., 1905.

Lewis, Naphtali, Yigael Yadin, and Jonas C. Greenfield, eds. *The Documents from the Bar Kokhba Period in the Cave of Letters: Greek Papyri.* Jerusalem: Israel Exploration Society, Hebrew University of Jerusalem, Shrine of the Book, 1989.

Liddell, Henry George, Robert Scott, and Sir Henry Stuart Jones, et al. *A Greek-English Lexicon.* 9th ed. Oxford: Clarendon, 1996.

Lightfoot, John. *A Commentary on the New Testament from the Talmud and Hebraica,* vol. 2: *Matthew — I Corinthians.* Peabody, Mass.: Hendrickson, 1989.

Lightman, Marjorie, and William Zeisel. "Univira: An Example of Continuity and Change in Roman Society." *Church History* 46 (1977): 19-32.

Lipinski, E. "The Wife's Right to Divorce in the Light of an Ancient Near Eastern Tradition." In *The Jewish Law Annual,* vol. 4, ed. B. S. Jackson, pp. 9-26. Leiden: Brill, 1981.

Little, Joyce A. "Paul's Use of Analogy: A Structural Analysis of Romans 7.1-6." *Catholic Biblical Quarterly* 46 (1984): 82-90.

Llewelyn, S. R., ed. *New Documents Illustrating Early Christianity,* vol. 6. North Ryde: The Ancient History Documentary Research Centre, Macquarie University, 1992.

Lövestam, Evald. "Divorce and Remarriage in the New Testament." In *The Jewish Law Annual,* vol. 4, ed. B. S. Jackson, pp. 47-65. Leiden: Brill, 1981.

Luck, William F. *Divorce and Remarriage: Recovering the Biblical View.* San Francisco: Harper and Row, 1987.

Lüddeckens, Erich. *Ägyptische Eheverträge.* Wiesbaden: Otto Harrassowitz, 1960.

Lundbom, Jack R. "Jeremiah, Book of." In *Anchor Bible Dictionary,* vol. 3, pp. 706-21. New York: Doubleday, 1992.

Lyttelton, E. "The Teaching of Christ about Divorce." *Journal of Theological Studies* 5 (1904): 621-28.

MacRory, Cardinal Joseph. *The New Testament and Divorce.* Dublin: Burns Oates and Washbourne Ltd., Publishers to the Holy See, 1934.

Madan, M. *Thelyphthora; or, A Treatise on Female Ruin, on Its Causes, Effects, Consequences, Prevention and Remedy, Considered on the Basis of the Divine Law.* 3 vols. London: J. Dodsley, 1780-81.

Malina, Bruce J. *The New Testament World: Insights from Cultural Anthropology.* Rev. ed. Louisville: Westminster/John Knox, 1993.

McKane, W. *Jeremiah 1–25.* Edinburgh: T. & T. Clark, 1986.

McNeile, Alan Hugh. *The Gospel according to St. Matthew: The Greek Text, with Introduction, Notes and Indices.* London: Macmillan, 1915.

Meissner, B. *Beiträge zum altbabylonischen Privatrecht.* Leipzig: Hinrichs, 1893.

Metzger, Bruce M. *A Textual Commentary on the Greek New Testament: A Companion Volume to the United Bible Societies' Greek New Testament.* 2nd ed. Stuttgart: Deutsche Bibelgesellschaft, 1994.

Meyer, Heinrich August Wilhelm. *Critical and Exegetical Handbook to the Gospel of Matthew.* Edinburgh: T. & T. Clark, 1877-79.

Milik, J. T. "Le travail d'édition des manuscrits Désert de Juda." In *Volume du Congres, Strasbourg, 1956,* pp. 17-26. Vetus Testamentum Supplements 4. Leiden: Brill, 1957.

Milligan, George, ed. *Selections from the Greek Papyri.* Cambridge: Cambridge University Press, 1912.

Montefiore, Hugh. "Jesus on Divorce and Remarriage." Appendix 1 in Anglican Synod, *Marriage, Divorce and the Church — the Report of a Commission Appointed by the Archbishop of Canterbury to Prepare a Statement on the Christian Doctrine of Marriage.* London: SPCK, 1971.

Montevecchi, Orsolina. *La papirologia.* Manuali universitari 1: Per lo studio delle scienze dell'antichità. Torino: Società editrice internazionale, 1973.

———. "Ricerche di sociologia nei documenti dell' Egitto greco-romano." *Aegyptus* 16 (1936): 3-83.

Morison, James. *A Practical Commentary on the Gospel according to St Matthew.* 8th ed. London, 1892.

Mortimer, Robert. "The Church and Divorce." *Theology* 32 (1936): 320-30.

Moulton, James Hope, and George Milligan. *The Vocabulary of the Greek Testament: Illustrated from the Papyri and Other Non-literary Sources.* London: Hodder & Stoughton, 1930.

Mueller, James R. "The Temple Scroll and the Gospel Divorce Texts." *Revue de Qumran* 10 (1980): 247-56.

Murphy-O'Conner, Jerome. "The Divorced Woman in 1 Cor. 7.10-11." *Journal of Biblical Literature* 100 (1981): 601-6.

———. "Remarques sur l'exposé du Prof. Y. Yadin." *Revue biblique* 79 (1972): 99-100.

———. "An Essene Missionary Document? CD II,14–VI,1." *Revue biblique* 77 (1970): 201-29.

Murray, John. *Divorce.* Philadelphia: Presbyterian and Reformed Publishing Co., 1961.

Murray, John. *Nuptiae Sacrae: An Inquiry into the Scriptural Doctrine of Marriage and Divorce Addressed to the Two Houses of Parliament.* London: 1821.

Nautin, Pierre. "Divorce et remariage dans la tradition de l'église latine." *Recherches de science religieuse* 62 (1974): 7-54.

Nemoy, Leon. *Karaite Anthology: Excerpts from the Early Literature.* New Haven and London: Yale University Press, 1952.

Neufeld, E. *Ancient Hebrew Marriage Laws: With Special Reference to General Semitic Laws and Customs.* London: Longmans, Green & Co., 1944.

The New Testament in the Apostolic Fathers, by A Committee of the Oxford Society of Historical Theology. Oxford: Clarendon, 1905.

Nickle, Keith F. *The Collection: A Study in Paul's Strategy.* London: SCM, 1966.

Nolland, John. "The Gospel Prohibition of Divorce: Tradition History and Meaning." *Journal for the Study of the New Testament* 58 (1995): 19-35.

Noth, Martin. *Exodus: A Commentary.* Trans. J. S. Bowden. London: SCM, 1962.

Okorie, A. M. "Divorce and Remarriage among the Jews in the Time of Jesus." *DELTION BIBLIKWN MELETWN* 25 (1996): 64-73.

Olsen, V. Norskov. *The New Testament Logia on Divorce — A Study of Their Interpretation from Erasmus to Milton.* Tübingen: Mohr (Paul Siebeck), 1971.

Olszowy-Schlanger, Judith. *Karaite Marriage Contracts from the Cairo Geniza: Legal Training and Community Life in Mediaeval Egypt and Palestine.* Leiden: Brill, 1998.

O'Mahony, Patrick J. *Catholics and Divorce.* London: Thomas Nelson & Sons Ltd., 1959.

Oppenheimer, L. H. "Divorce and Christian Teaching." *Theology* 60 (1957): 311-19.

Ortlund, Raymond C. *Whoredom: God's Unfaithful Wife in Biblical Theology.* Leicester: Apollos, 1996.

Osiek, Carolyn, and David L. Balch. *Families in the New Testament World: Households and House Churches.* Louisville: Westminster/John Knox, 1997.

Palmer, Paul F. "Christian Marriage: Contract or Covenant?" *Theological Studies* 33 (1972): 617-65.

Parker, D. *The Living Text of the Gospels.* Cambridge: Cambridge University Press, 1997.

Patte, D. *Early Jewish Hermeneutic in Palestine.* Society for Biblical Literature Dissertation Series 22. Missoula, Mont.: Scholars Press, 1975.

Paul, Shalom M. *Studies in the Book of the Covenant in the Light of Cuneiform and Biblical Law.* Supplements to Vetus Testamentum 17. Leiden: Brill, 1970.

———. "Exod. 21.10: A Threefold Maintenance Clause." *Journal of Near Eastern Studies* 28 (1969): 48-53.

Pearson, Birger A. *Exegesis: Gnosticism, Judaism and Egyptian Christianity.* Studies in Antiquity and Christianity. Minneapolis: Fortress, 1990.

Pelikan, Jaroslav, ed. *Luther's Works.* 55 vols. St. Louis: Concordia Publishing House, 1955-86.

Pestman, Pieter Willem. *Marriage and Matrimonial Property in Ancient Egypt: A Contribution to Establishing the Legal Position of the Woman.* Papyrologica Lugduno-Batava 9. Leiden: Brill, 1961.

Phillips, Anthony. "Another Look at Adultery." *Journal for the Study of the Old Testament* 20 (1981): 3-25.

Phipps, William E. "Is Paul's Attitude toward Sexual Relations Contained in 1 Cor. 7.1?" *New Testament Studies* 28 (1982): 125-31.

———. *Was Jesus Married? The Distortion of Sexuality in the Christian Tradition.* New York: Harper & Row, 1970.

Piattelli, Daniela. "The Marriage Contract and Bill of Divorce in Ancient Hebrew Law." In *The Jewish Law Annual,* vol. 4, ed. B. S. Jackson, pp. 66-78. Leiden: Brill, 1981.

Pickett, Winston H. "The Meaning and Function of T'B/TO'EVAH in the Hebrew Bible." Ph.D. thesis, Hebrew Union College, 1985.

Piper, Otto A. *The Biblical View of Sex and Marriage.* London: James Nisbit & Co., Ltd., 1960.

Pope, Leslie W. "Marriage: A Study of the Covenant Relationship as Found in the Old Testament." M.A. thesis, Providence Theological Seminary, 1995.

Pope, Marvin H. "Mixed Marriage Metaphor in Ezekiel 16." In *Fortunate the Eyes That See — Essays in Honor of David Noel Freedman in Celebration of His Seventieth Birthday,* ed. Astrid Beck, pp. 384-99. Grand Rapids: Eerdmans, 1995.

Porten, Bezalel. *Archives from Elephantine.* Berkeley: University of California Press, 1968.

Porten, Bezalel, and Ada Yardeni. *Textbook of Aramaic Documents from Ancient Egypt: Newly Copied, Edited and Translated into Hebrew and English.* 4 vols. Jerusalem: Hebrew University, 1986-96.

Powers, B. Ward. *Marriage and Divorce: The New Testament Teaching.* Concord, N.S.W.: Family Life Movement; Petersham, N.S.W: Jordan Books, 1987.

Prince, Derek. *God Is a Matchmaker.* Eastbourne: Kingsway, 1986.

Pritchard, James B., ed. *Ancient Near Eastern Texts relating to the Old Testament.* 3rd ed. Princeton: Princeton University Press, 1992.

Procter, Francis. *A History of the Book of Common Prayer: With a Rationale of Its Offices.* 4th ed. London: Macmillan, 1860.

Pummer, Reinhard. *Samaritan Marriage Contracts and Deeds of Divorce.* 2 vols. Wiesbaden: Otto Harrassowitz, 1993-97.

Rabello, Alfredo M. "Divorce of Jews in the Roman Empire." In *The Jewish Law Annual,* vol. 4, ed. B. S. Jackson, pp. 79-102. Leiden: Brill, 1981.

Rabin, Chaim. *The Zadokite Documents.* Oxford: Clarendon, 1954.

Rabinowitz, Jacob J. "The 'Great Sin' in Ancient Egyptian Marriage Contracts." *Journal of Near Eastern Studies* 18 (1959): 72-73.

———. "Marriage Contracts in Ancient Egypt in the Light of Jewish Sources." *Harvard Theological Review* 46 (1953): 91-97.

Retief, Bishop Frank J. *Divorce: Hope for the Hurting.* Cape Town: Struikhof, 1990.

Roberts, R. L. "The Meaning of *Chorizo* and *Douloo* in I Corinthians 7.10-17." *Restoration Quarterly* 8 (1965): 179-84.

Rosner, Brian S. *Paul, Scripture and Ethics: A Study of 1 Corinthians 5–7.* Arbeiten zur

Geschichte des antiken Judentums und des Urchristentums 22. Leiden: Brill, 1994.

Roth, M. T. *Babylonian Marriage Agreements: 7th-3rd Centuries* B.C. Kevalaer: Verlag Butzon & Bercker; Neukirchen-Vluyn: Neukirchener Verlag, 1989.

Rupprecht, Hans-Albert. "Marriage Contract Regulations and Documentary Practice in the Greek Papyri." *Scripta Classica Israelica* 17 (1998): 60-76.

Rushdoony, R. J. *The Institutes of Biblical Law.* Phillipsburg, N.J.: Presbyterian and Reformed Publishing Co., 1973.

Safrai, S. "Home and Family." In *The Jewish People in the First Century: Historical Geography, Political History, Social, Cultural and Religious Life and Institutions,* vol. 2, ed. S. Safrai and M. Stern, with D. Flusser and W. C. van Unnick, pp. 728-92. Section 1 of Compendia Rerum Iudaicarum ad Novum Testamentum. Philadelphia: Fortress, 1976.

Satlow, Michael L. *Jewish Marriage in Antiquity.* Princeton: Princeton University Press, 2001.

———. "'One Who Loves His Wife Like Himself': Love in Rabbinic Marriage." *Journal of Jewish Studies* 49 (1998): 67-86.

———. *Tasting the Dish: Rabbinic Rhetorics of Sexuality.* Brown Judaic Studies 303. Atlanta: Scholars Press, 1995.

———. "Reconsidering the Rabbinic *ketubah* Payment." In *The Jewish Family in Antiquity,* ed. Shaye J. D. Cohen, pp. 133-51. Atlanta: Scholars Press, 1993.

Sawyer, Deborah F. *Women and Religion in the First Christian Centuries.* London: Routledge, 1996.

Schaberg, Jane. *The Illegitimacy of Jesus: A Feminist Theological Interpretation of the Infancy Narratives.* San Francisco: Harper and Row, 1987.

Schaff, Philip, ed. *A Select Library of the Nicene and Post-Nicene Fathers of the Christian Church.* 38 vols. New York: Christian Literature Co., 1886-90. Reprinted Philip Schaff and Henry Wace, eds. *Nicene and Post-Nicene Fathers,* 2nd series. Grand Rapids: Eerdmans, 1979.

Schechter, Solomon. *Documents of Jewish Sectaries.* Cambridge: Cambridge University Press, 1910. Reprinted New York: Ktav, 1970.

Scheil, V. "Quelques contrats Ninivites." *Revue d'assyriologie et d'archéologie orientale* 24 (1927): 111-26.

Schereschewsky, Ben-Zion (Benno). "Agunah." In *Encyclopaedia Judaica,* vol. 2, pp. 430-34. Jerusalem: Keter Publishing House, 1972.

———. "Divorce." In *Encyclopaedia Judaica,* vol. 6, pp. 122-24. Jerusalem: Keter Publishing House, 1972.

Schiffman, Lawrence H. *Reclaiming the Dead Sea Scrolls: The History of Judaism, the Background of Christianity, the Lost Library of Qumran.* Philadelphia: The Jewish Publication Society, 1994.

———. "Laws Pertaining to Women in the Temple Scroll." In *The Dead Sea Scrolls: Forty Years of Research,* ed. D. Dimant and U. Rappaport, pp. 210-28. Leiden: Brill, 1992.

Schremer, Adriel. "Qumran Polemic on Marital Law: CD 4.20–5.11 and Its Social Background." In *The Damascus Document, a Centennial of Discovery: Proceedings of the Third International Symposium of the Orion Center for the Study of the Dead Sea Scrolls and Associated Literature, 4-8 February, 1998,* ed. J. M. Baumgarten et al., pp. 147-60. Leiden: Brill, 2000.

———. "Divorce in Papyrus Ṣe'elim 13 Once Again: A Reply to Tal Ilan." *Harvard Theological Review* 91 (1998): 193-202.

Schweizer, Eduard. *The Good News according to Matthew.* Trans. David E. Green. London: SPCK, 1976.

Selwyn, E. G. "Christ's Teaching on Marriage and Divorce: A Reply to Dr Charles." *Theology* 15 (1927): 88-101.

Seow, C. L. "Hosea, Book of." In *Anchor Bible Dictionary,* vol. 3, pp. 291-97. New York: Doubleday, 1992.

Shaner, Donald W. *A Christian View of Divorce.* Leiden: Brill, 1969.

Shields, Mary E. "Circumscribing the Prostitute: The Rhetorics of Intertextuality, Metaphor, and Gender in Jeremiah 3:1–4:4." Ph.D. thesis, Emory University, 1996.

Shilo, Shmuel. "Impotence as a Ground for Divorce: To the End of the Period of the Rishonim." In *The Jewish Law Annual,* vol. 4, ed. B. S. Jackson, pp. 129-43. Leiden: Brill, 1981.

Shreeve, Dr. Caroline. *Divorce — How to Cope Emotionally and Practically.* Wellingborough: Turnstone, 1984.

Sifre: A Tannaitic Commentary on the Book of Deuteronomy. Trans. Reuven Hammer. New Haven and London: Yale University Press, 1986.

Sigal, Philip. *The Halakah of Jesus of Nazareth according to the Gospel of Matthew.* New York, London, Lanham: University Press of America, 1986.

Sirat, Colette, P. Cauderlier, M. Dukan, and C. Friedman, eds. *La Ketouba de Cologne: un contrat de mariage juif à Antinoopolis.* Papyrologica Coloniensia 12. Opladen: Westdeutscher Verlag, 1986.

Skinner, John. *Genesis.* International Critical Commentary. Edinburgh: T. & T. Clark, 1930.

Smith, David L. "Divorce and Remarriage from the Early Church to John Wesley." *Trinity Journal* n.s. 11 (1990): 131-42.

Smith, Harold. *Ante-Nicene Exegesis of the Gospels.* Translations of Christian Literature Series 6. London: Society for Promoting Christian Knowledge; New York: Macmillan, 1925-29.

Snaith, Norman H. "Isaiah 40–66: A Study of the Teaching of the Second Isaiah and Its Consequences." In *Studies on the Second Part of the Book of Isaiah.* Supplements to Vetus Testamentum 14. Leiden: Brill, 1977.

Sohn, Seock-Tae. *The Divine Election of Israel.* Grand Rapids: Eerdmans, 1991.

Sprinkle, Joe M. "Old Testament Perspectives on Divorce and Remarriage." *The Journal of the Evangelical Theological Society* 40 (1997): 529-50.

———. *'The Book of the Covenant': A Literary Approach.* Journal for the Study of the

Old Testament Supplement Series 174. Sheffield: Sheffield Academic Press, 1994.

Stählin, Gustav. "χήρα." In *Theological Dictionary of the New Testament,* vol. 9, ed. Gerhard Kittel, pp. 440-65. Grand Rapids: Eerdmans, 1964-1995.

Stanton, Graham N. *The Gospels and Jesus.* Oxford: Oxford University Press, 1989.

Stern, Sacha. "The Concept of Authorship in the Babylonian Talmud." *Journal of Jewish Studies* 46 (1996): 183-95.

Stewart, Oliver. *Divorce Vatican Style.* London: Olifants, 1971.

Stienstra, Nelly. *YHWH Is the Husband of His People: Analysis of a Biblical Metaphor with Special Reference to Translation.* Kampen: Kok Pharos, 1993.

Stock, Augustine. "Matthean Divorce Texts." *Biblical Theology Bulletin* 8 (1978): 24-33.

Stone, Lawrence. *Road to Divorce, England 1530-1987.* Oxford: Oxford University Press, 1990.

Strack, H. L., and G. Stemberger. *Introduction to the Talmud and Midrash.* Trans. M. Bockmuehl. Edinburgh: T. & T. Clark, 1991.

Swanepoel, M. G. "Ezekiel 16: Abandoned Child, Bride Adorned or Unfaithful Wife?" In *Among the Prophets: Language, Image and Structure in the Prophetic Writings,* ed. Philip R. Davies and David J. A. Clines, pp. 84-104. Journal for the Study of the Old Testament Supplement Series 144. Sheffield: JSOT Press, 1993.

Tcherikover, Victor Avigdor, with Alexander Fuks, eds. *Corpus papyrorum Judaicarum.* 3 vols. Cambridge: Published for Magnes Press, Hebrew University by Harvard University Press, 1957-64.

Thiering, Barbara. "The Biblical Source of Qumran Asceticism." *Journal of Biblical Literature* 93 (1974): 429-44.

Thornes, Barbara, and Jean Collard. *Who Divorces?* London: Routledge, 1979.

Tigay, Jeffrey H. *The JPS Torah Commentary, Deuteronomy: The Traditional Hebrew Text with the New JPS Translation.* Philadelphia: Jewish Publication Society, 1996.

Tilborg, Sjef van. *The Jewish Leaders in Matthew.* Leiden: Brill, 1972.

Tomson, Peter J. *Paul and the Jewish Law: Halakha in the Letters of the Apostle to the Gentiles.* Compendia Rerum Iudaicarum ad Novum Testamentum 3.1. Minneapolis: Fortress, 1990.

Toorn, Karel van der. "Prostitution (Cultic)." In *Anchor Bible Dictionary,* vol. 5, pp. 510-13. New York: Doubleday, 1992.

Tosato, Angelo. "The Law of Leviticus 18.18: A Re-examination." *Catholic Biblical Quarterly* 46 (1984): 199-214.

———. "Joseph, Being a Just Man (Matt. 1.19)." *Catholic Biblical Quarterly* 41 (1979): 547-51.

Treggiari, Susan. "Divorce Roman Style: How Easy and How Frequent Was It?" In *Marriage, Divorce and Children in Ancient Rome,* ed. Beryl Rawson, pp. 31-46. Oxford: Clarendon, 1991.

Urbach, Ephraim E. *The Sages: Their Concepts and Beliefs.* Trans. Israel Abrahams.

Cambridge, Mass.: Harvard University Press, 1987 (2 vols.; Jerusalem: Magnes Press, Hebrew University, 1975).

Vanderkam, James C. "Zadok and the *spr htwrh hḥtwm* in Dam Doc 5:2-5." *Revue de Qumran* 11 (1984): 561-70.

Vawter, Bruce. "Divorce and the New Testament." *Catholic Biblical Quarterly* 39 (1977): 528-42.

———. "The Divorce Clause of Mt 5,32 and 19,9." *Catholic Biblical Quarterly* 16 (1954): 155-67.

Vermes, G. "Biblical Proof-Texts in Qumran Literature." *Journal of Semitic Studies* 34 (1989): 493-508.

———. "Sectarian Matrimonial Halakhah in the Damascus Rule." *Journal of Jewish Studies* 25 (1974): 197-202. Reprinted in *Post-Biblical Jewish Studies,* pp. 50-56. Leiden: Brill, 1975.

———. "The Qumran Interpretation of the Scripture in Its Historical Setting." *Annual of Leeds University Oriental Society* 6 (1969): 85-97.

Wacholder, B. Z. *The Dawn of Qumran: The Sectarian Torah and the Teacher of Righteousness.* Cincinnati: Hebrew Union College Press, 1983.

Wallace, Daniel B. *Greek Grammar beyond the Basics: An Exegetical Syntax of the New Testament.* Grand Rapids: Zondervan, 1996.

Walton, James H. "The Place of the *hutqattel* within the D-stem Group and Its Implications in Deuteronomy 24:4." *Hebrew Studies* 32 (1991): 7-17.

———. *Ancient Israelite Literature in Its Cultural Context: A Survey of Parallels between Biblical and Ancient Near Eastern Texts.* Grand Rapids: Zondervan, 1989.

Warren, Andrew. "Did Moses Permit Divorce? Modal *weqatal* as Key to New Testament Readings of Deuteronomy 24:1-4." *Tyndale Bulletin* 49 (1998): 39-56.

Washofsky, Mark. "The Recalcitrant Husband: The Problem of Definition." In *The Jewish Law Annual,* vol. 4, ed. B. S. Jackson, pp. 144-66. Leiden: Brill, 1981.

Watson, Alan. *Jesus and the Law.* Athens: University of Georgia Press, 1996.

Weder, H. "Perspective der Frauen." *Evangelische Theologie* 43 (1983): 175-78.

Weems, Renita J. *Battered Love: Marriage, Sex and Violence in the Hebrew Prophets.* Minneapolis: Fortress, 1995.

Wegner, Judith R. *Chattel or Person? The Status of Women in the Mishnah.* Oxford: Oxford University Press, 1988.

Weinfeld, M. "Berith." In *Theological Dictionary of the Old Testament,* vol. 2, ed. Johannes G. Botterweck, Helmer Ringgren, and Heinz-Josef Fabry, pp. 253-79. Grand Rapids: Eerdmans, 1974.

Wenham, G. J. "The Syntax of Matthew 19.9." *Journal for the Study of the New Testament* 28 (1986): 17-23.

———. "Matthew and Divorce: An Old Crux Revisited." *Journal for the Study of the New Testament* 22 (1984): 95-107.

West, Morris, and Robert Francis. *Scandal in the Assembly: A Bill of Complaints and a Proposal for Reform on the Matrimonial Laws and Tribunals of the Roman Catholic Church.* London: Pan, 1970.

Westbrook, Raymond. "Prohibition of Restoration of Marriage in Deuteronomy 24:1-4." In *Studies in Bible 1986*, ed. S. Japhet, pp. 387-405. Scripta Hierosolymitana 31. Jerusalem: Magnes, 1986.

Westermann, Claus. *Isaiah 40–66*. Old Testament Library. London: SCM, 1969.

Wilkins, J. J. *The History of Divorce and Re-Marriage for English Churchmen, Compiled from Holy Scripture, Church Councils and Authoritative Writers*. London: Longman, Green and Co., 1910.

Willans, Angela. *Divorce and Separation*. London: Sheldon, 1983.

Winter, B. W. "Secular and Christian Responses to Corinthian Famines." *Tyndale Bulletin* 40 (1989): 86-106.

———. "Providentia for the Widows of 1 Timothy 5.3-16." *Tyndale Bulletin* 39 (1988): 83-99.

———. "The 'New' Roman Wife and 1 Timothy 2.9-15: The Search for a Sitz im Leben." *Tyndale Bulletin* 51 (2000): 283-92.

Winter, J. G. *Life and Letters in the Papyri*. Ann Arbor, Mich.: University of Michigan Press, 1933.

Winter, P. "Sadoqite Fragments IV 20, 21 and the Exegesis of Gen I 27 in Late Judaism." *Zeitschrift für die alttestamentliche Wissenschaft* 68 (1956): 71-84.

Witherington, Ben, III. *Women in the Ministry of Jesus: A Study of Jesus' Attitudes to Women and Their Roles as Reflected in His Earthly Life*. Society for New Testament Studies Monograph 51. Cambridge: Cambridge University Press, 1984.

Wolff, Hans Julius. *Written and Unwritten Marriages in Hellenistic and Postclassical Roman Law*. Philological Monographs of the American Philological Association no. 9. Haverford, Pa.: American Philological Association, 1939.

Yadin, Yigael. *Masada: The Yigael Yadin Excavations, 1963-1965: Final Reports*. 5 vols. Jerusalem: Israel Exploration Society, 1989-99.

———. *The Temple Scroll*. 3 vols. Jerusalem: Israel Exploration Society, 1983.

———. "L'Attitude essénienne envers la polygamie et le divorce." *Revue biblique* 79 (1972): 98-99.

———. "Expedition D — the Cave of the Letters." *Israel Exploration Journal* 12 (1962): 227-57.

Yadin, Yigael, Jonas C. Greenfield, and Ada Yardeni. "Babatha's *Ketubba*." *Israel Exploration Journal* 44 (1994): 75-101.

Yamauchi, Edwin M. "Cultural Aspects of Marriage in the Ancient World." *Bibliotheca Sacra* 135 (1978): 241-52.

Yarbrough, O. L. *Not like the Gentiles: Marriage Rules in the Letters of Paul*. Atlanta: Scholars Press, 1985.

Yaron, Reuven. "The Restoration of Marriage [Deut. 24.1-4]." *Journal of Jewish Studies* 17 (1966): 1-11.

———. *Introduction to the Law of the Aramaic Papyri*. Oxford: Clarendon, 1961.

———. "On Divorce in Old Testament Times." *Revue Internationale des Droits de l'Antiquité* 3 (1957): 117-28.

Zakovitch, Yair. "The Woman's Rights in the Biblical Law of Divorce." In *The Jewish Law Annual,* vol. 4, ed. B. S. Jackson, pp. 28-46. Leiden: Brill, 1981.

Zimmerli, Walther. *Ezekiel.* 2 vols. Hermeneia. Philadelphia: Fortress, 1983.

Zodhiates, Spiros. *May I Divorce and Remarry? An Exegetical Commentary on 1 Corinthians 7.* Chattanooga, Tenn.: AMG Publishers, 1992.

———. *What about Divorce? An Exegetical Exposition from the Greek Text of Matthew 5:27-32; 19:3-12: Mark 10:2-12; Luke 16:18; Romans 7:1-3.* Chattanooga, Tenn.: AMG Publishers, 1992.

Index of Modern Authors

Index of Subjects

Index of Scripture and Other Ancient Texts

CLASSICAL & OTHER JEWISH AUTHORS